PENGUIN BOOKS

STRONG-MINDED WOMEN

Janet Horowitz Murray grew up in the Bronx and was educated at
the State University of New York, Binghampton, and Harvard. Since
1971 she has taught literature and women's studies at the
Massachusetts Institute of Technology. She lives in Cambridge,
Massachusetts, with her husband and two children, and is currently
working on a study of the creative process of nineteenth-century
novelists.

Janet Murray

STRONG-

and other lost voices from

MINDED

nineteenth-century England

WOMEN

Penguin Books

Penguin Books Ltd, Harmondsworth, Middlesex, England
Penguin Books, 40 West 23rd Street, New York, New York 10010, U.S.A.
Penguin Books Australia Ltd, Ringwood, Victoria, Australia
Penguin Books Canada Ltd, 2801 John Street, Markham, Ontario, Canada L3R 1B4
Penguin Books (N.Z.) Ltd, 182-190 Wairau Road, Auckland 10, New Zealand

First published in the United States of America by Pantheon Books,
a division of Random House, Inc., 1982
First published in Great Britain by Penguin Books 1984

Copyright © Janet Murray, 1982, 1984
All rights reserved

The acknowledgments on pages v and vi
constitute an extension to this copyright page

Made and printed in Great Britain by
Hazell Watson & Viney, Aylesbury, Bucks

A Fenland Chronicle by Sybil Marshall, copyright © 1967, by permission of Cambridge
University Press.
A Life's Work by Margaret Bondfield, copyright © 1966, by permission of Hutchinson
Publishing Group Ltd.

The author also makes grateful acknowledgment for the use of:

The "Petition of Ann Esther Thain," by permission of the Thomas Coram Foundation
for Children, London.
A letter from Josephine Butler to Albert Rutson, February 22, 1868, held in the Fawcett
Collection at the City of London Polytechnic.

For my daughter, Elizabeth

Contents

Acknowledgments

In the six years it has taken me to prepare this anthology I have received a great deal of help, which it is now my pleasure to acknowledge.

I became interested in recovering the experiences of nineteenth-century women while studying the English novel in graduate school during the late 1960s. It became apparent to me and to many others at that time that the classic fictional portrayals of women offered a much narrower record of their lives than the record we have of men's. I therefore began reading other material, both primary and secondary, and incorporating historical documents into my courses. But the specific inspiration for this anthology came from two sources. The first was Tillie Olsen, who was a visiting writer at the Massachusetts Institute of Technology in 1974, giving her remarkable, passionate lectures on the lives of literary women. The lingering spirit of those lectures, which made clear the extent of women's oppression while still honoring their courage and achievements, has been a fundamental source of my energy for this project. My second inspiration was the work of the new feminist historians—in particular, the essays in Martha Vicinus's two collections, including Barbara Kanner's ground-breaking bibliographies, and the imaginative and painstaking social history of Judith Walkowitz, Anna Davin, and Leonore Davidoff. Without this work, and the work of the other feminist historians whose books and articles appear in my bibliography, an anthology like this one would have been impossible.

In addition to the usefulness of their writings, I am personally grateful to the following feminist scholars for suggesting sources and for reading the manuscript: Joan Burstyn, Nancy Cott, Leonore Davidoff, Anna Davin, Louise Tilly, Martha Vicinus, and Judith

Walkowitz. In addition, Deborah Gorham, Dolores Hayden, Barbara Kanner, Jeanne L'Esperance, Mitzi Myers, and Liz Stanley generously gave me their help in locating material.

I owe a large debt of gratitude to the distinguished Victorian historian and bibliographer H. J. Hanham, Dean of Humanities and Social Science at M.I.T., whose expertise and encouragement were invaluable to me in shaping and sustaining this work. I am also grateful to Dean Hanham and to M.I.T. for making available the resources I needed to do the research and writing of this book, first as the holder of an Old Dominion Grant in the spring of 1976, and then as Research Associate in the School of Humanities and Social Science from 1978 to 1980.

When I began to do women's studies I was hampered, like other feminist scholars of that time, by the apathy or antipathy of older members of my profession and by the absence of women, especially of experienced feminist women scholars, to offer me guidance and support. I feel that I have been more than compensated for this early difficulty by the interest, enthusiasm, and hard work that I have received from younger women students, and particularly from a group of very dedicated researchers who worked for varying periods of time on this anthology. I want to thank Cheryl Allen, whose enthusiasm and hard work were crucial to the early stages of this project, Carol Moldaw, Louise Zanar, Linda Burcher Ramsay, Linda Jackson, Sharon Gill, and finally both Jan Lambertz and Anna Clark, who as Harvard undergraduates at the very beginning of their careers as historians offered me the benefit of their very considerable knowledge and professionalism.

After acknowledging all this help with the content of the anthology, I must add that any errors of fact or interpretation are entirely my own responsibility.

Among those whose careful work and good will were necessary to the physical preparation of the manuscript I want to express my thanks to Robin Carpenter, Marilyn Katz, Nancy Osborn, Elizabeth Rettner, Harriet Ritvo, Janet Romaine, Celia Slattery, Judith Wyckoff, and Linda Zieper. In particular I am very grateful to Nancy J. Werlin for her intelligence, speed, and meticulousness in typing the final manuscript.

I also wish to thank the staffs of the libraries I used in the United States and England: the M.I.T. interlibrary loan service; Widener, Schlesinger, Law School, Microtext, and Houghton libraries at Harvard; the Boston Athenaeum; the Boston Public Library; the New

York Public Library; the research libraries of the University of California at Los Angeles, the University of California at Berkeley, and Stanford University; the British Library in the British Museum; the Fawcett Collection, now housed in the City of London Polytechnic; and the library of Brontëana at Haworth Parsonage. For help with locating the illustrations for this volume I wish to thank the staffs of the Photograph Library and the Map and Print Collection at the Greater London Record Office and Library, the Labour History Museum, the BBC Hulton Collection, the British Library, and the Newberry Library in Chicago.

During the time I did much of the work on this book I belonged to two women's groups, one of college professors and one of professional writers. I wish to thank the members of these groups for their advice and support: Bernice Buresh, Naomi Chase, Patsy Cumming, Nancy Dworsky, Marcia Folsom, Lucy Horwitz, Gail Mazur, Beth O'Sullivan, Harriet Reisen, Claire Rosenfield, Trudy Rubin, Laura Shapiro, and Marjorie Shostak. In particular I want to thank Barbara Sirota for her warm friendship and her keen critical intellect, Ann Banks for her canny practical advice, Ruth Perry for the example of her intense energy and commitment, and Celia Gilbert for taking the time from her extraordinary poetry to read two chapters of this book in manuscript.

One of the great gifts of fortune I enjoyed in doing this anthology was the chance of working with my editor at Pantheon Books, Tom Engelhardt, whose intelligence and persistence helped to change an unwieldy grab-bag of juicy snippets and obsessively collected details into a proper and orderly anthology. Such a large and varied collection is a formidable challenge to any copyeditor, and Donna Bass rose to the occasion with great grace and skill. In England, Geraldine Cooke of Penguin Books was very encouraging and helpful to me. I am also very grateful to Elaine Markson and her assistant Geri Thoma, and to Leslie Gardner for their good judgment and efficiency in seeing this book into print.

Finally, I wish to thank my husband, Tom Murray, who has shared my excitement over this project from the very start, and whose love, wit, sanity, and generosity of spirit keep me going.

Some peculiarities of this anthology should be noted here lest they be taken as unintentional oversights. I have purposely left out some of the more lurid material associated with popular Victoriana either because its importance has not been assessed by responsible scholars (such as the infanticide scandals) or because it seemed clearly spurious (such as the notorious 1858 letter to the *Times* from a self-proclaimed prostitute). I have also violated chronological order when necessary to group selections in more meaningful sequences, such as a progression from the general to the particular. Although the text of all selections is as close as possible to the original, I have sometimes changed punctuation, including paragraphing, in order to enhance the fluidity of the excerpted passages. All omissions within the body of a selection are indicated by ellipses.

—JANET HOROWITZ MURRAY
Cambridge, Massachusetts
July 1981

A NOTE ABOUT CURRENCY

Nineteenth-century English currency was divided into pounds (£), shillings (s.), and pence (d.). There were twelve pence to a shilling, twenty shillings to a pound. In addition, farthings came four to a penny; crowns were five shillings apiece; sovereigns, a pound each; and guineas were equivalent to one pound, one shilling.

In terms of nineteenth-century American equivalents, one pound (£1), or twenty shillings (20s.), was worth about $4.80; one shilling (1s.), about $.25. In terms of buying power, a loaf of bread cost 6d., a pair of women's shoes 6s., rent on a three-room London tenement 8s. a week. A family earning an annual income of £100 could be considered members of the lower-middle class; among the working class, most men earned £50 or less a year, most women £25 or less.

STRONG-MINDED WOMEN

And Other Lost Voices

from Nineteenth-Century

England

Women and Womanhood in Nineteenth-Century England

When we look at photographs of nineteenth-century English women, we are teased by conflicting sensations, simultaneously aware of the immediacy and the distance of these women from us. There they are before us, the shapes of their faces, their smaller bodies, their long skirts, their eyes looking out at us over upholstered bosoms or from under nurses' caps or farm workers' bonnets. They did not live that long ago. We strain to hear their voices.

Instead we hear the voices of their literary contemporaries, the women we know so well from the great fiction of the era: the ironic playfulness of a Jane Austen heroine, the defiant passion of Jane Eyre, the moral intensity of a George Eliot character, or the humble and homiletic style of the Victorian literary poor. These familiar literary voices form most of our knowledge of the texture of women's experience in nineteenth-century England. Yet if we try to match them with photographs of women of the period, we see how much of women's experience has remained hidden. This anthology is an attempt to bring back the actual voices of nineteenth-century women—to place their lives before us with the distinctiveness of a photograph, the immediacy of a novel.

Each of the women who speaks here offers us a glimpse of what it meant to be alive and to be a woman at that time, in that place. The women speak about their families, their sexuality, their work, their friends, their sorrows, and their achievements. They also consider (often in response to male opinion) the nature of womanhood itself. Taken as a whole, these narratives are essentially telling three interrelated stories: the story of the middle-class or upper-class woman's struggle to escape the confinement of home, the story of the working-class woman's struggle to ensure her own and her family's survival, and the story of women's collective effort to redefine the boundaries and potentialities of the womanly life.

Historians have only just begun to consider the role played by women in the large economic and social changes that made England the first industrialized nation in the world. The pre-industrial and pre-capitalist world, which had all but disappeared by the early nineteenth century, was characterized by its relative lack of separation between home and work. Women had a clear role in the production of food and clothing and in the family's collective labor (which also included children), whether that labor was in artisan crafts, piecework manufacturing, or agricultural work. This home-centered economic life was disrupted by the changes associated with the Industrial Revolution: the elimination of small family farms after the enclosing of public grazing land; the removal of most manufacturing from the home to the factory (although women continued to take in piecework throughout the century); the shift to a wage-based economy that paid men at twice the rate of women; and the advent of ready-made goods, especially cloth, bread, and ale, all of which had previously been produced at home by the wives and daughters of the family. As a result, the mass of women lost some of the economic security that family life had given them in exchange for their diverse labor. It was now less advantageous to have an extra pair of female hands around the house and more likely that women, from early childhood on, would be required to work outside the home for wages. This change often meant a double load of duties for a married woman—a long workday at the factory preceded and followed by burdensome cooking, cleaning, and child care. Yet, young girls could also gain a measure of personal autonomy and mobility by becoming wage earners, a change that Marx and Engels hailed as the beginning of the breakdown of the patriarchal family.

The lives of economically privileged women were also disrupted by the changes accompanying the growth of the modern world. In the rapidly expanding middle class, women were increasingly cut off from the responsibilities that used to belong to the lady of a substantial household—the supervision of home baking, brewing, clothing production, and small-scale dairy and vegetable farming. Furthermore, many women from such families found themselves impoverished by an economic structure that concentrated both inherited wealth and the ability to earn money in the hands of their brothers and husbands. Marriage was almost the sole vocation open to middle-class and upper-class women, their "pleasantest preservative from want," in the words of one Jane Austen character. Housework and family life became their chief sources of occupation.

This economic dependency upon men gave rise to indirect means of exercising power. In the period from 1800 to 1840, in Evangelical circles in particular, women established the home as their "sphere," claiming moral authority over religious and sexual matters. Upper-class and upper-middle-class women made their own sphere of influence in "society," orchestrating the elegant dining-room and drawing-room life in which powerful connections were made. Women's economic isolation also gave rise to a new ideology—the cult of the domestic angel—which reached its peak in the first twenty years of Victoria's reign (1837–1857), exalting decorative idleness and dependency as virtuous, charming, and appropriate to women's essential role of ministration to men. Yet, many of these "domestic angels" longed to use their abilities and talents outside the home. As a result, by the late 1850s a feminist movement demanding wider opportunities for middle-class women was taking shape, seeking to replace the ideal of the self-sacrificing domestic angel with the ideal of the emancipated, educated, independent woman.

So many changes occurring within one century led to startling incongruities. Some women were considered too frail to walk alone in the streets, while others were working underground in coal mines. Middle-class women experienced a time of extreme economic dependency and social isolation followed by the first organized political movement of women in history. Working-class women were forced out of their homes to work and then subjected to a version of the domestic angel cult, which exhorted them to stay at home. The generational differences were dizzying. A mid-century Victorian "lady" who was taught refined accomplishments and modest manners in a proper finishing school might blush for the racy language of her Regency grandmother and live to be shocked once more by a bicycle-riding, university-educated "new woman" granddaughter. Womanhood as a social entity was reinvented several times in the course of the century, making it hard for individual women to place themselves, hard for them to understand what their role in society should be, hard for them to make clear the bases of their self-respect.

Compounding the confusion over women's roles was a system of potent cultural images that came to permeate art, literature, public controversy, and even the most private reflections of individual women and men. This imagery, which supported a view of women as docile, dependent, and self-sacrificing, was employed consciously or unconsciously by writers all across the political spectrum. It formed a kind of common vocabulary by which people identified the parts of women's lives.

This popular imagery of women fell into three categories. First, there were the images of happy and fulfilled womanhood: the angel in the house, the ivy-like wife clinging for protection to the oak-like husband, the modest bride, the doting and self-abnegating mother. Second, there were the images of corrupted womanhood: the gaudily dressed factory girl, the slatternly housewife, the mannish female laborer, the drunken virago, the negligent mother, the lascivious fallen woman, and the strong-minded feminist. Images like these expressed hostility toward women who were resisting the limits of their circumstances. They reinforced the belief that dissatisfied women were deviant and "unwomanly," that women who appeared to be seeking their own pleasure and happiness were behaving anti-socially. Third, and perhaps most importantly, were the images of suffering womanhood, sentimental renderings of situations in which women experienced pain and privation: the starving seamstress, the distressed gentlewoman, the agonized woman in childbirth, the lonely governess, the repentant prostitute, the homeless workhouse girl. Such images served to express widespread anxiety over the visible sufferings of women, while subtly reinforcing the notion that passive victimization or dependency was woman's natural and necessary lot. As an overall system, this imagery allowed for the collective expression of deeply held wishes, angers, and anxieties about women's changing situation, even as it falsified their actual experience of life.

This system of deceptive images of women's lives, which acted as a barrier when nineteenth-century women tried to grasp the truth of their experience, has that effect even today. After all, as twentieth-century readers, we too have absorbed these concepts. The popular imagery of women informs so much of our literary heritage that it takes a conscious effort to look beyond it, to try to see the actual seamstress, governess, wife, or reformer behind the language used to describe her, or even the language she is using to describe herself.

Because we have lost touch with some of the major coordinates by which women measured their lives a century ago, we are perhaps in even more danger than they were of allowing the lives presented here to collapse into these reductive images. Where today we think of personal decisions concerning family, education, work, and sexuality primarily in psychological terms, in Victorian England the same conflicts were understood primarily as moral problems. The moral coordinates of a woman's world were defined by religion, by a culturally specific understanding of the relationship between men and women, and by culturally specific assumptions about the duties of women to one another. In all of these matters the assumptions of the time differed greatly from those of our own day, although they were not necessarily more repressive (as we often assume them to be). This complex system of cultural values often led women into contradictory stances that are not easy for a modern reader to appreciate.

Religion was perhaps the most important cultural force affecting the lives of the women whose voices appear here. Its effects are probably most apparent to us in the shaping of the conservative ideology of home, the cult of the domestic angel. This notion of true womanliness as a sacred capacity for self-sacrifice often functioned merely as an excuse for expecting women to subordinate their needs to those of their male relatives. Yet the religious interpretation of women's domestic life also offered women a profound way to understand the suffering and helplessness that were so often a part of their experience. The deaths of young children and injury or death in childbirth were commonplace dangers calling forth intense speculation about the ultimate sources of human misery and solace. Therefore, when women themselves speak of the sacredness of maternal self-sacrifice or of renewing or abandoning their faith after a family illness or death, their feelings must be understood apart from the sentimental ideology of female piety.

Religion allowed women to give vent to their feelings with an otherwise forbidden intensity, providing a relatively safe arena for the release of potentially antisocial emotion. Thus, Harriet Martineau described her early religious enthusiasm as helping her through a very miserable childhood:

> I pampered my vain-glorious propensities by dreams of divine
> favour, to make up for my utter deficiency of self-respect: and
> I got rid of otherwise incessant remorse by a most convenient

> confession and repentance, which relieved my nerves without
> at all, I suspect, improving my character.*

Similarly, Florence Nightingale believed her youthful restlessness and
undefined sense of social isolation derived from her special calling
from God. To one degree or another, many other women experienced
such an enhancement of self-esteem by identifying their goals with
those of Omnipotence itself.

In addition to its emotional value, religion provided women with
an intellectual and moral context that transcended the secular world
in which they were so undervalued, a higher religion gave them a
higher plane of values from which they could examine and judge social
customs. Many of the most accomplished women of the time (Charlotte Brontë, George Eliot, Josephine Butler, Frances Power Cobbe)
experienced important religious crises early in life. Their later certainty of the rightness of their unconventional behavior, their willingness to risk independent judgments in crucial areas of their lives,
was directly traceable to their early ability to address their personal
situations in the highest, most solemn, and most universal terms.

Feminists often used religious associations, quite sincerely, in
political and personal contexts. For instance, the New Testament
story of the unworthy steward whom Christ condemns for hiding his
talents rather than causing them to multiply was frequently and feel-
ingly invoked by women seeking justification for using their minds
and developing their skills. Such a parallel turned a socially rebellious
act into a sacred duty. Moreover, progressive religious movements,
like Unitarianism and Quakerism, strengthened women's sense of
equality with men while giving them experience in public debate.

Religion was therefore not merely a source of antifeminist ideology, but an important means by which women transcended the
narrow limits of their physical and economic lives. Imaginatively
employed, it helped them cope with the stresses of motherhood and
with the psychological damages of powerlessness. It could, in fact,
even form the basis for an activist or emancipationist approach to
the world.

Second only to religion in its influence, and intertwined with it,
was an elaborate and often contradictory edifice of popular beliefs
concerning women's rightful relationship to men. The new industrial

---

* Maria Weston Chapman, ed., *Harriet Martineau's Autobiography* vol. 1,
   p. 12 (1877)

and capitalist order brought with it a redefinition of manhood as well as of womanhood. It was the Victorians who in large part created the modern myth of the middle-class successful man—self-sufficient, aggressive, competitive, a good "provider" for his sheltered family. Womanhood was largely understood only as it contrasted with this view of manhood, and many of the traits most often praised in women were merely inversions of male self-images. The more men felt themselves to be selfishly competitive in the commercial world, the more they idolized women as self-sacrificing and divinely maternal; the more men experienced their own sexuality as animalistic and intrusive, the more they praised the essential "purity" of women. The presumed female vices were the same ones women had been charged with for centuries (the traditional vices subject people are accused of by their rulers): frivolity, laziness, fickleness, vanity, and untruthfulness. Yet, such "sins" were now not only tolerated as inevitable but often actually encouraged. Women who emulated either the virtues or the vices of men, however, were attacked and loudly accused of "unsexing" themselves.

Both reinforcing and to some degree mitigating this starkly defined separation of the sexes was the Victorian middle-class notion of the sanctity of home life. Home was considered to be the center for both men's and women's lives, the abode of moral decency and peace of mind. In the course of the century, home displaced the church itself as a refuge and spiritual haven, with religious observances, most notably Christmas, changing from public to domestic rituals. Within the ideally sanctified home, a husband and wife were seen as enjoying a complementary relationship in which each benefited from the peculiar strengths of the other sex. A firm faith in the moral purpose of complementary marriage was common to the thinking of such diverse writers as John Ruskin, Eliza Lynn Linton, Charles Dickens, and Harriet Taylor Mill—despite their political differences and their painful private experiences of marriage.

Taken together, these related cultural assumptions involved women in complicated psychological and moral conflicts. On the one hand, it was flattering to be considered the moral superiors of men, and many women accepted this superiority as a plain truth of family life. On the other hand, the qualities upon which that superiority was based were hard to sustain. Since womanliness was as much defined by the absence of male qualities as by the presence of the conventionally feminine graces and virtues, to be womanly required a total ignorance of male concerns, from politics to higher mathematics to sexuality. Such extensive ignorance was hard to achieve or even to pretend to. Then, too, the male expectation of self-sacrificing maternal care also meant that women in their most intimate relationships were encouraged to see themselves as sources of unlimited energy for the emotional and physical nurturance of others. In effect, women could only gain the moral luxury of looking down on their more powerful male relatives by serving them with slavish devotion.

The tension between the image of women as domestic angels and their real lives as domestic servants created a great deal of confusion in sexual matters. As feminist writers often pointed out, a woman's sexual feelings were necessarily corrupted by her economic dependency upon men. Ann Lamb put it this way:

> It is said that woman cannot exist without love; that she is perpetually in search of something to look up to, something for which to sacrifice herself, something to guide and lead and keep her out of the way of temptation! But is she not at the same time in search of something to support her? To give her food and clothes and fire? It is difficult to sound the depths of the heart, and women often deceive themselves as well as others upon this subject.*

The belief in women's virtuous asexuality added to women's confusions. Imagine, for instance, a middle-class girl of the 1850s at age eighteen—the age at which Victorian boys were supposed to "sow their wild oats" and Victorian girls were expected to marry. Unlike her brother, however romantically inclined she might be, she could not allow herself to let her desires show. A single woman who was eager for love (even married love) might well be condemned as improper or absurd. If some likely young fellow attracted her, she was to wait for him to declare himself and not frighten him off by appearing either too cold or too warm. Marriageable young ladies in such circumstances were often depicted in melodrama as cruelly separated from the poor suitors who loved them truly, and in popular cartoons as heartlessly choosing a mate by his bank account. The reality was a less exaggerated, more ordinary form of misery and confusion.

Once married, a woman faced further conflicts and ambivalences. If she betrayed too much passion for her husband she might well be considered indecent. Male feminist William Thompson, writing in

* Ann Richelieu Lamb, *Can Woman Regenerate Society?* (1844)

1825 in collaboration with fellow radical Anna Wheeler, described the sex life of a married woman in these terms:

> She is not permitted to feel, or desire. . . . The obedient instrument of man's sensual gratification, she is not permitted even to wish for gratification for herself.†

Since sexuality was widely believed to be natural only to men, fallen women, and the most disreputable poor people, a woman who was conscious of her own unsatisfied sexual needs faced a problem of self-definition. Narratives included here give evidence of some women in both the privileged and the lower classes denying their sexuality or being raised in an atmosphere of protective sexual ignorance. Others (like Charlotte Brontë, for instance) were tortured by sexual desires they felt all too clearly and yet could not directly express. Even assuming a woman felt no conflict between her inner needs and social and cultural pressures, she was left in the unpleasant situation of thinking of herself as a bodiless angel who was nevertheless duty bound to submit to her husband's animal desires. Many women found it convenient and even comforting to follow the solution urged upon them by the culture: channeling their sexual energies into motherhood and treating their husbands with only a distant affection, which at times could be manipulative rather than sincere. Then, too, sexual coldness could be a guard against frustration, the dangers of childbirth, or the sheer exhaustion of caring for a large family. In short, the Victorian mystification of sexuality served in many ways to increase antagonism between the sexes.

In the political sphere, the moral idealization of women had a strong effect on contemporary feminism. Like other women, feminists were accustomed to thinking of themselves as making up for the deficiencies of men. They therefore tended to insist upon emancipation as a means of making women better wives and mothers rather than as a way of liberating them from the constriction of family roles. They were less likely than twentieth-century feminists to express a direct desire for the emulation of male achievements or for admission to male privileges. Instead they often claimed a right to equal participation in the wider world in order to make up for the errors of men.

Women defined themselves most clearly perhaps in relationship to one another, as members almost of a class with interests different

† William Thompson, *Appeal of One-Half the Human Race, Women, Against the Pretensions of the Other Half, Men, to Restrain Them in Political and Thence in Civil and Domestic Slavery* (1825)

from, if not actually opposed to, those of men. Because of the precariousness of their economic situation and their segregation in the "woman's sphere," women necessarily relied upon one another for comfort and advice, pooling their physical, financial, and intellectual resources to make up for the difficulties of their position. Friendships were expected to be much closer and more exuberantly expressed, more like what we now think of as family or even romantic relationships. Activists made use of the bonds between women to form groups in which friendship and sometimes kinship reinforced political commitment. Emily Davies, for instance, drew upon the combined resources of such a group in her battle to found Girton College, Cambridge. However, this ethic of female comradeship broke down in the relations between women of different classes. The rigid class structure of nineteenth-century English society did much to prevent women from identifying with one another across class lines. Opposing interests, as between servants and mistresses, often proved to be insurmountable obstacles. Even the best efforts of privileged women to be helpful to poor women were frequently colored by the condescension, paternalism, and desire for social control that characterized much of nineteenth-century philanthropy and social reform. There were, however, notable exceptions to this division by class. The women's trade union movement, for instance, received much stimulus and support from middle-class feminists and socialists.

Public debate on specific questions concerning women took place within the context of these cultural assumptions about women's relationships to God, to men, and to one another. Whether the issue was corsets, coal mines, or college educations, these general assumptions often determined the range of the discussion. Even in women's private debates, in their inner conflicts over imagining their place in the disjointed world of nineteenth-century England, these assumptions were tremendously influential.

Josephine Butler is a fascinating case in point. In her personal life, she combined an independence of action with a strong faith in God and a close relationship with her husband. Out of their conventional religious faith came the Butlers' sense of their marriage as both a sanctuary in the secular world and a bulwark against other social conventions of the time. Similarly, in her iconoclastic public life as a defender of prostitutes against compulsory examination for venereal disease, Butler called upon conventional Victorian notions of religion, marriage, and womanly solidarity to challenge Parliament itself and to speak out on issues it was considered disgraceful for a woman to understand, let alone mention. The following excerpt from Butler's 1882 Parliamentary testimony makes clear the ways in which she understood her feminist championing of prostitutes within a conventionally Victorian moral framework:

> Permit me to remind you that there is nothing answering in the physical being of a man to the sacredness of the maternal functions in a woman, and that these functions and every organ connected with them ought to be held in reverence by man. . . . I am not here to represent virtuous women alone: I plead for the rights of the most virtuous and the most vicious equally, and I speak for the womanhood of the world. We are *solidaire*. You will find us so. . . . The moral character of a woman, though it be of the lowest, does not alter the sacrilegious character of an indecent assault upon her person; and no enactment or law in the land can ever make such an assault other than morally criminal. The part assigned to woman in the physiology of the race is higher, much more delicate, and more to be respected than that of man. The line of human descent is continued corporeally on the woman's side. The fact of the greater physical weakness of women results from their forces being diverted to the maternal functions, and this very weakness gives a stronger title to the respect of their persons than men can have, who are able, by their superior physical strength, to protect themselves. . . . Every woman has a right, a Divine right, to protect the secrets of her own person; it is her inalienable right. . . . It may be said that this is sentiment; I grant that it is sentiment, but it is a sentiment which governs the world; it is a sentiment as deep as our faith in God; it is the deepest of human sentiments. Parliament cannot afford, on this question, to set aside the sentiment of the motherhood of England.*

Butler's sincere appeal to the "weakness" of women, their loyalty to one another, their need of male protection, and the sacredness of their motherly functions, could all form a part of any hymn to the angel in the house. Yet, at the same time, Butler's position is informed by a radical energy, a commitment to resist male power over

* Testimony, Friday, May 5, 1882, in *Report of the Select Committee on the Contagious Diseases Acts* 9, P.P. (1882)

women's bodies, and male political power over the "motherhood" of England. Unlike a modern feminist, Butler emphasizes women's weakness and maternal role rather than their strength and resistance. But her stance is no less feminist, or even radical, for its grounding in Victorian conventions.

Similar difficulties of interpretation surround our understanding of working-class women's lives. Much of what we know of the working class was recorded for us by middle-class men, who brought to their accounts the prejudices of their own class and gender. In reports collected by journalists, reformers, or government investigators, people are often stereotyped as belonging to either the "respectable" or the "rough" poor. In their middle-class male eyes, "respectability" for a woman meant keeping a clean house, not working for wages outside the home, caring for the meals and clothing of her family, making sure the family attended church, school, and employment regularly and displayed proper deferential behavior to their class superiors. Most of all, a respectable poor woman was expected to imitate the manners of middle-class women as far as she was able without their resources or leisure.

In effect, the ethic of respectability was a way of blaming the poor for the misery of their lives. Horrendous sanitation and malnutrition were often viewed as the fault of the sufferers, particularly of women housekeepers. Ill health itself was seen as evidence of ignorance rather than as a symptom of near starvation. In a time when exhausting, lifelong labor was the norm, the poverty of the working class was often attributed to reprehensible laziness. Moreover, to many observers poverty suggested immorality of all sorts. Middle-class investigators were particularly suspicious of the sexual behavior of poor people: Were the women using coarse language, dressing in a revealing way, thrown into contact with male workers after dark, having too many illegitimate children, or too few due to the secret practice of abortion?

At the same time, working-class women themselves often embraced "respectability" as a means of enhancing pride and morale, a means of insisting upon a certain level of comfort and dignity, even if it came with painful extra labor. Reading accounts of women who took pride in hiding their misery from their neighbors or in cleaning their front doorsteps or in sending their children to often inadequate schools, we have to bear in mind the real gain in self-respect that such practices offered. But we also have to be careful not to accept uncritically the frequent middle-class laments at the slovenliness of poor housewives or the unmotherly behavior of factory workers.

Once we are aware of the historical and cultural context in which nineteenth-century English women lived their lives, we can begin to see them for themselves, as individuals, and to claim some knowledge of their life experiences. The closer we come to seeing them as part of their circumstances, but not wholly defined by them, the more aware we become of a different kind of imagery, one that contrasts strongly with the pervasive cultural images of passivity, victimization, and dependency. This truer collection of images arises out of the women's own stories of significant moments in their lives. Among these moments are Mary Taylor opening her shop; Annie Besant giving her first oration in an empty church; an anonymous mother of five sedating her ailing husband so he would not be disturbed by her cries in childbirth; Nelly Weeton obsessively writing and erasing her forbidden stories on her small but treasured slate; Elizabeth Dickson soothing the cold and damp from the legs of her young gang-worker daughter with a petticoat and a warming pan; Mary Somerville struck by the algebraic symbols in a fashion magazine; Charlotte Brontë taking her first look at the ocean; Isabella Bird Bishop battling her way to the summit of Long's Peak; and Josephine Butler facing a hostile mob in a smoldering hayloft.

All of these moments seem to me to represent the true history of women in this period, the struggle to realize their potential as human beings, to care for themselves and their families, to find their work in the world and to do it conscientiously despite the enormous limitations of their circumstances. Faced with an inhospitable and often dangerous world, they took it on with the full measure of their vitality. These women display a wide range of admirable characteristics—courage, kindness, curiosity, persistence, endurance. But most of all they display the relentless struggle against circumstances which makes up nobility in any human situation but which is so often ignored in the lives of women.

Hearing these voices today, we inevitably become aware of the bonds that link the experiences of women across the generations. Patterns of subjection and sexual politics that are muted or confused in contemporary society appear in bold relief in the Victorian world where men frankly stated that women must be kept in the home in order to serve male needs, or that they should be given employment as clerks primarily because they were so much cheaper and more expendable than men. Some arguments, like those over state control of prostitution or protection of battered women, are much the same today as they were one hundred years ago. But these voices are valuable most of all because women are once more living in a time of disruptive change and are once again facing the task of imagining a new ideal of womanhood while coping with economic and social upheavals. In meeting this situation we are in need of the wisdom, the strategies, the life experiences of those women who have gone before us. We need to recover the history of these women in order to be renewed by an awareness of their vitality, and to replace in our own imaginations the false images of passive victimization with our true heritage of women's struggles and women's strengths.

Part I

THE WOMANLY
WOMAN

In nineteenth-century England men and women were usually regarded as belonging to two different species. Not only were they confined to the separate "spheres" of business and home, but their very characters were assumed to operate on separate principles. Of the two, women were the less clearly defined. But throughout the century, and especially from the time of Victoria's accession in 1837, there were repeated attempts to describe true womanliness in moral terms and to set appropriate boundaries for female behavior. The four popular controversies represented in this section are part of that long and lively public debate.

Underlying these attempts was a relatively new situation—women's extreme economic dependence upon men, specifically, upon marriage as their chief means of support, particularly in the middle classes. In defining womanly goodness, nineteenth-century writers looked at this central fact of woman's dependence in one of two ways. There were those, male and female, who extolled this dependency as ennobling and found that woman's loving maternality, purity of heart, disinterestedness, and capacity for self-sacrifice all happily stemmed from her powerlessness in the outside world. For such conservative moralists, women were most appropriately womanly when praying for men's souls or sacrificing themselves for their children. This "angel in the house," as she was popularly called, was expected to be safely sheltered in marriage, sexually passive, and dressed in confining, ornamental clothes. Unmarried women, flirtatious women, women in divided skirts, were condemned as "unwomanly" or "unsexed."

There were, however, those who espoused an ethic of emancipation. These writers found woman's dependence upon man to be degrading and her character to be corrupted rather than enhanced by her powerlessness. Emancipationist or feminist writers, including some men, saw mercenaries and parasites where the conservative writers saw domestic angels. The ideal of womanliness for these feminists was similar to the Victorian ideal of masculine character: self-reliance, industry, forthrightness, and independence. Feminist writers defended the unmarried, and thought there was more womanly dignity in comfortable clothing and paid occupations than in the "shelter" of home.

The selections in this chapter are mostly by women, some of whom thought that women were ennobled rather than degraded by their dependency upon men. Whatever their differences, these women shared a common effort to create for themselves and for their fellow women a model of womanly dignity at a time when, as they all agreed, men were encouraged to be selfish and women were without direct power in the world. Furthermore, although feminists found it unpleasant to have women raising public voices in favor of dependency and domesticity, conservative arguments could sometimes be used to advance women's rights. The advocates of woman's mission, for instance, laid the basis for later feminist arguments on the need for women's moral energy in the wider political and social world. Even such a castigator of her sex as Eliza Lynn Linton was closer to feminists like Ann Richelieu Lamb or Harriet Taylor Mill in her disgust with women's trivial occupations and dishonesty toward men than she was to her fellow conservative William Rathbone Greg, who urged single women to adopt the pleasing manners of expensive prostitutes in order to marry their way out of their economic "redundancy." In a culture in which women were brought up to pride themselves on their selflessness, the creation of any standard by which they could affirm a strong moral character was one of the most basic ways to resist the limitations of their position.

ONE

Woman's Mission

Sarah Lewis's widely read book *Woman's Mission* (1839) ambitiously suggested that "women may be the prime agents in the regeneration of mankind." The "mankind" that needed regeneration was composed mainly of men, whose selfishness and profligacy were to be corrected by the selfless, maternal purity of their female family members, particularly their mothers and wives. At the heart of Lewis's argument was a sentimental celebration of women's "influence." For over a century women had been told that they were given "influence" over men to compensate them for their lack of direct power in the world. Lewis, however, exalted this mysterious faculty by equating it with the ability to effect evangelical conversion. In her view, every woman's home life should be a strenuous colonial mission to the barbaric males around her, a mission in which glory awaited the outwardly meek but inwardly triumphant female emissary of God. This concept of woman's influence rested upon the assumption that power was necessarily corrupting and that goodness was nurtured by impotence. Woman's dependency upon man, then, was necessary if she were to retain her high moral character and perform her great mission of regenerating society.

Lewis expected women to glory in their ability to endure pain in the service of others. She identified the mother's willingness to suffer for the sake of her child as the quintessential form of self-sacrificing Christian love. The mother's direct pleasure in the child was not part of the picture Lewis painted. Instead, Lewis assumed that women experienced the painful aspects of motherhood in an ecstasy of self-denial—a spiritual state that she recommended as an antidote to the selfishness of men as well as to the materialism and aggression of the male-created social and economic world. Lewis stressed the intensity and endurance of motherly feeling, and the irritations of daily life with demanding male relatives, giving her argument the strength of emotional familiarity. Moreover, she appealed to women in the one relationship in which they felt dominance over their male relatives: as mothers of young sons. Because her arguments flattered women's sense of superiority to men, recognized the difficulties of their lives, and appealed to their common emotional experience, Lewis's vision of woman's mission had an immediate popularity and today remains an interesting example of profemale yet antifeminist thought.

In her book-length refutation of Lewis, *Can Woman Regenerate Society?* (1844), Ann Richelieu Lamb called upon women to be discontented with their dependence upon men and ashamed of their moral state. Lamb argued that marriage, women's primary economic relationship, turns men into tyrants and women into mercenaries. Under such circumstances friendship and love are impossible and regeneration a mockery, since women are degraded rather than ennobled by their subservience to men. Lamb's was one of several feminist voices raised in the 1840s against the doctrine of woman's mission and woman's influence.

Harriet Taylor Mill raised a harsher voice than Lamb's in 1851 when she denounced woman's moral state as one of debased servility. She turned Lewis's argument upside down by focusing on how women's mercenary tendencies actually corrupted the men they lived with by allowing them to forego social responsibilities for family-centered greed. For Mill, abnegation of self was not noble at all but merely the submission of the weak to the demands of the strong. Moreover, Mill claimed that women were corrupted in their public lives just as they were at home by their inescapable economic dependence upon the good will of men. Such beliefs were in direct opposition to some of the more passionately held sentiments of the age, as is dramatically illustrated by Charlotte Brontë's horrified reaction to Mill's article. To Brontë, any woman who "longed for power" must have "never felt affection."

John Ruskin took the doctrine of woman's spiritual influence to its emotional and logical extreme in his influential 1865 lecture to girls, "Of Queens' Gardens." Pursuing Lewis's suggestion that women could affect the political sphere by advocating Christian values, Ruskin extends the argument, holding them responsible for all wars made by men. His essay represents a high-water mark for the belief in women's influence. At roughly the same time, feminist writer Mary

Taylor, best friend to Charlotte Brontë and advocate of women's economic self-sufficiency, dismissed the very concept of "influence" in this down-to-earth manner:

> I should like to see a human being, man or woman, whose main business was in influencing people. How do they make a business of it? What time does it begin in the morning? And how do they fill, say, a few hours every day, in the doing of it? Not commanding or teaching, but influencing.*

From her point of view, a woman with no better job in life than influencing others was by her very idleness a contemptible being.

By the late 1860s, the focus of public controversy had begun to shift toward the question of what was to be the business of women's lives if they could not be persuaded to regenerate humanity. However, belief in the moral superiority of woman remained popular, both among those who would have her act the domestic angel and those who wanted her to bring her sanctified maternal care to the world at large.

From WOMAN'S MISSION (1839)
Sarah Lewis

Sarah Lewis's Woman's Mission began as a translation of a work by Louis-Aimé Martin in which he presented a Rousseauist view of woman as man's spiritual guide, with heavy emphasis on the importance of maternal love. Lewis adapted Martin's ideas for English protestant tastes, eliminated most of his references to male profligacy, and wrote a shorter, tighter book from a female viewpoint. By 1849, her book had gone through thirteen editions.

The missionary spirit . . . may, in some degree, be acquired by cultivation; but there is one natural manifestation of it, and that is placed in woman's heart—maternal love—the only truly unselfish feeling that exists on this earth. . . . By intrusting to woman such a revelation of himself, God has pointed out whom he intends for his missionaries upon earth—the disseminators of his spirit, the diffusers of his word. Let men enjoy in peace and triumph the intellectual kingdom which is theirs, and which doubtless, was intended for them. . . . The moral

* Mary Taylor, *The First Duty of Women* (1870), p. 14

world is ours—ours by position; ours by qualification; ours by the very indication of God himself. . . .

But women who are not mothers have a mission likewise. . . . Their mission is the establishment of peace, and love, and unselfishness, to be achieved by any means, and at any cost to themselves; in the cultivation first in themselves, then in all over whom they have any influence, of an unselfish and unworldly spirit; the promotion even in the most minute particular of elegance, of happiness, of moral good. The poor, the ignorant, the domestic servant, are their children; and on them let them lavish the love which God has denied to flow in its natural channel. . . .

Christianity once received—the condition of women is ascertained never to be altered; they, equally with man, have received the spirit of adoption, whereby they cry, Abba* Father! What a deep meaning is hidden in those words—peculiarly touching to woman, since they proclaim her no longer the slave of man, but the servant of God. If we are sensible of the benefits conferred upon us by our share in this great redemption, what ought to be our conduct? The adoption into our hearts, and the dissemination, by our influence, of this most holy spirit of Christianity. . . . There is a kind of quiet consistency of conduct in truly Christian people, which begins by exciting wonder, and ends by securing respect. It is very puzzling to a selfish and worldly mind to see the action of an immutable principle of right as frequently operating *against* the worldly interests of the individual as not. This is the peculiar form of Christianity which we, as women, ought to cultivate. . . . Christian virtues, in this form, are more easy of practice to women than to men, because women have fewer worldly interests, and are by nature and education less selfish. . . . Let women begin this good work; they are eminently qualified for the acceptance of the two great truths of the gospel, love and self-renunciation, which qualities are more or less placed in the hearts of all women; they are naturally disposed to reverence, to worship, to self-sacrifice, for the sake of a beloved object. These peculiar qualities, accompanied by unenlightened intellect and narrow views, lead them to minute devotional practices, to the unlimited indulgence of religious sensibility, and partial unintelligent obedience. Grafted on enlightened Christianity, they may accomplish—what may they *not* accomplish?

The women, then, who are to be the regenerators of society must

* Hebrew, "father"

BBC Hulton Picture Library

Prime Minister William Gladstone with his wife, Catherine Glynne Gladstone

be Christian women—Christian wives and Christian mothers, but enlightened Christians, deeply imbued with the spirit of Christ. . . . They must show forth that it is a grand comprehensive principle, which embraces all things, from the greatest to the least, not only our safety, but our honour, our happiness, our ultimate glory. Let them deeply engrave these principles on the hearts of their children. It is true they cannot command results, but they will have done their duty. . . .

Most great men have had extraordinary mothers, and it seems as though by some peculiar influence, the nature of the mother acts upon the son. . . . But even those who do take some heed to preserve boys from the contaminating influence which makes them an easy prey to flagrant immorality, seem to have no conception that it is their place to watch over the minor points of character, which, though they may not affect a man's good fame, and hinder his worldly advancement, materially influence his happiness and his virtue. The regulation of temper, the repression of selfishness, the examination of motive—how seldom do they form any part of the training of boys! The neglect has a most fatal effect on their happiness, and the happiness of all connected with them. We may see it illustrated in that curious popular paradox, which allows a man to be by his unregulated temper the torment of all around him, and yet retain the name of a "thoroughly good-hearted fellow."—How far the good heart brings forth good fruits, may be read in the anxious looks of the timid wife—the unchild-like, and joyless manners of frightened children—the obsequious but unloving obedience of domestics—all fearing to awake the lion's wrath. A woman with such a temper is deservedly called a vixen, but a man is "a good-hearted fellow"; except it can be proved that there is a very different moral code for the two sexes, it is very puzzling to simple-minded people to know why that which excites merited dislike in a woman, is so leniently passed over in a man: nay, of the two, we should say that the ill temper of a man has less excuse than that of a woman, because he has more power to escape from domestic annoyances. The error here is in the fundamental principle, which makes the regulation of temper no part of the education of boys. . . .

Again, men are said to be more selfish than women. How can they help it? no pains are taken in their education to make them otherwise. That pugnacity which is so admired as a proof of *spirit*, is the very embodiment of the selfish principle—a fighting for their *own* rights—an assertion of their *own* superiority. They are taught at school to despise the weak, and practise the lesson at home in petty domestic torments to the weak of their circle—their sisters; receiving, at the same time, from those very sisters, a thousand little services, without consciousness and without gratitude. Is it astonishing that these boys should hereafter be selfish husbands and tyrannical fathers? . . .

Oh, why are mothers in such haste to delegate to others the delightful task which Providence has assigned to them? . . . They, as the guardian angels of man's infancy, are charged with a mission—to them is committed the implanting of that heavenly germ, to which God must indeed give the increase, but for the early culture of which they are answerable. . . .

It is of the utmost importance to the virtue and happiness of men, that they enter life with exalted notions of female character, and that they be not satisfied with the semblance without the reality of virtue. Let each mother then engrave upon the heart of her son such an image of feminine virtue and loveliness, as may make it sufficient for him to turn his eyes inward in order to draw thence a power sufficient to combat evil, and to preserve him from wretchedness. And here, I may observe, is a great inducement for mothers to cultivate their intellectual powers, for those powers will materially affect their influence over grown-up sons. . . .

It is by no means my intention to assert, that women should be passive and indifferent spectators of the great political questions, which affect the well-being of the community, neither can I repeat the old adage, that "women have nothing to do with politics"; they have, and ought to have, much to do with politics. But in what way? It has been maintained, that their public participation in them would be fatal to the best interests of society. How, then, are women to interfere in politics? As moral agents; as representatives of the moral principle; as champions of the right in preference to the expedient; by their endeavours to instil into their relatives of the other sex the un-compromising sense of duty and self-devotion, which ought to be *their* ruling principles! The immense influence which women possess will be most beneficial, if allowed to flow in its natural channels, viz., domestic ones, because it is of the utmost importance to the existence of influence, that purity of motive be unquestioned. It is by no means affirmed, that women's political feelings are always guided by the abstract principles of right and wrong; but they are surely more likely to be so, if they themselves are restrained from the public expression of them. Participation in scenes of popular emotion has a natural tendency to warp conscience and overcome charity. Now conscience and charity (or love) are the very essence of woman's beneficial influence, therefore everything tending to blunt the one and sour the other is sedulously to be avoided by her. It is of the utmost importance to men to feel, in consulting a wife, a mother, or a sister, that they are appealing *from* their passions and prejudices, and not *to* them as embodied in a second self: nothing tends to give opinions such weight as the certainty, that the utterer of them is free from all petty or personal motives. The beneficial influence of woman is nulli-fied if once her motives, or her personal character, come to be the subject of attack; and this fact alone ought to induce her patiently to acquiesce in the plan of seclusion from public affairs.

It supposes, indeed, some magnanimity in the possessors of great powers and widely-extended influence, to be willing to exercise them with silent unostentatious vigilance. There must be a deeper principle than usually lies at the root of female education, to induce women to acquiesce in the plan which, assigning to them the responsibility, has denied them the *éclat* of being reformers of society. Yet it is, probably, exactly in proportion to their reception of this truth, and their adoption of it into their hearts, that they will fulfil their own high and lofty mission; precisely because the manifestation of such a spirit is the one thing needful for the regeneration of society. . . . Now it is proverbially as well as scripturally true, that love "seeketh not its own" interest, but the good of others, and finds its highest honour, its highest happiness, in so doing. This is precisely the spirit which can never be too much cultivated by women, because it is the spirit by which their highest triumphs are to be achieved: it is they who are called upon to show forth its beauty, and to prove its power; everything in their education should tend to develope self-devotion and self-renunciation.

From CAN WOMAN REGENERATE SOCIETY? (1844)
Ann Richelieu Lamb
(See pp. 49 and 108.)

Unlike Mrs. Lewis, Ann Lamb believed that woman's spirituality was the result of training and circumstance rather than the mark of her special God-appointed mission. "Those who have been so ungraciously treated in this lower world," she wrote, "would be unwise indeed if they did not comfort themselves with continual thoughts of that better one . . . where man dares no longer oppress the weak or insult the defenseless."

As far as manners and morals are concerned, a book can scarcely be opened without meeting therein the assertion, that woman is the secret and silent spring which keeps us all right; that in her hands is placed that mighty engine "the morals of society"; that she is the keeper of the soul of the social system, &c. All this sounds well, and it would be gratifying to know that we are so much honoured, did the words convey aught to us but sound; for if they are truth, how comes it that under such guardianship, society is what we behold it?

—its surface fair because whitewashed; but below full of darkness and vice.

The guardian angel must either be false to her trust, which not for a moment can we believe, or there must be a stronger influence at work, which it is beyond the possibility of woman to counteract. We are daily told that our power is great, if we only knew how to use it; I regret to say that for my own part I have never yet been fully made aware of this power, and therefore cannot recognise the influence of woman to be what it is represented. The little she has of either power or influence is crippled by the obstacles placed in her path. When she leads the way to pleasure or amusement, she is followed, and for a day, a short-lived day, is admired; when she points to stern duties, and speaks of man as the being of immortality, rather than the pleasure-hunter, or lover of the world; when she reasons of self-government, or the principles of self-regulation; what is the result? She is tolerated, perhaps, but laughed at for her pains; she may dance, sing, and be a child as long as she pleases, write pretty stories, string rosy words in rhyme—but to help in devising or practising such schemes, as may be for the real benefit of mankind, becomes in her, a matter for ridicule, a subject for merriment, impertinence not to be endured! . . .

We hear forever of the self-devotion of our sex. In nine cases out of ten such a feeling would be more aptly named by the designation of self-abasement or self-annihilation; since the thing so much lauded is neither more nor less than the act of the devoted one losing her self-identity in that of a being composed of no better materials than herself; whose will, no matter what! becomes her law. . . . The consequence of course being, that in losing herself she loses her self-respect, and becomes the veriest slave of another, whose selfish wishes she fulfils *au pied de la lettre*; whose every whim and caprice she pampers to their fullest extent, and in some instances whose evil passions she helps to run riot, because "he is far too much loved to be contradicted." Such is woman's devotion! lowering her own character and demoralizing that of another! . . .

Woman not being permitted by our present social arrangements and conventional rules, to procure a livelihood through her own exertions, *is compelled* to unite herself with some one who can provide for her; therefore in contracting matrimony she thinks principally of this necessary requisite. I fear I annoy the vanity of man in saying this, but I cannot help it, for it is the truth. Man, on the other hand, being educated to regard woman as a something made merely for his benefit, with which he can do as he pleases, amusing himself with the toy the one moment, and neglecting it, if he chooses, the next, seeks to find in his wife, a sort of upper servant, or female valet, who is to wait upon him, attend to his wants, instinctively anticipate his wishes, and study his comfort, and who is to live for the sole purpose of seeing him well-fed, well-lodged, and well-pleased! Companionship, friendship, neither of them bargain for. As long as the female looks pretty, dresses well, and waits assiduously upon her liege lord, he is polite and attentive enough; but if from the multiplicity of her cares and petty annoyances, she smiles less frequently, and finds little time to adorn herself—except on state occasions—then the manner begins to change somewhat on the part of the once devoted admirer. He wonders how she manages so badly, is amazed at her want of equability, and declares that she often looks very like the opposite of what he always expects *his* wife to appear. On the other hand, the lady meeting with no participation in her cares, but rather a perpetual fault-finding, and blame-giving, for things she cannot help, begins to think she may have purchased a station in society at too dear a cost; one regret leads to another, until she feels her situation all but unendurable—the very antipodes of her inexperienced expectation.

She has no one to blame, as she entered voluntarily into such an engagement (if indeed we can speak of a woman having power to do any action voluntarily, when a stern necessity is on her right hand and on her left, when she has before her indeed only a choice of evils); she smothers her grief and disappointment; heartlessly, and cheerlessly performing her appointed tasks; getting hardened, if not accustomed to the frowning, grumbling, and never ending hints, that she is always in the wrong. In this manner that existence passes wearily away, which under better circumstances, and a more elevated and enlightened social system, might have been one of happiness to both parties; especially were the relationship and duties of married persons towards each other better understood and more clearly defined.

Nothing, however, seems at present to be known, than the rule of "Wives *obey* your husbands!" no matter how silly, how absurd—nay, indeed, in many instances, how ruinous the command may be. The duty of the wife *means* the obedience of a Turkish slave, while the husband believes himself empowered to be of a like imperiousness with the follower of the turbaned prophet. It is a curious fact, that we never hear the faintest echo of that equally distinct command,

"Men, love and *honour* your wives!" It seems to be taken for granted, that women have many obligations in this state to perform, from which men are free; but this is far from being the case: the obligations being the same, and equally binding upon both, though from the perverse training to which the sexes are subjected, the whole weight is laid upon those who, from the very falsehood of their education, are the least able to bear it. Woman, chained and fettered, is yet expected to work miracles. Man, however, deems himself free to do as he likes; to spend his money and time as he pleases, and to scold his *patient Griselda,** should she dare to remonstrate about extravagance, waste, indolence, or idleness. Her business is to love! suffer!! and obey!!! the three articles of woman's creed. She must on no account reason or suppose herself wiser than her protector and legislator, even should he bring her and her children to beggary.

THE EMANCIPATION OF WOMEN (1851)
Harriet Taylor Mill
(See p. 123.)

Harriet Hardy was born in 1807, daughter of a domineering surgeon and male midwife, whose wife bore him seven children. When Harriet was eighteen years old she married John Taylor, a manufacturer and Unitarian Radical eleven years older than she. Harriet and John had three children, including one daughter, Helen, who grew up to be an outspoken feminist during the activist years of the later nineteenth century. In 1830 Harriet Hardy Taylor met John Stuart Mill, who was also in his early twenties; and the intense intellectual and emotional bond that developed between them quickly became central to both their lives. Honoring her duty to her husband and children, as well as her profound attachment to Mill, Harriet worked out an arrangement suitable to all: she functioned as John Taylor's wife to outward appearances (bearing him their last child in July 1831), but met with John Stuart Mill for private dinners in her home and went off with him for occasional trips to the seaside. Their lifelong interchange of ideas and shared process of intellection was stimulating in the extreme to Harriet herself; and in an age in which women were so

* Patient Griselda was a legendary woman who was rewarded for enduring her husband's cruelties without resistance or complaint.

badly educated, it marked perhaps the highest degree of intellectual development she could have attained.

After twenty years of this unconventional triangle, John Taylor died. Two years later, in April 1851, John Stuart Mill and Harriet Taylor were married. When Harriet died in Avignon, France, in 1858, Mill bought a cottage "as close as possible to the place where she is buried" and made daily pilgrimages to her grave. Mill credited Harriet with rescuing him from a life of emotional aridity and with creating in conversation many of the insights that he went on to develop in print. After her death he dedicated his most important work, On Liberty, to her, writing:

> Were I but capable of interpreting to the world one half the great thoughts and noble feelings which are buried in her grave I should be the medium of a greater benefit to it than is ever likely to arise from anything that I can write, unprompted and unassisted by her all but unrivalled wisdom.

Of more lasting significance is the landmark study The Subjection of Women (1869), which he wrote at the request of Harriet's daughter, Helen, in homage to his wife's memory and in an effort to record their shared belief in the necessity for women's emancipation. Mill's classic essay had an international impact on nineteenth-century feminism, but many of the same ideas and arguments appear in Harriet's shorter 1851 article written anonymously as a response to the birth of the American suffrage movement, and published a few months after their marriage.

When . . . we ask why the existence of one-half the species should be merely ancillary to that of the other—why each woman should be a mere appendage to a man, allowed to have no interests of her own that there may be nothing to compete in her mind with his interests and his pleasure; the only reason which can be given is, that men like it. It is agreeable to them that men should live for their own sake, women for the sake of men: and the qualities and conduct in subjects which are agreeable to rulers, they succeed for a long time in making the subjects themselves consider as their appropriate virtues. . . . [H]ow wonderfully the ideas of virtue set afloat by the powerful, are caught and imbibed by those under their dominion, is exemplified by the manner in which the world were once persuaded that the supreme virtue of subjects was loyalty to kings, and are still persuaded that the paramount virtue of womanhood is loyalty to men. Under a nominal recognition of a moral code common to both, in practice self-will and self-assertion form the type of what are designated as manly virtues, while abnegation of self, patience, resignation, and submission to power, unless when resistance is commanded by other interests than their own, have been stamped by general consent as pre-eminently the duties and graces required of women. The meaning being merely, that power makes itself the centre of moral obligation, and that a man likes to have his own will, but does not like that his domestic companion should have a will different from his.

The common opinion is, that whatever may be the case with the intellectual, the moral influence of women over men is almost salutary. It is, we are often told, the great counteractive of selfishness. However the case may be as to personal influence, the influence of the position tends eminently to promote selfishness. The most insignificant of men, the man who can obtain influence or consideration nowhere else, finds one place where he is chief and head. There is one person, often greatly his superior in understanding, who is obligated to consult him, and whom he is not obliged to consult. He is judge, magistrate, ruler, over their joint concerns; arbiter of all differences between them. . . . If there is any self-will in the man, he becomes either the conscious or unconscious despot of his household. The wife, indeed, often succeeds in gaining her objects, but it is by some of the many various forms of indirectness and management.

Thus the position is corrupting equally to both; in the one it produces the vices of power, in the other those of artifice. . . .

We are not now speaking of cases in which there is anything deserving the name of strong affection on both sides. . . . That, where it exists, is too powerful a principle not to modify greatly the bad influences of the situation; it seldom, however, destroys them entirely. Much oftener the bad influences are too strong for the affection, and destroy it. The highest order of durable and happy attachments would be a hundred times more frequent than they are, if the affection which the two sexes sought from one another were that genuine friendship, which only exists between equals in privileges as in faculties. But with regard to what is commonly called affection in married life—the habitual and almost mechanical feeling of kindliness, and pleasure in each other's society, which generally grows up between persons who constantly live together, unless there is actual dislike—

there is nothing in this to contradict or qualify the mischievous influence of the unequal relation. Such feelings often exist between a sultan and his favourites, between a master and his servants; they are merely examples of the pliability of human nature, which accommodates itself in some degree even to the worst circumstances, and the commonest natures always the most easily. . . .

[T]he assertion, that the wife's influence renders the man less selfish, contains, as things now are, fully as much error as truth. Selfishness towards the wife herself, and the children, the wife's influence, no doubt, tends to counteract. But the general effect on him of her character, so long as her interests are concentrated in the family, tends but to substitute for individual selfishness a family selfishness, wearing an amiable guise, and putting on the mask of duty. How rarely is the wife's influence on the side of the public virtue; how rarely does it do otherwise than discourage any effort of principle by which the private interests or worldly vanities of the family can be expected to suffer. Public spirit, sense of duty towards the public good, is of all virtues, as women are now educated and situated, the most rarely to be found among them; they have seldom even, what in men is often a partial substitute for public spirit, a sense of personal honour connected with any public duty. . . . In England, the wife's influence is usually the illiberal and anti-popular side: this is generally the gaining side for personal interest and vanity; and what to her is the democracy of liberalism in which she has no part—which leaves her the Pariah it found her? The man himself, when he marries, usually declines into Conservatism; begins to sympathize with the holders of power, more than with its victims, and thinks it his part to be on the side of authority. . . .

Custom hardens human beings to any kind of degradation, by deadening the part of their nature which would resist it. And the case of women is, in this respect, even a peculiar one, for no other inferior caste that we have heard of have been taught to regard their degradation as their honour. . . . They are taught to think, that to repel actively even an admitted injustice done to themselves, is somewhat unfeminine, and had better be left to some male friend or protector. To be accused of rebelling against anything which admits of being called an ordinance of society, they are taught to regard as an imputation of a serious offence, to say the least, against the proprieties of their sex. It requires unusual moral courage as well as disinterestedness in a woman, to express opinions favourable to women's enfranchisement, until, at least, there is some prospect of obtaining it. The comfort of her individual life, and her social consideration, usually depend on the good-will of those who hold the undue power; and to possessors of power any complaint, however bitter, of the misuse of it, is a less flagrant act of insubordination than to protest against the power itself. The professions of women in this matter remind us of the State offenders of old, who on the point of execution, used to protest their love and devotion to the sovereign by whose unjust mandate they suffered. Griselda herself might be matched from the speeches put by Shakespeare into the mouths of male victims of kingly caprice and tyranny. . . .

The literary class of women, especially in England, are ostentatious in disclaiming the desire for equality or citizenship, and proclaiming their complete satisfaction with the place which society assigns to them; exercising in this, as in many other respects, a most noxious influence over the feelings and opinions of men, who unsuspectingly accept the servilities of toadyism as concessions to the force of truth, not considering that it is in the personal interest of these women to profess whatever opinions they expect will be agreeable to men. . . . They depend on men's opinion for their literary as well as for their feminine successes; and such is their bad opinion of men, that they believe there is not more than one in ten thousand who does not dislike and fear strength, sincerity, or high spirit in a woman. They are therefore anxious to earn pardon and toleration for whatever of these qualities their writing may exhibit on other subjects, by a studied display of submission on this: that they may give no occasion for vulgar men to say (what nothing will prevent vulgar men from saying), that learning makes women unfeminine, and that literary ladies are likely to be bad wives.

In "The Emancipation of Women," *Westminster Review,* July 1851

ON HARRIET TAYLOR MILL'S
VIEWS OF WOMEN (1851)
Charlotte Brontë
(*See pp.* 95, 109, 115, 151, 160, 272, *and* 273.)

When Charlotte Brontë (1816–1855) wrote the following letter to Elizabeth Gaskell, she was under the impression that Harriet Taylor

Mill's anonymous Westminster Review *article was written not by a woman as she had originally assumed, but by John Stuart Mill. Gaskell published the letter after Brontë's death in her biography of her friend, provoking J. S. Mill to protest Brontë's remarks as an insult not to himself but to his wife, whom he indignantly defended as "the most warm-hearted woman, of the largest and most genial sympathies, and the most forgetful of self in her generous zeal to do honour to others, whom I have ever known."*

Of all the articles respecting which you question me, I have seen none except that notable one in the *Westminster* on the Emancipation of Women. But why are you and I to think (perhaps I should rather say to *feel*) so exactly alike on some points that there can be no discussion between us? Your words on this paper express my thought. Well-argued it is—clear, logical—but vast is the hiatus of omission; harsh the consequent jar on every finer chord of the soul. What is this hiatus? . . . I think the writer forgets there is such a thing as self-sacrificing love and disinterested devotion. When I first read the paper, I thought it was the work of a powerful, clear-headed woman, who had a hard, jealous heart, and nerves of bend [thick, strong, shoe-sole] leather; of a woman who longed for power, and had never felt affection. To many women affection is sweet, and power conquered indifferent—though we all like influence won. I believe J. S. Mill would make a hard, dry, dismal world of it; and yet he speaks admirable sense through a great portion of his article, especially when he says that if there be a natural unfitness in women for men's employment, there is no need to make laws on the subject; leave all careers open; let them try; those who ought to succeed will succeed, or, at least, will have a fair chance; the incapable will fall back into their right place. . . . In short, J. S. Mill's head is, I dare say, very good, but I feel disposed to scorn his heart. You are right when you say that there is a large margin in human nature over which the logicians have no dominion; glad am I that it is so.

From Charlotte Brontë to Elizabeth Gaskell, September 20, 1851, in *The Brontës: Their Lives, Friendships and Correspondence in Four Volumes*, ed. Thomas J. Wise and J. Alexander Symington (Oxford: Shakespeare Head Press, 1932), letter no. 708.

"OF QUEENS' GARDENS" (1865)
John Ruskin

Art critic, painter, writer, and Christian social reformer, John Ruskin (1819–1900) was the only son of wealthy and indulgent parents. Sarah Lewis would have approved of his upbringing, since his evangelical mother read the Bible with him every day, educated him until he was ten, and then kept him at home with a private tutor. When it became time for Ruskin to attend Oxford, his mother rented rooms nearby, while his equally attached father traveled out on weekends. Ruskin remained close to his parents throughout their lives, writing to them daily during the brief periods when the family did not live together. A year before Ruskin delivered this lecture, his marriage of five years ended in annulment due to his inability to consummate the union. Ruskin's intense, rapturous evocation of the perfect woman secluded in her home and garden, always available to praise and inspire men, captures the primitive longing for peace and nurturance that underlay much male encouragement for women to make domestic love into a religious mission.

The man's power is active, progressive, defensive. He is eminently the doer, the creator, the discoverer, the defender. His intellect is for speculation and invention; his energy for adventure, for war, and for conquest, wherever war is just, wherever conquest necessary. But the woman's power is for rule, not for battle—and her intellect is not for invention or creation, but for sweet ordering, arrangement, and decision. She sees the qualities of things, their claims, and their places. Her great function is Praise: she enters into no contest, but infallibly judges the crown of contest. By her office, and place, she is protected from all danger and temptation. The man, in his rough work in [the] open world, must encounter all peril and trial: to him, therefore, must be the failure, the offence, the inevitable error: often he must be wounded, or subdued; often misled, and *always* hardened. But he guards the woman from all this; within his house, as ruled by her, unless she herself has sought it, need enter no danger, no temptation, no cause of error or offence. This is the true nature of home—it is the place of Peace; the shelter, not only from all injury, but from all terror, doubt, and division. In so far as it is not this, it is not home:

so far as the anxieties of the outer life penetrate into it, and the inconsistently-minded, unknown, unloved, or hostile society of the outer world is allowed by either husband or wife to cross the threshold, it ceases to be home; it is then only a part of that outer world which you have roofed over, and lighted fire in. But so far as it is a sacred place, a vestal temple, a temple of the hearth watched over by Household Gods, before whose faces none may come but those whom they can receive with love, . . . so far it vindicates the name, and fulfils the praise, of home.

And wherever a true wife comes, this home is always round her. The stars only may be over her head; the glow-worm in the night-cold grass may be the only fire at her foot: but home is yet wherever she is; and for a noble woman it stretches far round her, better than ceiled with cedar, or painted with vermilion, shedding its quiet light far, for those who else were homeless.

This, then, I believe to be—will you not admit it to be—the woman's true place and power? But do not you see that to fulfil this, she must—as far as one can use such terms of a human creature—be incapable of error? So far as she rules, all must be right, or nothing is. She must be enduringly, incorruptibly good; instinctively, infallibly wise—wise, not for self-development, but for self-renunciation: wise, not that she may set herself above her husband, but that she may never fail from his side: wise, not with the narrowness of insolent and loveless pride, but with the passionate gentleness of an infinitely variable, because infinitely applicable, modesty of service—the true changefulness of woman. . . .

We come now to our last, our widest question—What is her queenly office with respect to the state? . . . What the woman is to be within her gates, as the centre of order, the balm of distress, and the mirror of beauty, that she is also to be without her gates, where order is more difficult, distress more imminent, loveliness more rare. . . . There is not a war in the world, no, nor an injustice, but you women are answerable for it; not in that you have provoked, but in that you have not hindered. Men, by their nature, are prone to fight; they will fight for any cause, or for none. It is for you to choose their cause for them, and to forbid them when there is no cause. There is no suffering, no injustice, no misery in the earth, but the guilt of it lies with you. Men can bear the sight of it, but you should not be able to bear it. Men may tread it down without sympathy in their own struggle; but men are feeble in sympathy, and contracted in hope; it is you only who can feel the depths of pain; and conceive the way of its healing. Instead of trying to do this, you turn away from it; you shut yourselves within your park walls and garden gates; and you are content to know that there is beyond them a whole world in wilderness—a world of secrets which you dare not penetrate; and of suffering which you dare not conceive.

In John Ruskin, *Sesame and Lilies* (1865)

TWO

The Girl of
the Period

In the final third of the nineteenth century, as women were making
political and economic gains, conservative sentiment turned from ex-
tolling their selfless, missionary love to damning them for unfeminine
moral license of all sorts. Fashionable middle-class women of the late
1860s who were becoming overtly flirtatious and sexually assertive (as
upper-class women had certainly been in the very early part of the
century), were attacked with as much horror as were those women
seeking an education or a political voice. For many Victorians, this
decline in feminine modesty was akin to the demand for a wider
sphere for women, another sign of the steady degradation of the sex.
One of the most prolific writers of such antifemale and antifeminist
polemic was an individualistic, independent, rebellious, middle-aged
woman named Eliza Lynn Linton. On March 14, 1868, Mrs. Linton
used the pages of the *Saturday Review*, a popular conservative weekly
that became famous for its attacks on women's rights advocates, to
accuse upper-middle-class girls of behaving like prostitutes. With her
forceful and carefully aimed satire, Mrs. Linton inaugurated a lively
magazine controversy and a cultural fad that took the form of "Girl
of the Period" products, jokes, and household quarrels. The article
caused a sensation not only because of its risqué innuendos, but also
because it was an accurate if exaggerated account of the effects of the
marriage market upon manners and character. Linton's article, like
most contemporary journalism by women, was published anonymously and written in male persona.

Among the most thoughtful responses to Linton's attack was
Penelope Holland's article published in *Macmillan's Magazine*,
written as a self-defense by "a Belgravian young lady." The article
rings true in its description of the demoralization of young women

of the privileged classes, who were exhorted to live lives of high spiritual and philanthropic purpose, yet who were locked up at home with nothing to do but plan for the next ball and hope for a good husband. For Holland, the way to improve the moral situation of women was to release them from confining, time-consuming domestic rituals and allow them to develop their minds in the service of others. Such arguments, however, did not capture the popular imagination with the same force as Linton's original satire, which (as the feminist *Englishwoman's Review* lamented in October 1868), was even translated into Hindustani and used as an argument against the education of women in India.

"THE GIRL OF THE PERIOD" (1868)
Eliza Lynn Linton

Eliza Lynn Linton (1822–1898) was the youngest of twelve children. Her mother died when she was five months old. Nearsighted, dreamy, and victimized by her siblings, Eliza was considered the unwomanly rebel of the family, lost her religious faith in her teens despite her bishop grandfather, and found her vocation as a writer in her early twenties. After a lengthy struggle she convinced her father to support her for a year's test period in London, where she researched and wrote a historical novel, Azeth the Egyptian *(1846). This first effort was a success, and on the strength of it she established herself with the Morning Chronicle as the first salaried woman journalist in England. In her late thirties she married W. J. Linton, a radical engraver and widower whose four young children had been raised in a rather bohemian fashion. Eliza took the family to London and introduced the children to conventional clothing and regular lessons. She had less success with their father, however, since W. J. Linton had a messianic faith in the imminence of revolution, which rendered him careless with money and indifferent to work. The family ran through Eliza's resources quickly; and between household responsibilities and financial anxiety, her usually extraordinary productivity dropped off dramatically. Finally the Lintons separated, and he took the children to America.*

It was about a year after Linton's departure that Eliza Linton published "The Girl of the Period." So commenced the second part of her professional life, which was largely devoted to misogynist broad-

sides written with great energy and conviction. Her characteristic targets were undutiful and unmotherly women, from the "Fashionable Lady" to the "Shrieking Sisterhood" of suffragists. Her ideal remained a nostalgically conceived domestic angel, although her own angry and assertive writing bore the stamp of a very different kind of character.

Eliza Linton's personal life reflected the same contradictions. A self-proclaimed hater of women "as a race," she was a devoted and sympathetic friend to many individual women, a reliably tender counselor in times of stress. Despite her strong opposition to higher education for women, she made a protégée of the young feminist writer Beatrice Harraden, an early university graduate, whom Linton lovingly referred to as "my little B.A." Throughout her extraordinarily energetic and zestful life, to her pain and confusion the traditionally womanly forms of satisfaction eluded her, particularly the pleasures of motherhood. When she came to write her autobiography, she did it as a novel with a male protagonist (Christopher Kirkwood, 1885).

Time was when the phrase, "a fair young English girl," meant the ideal of womanhood . . . a girl who could be trusted alone if need be, because of the innate purity and dignity of her nature, but who was neither bold in bearing nor masculine in mind; a girl who, when she married, would be her husband's friend and companion, but never his rival; one who would consider his interests as identical with her own, and not hold him as just so much fair game for spoil; who would make his house his true home and place of rest, not a mere passage-place for vanity and ostentation to pass through; a tender mother, an industrious housekeeper, a judicious mistress [to her servants]. . . .

This was in the old time, and when English girls were content to be what God and nature had made them. Of late years we have changed the pattern, and have given to the world a race of women as utterly unlike the old insular ideal as if we had created another nation altogether. . . .

The Girl of the Period is a creature who dyes her hair and paints her face, . . . a creature whose sole idea of life is fun; whose sole aim is unbounded luxury; and whose dress is the chief object of such thought and intellect as she possesses. Her main endeavour is to outvie her neighbours in the extravagance of fashion. . . . What the *demi-monde* [world of fashionable mistresses] does in its frantic efforts to excite attention, she also does in imitation. If some fash-

BBC Hulton Picture Library

Eliza Lynn Linton

ionable *dévergondée en évidence* [obviously debauched woman] is reported to have come out with her dress below her shoulder-blades, and a gold strap for all the sleeve thought necessary, the Girl of the Period follows suit the next day; and then she wonders that men sometimes mistake her for her prototype, or that mothers of girls not quite so far gone as herself refuse her as a companion for their daughters. . . .

This imitation of the *demi-monde* in dress leads to something in manner and feeling, not quite so pronounced perhaps, but far too like to be honourable to herself or satisfactory to her friends. It leads to slang, bold talk, and general fastness; to the love of pleasure and indifference to duty; to the desire of money before either love or happiness; to uselessness at home, dissatisfaction with the monotony of ordinary life, horror of all useful work; in a word, to the worst forms of luxury and selfishness—to the most fatal effects arising from want of high principle and absence of tender feeling.

The Girl of the Period envies the queens of the *demi-monde* far more than she abhors them. She sees them gorgeously attired and sumptuously appointed, and she knows them to be flattered, fêted, and courted with a certain disdainful admiration of which she catches only the admiration while she ignores the disdain. . . . It is this envy of the pleasures, and indifference to the sins, of these women of the *demi-monde* which is doing such infinite mischief to the modern girl . . . though she is not yet prepared to pay quite the same price. Unfortunately, she has already paid too much—all that once gave her distinctive national character.

No one can say of the modern English girl that she is tender, loving, retiring or domestic. . . . The legal barter of herself for so much money, representing so much dash, so much luxury and pleasure—that is her idea of marriage; the only idea worth entertaining. For all seriousness of thought respecting the duties or the consequences of marriage, she has not a trace. If children come, they find but a stepmother's cold welcome from her; and if her husband thinks that he has married anything that is to belong to him . . . the sooner he wakes from his hallucination . . . the less severe will be his disappointment. She has married his house, his carriage, his balance at the banker's, his title; and he himself is just the inevitable condition clogging the wheel of her fortune; at best an adjunct, to be tolerated with more or less patience as may chance. . . .

But the Girl of the Period does not marry easily. Men are afraid of her; and with reason. They may amuse themselves with her for an evening, but they do not readily take her for life. Besides, after all her efforts, she is only a poor copy of the real thing; and the real thing is far more amusing than the copy, because it is real. Men can get that whenever they like; and when they go into their mothers' drawing-rooms, with their sisters and their sisters' friends, they want something of quite a different flavour.

In *Saturday Review*, March 14, 1868

"OUR OFFENCE, OUR DEFENCE,
AND OUR PETITION" (1869)
Penelope Holland

Penelope Holland (d. 1873), wife of an Anglican clergyman, feared that the idleness of domestic life combined with exhortations to fulfill a great spiritual mission would lead young girls into High Church philanthropic sisterhoods modeled on Catholic orders of nuns.

It may be pleasant to write a pointed, stinging satire on the frivolity and the vices of women, seasoning it with that flavour of impropriety which the public takes for wit, and then to hug oneself with the feeling that a duty to society has been performed; but the matter changes its aspect altogether when looked at from *our* point of view. . . .

Let us, then, imagine the case of a girl who at seventeen finds herself a member of a prosperous and wealthy family, with a father and mother still in the prime of life. Let us also suppose her . . . intelligent, high-minded, and warm-hearted. A desultory education has shown her glimpses of much that is interesting in the world around her, and probably the poetry of three or four modern languages has left the traces of many a noble thought and aspiration in her mind. The newspapers lying on her father's table show her each morning the great world with all its sorrow and all its needs. The religious revival, too, affects her powerfully, as in sermon after sermon she hears the preacher extol the merits of self-denial and the glories of self-sacrifice. She is stirred with enthusiasm, and she looks about her for her own personal duties, and asks to have a post assigned her in the battlefield of life. Strange, while all around are up and stirring, there seems to be no place left for her. She reads in stilted phrases in many a "good" book that woman's work is home work and home influence, but this is scarcely applicable to herself. Her home is a luxurious one, and servants are at hand, often in unnecessary numbers, to perform every household duty; and her mother, blessed with many daughters, only asks for her occasional society. . . .

Finding no field for the exercise of her energies inside her father's house, she will probably direct her attempt toward the parish-school. Often, however, she finds it well supplied with trained teachers, who look upon her amateur labours with contempt . . . or . . . her mother finds out . . . that scarlatina, measles, or whooping-cough are prevalent, and forbids her attendance on that score. The same objections are raised against her visiting the poor, even if she feels that her youth and inexperience fit her to comfort the misery and cope with the vice of which she knows nothing. . . . Feeling, however, that she must do something, she pulls out her old schoolbooks, and determines to study by herself, but she presently becomes dissatisfied with her work, discovering her original grounding to be so indifferent that she is building on very insecure foundations. . . . Lastly—and this discourages her more than anything—she reflects that her education and her accomplishments can never be of the slightest use to any one save herself, and she cannot see clearly that they will even help her.

Her mother, distressed at perceiving in her the germ of such unorthodox and troublesome tastes, calls her "morbid," and thinks it right to "rouse" her, by a course of gaiety, probably beginning with a ball at home. . . . The mere physical exertion of dancing for five hours together is a pleasant change from the listless torpor of her life. She enjoys it thoroughly, and when it is over finds that it has left a hundred amusing reminiscences. The little trivial flatteries and compliments which she received would not hurt her if she had anything else to think about; but, as it is, she finds that she dwells more upon them than she at all desires. She begins to despise herself. . . .

The pleasures of society soon pall upon her. From week to week, and month to month, there is no cessation from the weary, purposeless round of gaiety. . . . She no longer cares for dancing for its own sake, she must relieve its monotony with flirtation. Then gradually as she feels herself falling farther and farther away from her own girlish ideal, she clings the more desperately to the only excitement with which she can kill time and smother conscience. Hence arises all the evil against which the moralist and satirist alike inveigh. Hence also the wretched extravagances of tasteless fashion (whose only object is to attract attention), and, worse still, the low tone of morality which all agree in declaring to be daily gaining ground. The affection of schoolboy slang which was in vogue ten years ago is fast being superseded by conversation of a far more dangerous type, and she who would earn the reputation for being fashionably "fast" must stifle every feeling of delicacy and amuse herself by making good men blush while bad men laugh. . . .

She sees some of her friends saved all this degradation by a happy marriage, and wishes to change her lot for one in which she might have some object to live for besides herself, some purpose in life not wholly selfish. Hence proceed many unhappy marriages, when the bride only flies to marriage to save her from the insipid uselessness of her life. Hence also many mercenary marriages which often tempt girls by offering them a larger sphere of action. We think if men oftener had themselves the chance of winning power, wealth, independence, and rank, by a flattering word or an expressive smile, we should hear fewer hard words on this subject. . . . We ask any intelligent man to put himself for a moment into the place of any unmarried woman of his acquaintance. Treated up to the very confines of middle age as if still a child, with no more liberty or independence than at sixteen, obliged to conform to the habits and practices of her father's house, whether congenial or not to her own temper and principles, with no definite object in view, and no prospect of being able to form larger interests till the breaking up of her home (often late in life) leaves her more desolate than before, can we wonder that with many fear overcomes delicacy in their struggle to escape? . . .

In the name therefore of a large class, we demand for girls growing to womanhood the opportunity of spending a portion of their young lives in the service of their God and of their fellow creatures. We implore for them a release from their present bondage of idle selfishness, and the means not only of cultivating their talents, but of exercising them in the cause of good and not of evil. . . . We implore it for the sake of those who are still young, that they may be saved the dreariness and degradation which we have undergone. . . . Grant us a fair trial, and it shall be our fault if at the close of the present century it continues to be a reproach to be called

"A Girl of the Period."

In *Macmillan's Magazine*, February 1869

THREE

Redundant Women

At the heart of the woman's-mission ideology lay the assumption that there was no respectable occupation for women outside of marriage, that true moral purity demanded the shelter of home and economic dependency upon a husband. The difficulties of applying this ideology to the experiences of the working class, where women were necessarily working for their living at age thirteen or younger, became apparent in the controversies detailed in Part IV. Yet, even among middle-class women, whose enforced domesticity gave rise to the ideal of the domestic angel, there were jarring reminders that not every woman had a husband to whose comfort and salvation she could devote her energies. As Ann Lamb bitterly lamented, unmarried women were the victims of pervasive popular prejudice. Jeered at as "social failures," they were treated with alternating contempt and pity. Most of all, they were considered anomalies whose very existence challenged the prevailing view of angelic wifedom as the natural fate of all women.

The census for 1851 revealed that as many as 30 percent of all English women between the ages of twenty and forty were unmarried. Such women were considered "redundant," i.e., excessive in that they overflowed the conventional boundaries of marriage. Since there were only about 6 percent more women than men in this age group, people worried over the reasons why the remaining women, numbering over a million, should be unmarried. Such a large number of adult women leading husbandless lives seemed to indicate a breakdown in the general social system. It is this problem that W. R. Greg boldly addressed in his 1862 essay "Why Are Women Redundant?" The article was reprinted and quoted many times during the following decade.

Greg's recommendations for alleviation of the problem were based on the assumption that women who did not marry were unnatural freaks guilty of neglecting their social duty toward men. The brutal impracticality of his proposals, particularly his suggestion that redundant females be encouraged to emigrate in large numbers to seek husbands in the colonies, led to several feminist rebuttals. Such writers as Jessie Boucherett and Mary Taylor, who were single themselves, responded to Greg by urging women to look to their own efforts for support, and by faulting society for not allowing women access to the education and work that would allow them to be independent. For writers on both sides of the controversy, the question of women's redundancy raised the issue of what value society as a whole might see in the lives of women who remained outside of marriage.

"OLD MAIDISM!" (1844)
Ann Richelieu Lamb
(See pp. 28 and 108.)

Ann Lamb devoted a chapter of her feminist response to Sarah Lewis, Can Woman Regenerate Society? to the social and economic penalties imposed on women without husbands. Her argument is notable for its early insistence upon the personal advantages of remaining single.

That some women remain unmarried from choice, there can be no doubt; and there would be many more . . . were it not for the opprobrium which is generally attached to the name of old maid, from childhood held up before our eyes as a bugbear, perpetually reminding us that marriage is not only admirable and excellent, but *indispensable*; and, on the other hand, single life abominable, hideous; a very violation of the commands of God! Many, not having sufficient stamina to endure the reproach, rush blindly into matrimony, who would have been a thousand times better off had they remained single. . . .

For it is unquestionable, that nowhere can we meet with more kind-hearted, happier, and more *intelligently* contented women, than among those who from different motives have *chosen* to remain single, instead of encountering the arduous task, the unceasing toil and anxiety, which attend the votaries of Hymen. . . .

For surely it is nobler to be looked upon as able to stand upon our own feet, and manage our own affairs, than to be so completely merged in the existence of another, that the law takes no cognizance of us. The unmarried woman is *somebody*; the married, *nobody*! The former shines in her own light; the latter is only the faint reflection of her husband's, in whom both law and public opinion suppose her "to be lost." She can have no will in her half-sort of existence, is utterly without power, a mere derivative, scarcely held responsible for her own actions! Surely the state of the much-ridiculed spinster is better than this very equivocal position, in which there is a great risk of losing our very identity. . . .

Nothing is more ridiculous and unjust than the marked difference which is made between the married and unmarried woman; in consequence of which, we often see some conceited young girl, dressed in all the exuberance of bad taste, and chattering like a magpie, take the precedence of an older and wiser person, for no other reason than because she has happened to find some one to dress her, and keep her, and call her wife. . . . Why are people not respected for what they are as human beings, rather than flattered and caressed for their trappings, or the names they happen to bear? There is no disgrace in being a bachelor; then why should there be such attached to the feminine gender of the same class? . . .

Why so many unmarried women are unhappy, is *not* because they are old maids, but in consequence of *poverty*, and of the difficulty they encounter in maintaining a decent position in society, which we know in this country depends upon the value of our property, not upon our mental endowments and moral worth. It is the want often of the common comforts of life which gives to so many unmarried women that anxious look of care and grief which is seen in the expression of their countenances. This is the evil which distresses and undermines their existence.

"WHY ARE WOMEN REDUNDANT?" (1862)

William Rathbone Greg
(See p. 409.)

William Rathbone Greg (1809–1881) gave up his unsuccessful Cheshire mill in 1850 to begin a prolific career as a political writer. He was among those who believed that social problems could be solved by reference to the operation of the laws of nature, laws that revealed

*themselves in statistical tables. In this influential article, he assumes
that the only natural sources of support for women are marriage and
domestic service.*

There is an enormous and increasing number of single women in the
nation, a number quite disproportionate and quite abnormal. . . .
There are hundreds of thousands of women— . . . proportionally
most numerous in the middle and upper classes—who have to earn
their own living, instead of spending and husbanding the earnings of
men; who, not having the natural duties and labours of wives and
mothers, have to carve out artificial and painfully-sought occupations
for themselves; who, in place of completing, sweetening, and em-
bellishing the existence of others, are compelled to lead an independent and incomplete existence of their own. . . .

There are women, though we believe they are more rare than any
other natural anomalies, who seem utterly devoid of the *fibre féminin*,
to whom Nature never speaks at all, or at least speaks not in her
tenderest tones. There are others too passionately fond of a wild
independence to be passionately fond of any mate. . . . There are
some who seem made for charitable uses; whose heart overflows with
all benevolent emotions, but the character of whose affection is
rather diffusive than concentrated—ideal old maids—old maids *ab
ovo* [from the beginning]. There are women . . . in whom the spiritual
so predominates . . . that human ties and feelings seem pale and poor
by the side of the divine; and to such marriage would appear a profa-
nation, and would assuredly be a mistake. . . . Lastly, there are
women . . . whose brains are so analogous to those of men that they
run nearly in the same channels, are capable nearly of the same toil,
and reach nearly to the same heights; women . . . of hard, sustained,
effective *power*; women who live in and by their intelligence alone,
and who are objects of admiration, but never of tenderness, to the
other sex. Such are rightly and naturally single; but they are abnormal
and not perfect natures. The above classes . . . constitute the *natural
celibates* among the female sex; to all others who go through life unmarried, celibacy is unnatural, even though it may in one sense be
voluntary. . . .

We have now to consider to what causes this startling anomaly
is to be traced, and by what means it may be cured. . . . The chief
causes we shall find to be three in number: the first we shall notice
is EMIGRATION.

I. In the last forty-five years, upwards to 5,000,000 persons have definitely left our shores to find new homes either in our various colonies or in the United States. Of this number we know that the vast majority were men. . . . We must redress the balance. We must restore by an emigration of women that natural proportion between the sexes in the old country and in the new ones. . . . It is not easy to convey a multitude of women across the Atlantic, or to the antipodes, by any ordinary means of transit. To transport the half million from where they are redundant to where they are wanted, at an average rate of fifty passengers in each ship, would require 10,000 vessels, or at least 10,000 voyages. . . . Still, it would be feasible enough to find passenger ships to take out 10,000, 20,000, or 40,000 every year, if they were men. But to contrive some plan to take out such a number of women, especially on a three months' voyage, in comfort, in safety, and in honour, is a problem yet to be solved.

The second difficulty is of a different character. . . . The *class* of women who are redundant here is not exactly the class that is wanted in the colonies, or that is adapted for colonial life. The women most largely wanted there would be found among the working classes, and in the lower ranks of the middle classes: the women who are mostly redundant, the "involuntary celibates" in England, are chiefly to be found in the upper and educated sections of society . . . those *immediately* above the labouring poor, those who swell the ranks of "distressed needlewomen," those who as milliners' apprentices so frequently fall victims to temptation or to toil, the daughters of unfortunate tradesmen, of poor clerks, or poorer curates. Now these, though neither as hardy nor as well trained for the severe labours of a colonial life as dairy-maids, have all been disciplined in the appropriate school of poverty and exertion, and if their superior instruction and refinement added to their difficulties in one way, it would certainly smooth them in another; for of all qualities which education surely and universally confers, that of *adaptability* is the most remarkable. . . .

II. The second cause for this vast amount of super-normal celibacy is undoubtedly to be found in the growing and morbid Luxury of the age. The number of women who remain unmarried, because marriage—such marriage, that is, as is within their reach, or may be offered them—would entail a sacrifice of that "position," which they value more than the attractions of domestic life, is considerable in the middle ranks, and is enormous in the higher ranks. Quite as many

men—probably far more—share these sentiments. . . . They are loth
to resign the easy independence, the exceptional luxuries, the habitual
indulgence of a bachelor's career, for the fetters of a wife, the burden
and responsibility of children, and the . . . monotony of the domestic
hearth. They dread family ties more than they yearn for family joys.

Connected with this part of the subject we must enumerate one
more fruitful source of female celibacy—*domestic service*. The number of women servants in Great Britain, nearly all of whom are necessarily single, is astonishing. In 1851, it reached 905,165, and must
now reach at least a million. Of these 905,165, 582,261 were twenty
years of age and upwards. This is a social phenomenon in all civilised
countries, though probably nowhere on so great a scale as with us;
it would appear to be a permanent and a necessary one; and probably
in its essence and within due limits is not to be found fault with or
deplored. . . . No doubt many of these girls are exposed to considerable hardships. . . . The special remark, however, which we have to
make upon this matter, as bearing on our present subject, is that *female servants do not constitute any part* (or at least only a very small
part) *of the problem we are endeavouring to solve*. They are in no
sense redundant; we have not to cudgel our brains to find a niche or
an occupation for *them*; they are fully and usefully employed; they
discharge a most important and indispensable function in social life;
they do not follow an obligatorily independent, and therefore for
their sex an unnatural, career:—on the contrary, they are attached to
others and are connected with other existences, which they embellish,
facilitate, and serve. In a word, they fulfil both essentials of a woman's being; *they are supported by, and they minister to, men*. We
could not possibly do without them. Nature has not provided one too
many. . . .

III. We have now to treat the last chief cause of the abnormal extent of female celibacy in our country, a cause respecting which . . .
silence would be undutiful and cowardly. We will be plain, because
we wish both to be brief and to be true. So many women are single
because so many men are profligate. . . . Few men—incalculably
few—are truly celibate by nature or by choice. If therefore, every
man among the middle and higher ranks were compelled to lead a
life of stainless abstinence till he married, and unless he married,
we may be perfectly sure that every woman in those ranks would
have so many offers . . . that no one would remain single except those
to whom nature dictated celibacy as a vocation, or those whose cold

hearts, independent tempers, or indulgent selfishness, made them select it as a preferable and more luxurious career. Unhappily, as matters are managed now, thousands of men find it perfectly feasible to combine all of the freedom, luxury, and self-indulgence of a bachelor's career with the pleasures of female society and the enjoyments they seek for there. As long as this is so, so long, we fear, a vast proportion of the best women in the educated classes—women especially who have no dowry beyond their goodness and their beauty—will be doomed to remain involuntarily single. . . .

Celibacy, within the limits which Nature has prescribed, and through her statistical interpreters has clearly proclaimed, is a wholesome and not unlovely feature in the aspect of society. Celibacy, when it transcends these limits . . . is one of the surest and most menacing symptoms of something gravely and radically wrong. Therefore it is that all those efforts, on which chivalric or compassionate benevolence is now so intent, to render single life as easy, as attractive, and as lucrative to women, as unhappily other influences to which we have alluded have already made it to men, *are efforts in a wrong direction*. . . . To endeavour to make women independent of men; to multiply and facilitate their employments; to enable them to earn a separate and ample subsistence by competing with the hardier sex in those careers and occupations hitherto set apart for that sex alone; to induct them generally into avocations, not only as interesting and beneficent, and therefore *appropriate*, but specially and definitely as *lucrative*; to surround single life for them with so smooth an entrance, and such a pleasant, ornamented, comfortable path, that marriage shall almost come to be regarded, not as their most honourable function and especial calling, but merely as one of many ways open to them, competing on equal terms with other ways for their cold and philosophic choice:—this would appear to be the aim and theory of many female reformers, and of one man of real preeminence [J. S. Mill]—wise and farsighted in almost all things else, but here strangely and intrinsically at fault. Few more radical or more fatal errors, we are satisfied, philanthropy has ever made, though her course every where lies marked and strewn with wrecks, and failures, and astounding theories, and incredible assumptions. . . .

In *National Review*, April 1862

"HOW TO PROVIDE FOR
SUPERFLUOUS WOMEN" (1869)
Jessie Boucherett

Jessie Boucherett (1825–1905) was a lifelong feminist who devoted her energies to the extension of employment opportunities for women, particularly women of the lower middle class. Born into the landed gentry, she made her way to London in the late 1850s to seek out the editors of the English Woman's Journal. When she met Barbara Leigh Smith Bodichon and Bessie Rayner Parkes in their Langley Place office, she was surprised and delighted to find them elegant beauties as well as strong-minded feminists. Working with the Langley Place circle, Boucherett helped found the Society for Promoting the Employment of Women, which acted as a training school and employment bureau for women seeking clerical work, then almost wholly a male occupation. Boucherett worked as editor, writer, and proprietor of the Englishwoman's Review, which she founded in 1866 and carried on at her own expense as the successor to the English Woman's Journal. The Englishwoman's Review was the magazine of record for the feminist movement in England and abroad until 1910, always paying special attention to questions surrounding women's work.

There is a general impression that the difficulty now experienced in providing for single women in England is occasioned by a disparity in the number of the sexes caused by the emigration of a larger number of men than of women. This view is very forcibly expressed by Mr. Greg. . . . [Yet in] countries where the men exceed the women in number, as in our own colony of Melbourne and in the United States, the women still find it difficult to live. Mr. Greg estimates the excess of men over women in the United States at 250,000. . . . [Yet the] fact appears to be that the men from the Eastern side of the United States migrate towards the West, leaving a surplus number of women behind them. . . .

I deduct from these facts, that if Mr. Greg's plan for draughting off half a million of English women to the United States and our own colonies could be put into execution, it would be of no advantage to the women exported, as they would merely add to the numbers of superfluous women already existing there. Their departure would be

an immense relief to the women remaining at home, but unfortunately there is nowhere to send them, for nobody wants them, either
in the Old World or the New. It comes to this, that unless Heaven
should send a new planet alongside us to export our superfluous
women to, we must make up our minds to keep them at home. Let
us, then, proceed to consider by what means we can provide for the
superfluous women in England, since it is evident we cannot hope
to get rid of them.

Now let us see what would happen if the opposite system were
pursued, and every young man was compelled to emigrate as soon as
he reached the age of twenty-one. The wages of the men who remained behind would immediately rise, there would no longer be any
necessity for married women to go to work, and of those who are now
in the habit of working many would be withdrawn from the labour-
market.

In consequence of the scarcity of male labour women would be
employed in many occupations now considered not to be women's
work; and, if the system were persevered in, as years went by, and the
men grew old and died off, women would be more and more employed in men's work. The country would at last contain a vast excess of women and a prodigious number of single women, but there
would not be one superfluous woman, as every one would be valuable
in the labour-market. . . .

My belief is that it would be for the ultimate advantage of men
to emigrate more, and so leave enough easy work to the women to
enable them to live; but if I am mistaken in this opinion, and if it
really is the fact that men are happier following easy trades in England than doing hard work in the Colonies, I still hold that they
ought to go; for it cannot be denied that a man is less unhappy cutting
down trees in Canada or tending sheep in Australia, than a woman is
who has no means of earning an honest livelihood. If, then, it is
recognised that the happiness of women is of as much importance as
the happiness of men, it follows that men ought to encounter the
minor evil of hard work rather than expose women to the greater evil
of having no work at all. . . .

The plan then which I advocate for providing for superfluous
women is that of allowing them to engage freely in all occupations
suited to their strength. The great merit of this plan is, that it would
put an end to superfluous women altogether, by converting them
into useful members of society. This is without doubt the plan in-

tended by nature all along, and it is from failing to fulfil it that we have fallen into such difficulties.

But though the plan may be the right one, let it not be imagined that it is an easy one to carry out. The accomplishment of the plan requires no small amount of good feeling and generosity on the part of working men. Let us suppose that a ladies' hairdresser brings up his daughter to succeed him instead of his son. What is the son to do? There is no room for more men in other trades, so he will be obliged to emigrate; and if he loves ease, if he has no spirit of adventure, if he shrinks from leaving his friends, if, in short, he is not a hero, he will prefer to remain at home dressing fine ladies' hair and manufacturing chignons, to roughing it in the bush with his axe in his hand and his gun on his shoulder. So, if he is not generous and manly, he will beg his father to leave the business to him, and to let his sister take her chance like other girls, and marry or starve, sink or swim, as chance may decide.

We have all laughed at the story of the New Zealand chief who, when asked how he had provided for his second wife, from whom he had parted at the recommendation of the Missionary, replied, "Me eat her." It was but his way of providing for superfluous women, and, if it had the disadvantage of being disagreeable to the woman herself, the same may be said of other plans proposed by much better instructed men than the chief.

If he would have allowed his discarded wife a house and some land, as no doubt the Missionary expected, she might have provided for herself; but then, he wanted all the land for himself, and besides, he probably thought that to give women land and let them support themselves might raise up in them a dangerous spirit of independence, and quite destroy all their feminine charms and characteristics; so it seemed to him better to eat her, according to the ancient and venerable custom of the country. Is not the same principle acted on in England? Do not many people think it better that women should suffer than that professions and trades should be opened to them, on the ground that they would be "unsexed" by engaging in them?

It appears to me that our continuance in the present system can only be justified on the principle of the lady who said, "It is natural that *women* should suffer, but it is sad indeed when *men* have to endure privation."

In *Woman's Work and Woman's Culture*, ed. Josephine Butler (1869)

"REDUNDANT WOMEN" (1870)
Mary Taylor
(See p. 151.)

(See p. 151.)

Mary Taylor (1817–1893) was born into the lively household of a Yorkshire manufacturing family with radical politics. She decided early in life that she wanted to earn her way in the world. First, she scandalized her friends by teaching young boys in Germany, then astonished them by setting off for New Zealand with her youngest brother, Henry, in 1845. Mary remained there for fifteen years, running a successful dry-goods store in the frontier city of Wellington, but she missed the intellectual stimulation of England. When she returned she discovered that a feminist movement had begun in earnest. Her way of joining it was to contribute articles to Emily Faithfull's woman-published Victoria Magazine.

Although young women found Mary Taylor to be a loving and encouraging friend, she lived in a reclusive manner after her return to Yorkshire from New Zealand and was rumored to carry a gun. In 1890, near the end of her life, she brought out her feminist novel Miss Miles, on which she had been working throughout her adulthood. Her writing has a peculiarly modern ring because of her insistence on women earning their own way, her directly expressed anger at men and male authority, and her exhilarating adventurousness in urging women on to new experiences. She is best known today as a friend of Charlotte Brontë's.

It gives a curious feeling to a person of the wrong sex to hear for the first time the question—why are women redundant? . . .

The reason why Mr. Greg and a great many other people cannot let the question alone is, that the phrase redundant women really means starving women very often, and almost always women whose means have fallen so much below their position that they are miserably poor. . . . The remedies he proposes amount to this—they are to marry. If the complaint is that they are single, the remedy is unobjectionable. With the poverty that makes marriage impossible he does not propose to deal. . . . [In fact,] he wishes to keep single women poor. He wants their life not to be so easy and attractive as that of the married.

If a moral teacher wished to show mankind the necessity that exists for every one to undertake the management of their own interests, seeing that their knowledge of their own affairs will help them better than the advice of the wisest and most beneficent of mankind, and if he looked out for an example to show him how the imperfect sympathy and the selfishness of even the most cultivated men lead them into unconscious cruelty, he could hardly find one more to his purpose than Mr. Greg's urgent insistence that women who are prevented by poverty from marrying should be kept poor lest their lives should be too easy. If the prescription is intended to force women into matrimony who prefer a single life, it is offensively unjust; if women in general prefer matrimony, as he says they do, it is wantonly cruel. . . .

It is surprising how often in men's schemes for ameliorating feminine evils one meets with this contradiction. Never a philanthropist takes the subject in hand but he begins by vigorously asserting that [women's] first wish is for marriage, and that their main happiness in life must come from their husbands and children, as if the point were doubtful. Seldom, however, does he write long without betraying the belief that they adopt this career because all others are artificially closed to them, and that if a single life is made too pleasant they will not adopt it at all. . . .

God save us from our friends! . . .

After deciding that the number of women who deliberately resolve upon celibacy as "that which they like for itself," will not exceed three or four per cent of the whole, and declaring that the remainder of single women, about thirty per cent, "constitute the problem to be solved; the evil and anomaly to be cured," he finds that two-thirds of these* consist of domestic servants, concerning whom he comes to the following decisions. . . . Their state of celibacy, though it would not be deliberately chosen by above four or five per cent of them, need not be interfered with because "we want them." Their "incomplete existence" need not be remedied, their own inclinations notwithstanding, because "they are supported by, and they minister to, men"; and so "fulfil the essential conditions of a woman's being." . . .

The object of Mr. Greg's pamphlet, he declares, is to protest against "calling the malady by a wrong name, and seeking in a wrong

* 582,261 of the 750,000 women Greg considered truly "redundant"

direction for a cure." The "wrong direction" is in the endeavour to alleviate their poverty by working. A woman then seeking counsel and help from this author is met by a prohibition instead of encouragement. Of ways and means to help herself there are two pointed out. One is not to claim so high a position in marriage, and so make it easier for a husband to maintain her. The other is emigration. . . . [But] though a servant may improve her chances of finding employment by asking lower wages, a woman is not more easily married by being content with an inferior position. The man desires to raise not to lower her. That she must come down in the world to marry him must always be an objection to his choosing her, and a sore point afterwards.

With regard to the other remedy proposed, emigration: The men who emigrate without wives, do so because in their opinion, they cannot afford to marry. The curious idea that the women, whom they would not ask in England, should run after them to persuade them would be laughable if it were not mischievous. . . .

So it appears that to the question, what is to be done with our redundant women? or rather, what is to be done with their poverty? the answer is—they must try and get married. Could any woman, after realising with sorrow how small her chances of such a consummation were, and looking round with terror to the hopeless poverty that was her destiny, receive comfort or encouragement from such futile advice? Something she might perhaps learn from it, though not the lesson it is intended to convey. She would learn that her adviser did not enter into her position, did not care for her suffering; nay that he was ready to lay a still greater burden upon her. Her wants, her choice, her nature, are to be gratified if they accord with the wants and wishes of the other sex; if not, they are to be forced or neglected.

Nor can she fail to see that this thwarting of her wishes, this indifference to her happiness, is not guided by any consistent principle. She is, or she is not, to be dependent; she is, or she is not, to earn a livelihood, for reasons quite foreign to her interests; and when "we want," or "we do not want" her, they are not even taken into consideration. The definition of her "nature" is given only to be ignored, and a great part of what constitutes her real self is left out of it. It is as natural to a woman to help herself as to take help when she can get it; the first may involve labour, hardship, unpleasantness—and so may the other. It is as natural for her to depend on herself as on others, and most natural of all that she should choose which it shall be. And she herself, aided by the deeper interest she feels in the question, can hardly fail to advance further towards its solution, if once she takes it in hand, than her would-be helpers. No conscientious woman fairly takes up the question without seeing that if she has no maintenance she ought to earn one, and if she knows anything of the world at all, knows that there are legal disabilities that interfere with her doing so. So long as the majority of her sex cannot own money, they will not be taught those trades that require the use of it, nor will any woman be in a position to take clerks or apprentices. She has therefore no means of learning from her own sex, and no permission (if it were practicable) to learn from the other. She will see, too, that the selfishness of trade unions, and the various interested motives that make men wish to keep women poor, and desire them to be dependent, are the main causes why these disabilities were inflicted, and why they are not removed. She will know that only those are her friends who are willing to help her to the unrestricted use of her own powers. Those only preach a true morality who urge upon her the duty of looking to herself, and herself only, for subsistence, and the perfect right she has to make her life as "easy, pleasant, and lucrative" as she can.

She may infer also one or two things, the knowledge of which will give her encouragement. When once she has become aware of the strong desire that some men have to prevent her acquiring the power of earning money, she will see that the difference of faculty, the weaker intellect, the sensitive brain, &c., that are attributed to women, were discovered when an argument was needed for a certain conclusion, not used in order to arrive at it.

In Mary Taylor, *The First Duty of Women* (1870), reprinted from *Victoria Magazine*, June 1870

FOUR

Suffering for Beauty

As the nineteenth century began, fashionable English women were wearing relatively comfortable Empire dresses, which emphasized the bustline and flowed in loose, soft lines from a high waist. By the 1820s, however, the newly popular fashion magazines were showing the way toward tighter waists, more confining corsets, and puffy skirts. By the time Victoria took the throne, wasp waists, molded bosoms, and rounded skirts were the established rule. The following decades worked superficial changes on this pattern, but the essential quality of dress remained the same. For the middle- and upper-class woman, being fashionably dressed meant resembling a kind of ambulatory armchair. Well-stuffed, sculptured, and upholstered clothes parodied the basic body shape, immobilized the body itself, and necessitated many yards of costly fabrics and many hours of seamstresses' labor.

The financial and physical extravagance of women's clothing was commented on throughout the period. Crinolines were criticized for being absurdly cumbersome and for making traveling in small carriages or going to the theater inconvenient for male companions as well as for the women, whose skirts were dramatically extended by the hoops. But crinolines were merely one expression of the overall trend toward exaggerating the shape of a woman's body into unnatural and encumbering forms. Sheaths, tubular skirts that in the last quarter of the century replaced the wide bells and cones, were also highly constricting and overupholstered. Sleeves varied dramatically throughout the century, but whether they were tight off the shoulder, puffy mutton chops, layered pagodas, or closely fitted, it was always difficult to move one's arms in them. The bosom was flattened into a pillowlike, undifferentiated swelling. The rear was exaggerated under shaped horsehair or steel bustles. Because legs were taboo, even bathing costumes (which were meant never to be seen) were in the shape of gowns until late in the century, and underpants (which were not worn by women before the 1840s) were at first slit at the crotch and down the inseams to avoid resemblance to trousers. The only trace of natural form was the décolletage of evening dress, which was denounced by Eliza Lynn Linton and many others. But worst of all, from the point of view of many observers and female sufferers, was the compression of the waist into seventeen or eighteen inches by the tight lacing of corsets.

One of the defenses offered for the delicate fabrics and extreme restrictiveness of fashionable dress was that it was made to be worn by women who walked on soft carpets and traveled by private carriage, had servants to help them dress and keep their clothes clean, and were never troubled by dirty pavement, rain, or even the necessity to bend down. In other words, fashionable women's dress was meant to be a sign of class and emphasized the prerogatives of wealth.

Working-class women dressed more practically by necessity. They wore short dresses, the toughest shoes they could afford, and as many layers of clothes as would keep them warm. They often went without shoes or outer clothes so that the men of the family could dress more sturdily or more respectably (depending on their jobs) or so that the family could eat better. Much of their clothing was bought second-hand. Better-off young factory girls who wished to imitate the clothing of the middle class could buy one-shilling crinolines or club together for a fancy accessory like impractically thin boots or colored ostrich feathers for hats. Servants sometimes acquired their mistresses' castoffs. Such fortunate working-class girls were criticized by middle-class observers for dressing garishly or above their station.

In the privileged classes, the less work women did, the wider they swelled, the more their clothing absorbed the work of others, and the more they were employed as billboards of their fathers' or husbands' wealth. The clothing of nineteenth-century fashionable women simultaneously announced their importance and their lack of activity. It fit the ideal of the dependent domestic angel just as the plain black business suit fit the new ideal of the industrious businessman.

Feminists first attempted to introduce healthier and more comfortable clothes in 1851 with the bloomer costume. The outfit was immediately and brutally ridiculed because of its daringly trouserlike design. In the 1880s, the Rational Dress movement took up the call for two-legged clothing and a simpler corseting. At the same time, loose, flowing, pseudo-medieval dress was introduced in university towns through the influence of the Pre-Raphaelite painters and models. But the real change came in the 1890s with the introduction of the well-balanced bicycle, which created a demand for clothes that allowed women mobility. Although most women cyclists continued to wear long skirts kept down by skirt holders and weights, knickerbockers and divided skirts were sometimes worn despite the jeers and even physical attacks they provoked on the street. As one reformer pointed out, the ridicule of men for the new and comfortable clothing was coarse and vulgar in a way that their laughter at the extravagances of fashion never was. Male objections were often contradictory. Women were told that they were desexualizing themselves and that they were being dangerously provocative. Common to both of these complaints, however, was the root difficulty: by wearing clothes that imitated the easy mobility of men's dress, women were claiming control of their own bodies, whether to offer or withhold them.

Although divided skirts did not become popular among noncyclists, the 1890s did usher in a looser, plainer style of dress, suitable to the lives of women who rode railways and omnibuses, walked pavements, worked in offices and schools, and took more exercise. The loose straight skirt and blouse, which did not require stiff corseting, became the new style. Women were still expected to dress in a way that distinguished them from men and emphasized their decorative function, but they were no longer willing to suffer severe discomfort or immobility for the sake of beauty.

PERILS OF THE CRINOLINE (1850)
Lady Dorothy Nevill

Crinolines were introduced in 1857 as the culmination of thirty years of ever-expanding women's skirts. A reinvention of an eighteenth-century device, the crinoline was made of a light steel wire covered with tape, arranged in rows of increasing circumference. The wires were initially attached to a petticoat, but later they were interconnected without fabric as a steel "cage," which left the woman's legs relatively unencumbered within the wide circle of hoops.

At first, the crinoline was hailed by women as a relief from the

Getting dressed in the era of the crinoline

heavy layers of petticoats, some stiffened with horsehair, which had previously provided their skirts with bulk. But crinolines were soon attacked from several sides: they made it hard to sit down, indecent to bend over, and, as Lady Dorothy Nevill (1826–1913) and others could testify, treacherous to stand near the fire. One must picture Lady Dorothy Nevill at the time of this incident clothed in a stiff yet billowing silken tent three to five yards in circumference.

That was the day of that monstrosity "the crinoline," which once came near to costing me my life; in fact, I only escaped a terrible fate through mercifully retaining my presence of mind. I was in the drawing-room one evening after dinner at Dangstein before the gentlemen had joined us, and at the time my dress caught fire I was showing a lady an engraving of Mr. Cobden which he had just given me, and which hung near the fireplace. Somehow or other my voluminous dress caught fire, and in an instant I was in a blaze, but I kept my presence of mind, and, rolling myself in the hearthrug, by some means or other eventually beat out and subdued the flames. I was rather badly burnt about one of my arms, where the marks remain to this day, but otherwise I was unhurt, and, oddly enough, not at all frightened; in fact, after having common whitening, made into a paste with water, applied to my arm—an excellent receipt for burns of which I had but a day or two before been reading—I came downstairs again in time to meet the gentlemen coming from their coffee. My not having been frightened is rather puzzling, but I have an idea that the thought of trying this new receipt took up my attention. None of the ladies present could of course do much to assist me, for their enormous crinolines rendered them almost completely impotent to deal with fire, and had they come very close to me, all of them would have been in a blaze too.

In Lady Dorothy Nevill, *Reminiscences of Dorothy Nevill* (1906)

A LETTER ON CORSETS (1870)
Englishwoman's Domestic Magazine

Corsets of the time—which functioned as brassieres and girdles in one—were made with whalebone stays and a wooden or whalebone "busk," a stiff slat of about an inch in width running down the center front of the corset to keep it flat. By tightening the laces that held the corset together, women could achieve the very small waist that was part of the nineteenth-century ideal of feminine beauty. Tight-lacers extolled both the sensual pleasures and bracing moral benefits of compression, while some doctors warned women that their slavery to fashion was producing a multitude of disorders such as stomach ulcer, gallstones, dislocation of the ribs, headache, dizziness, curvature of the spine, lung disease, and deterioration of the race through sickly offspring. In 1869 and 1870 the reader's-advice columns of the Englishwoman's Domestic Magazine were filled with letters about the difficulties and advantages of tight lacing, as well as suggestions on how to adapt pubescent girls to such routines of womanliness.

When my sisters were, the one sixteen, the other nearly two years younger, our mother considered it was time that their figures, hitherto unrestrained, should be subjected to some control, and accordingly she laced them, rather tightly, in stiff new stays, both day and night. They tried the usual expedients of cutting laces, and so forth, at first, but were entirely frustrated by mamma procuring a steel belt, fitted with a lock and key, to be worn at night outside the corset. I had then just left school, and the poor girls came to me in great trouble to know what they were to do. They confessed themselves doubly beaten; for the pressure of the stays, being an equal pressure, they were obliged to allow was not altogether unpleasant (although they could not racket about quite so easily); but the pressure of the belt, being unequal, was very uncomfortable indeed. Mamma was inexorable. I proposed a compromise. The girls should be relieved from the belts, and presented with very tiny-waisted riding habits (they were mad to be allowed to ride), which they should have facilities for using as soon as they could fit them on. They, on their part, should promise that their corsets should be always tightly laced. The compromise was agreed to, but, although they tried their hardest—at first somewhat under protest—it was six months before the habits could be worn. When I supervised their first mount, I can assure you I was very proud of my sisters' figures; and—dare I say— with the charming inconsistency of their sex, I believe they were, and still are, as proud of them themselves. When the subject is mentioned they will laughingly quote "*Qu'il faut souffrir pour être belle*" [One must suffer to be beautiful], but they declare that the very slight suffering at first is fully compensated by the delicious sensation of perfect compression when once accustomed to it, and that they would go through it all again for that end alone if appearance were no consideration at all.

In *Englishwoman's Domestic Magazine*, June 1870

A MEMORY OF "BLOOMERS" (ca. 1851)
Jane Ellen Panton

The first organized dress reform for women was the bloomer costume. Invented in 1851, it lasted some six or seven years among American feminists. Although Amelia Jenks Bloomer did not herself bring it to England as Jane Ellen Panton (1848–1923) remembers, the patterns and daguerrotypes from her newspaper The Lily were reproduced by the English press and promptly ridiculed, as were the brave adopters of the costume. Subsequent dress reformers were always careful to dissociate themselves from the Bloomers, who were considered shockingly unwomanly in their advocacy of ugly clothing and the vulgar display of the legs.

One or two more pictures are hung round the walls, and belong to the special time of Park Village West. One is a curious one of two females, in long trousers tied in at the ankles, and with a short species of stuck-out skirt similar to the one a ballet dancer used to wear. They had hats and feathers and soft grey boots with shiny leather toes, and were altogether awesome specimens of humanity. They were turning round the corner at the end of our crescent, and we were told that the females were called "Bloomers," so it must have been the year of the great exhibition, when the original Mrs. Bloomer first came over from America to teach her doctrine of hygienic clothing. I have lived to see many attempts at so-called rational dress, have gazed at the divided skirt dear to the heart of the inventor, have seen women, who ought to know better, careen round the park on bicycles, clad in check stockings, knickerbockers, and men's coats, shirts, and ties; while others drag yards of skirts after them through the muddy germ-laden streets, but not one of them do I recollect so well as I do these Bloomers, more especially as they were followed by the ubiquitous street-boy making use of all possible opprobrious terms. At the same time, absurd as it may sound, these erratic females were the first persons who ever made women aware of the fact that they possessed legs, and that they should use them more than they did in those days. . . . [W]hen I recollect the walks I used to take, holding yards of material in my cramped hand, while petticoats twisted and twined themselves round my unfortunate limbs, and that I used to skate in

BLOOMERISM—AN AMERICAN CUSTOM.

Punch's *response to the first attempts at dress reform*

BBC Hulton Picture Library

a similar garb, the long skirt being then drawn by pulleys into folds so that it did not entirely impede one's progress, I envy the girls of to-day. . . .

In Jane Ellen Panton, *Leaves from a Life* (1908)

"RATIONAL DRESS FOR WOMEN" (1882)
Florence Pomeroy, Viscountess Harberton

In March 1882, the National Health Society held an exhibition at which Viscountess Harberton introduced her invention of the divided skirt. The skirt itself was cut to clear the ground, with three quarters of a yard to a yard of material at the ankle of each half of the dual skirt. The adoption of this skirt was one of the most important aims of the Rational Dress movement, of which Viscountess Harberton (d. 1911) was president.

Along with its emphasis on the divided skirt, members of the Rational Dress movement advocated the abandonment of the corset and the shifting of the weight of women's clothing from the waist to the shoulders and hips. They pointed out repeatedly that it was contemporary clothing and not nature that formed the upper part of a woman's body in the shape of the letter V.

Bearing in mind the determination of the world, as far as possible, to misunderstand every new idea presented to it, it may be as well to preface the remarks put down here by stating distinctly that I neither wish to wear men's clothes myself, nor to see other women do so. One of the most curious circumstances connected with the subject of reform in dress is this: As soon as any one says some considerable change is advisable, the world at large—either from excess of imaginative power or the want of it—exclaims aloud that that person wishes women to wear men's clothes. "Bloomerism" still lurks in many a memory. . . .

In order to justify an attempt to change the present style of women's dress, it would not be a difficult task to show that the clothing now in vogue, instead of fulfilling its original purpose and being a useful servant, has become a species of tyrant or idol, subjecting the human form to an inconvenient, unsightly, and tormenting control, and indeed standing almost in the same relation to reason that superstition may be said to do to religion. A curious sort of conventionality is thoughtlessly and blindly followed, and no one seems to think they have the slightest responsibility in the matter, however strange and incongruous the result may be. . . .

Now that our daughters are being properly educated, and much on the same lines as our sons, it is likely to have a very serious effect on their health if they cannot also have the counteracting influence of really stirring interesting games. In their present clothes this is neither possible nor desirable. . . .

Now that women are being gradually allowed to take their place in Society as rational beings, and are no longer looked upon as mere toys and slaves; and now that their livelihood is becoming more and more to be considered their own affair, the question of dress assumes proportions which it did not use to have. Physically rather weaker than men we undoubtedly are, but why exaggerate this weakness by literally so tying ourselves up in clothing that the muscles in some parts of the body dwindle till they become useless? . . . Observe simply the extra fatigue which is ensured to every woman, in merely carrying a tray up stairs, from the skirt of the dress. Ask young women who are studying to pass examinations whether they do not find loose clothes a *sine qua non* while poring over their books, and then realize the harm we are doing ourselves and the race by habitually lowering our powers of life and energy in such a manner. . . .

The well-worn saying that ornament preceded dress is doubtless true, and many people at present draw the inference that because women's dress appears designed for ornament rather than convenience, women must be immeasurably lower in the intellectual scale than men whose dress has not this fault. There perhaps they judge hastily. For one thing, it affords to many men quite as keen a delight to see their wives and daughters decked out in absurd costumes, trailing yards of material on the floor after them about a room (and possibly a mat or two accidentally caught up on the way), or tottering feebly along a street on high heels, as it ever afforded any woman to wear such things. Hence it is that we do not have the help from men in the matter of dress reform which reason would lead us to expect; and then the question arises whether they are after all so much in advance as at first appears. Possibly they are not aware of the daily and hourly discomfort inflicted by the garments they admire so much, as even women often say they consider their dresses quite comfortable for walking! However, as it is well known that those born blind know little about the charm of colour, so those who have never tried a divided skirt, or freedom of lung power, may not be aware of the drag they are subject to, and may believe the fatigue they feel to be inseparable from the act of walking, which is a very comprehensible error. . . .

And as for the men not liking it! Where is our common sense? Where is our self-respect? Why, men have admired the queer and scanty garments of the beginning of this century, they have admired the huge and outrageous crinolines of twenty years ago, and the ludicrous tied-in dresses of later days . . . and whatever women wear it is very certain men will go on admiring it still. Unconscious as their admiration may be, it is none the less real, for it is the women they admire, and the clothes for their sakes, but never the women for the sake of the clothes. No one ever saw men in rows in front of shop windows admiring the dresses on stands, but every one sees beautiful women gazed at with admiration and delight wherever they go; and so far from such changes as are here advocated taking beauty out of the world, it would, as far as men are concerned, be doing them good service by giving them something worthy of admiration in a graceful natural walk and carriage; in the general harmony of appearance that accompanies health and strength; and in the true beauty of nature which makes a real flower so incomparably more beautiful than an artificial one.

In *Macmillan's Magazine*, April 1882

THE DANGERS OF BICYCLING (1891)
Helena Swanwick
(See p. 239.)

Helena Swanwick (1864–1939) benefitted from the social and educational reforms of the last third of the century, attending Girton College and going on to become a feminist, pacifist, and writer.

In 1891 [my husband] Fred and I took to bicycling and our lives were greatly enlarged thereby. The so-called "safety bicycles" attracted my husband more than the "penny-farthing" had, and the dropped frame adapted it to the skirted sex. By means of these machines we were able, in ten minutes, to leave Manchester behind, and we scoured the Cheshire and Derbyshire lanes within a radius of twenty miles. There was only one other woman in our part of Manchester who took to bicycling in the same year, and I was frowned on by some of the college ladies, until royal ladies took to riding round a London park, and I was suddenly in the fashion.

Near Manchester the boisterous mill-hands would play pranks on me, linking arms across the road to upset me. The only way to cope with this was to avoid looking at them and, putting down my head, charge full tilt, when they would scatter. In London, bus drivers were not above flicking at me with the whip, and cabmen thought it fun to converge upon me from behind. I was pulled off by my skirt in a Notting Hill slum, and felt a bit scared till a bright idea struck me. I said to the loutish lad who had seized my handle-bar, "I say, they seem rather a rough lot here. I wonder whether you would kindly help me out?" He instantly clutched my arm with his other hand, and bustling along with great dignity, shouted, "Nah then! Mike room for the lidy, can'tcher?" He saw me through, and helped me to re-mount with the recommendation, "Cut away nah, quick!" And I did.

My long skirt was a nuisance and even a danger. It is an unpleasant experience to be hurled on to stone setts [paving stones] and find that one's skirt has been so tightly wound round the pedal that one cannot even get up enough to unwind it. But I never had the courage to ride in breeches except at night. Then, oh then, I sang, jubilating with Clärchen:

"Welch Freud' ohne Ende
Ein Mannsbild zu sein!"

(What glorious rapture to be a he-man!) In Dieppe we saw fashionable women in wide breeches like Dutchmen, strolling about the Casino grounds. But that fashion never caught on here.

In Helena Swanwick, *I Have Been Young* (1935)

Part II

WOMAN'S
SPHERE

"Making the Pudding," from the Girl's Own Paper, *1883*
British Library

Woman's proper sphere was the home—the shrine and shelter of the domestic angel. Yet home was more than a bower for even the most privileged of women. It was a workplace. Womanly goodness was expected to demonstrate itself in a regular round of duties, duties which blurred the distinction between acts of love and obligation. The preeminent womanly virtues of self-sacrifice and ministration to the needs of others were called into play by the unremitting round of domestic chores. Not only ˅ housework itself extremely burdensome and time-consuming, ʔ much of the work that fell to women in the home derived from thᴄ ᵢ responsibility for the well-being and comfort of family membeɪ Such duties were particularly emotionally draining since the demanᴄᵢꜱ on a woman's time came from those who claimed her love as well as her services.

These demands were aggravated by the extreme powerlessness of women. They had very limited rights to support, to property, even to their own children. Widowhood, bankruptcy, or simply the displeasure of father or husband could strip a woman of the home ties upon which her economic and emotional security rested. At the same time, legal, economic, and social institutions made it difficult for a woman to survive outside the family structure. In her proper sphere, woman was essentially a prisoner.

Household work was especially burdensome for working-class women, who fought for their families' survival with every meal, every new illness, and every extra sixpence earned in the odd moment. They had the impossible job of trying to make up for the ravages of poverty, miserable housing, malnutrition, and brutal working conditions, by their own efforts. With less food than their brothers or husbands and with the added physical strain of frequent childbearing, they worked as hard as their men at paid and unpaid occupations.

All the women in this chapter struggled in one way or another to cope with the limitless demands of family life. Some of them, wishing to be independent and self-reliant, attempted to rid themselves of family responsibilities altogether. However, the emotional, moral, and material ties that bound women to abusive husbands, hungry children, dictatorial fathers, and aged grandmothers made overt rebellion against the demands of domestic life quite rare. Nineteenth-century feminism offered little support for daughters to disobey their fathers or wives to refuse to run their households. Those who sought lives outside the boundaries of home either had to combine domestic duties with more autonomous work by greater exertion and force of will, or to invent ways of evading the burdens of domestic life without challenging the established order. On the other hand, as several of these narratives show, even independent women could find spiritual satisfaction and personal pleasure in serving the needs of others.

But neither the ideal of the self-sacrificing domestic angel nor the counter ideal of the rational, self-reliant, emancipated woman adequately describes the moral qualities so apparent in almost all these narratives, the peculiar combination of pliability and resolution that women needed to meet the circumstances of their lives. Nineteenth-century women demanded of themselves tireless tolerance and sympathy for others, physical courage and strength (especially in childbirth or sick nursing), loyalty to friends and family members in difficulty and suffering, and acceptance of inevitable pain and hardship without paralyzing despair. These are the virtues of oppression, but together they form a pattern of endurance and resourcefulness that constituted, through sheer strength of character, women's resistance to the conditions of their lives.

Love and Duty

The readings in this section comprise a collective job description of the middle-class domestic angel. Middle-class women had three kinds of obligations in the home: tasks of decorum, housework, and ministration to the needs of others. The first category, and to some extent the second, derived from the new sense of home, which epitomized nineteenth-century English life. With the growth in middle-class wealth and numbers, the home as status object and as emotional bulwark against a rude commercial world gained the importance of a cultural institution. The rituals that governed this institution were the province of women. In their most idealized form, these rules were definitively codified in 1861 by Isabella Beeton in her enormously popular *Beeton's Book of Household Management*.

Housework itself was done on an institutional scale in the Victorian home. If the family could afford it, the home was staffed by an army of servants, hierarchically organized, carefully specialized, and disciplined in imitation of the staffs employed by the aristocracy on their great country estates. Servants' work derived from several sources. Houses were large and water was generally available only in the basement, necessitating elaborate heating and carrying operations for cleaning as well as for the bathing and toilet needs of the family. A multiplicity of fireplaces meant daily cleaning and frequent re-making of fires in all the rooms of the house. Elaborate meals meant daily shopping and laborious cooking complicated by cumbersome stoves. Families with five or six children required the services of nursery maids, governesses, and tutors. Victorian taste in furnishings, clothing, and upholstery emphasized the ornate and delicate, while perfect cleanliness was considered of supreme importance. Finally, there were the rituals of status, which demanded servants in livery to run errands and generally to "wait upon" the family. (See pp. 328–339 for more about the work and position of servants.)

The woman's role was to manage this institution, using her charm, cleverness, and empathy to make the home a kind of cozy monument to the family's financial well-being. Mrs. Beeton advised her on how to accomplish this with recipes, meal plans, etiquette suggestions, and specific directions for the performance of all household chores. Her book gives us a picture of a woman at the head of a complicated enterprise who nevertheless preserves the decorative pursuits of idleness; a woman who knows how to scrub a grate but spends her time practicing the piano.

Of course, the reality of household life deviated widely from this ideal. Those few who could afford Mrs. Beeton's army of servants were probably without interest in or knowledge of household chores. Moreover, even among the middle class, most women could afford only one servant, and she was usually in her teens without much experience or skill. Most of the housework therefore fell on the housewife herself, who could count on assistance only with heavier tasks.

One of the most demanding domestic responsibilities was nursing, since, as Mrs. Beeton points out, every woman could expect to be called upon to act as a nurse at some point in her life. In an age when sickness was treated primarily at home and professional nursing was just getting started (see Part IV), the job of administering the medicine prescribed by doctors and of keeping patients comfortable fell to the women in a family. Nursing could be an exhilarating task. Annie Besant, for instance, relished the fight for life against death, but only when she was caring for strangers. More often, it was emotionally draining, physically exhausting, and tragically frustrating. With no antibiotics and many medical procedures that did more harm than good, nursing often meant a long witnessing of suffering ending in death. It also carried with it the danger of contagion. Even in less dramatic circumstances nursing took its toll on women. Any unmarried woman was considered available for the invalided or merely lonely older relative. As Charlotte Brontë, Ellen Nussey, Rachel McMillan, and Harriet Martineau all knew, the claims of a sickly or demanding relative superceded any personal plans.

Self-sacrifice and obedience to family rituals of service was demanded of girls quite early. In ornamental tasks, such as the hand sewing of love gifts for relatives, particularly for fathers and brothers, or in the sharing of mother's ceremonial duties and her housework, girls were soon trained to be comfort-givers and to sacrifice their needs for others. By custom, they were encouraged to indulge their brothers' selfishness, custom being amply reinforced by affection, self-interest, and even simple envy turned into hero-worship.

Though duties to parents and brothers were considered preparation for wifehood, the sheltered atmosphere of home often made the actual transition to marriage difficult. The encouragement of close ties between parents and children and among siblings intensified this particularly painful separation. Some women refused marriage in the hope of continuing to live with family members, while others found it hard to reconcile their strong feelings of filial duty with their desire to marry. In addition, the unworldly ignorance cultivated in young girls left them ill-prepared to choose among suitors, to interpret the advances of men, or to comprehend matters of sexuality and child-bearing. At the same time, marriage was seen as the only escape from the monotony and lifelong infantilization of unmarried life at home.

Marriage was a political and social institution as well as a personal relationship, and the rights—or lack of rights—of married women were clearly defined by law and custom. A wife was subservient to a husband in law, and unable to own her own property or to protect herself from physical abuse. Advice offered to husbands and wives— exemplified here by that of Mrs. Sarah Ellis and Dr. William Acton— emphasized differences in what was expected of them. Women were told how to mollify difficult husbands by pampering their appetites and bolstering their egos; men were reassured that women did not need satisfaction beyond the provision of children, and that in the key area of sexuality, they were devoid of appetite altogether. Those who deviated too strongly from this ideal could be treated as mad-women or criminals, and subjected to institutionalized violence, such as the clitoridectomies performed by Isaac Baker Brown.

The experiences of Caroline Norton and Josephine Butler mark the two extremes that marriage could take for an intelligent and asser-tive woman living in a culture that stressed wifely subservience. Caro-line Norton's husband, goaded by her very superiority of intellect and charm, used all the abusive powers of a Victorian husband against her, including the removal of her children from her care. Josephine Butler's husband, on the other hand, shared her values and admired her talents to such an extent that he helped her find her vocation as leader of the controversial campaign against the regulation of prosti-tution.

The legal and social restrictions of marriage were reinforced by the biological pressures of childbearing. Lack of information about contraception—which was considered immoral—left women prey to frequent pregnancies. Childbirth itself was much more hazardous than it is today. (Maternal mortality was greater than one in two hundred births, as against one in sixty thousand in contemporary England.) By the early nineteenth century, doctors had replaced mid-wives for those who could afford it; but the doctor-attended births were not necessarily safer (see p. 307). Doctors knew how to use forceps for difficult deliveries, but they sometimes injured the baby or the mother through too violent employment of the instruments. In most complications of childbirth they were powerless. In addition, because of their ignorance of the principles of contagion, doctors could easily infect women at the time of childbirth by introducing germs from other patients.

Young children's lives were also at risk, with as many as one in six children dying before the age of five, half of them before they were one year old. Good nutrition and housing greatly increased a child's chance of survival, but the childhood diseases could sweep family nurseries, leaving a family childless in a relatively short time. Annie Besant and Elizabeth Gaskell, both very affectionate mothers, expressed some of the terrors and anxieties, the "mother's fears," as Gaskell termed them, that were endemic to motherhood. For them, and even for Queen Victoria, who was the proverbial doting wife, the pains of childbearing and motherhood were increased by a sense that their husbands could not understand or participate in their suffering.

In negotiating their way through the seemingly limitless obligations to family, the transition to marriage, and the cares of motherhood, women relied on one another for support and advice. Although it was popularly assumed that women were incapable of sisterly affection or friendship because of their rivalry for men, sisters and friends often shared intense emotional commitments. These relationships could become more reciprocal and mutually supportive than the economically unequal relations with parents, brothers, and husbands. Harriet Martineau was not unusual in her powerful love for her younger sister; and the reclusive Emily Brontë lavished on her sister Anne an intensity of affection she shared with no one else. Sometimes the intensity of such an emotional bond could become unhealthy, as it did between Parthe and Florence Nightingale. Florence claimed to be "devoured" by her possessive sister, who tried to prevent her from undertaking her career through a series of attacks of hysteria. But sisters often shared their work lives, as did the Brontës, Rachel and Margaret McMillan, educational reformers Emily Shirreff and Maria Grey, and Josephine Butler and her sister Harriet Meuricoffre. Similarly, in the correspondences of Charlotte Brontë, Ellen Nussey, and Mary Taylor we can see how strongly the advice and support of friends affected women wavering between domestic duty and the need for personal fulfillment.

Few women openly rejected domestic responsibilities and conventional occupations as did Mary Taylor, who fled to New Zealand. It was more common to evade the responsibilities of domestic life through invalidism (as did Elizabeth Barrett Browning, Florence Nightingale, and Isabella Bird Bishop) or through a denial of sexual or romantic feelings (as did Harriet Martineau and Frances Power Cobbe). Women who managed to have careers, including McMillan, Martineau, and Cobbe, or adventures, as Bird Bishop had, generally did so after the death of their parents.

The selections in this chapter dramatize the experiences of individual women. They also suggest the nature of the collective struggle against the limitations of "woman's sphere": the campaign for women's legal and social rights, waged by activists like Bodichon, Cobbe, Besant, and Norton, and the gains in educational and vocational opportunity described in Parts III and IV, which gradually opened the doors of home wide enough to allow larger numbers of women to find productive work and a greater measure of independence.

THE HOUSEHOLD GENERAL

DUTIES OF THE MISTRESS OF THE HOUSE (1861)
Isabella Beeton
(See pp. 93, 150, and 335.)

Isabella Mayson Beeton (1836–1865) was the wife and business partner of Samuel O. Beeton, publisher and editor of the very popular Englishwoman's Domestic Magazine. Isabella did translations, cookery, and fashion notes for the magazine, which led to her writing Beeton's Book of Household Management. Because of its practicality and good recipes, the book was an instant success and continued to be valued into the twentieth century. Married at age twenty, Isabella Beeton bore four sons, two of whom died in infancy. She died a week before her twenty-ninth birthday, a victim of puerperal fever caused by lack of aseptic procedures in childbirth.

As with the Commander of an Army, or the leader of any enterprise, so is it with the mistress of a house. Her spirit will be seen through the whole establishment; and just in proportion as she performs her duties intelligently and thoroughly, so will her domestics follow in her path. Of all those acquirements, which more particularly belong to the feminine character, there are none which take a higher rank, in our estimation, than such as enter into a knowledge of household duties; for on these are perpetually dependent the happiness, comfort, and well-being of a family. . . .

Having risen early, . . . and having given due attention to the bath, and made a careful toilet, it will be well at once to see that the children have received their proper ablutions, and are in every way clean and comfortable. . . .

After breakfast is over, it will be well for the mistress to make a round of the kitchen and other offices, to see that all are in order, and that the morning's work has been properly performed by the various domestics. The orders for the day should then be given, and any questions which the domestics desire to ask, respecting their several departments, should be answered, and any special articles they may require, handed to them from the store-closet. In those establishments where there is a housekeeper, it will not be so necessary for the mistress, personally, to perform the above-named duties.

After this general superintendence of her servants, the mistress, if a mother of a young family, may devote herself to the instruction of some of its younger members, or to the examination of the state of their wardrobe, leaving the later portion of the morning for reading, or for some amusing recreation. . . . Unless the means of the mistress be very circumscribed, and she be obliged to devote a great deal of her time to the making of her children's clothes, and other economical pursuits, it is right that she should give some time to the pleasures of literature, the innocent delights of the garden, and to the improvement of any special abilities for music, painting, and other elegant arts, which she may, happily, possess. . . .

After luncheon, morning calls and visits may be made and received. . . . Visits of ceremony, or courtesy . . . are uniformly required after dining at a friend's house, or after a ball, picnic, or any other party. These visits should be short, a stay of from fifteen to twenty minutes being quite sufficient. A lady paying a visit may remove her boa or neckerchief; but neither her shawl nor bonnet. . . .

The morning calls being paid or received, and their etiquette properly attended to, the next great event of the day in most establishments is "The Dinner." . . .

PLAIN FAMILY DINNERS FOR FEBRUARY

Sunday.—1. Ox-tail soup. 2. Roast beef, Yorkshire pudding, broccoli, and potatoes. 3. Plum-pudding, apple tart. Cheese.

Monday.—1. Fried soles, plain melted butter, and potatoes. 2. Cold roast beef, mashed potatoes. 3. The remains of plum-pudding cut in slices, warmed, and served with sifted sugar sprinkled over it. Cheese.

Tuesday.—1. The remains of ox-tail soup from Sunday. 2. Pork cutlets with tomato sauce; hashed beef. 3. Rolled jam pudding. Cheese.

Wednesday.—1. Boiled haddock and plain melted butter. 2. Rump-steak pudding, potatoes, greens. 3. Arrowroot, blancmange, garnished with jam.

Thursday.—1. Boiled leg of pork, greens, potatoes, pease pudding. 2. Apple fritters, sweet macaroni.

Friday.—1. Pea soup made with liquor that the pork was boiled in. 2. Cold pork, mashed potatoes. 3. Baked rice pudding.

Saturday.—1. Broiled herrings and mustard sauce. 2. Haricot mutton. 3. Macaroni, either served as a sweet pudding or with cheese.

Sunday.—1. Carrot soup. 2. Boiled leg of mutton and caper sauce, mashed turnips, roast fowls, and bacon. 3. Damson tart made with bottled fruit, ratafia pudding.

Monday.—1. The remainder of fowl curried and served with rice; rump-steaks and oyster sauce, cold mutton. 2. Rolled jam pudding.

Tuesday.—1. Vegetable soup made with liquor that the mutton was boiled in on Sunday. 2. Roast sirloin of beef, Yorkshire pudding, broccoli, and potatoes. 3. Cheese.

Wednesday.—1. Fried soles, melted butter. 2. Cold beef and mashed potatoes: if there is any cold boiled mutton left, cut it into neat slices and warm it in a little caper sauce. 3. Apple tart.

Thursday.—1. Boiled rabbit and onion sauce, stewed beef and vegetables, made with the remains of cold beef and bones. 2. Macaroni.

Friday.—1. Roast leg of pork, sage and onions and apple sauce; greens and potatoes. 2. Spinach and poached eggs instead of pudding. Cheese and water-cresses.

Saturday.—1. Rumpsteak-and-kidney pudding, cold pork and mashed potatoes. 2. Baked rice pudding.

BILL OF FARE FOR A BALL SUPPER,

Or a Cold Collation for a Summer Entertainment, or Wedding or Christening Breakfast for 70 or 80 Persons (July).

Left margin (vertical): 3 Compôtes of Fruit.   4 Blancmanges, to be placed down the table.   3 Dishes of Small Pastry.   3 Fruit Tarts.   3 English Pines.   4 Jellies, to be placed down the table.   3 Fruit Tarts.   3 Cheesecakes.   20 Small Dishes of various Summer Fruits.

Right margin (vertical): 4 Blancmanges, to be placed down the table.   3 Cheesecakes.   20 Small Dishes of various Summer Fruits.   4 Jellies, to be placed down the table.   3 Dishes of Small Pastry.   3 English Pines.   3 Compôtes of Fruit.

Left column	Centre column	Right column
Dish of Lobster, cut up.	Tongue.	Veal-and-Ham Pie.
	Ribs of Lamb.	
	Two Roast Fowls.	
Charlotte Russe à la Vanille.	Mayonnaise of Salmon.	Savoy Cake.
(Lobster Salad)	Epergue, with Flowers. *(Lobster Salad)*	
	Mayonnaise of Trout.	Dish of Lobster, cut up.
Pigeon Pie.	Tongue, garnished.	
	Boiled Fowls and Béchamel Sauce.	
	Collared Eel.	
	Ham.	
(Lobster Salad)	Raised Pie.	*(Lobster Salad)*
	Two Roast Fowls.	
(Larded Capon)	Shoulder of Lamb, stuffed.	
Dish of Lobster, cut up.	Mayonnaise of Salmon.	Pigeon Pie.
	Epergue, with Flowers. *(Boar's Head)*	
(Lobster Salad)	Mayonnaise of Trout.	*(Lobster Salad)*
	Tongue.	
Pigeon Pie.	Boiled Fowls and Béchamel Sauce.	Dish of Lobster, cut up.
	Raised Pie.	
	Ham, decorated.	
	Shoulder of Lamb, stuffed.	
Dish of Lobster, cut up. Savoy Cake.	Two Roast Fowls.	Charlotte Russe à la Vanille. Veal and Ham Pie.
(Lobster Salad)	Mayonnaise of Salmon.	
	Epergue, with Flowers. *(Lobster Salad)*	
	Mayonnaise of Trout.	Dish of Lobster, cut up.
	Tongue, garnished.	
	Boiled Fowls and Béchamel Sauce.	
	Collared Eel.	

Note.—The length of the page will not admit of our giving the dishes as they should be placed on the table; they should be arranged with the large and high dishes down the centre, and the spaces filled up with the smaller dishes, fruit, and flowers, taking care that the flavours and colours contrast nicely, and that no two dishes of a sort come together. This bill of fare may be made to answer three or four purposes, placing a wedding cake or christening cake in the centre on a high stand, if required for either of these occasions. A few dishes of fowls, lobster salads, &c. &c., should be kept in reserve to replenish those that are most likely to be eaten first. A joint of cold roast and boiled beef should be placed on the buffet, as being something substantial for the gentlemen of the party to partake of. Besides the articles enumerated in the bill of fare, biscuits and waters will be required, cream-and-water ices, tea, coffee, wines, liqueurs, soda-water, ginger-beer, and lemonade.

FEBRUARY.
DINNER FOR 18 PERSONS.

First Course.

Fried Eels.

Hare Soup,
removed by
Turbot and Oyster Sauce.

Vase of
Flowers.

Oyster Soup,
removed by
Crimped Cod à la Maitre
d'Hôtel.

Fried Whitings.

Entrées.

Lobster Patties.

Lark Pudding.

Vase of
Flowers.

Fricasseed Chicken.

Filets de Perdrix.

Second Course.

Roast Fowls, garnished
with Water-cresses.

Braised Capon.
Boiled Ham, garnished.

Vase of
Flowers.

Pâté Chaud.
Haunch of Mutton.

Boiled Fowls and
White Sauce.

Third Course.

Meringues.

Orange Jelly.
Victoria
Sandwiches.

Ducklings,
removed by
Ice Pudding.

Coffee Cream.

Vase of
Flowers.

Blancmange.

Partridges,
removed by
Cabinet Pudding.

Clear Jelly.

Gâteau de
Pommes.

Cheese-
cakes.

Dessert and Ices.

DINNER FOR 12 PERSONS (February).
First Course.
Soup à la Reine.   Clear Gravy Soup.
Brill and Lobster Sauce.   Fried Smelts.

Entrees.
Lobster Rissoles.   Beef Palates.   Pork Cutlets à la Soubise.
Grilled Mushrooms.

Second Course.
Braised Turkey.   Haunch of Mutton.   Boiled Capon and Oysters.
Tongue, garnished with tufts of Broccoli.   Vegetables and Salads.

Third Course.
Wild Ducks.   Plovers.
Orange Jelly.   Clear Jelly.   Charlotte Russe.   Nesselrode Pudding.
Gâteau de Riz.   Sea-kale.   Maids of Honour.

Dessert and Ices.

The half-hour before dinner has always been considered as the great ordeal through which the mistress, in giving a dinner-party, will either pass with flying colours, or, lose many of her laurels. The anxiety to receive her guests, her hope that all will be present in due time, her trust in the skill of her cook, and the attention of the other domestics, all tend to make these few minutes a trying time. The mistress, however, must display no kind of agitation, but show her tact in suggesting light and cheerful subjects of conversation. . . .

When fruit has been taken, and a glass or two of wine passed round, the time will have arrived when the hostess will rise, and thus give the signal for the ladies to leave the gentlemen, and retire to the drawing-room. . . .

Of the manner of passing evenings at home, there is none pleasanter than in such recreative enjoyments as those which relax the mind from its severer duties, whilst they stimulate it with a gentle delight. Where there are young people forming a part of the evening circle, interesting and agreeable pastime should especially be promoted. . . . It ought . . . to enter into the domestic policy of every parent, to make her children feel that home is the happiest place in the world; that to imbue them with this delicious home-feeling is one of the choicest gifts a parent can bestow.

Light or fancy needlework often forms a portion of the evening's recreation for the ladies of the household, and this may be varied by an occasional game at chess or backgammon. It has often been remarked, too, that nothing is more delightful to the feminine members of a family, than the reading aloud of some good standard work or amusing publication. . . .

In retiring for the night, it is well to remember that early rising is almost impossible, if late going to bed be the order, or rather disorder, of the house. The younger members of a family should go early and at regular hours to their beds, and the domestics as soon as possible after a reasonably appointed hour. Either the master or the mistress of a house should, after all have gone to their separate rooms, see that all is right with respect to the lights and fires below; and no servants should, on any account, be allowed to remain up after the heads of the house have retired.

In Isabella Beeton, *Beeton's Book of Household Management* (1861)

HOUSEHOLD ADVICE TO AN
ASPIRING WOMAN WRITER (1862)
Elizabeth Gaskell
(See p. 148.)

The limitlessness of women's home duties made it difficult for them to develop their own interests in a serious way. Elizabeth Gaskell (1810–1865), who bore the burdens of a minister's wife in addition to the usual domestic routines and who still managed to be a prolific writer, worried about the conflict between responsibilities to family and the duty to develop one's own talents. In this letter of advice to a young woman struggling to write novels while raising young children, Gaskell comes down strongly on the side of domestic responsibilities. She herself bore six children, the first of whom was stillborn; the second, a much loved son, died at ten months.

I feel very sorry for you, for I think I can see that, at present, at least you are rather overwhelmed with all you have to do; and I think it possible that the birth of two children, one so close upon another, may have weakened you bodily, and made you more unfit to cope with your many household duties. Try . . . to strengthen yourself by every means in your power; by being very careful as to your diet; by cold-bathing, by resolute dwelling on the cheerful side of everything; and by learning to economize strength as much as possible in all your household labours. . . . I hope (for instance) you soap and soak your dirty clothes well for some hours before beginning to wash; and that you understand the comfort of preparing a dinner and putting it on to cook *slowly*, early in the morning, as well as having *always* some kind of sewing ready arranged to your hand, so that you can take it up at any odd minute and do a few stitches. I dare say at present it might be difficult for you to procure the sum that is necessary to purchase a sewing machine; and indeed, unless you are a good workwoman to begin with, you will find a machine difficult to manage. But *try*, my dear, to conquer your "clumsiness" in sewing; there are thousand little bits of work, which no sempstress ever does so well as the wife or mother who knows how the comfort of those she loves depends on little peculiarities which no one but she cared enough for the wearers to attend to.

My first piece of advice to you would be *Get strong.* . . . Did you ever try a tea-cup full of *hop-tea* the first thing in the morning? It is a very simple tonic, and could do no harm. Then again try *hard* to arrange your work well. That is a regular piece of headwork and taxes a woman's powers of organization; but the reward is immediate and great. I have known well what it is to be both wanting money, and feeling weak in body and entirely disheartened. I do not think I ever cared for literary fame; nor do I think it *is* a thing that ought to be cared for. It comes and it goes. The exercise of a talent or power *is* always a great pleasure; but one should weigh well whether this pleasure may not be obtained by the sacrifice of some duty. When I had *little* children I do not think I could have written stories, because I should have become too much absorbed in my *fictitious* people to attend to my *real* ones. I think you would be sorry if you began to feel that your desire to earn money, even for so laudable an object as to help your husband, made you unable to give your tender sympathy to your little ones in their small joys and sorrows. . . . Besides viewing the subject from a solely artistic point of view a good writer of fiction must have *lived* an active and sympathetic life if she wishes her books to have strength and vitality in them. When you are forty, and if you have a gift for being an authoress you will write ten times as good a novel as you could do now, just because you will have gone through so much more of the interests of a wife and a mother.

From Elizabeth Gaskell to unknown correspondent, September 25 [1865?], in *The Letters of Mrs. Gaskell,* ed. J. A. V. Chapple and A. Pollard (Cambridge, Massachusetts: Harvard University Press, 1964), letter no. 515

THE HOUSEHOLD PRISONER (1852)

Florence Nightingale
(See pp. 301, 303, and 304.)

Florence Nightingale (1820–1910) was thirty years old before she won her release from family duties to begin her career as the founder of the nursing profession. Her well-educated family was widely traveled, and part of an active political and intellectual circle of progressive people. Florence was treated as the family beauty and sought in marriage by men she cared about. But even in such relatively favorable circumstances she experienced family life as an agony of suffocation. She wrote Cassandra, from which this excerpt is taken, as a *meditation on the spiritual and intellectual costs of women's domestic confinement, but on the advice of friends she never published it. The disjunction of her thoughts—evident even in this brief excerpt— testifies to the difficulties of clear thinking in a world that encouraged interruptability, passivity, and the cheerful inanities of drawing-room conversation.*

Look at the poor lives we lead. It is a wonder that we are so good as we are, not that we are so bad. . . . Mrs. A. has the imagination, the poetry of a Murillo, and has sufficient power of execution to show that she might have had a great deal more. Why is she not a Murillo? From a material difficulty, not a mental one. If she has a knife and fork in her hands for three hours of the day, she cannot have a pencil or brush. Dinner is the great sacred ceremony of this day, the great sacrament. To be absent from dinner is equivalent to being ill. Nothing else will excuse us from it. Bodily incapacity is the only apology valid. If she has a pen and ink in her hands during other three hours, writing answers for the penny post, again, she cannot have her pencil, and so *ad infinitum* through life. . . .

Women are never supposed to have any occupation of sufficient importance *not* to be interrupted, except "suckling their fools"; and women themselves have accepted this, have written books to support it, and have trained themselves so as to consider whatever they do as *not* of such value to the world or to others, but that they can throw it up at the first "claim of social life." They have accustomed themselves to consider intellectual occupation as a merely selfish amusement, which it is their "duty" to give up for every trifler more selfish than themselves. . . .

Women never have an half-hour in all their lives (excepting before and after anybody is up in the house) that they can call their own, without fear of offending or of hurting someone. Why do people sit up so late, or, more rarely, get up so early? Not because the day is not long enough, but because they have "no time in the day to themselves."

If we do attempt to do anything in company, what is the system of literary exercise which we pursue? Everybody reads aloud out of their own book or newspaper—or, every five minutes, something is said. And what is it to be "read aloud to"? The most miserable exercise of the human intellect. Or rather, is it any exercise at all? It is like lying on one's back, with one's hands tied and having liquid

poured down one's throat. Worse than that, because suffocation
would immediately ensue and put a stop to this operation. But no
suffocation would stop the other. . . .

' The family? It is too narrow a field for the development of an
immortal spirit, be that spirit male or female. . . .

The family uses people, *not* for what they are, not for what they
are intended to be, but for what it wants them for—its own uses. It
thinks of them not as what God has made them, but as the something
which it has arranged that they shall be. If it wants someone to sit
in the drawing-room, *that* someone is supplied by the family, though
that member may be destined for science, or for education, or for
active superintendence by God, i.e., by the gifts within.

This system dooms some minds to incurable infancy, others to
silent misery.

In Florence Nightingale, *Cassandra* (1852)

UPROOTED (1840s)
Frances Power Cobbe
(*See pp.* 121, 162, 198, *and* 261.)

*Frances Power Cobbe (1822–1904) spent her Dublin girlhood study-
ing history, astronomy, philosophy, and Greek. Born to a family of
clerics, she underwent a religious crisis at fourteen, becoming first a
Kantian and eventually a Unitarian preacher. Her earliest publication,
an essay on Kant's theory of intuitive morals that she wrote in her
twenties, was published anonymously in order not to offend her
father. With an inherited income of £200 a year, she was free not to
marry, and chose instead to pursue a career as a writer and social reformer. With Mary Carpenter and Margaret Elliot she established and
ran various reformatories for young girls. She was a defender of battered wives and an advocate of women's suffrage, as well as a leader in
the cause of antivivisectionism.*

I draw now to the closing years of my life at Newbridge, after I had
published my first book and before my father died. They were happy
and peaceful years, though gradually overshadowed by the sense that
the long tenure of that beloved home must soon end. It is one of the
many perversities of woman's destiny that she is, not only by heredi-

tary instinct a home-making animal, but is encouraged to the utter-most to centre all her interests in her home; every pursuit which would give her anchorage elsewhere (always excepting marriage) being more or less under general disapproval. Yet when the young woman takes thoroughly to this natural home-making, when she has, like a plant, sent her roots down into the cellars and her tendrils up into the garrets, and every room bears the impress of her personality, when she glories in every good picture on the walls or bit of choice china on the tables and blushes for every stain on the carpets, when, in short her home is, as it should be, her outer garment, her nest, her shell . . . then, almost invariably comes to her the order to leave it all, tear herself out of it—and go to make (if she can) some other home elsewhere. Supposing her to have married early, and that she is spared the late uprooting from her father's house at his death, she has usually to bear a similar transition when she survives her husband; and in this case often with the failing health and spirits of old age. I do not know how these heartbreaks are to be spared to women of the class of the daughters and wives of country gentlemen or clergymen; but they are hard to bear. Perhaps the most fortunate daughters (harsh as it seems to say so) are those whose fathers die while they are themselves still in full vigor and able to begin a new existence with spirit and make new friends; as was my case. Some of my contemporaries whose fathers lived till they were fifty, or even older, had a bitterer trial in quitting their homes and were never able to start afresh.

In Frances Power Cobbe, *Life of Frances Power Cobbe* (1894)

SERVING THE COMFORT
OF OTHERS

DUTIES OF THE SICK-NURSE (1861)
Isabella Beeton
(See pp. 83, 150, and 335.)

All women are likely, at some period of their lives, to be called on to perform the duties of a sick-nurse, and should prepare themselves as much as possible, by observation and reading, for the occasion when they may be required to perform the office. The main requirements are good temper, compassion for suffering, sympathy with sufferers,

"Good for a Cold": Nursing a sick relative as it was construed in 1857

BBC Hulton Picture Library

which most women worthy of the name possess, neat-handedness, quiet manners, love of order, and cleanliness. With these qualifications there will be very little to be wished for; the desire to relieve suffering will inspire a thousand little attentions, and surmount the disgusts which some of the offices attending the sick-room are apt to create. Where serious illness visits a household, and protracted nursing is likely to become necessary, a professional nurse will probably be engaged, who has been trained to its duties; but in some families, and those not a few let us hope, the ladies of the family would oppose such an arrangement as a failure of duty on their part. There is, besides, even when a professional nurse is ultimately called in, a period of doubt and hesitation, while disease has not yet developed itself, when the patient must be attended to; and, in these cases, some of the female servants of the establishment must give their attendance in the sick-room. There are, also, slight attacks of cold, influenza, and accidents in a thousand forms, to which all are subject, where domestic nursing becomes a necessity; where disease, though unattended with danger, is nevertheless accompanied by the nervous irritation incident to illness, and when all the attention of the domestic nurse becomes necessary. . . .

The sick-room should be quiet; no talking, no gossiping, and, above all, no whispering—this is absolute cruelty to the patient; he thinks his complaint the subject, and strains his ear painfully to catch the sound. No rustling of dresses, nor creaking shoes either; where the carpets are taken up, the nurse should wear list shoes, or some other noiseless material, and her dress should be of soft material that does not rustle. Miss Nightingale denounces crinolines, and quotes Lord Melbourne on the subject of women in the sick-room, who said, "I would rather have men about me, when ill, than women; it requires very strong health to put up with women." Ungrateful man! but absolute quiet is necessary in the sick-room.

In Isabella Beeton, *Beeton's Book of Household Management* (1861)

DUTY TO PARENTS (1846)
Charlotte Brontë
(See pp. 35, 109, 115, 151, 160, 272, and 273.)

In this letter to her close friend Ellen Nussey, Charlotte Brontë expressed her credo of self-sacrifice. Brontë was at this time living unhappily at home, taking care of her sick father. In late August 1846, she took him to Manchester and stayed with him during his unanesthetized operation for cataracts. During the period of her father's blindness and recovery she turned down opportunities to earn substantial wages as a teacher—better opportunities than the ones she advised Ellen to forego in favor of caring for her aging mother.

I see you are in a dilemma, and one of a peculiar and difficult nature. Two paths lie before you, you conscientiously wish to choose the right one, even though it be the most steep, strait and rugged; but you do not know which is the right one; you cannot decide whether duty and religion command you to go out into the cold and friendless world, and there to earn your bread by governess drudgery, or whether they enjoin your continued stay with your aged mother, neglecting, *for the present*, every prospect of independency for yourself, and putting up with daily inconvenience, sometimes even with privations. Dear Ellen, I can well imagine, that it is next to impossible for you to decide for yourself in this matter, so I will decide it for you. At least I will tell you what is my earnest conviction on the subject; I will show you candidly how the question strikes me. The right path is that which necessitates the greatest sacrifice of self-interest—which implies the greatest good to others; and this path, steadily followed, will lead, I believe, in time, to prosperity and to happiness; though it may seem, at the outset, to tend quite in a *contrary direction*. Your mother is both old and infirm; old and infirm people have few sources of happiness, fewer almost than the comparatively young and healthy can conceive; to deprive them of one of these is cruel. If your mother is more composed when you are with her, stay with her. If she would be unhappy in case you left her, stay with her. It will not apparently, as far as short-sighted humanity can see, be for *your* advantage to remain at Brookroyd, nor will you be praised and admired for remaining at home to comfort your mother; yet, probably, your own conscience will approve, and if it does, stay with her. I recommend you to do what I am trying to do myself.

From Charlotte Brontë to Ellen Nussey, July 10, 1846, in *The Brontës*, letter no. 257

DUTY TO HER MOTHER (1829)
Harriet Martineau
(See pp. 149, 161, 216, 291, and 330.)

A prolific writer on public issues and pioneer in the social sciences, Harriet Martineau (1802–1876) was among the most respected women of her age, one of the few always cited as an example of what women were capable of achieving in intellectual life. Her passion for social justice had its roots in her unhappy childhood, which she recorded with unusual detail in her monumental autobiography, written in 1855 in the mistaken belief that she was about to die. She claimed to have cried every day of her childhood, in large part because of the coldness of her mother and the favoritism shown to her sister Rachel, who was more conventionally domestic. When Martineau was twenty-seven her father died, and the family suffered severe financial reverses. Martineau relished the change to relative impoverishment for the reasons described here. She immediately turned her hand to writing, selling her clothes when necessary to keep at it. But as this passage shows, she was still hampered by her family responsibilities.

While I was at Newcastle, a change, which turned out a very happy one, was made in our domestic arrangements. . . . I call it a misfortune, because in common parlance it would be so treated; but I believe that my mother and all her other daughters would have joined heartily, if asked, in my conviction that it was one of the best things that ever happened to us. My mother and her daughters lost, at a stroke, nearly all they had in the world by the failure of the house—the old manufactory—in which their money was placed. We never recovered more than the merest pittance; and at the time, I, for one, was left destitute —that is to say, with precisely one shilling in my purse. The effect upon me of this new "calamity," as people called it, was like that of a blister upon a dull, weary pain, or series of pains. I rather enjoyed it, even at the time; for there was scope for action. . . . In a very short time, my two sisters at home and I began to feel the blessing of a wholly new freedom. I, who had been obliged to write before breakfast, or in some private way, had henceforth liberty to do my own work in my own way; for we had lost our gentility. Many and many a time since have we said that, but for that loss of money, we might have lived on in the ordinary provincial method of ladies with small means, sewing, and economizing, and growing narrower every year: whereas, by being thrown, while it was yet time, on our own resources, we have worked hard and usefully, won friends, reputation and independence, seen the world abundantly, abroad and at home, and, in short, have truly lived instead of vegetated. . . .

My griefs deepened towards the close of [my] London visit. While failing in all my attempts to get my articles even looked at, proposals were made to me to remain in town, and undertake proof-correcting and other literary drudgery, on a salary which would, with my frugal habits, have supported me, while leaving time for literary effort on my own account. I rejoiced unspeakably in this opening, and wrote home in high satisfaction at the offer which would enable my young sister, then only eighteen, to remain at home, pursuing her studies in companionship with a beloved cousin of nearly her own age, and gaining something like maturity and self-reliance before going out into the cold dark sphere of governessing. But, to my disappointment—I might almost say, horror—my mother sent me peremptory orders to go home, and to fill the place which my poor young sister was to vacate [as Mother's companion]. I rather wonder that, being seven and twenty years old, I did not assert my independence, and refuse to return—so clear as was, in my eyes, the injustice of remanding me to a position of helplessness and dependence, when a career of action and independence was opening before me. If I had known what my young sister was thinking and feeling, I believe I should have taken my own way, for her sake: but I did not know all: the instinct and habit of old obedience prevailed, and I went home, with some resentment, but far more grief and desolation in my heart. My mother afterwards looked back with surprise upon the peremptoriness with which she had assumed the direction of my affairs; and she told me (what I had suspected before) that my well-meaning [London] hostess, who knew nothing of literature, and was always perplexing me with questions as to "how much I should get" by each night's work, had advised my return home, to pursue—not literature but needlework, by which, she wrote, I had proved that I could earn money, and in which career I should always have the encouragement and support of herself and her family. . . . I went down to Norwich, without prospect—without any apparent chance of independence; but as fully resolved against being dependent as at any time before or after.

In *Harriet Martineau's Autobiography*, ed. Maria Weston Chapman (1877)

NURSING AN AGED GRANDMOTHER (1877)
Margaret McMillan

When Rachel McMillan (1859–1917) was eighteen years old, she was called home from a school run by some progressive aunts to take care of her grandmother. She devoted eleven years to the task. Margaret McMillan (1860–1931) wrote the biography of her sister, Rachel, from which this excerpt is taken, as a tribute to their long years of partnership and as a memorial to her sister's loving and noble nature. Socialist activists and educational reformers, they opened and ran children's health clinics, open-air schools, and nurseries for the poor.

They also helped establish the practice of state medical inspection of schoolchildren.

Happily our grandmother, now seventy years old, never grew old in spirit. She had the cheerful temperament that comes not from inner joy, but from inner movement—unresting and keen intelligence. It was impossible to stagnate in her vicinity. She had lost all her early friends, and nearly all her children, and, greatest loss of all, she had outlived her adored husband. Nevertheless, her dark eyes still shone like black stars and every part of her dwelling seemed to be vitalised by her mere presence. She had never, perhaps, felt any great affection for her granddaughter, but now that she was flung back on her for companionship and service, she faced the new situation with courage and tolerance.

Among Rachel's hopeful plans and aims during her school life there was an inner purpose that swept through and vitalised every experience, even the saddest experience. She may and did, in fact, dream of a career, or rather a mission, which would be revealed to her in time, and would make her life a real and great thing, worth something not merely to her own family, but to the world. In spite of modesty, she had a naïve courage, and she dreamed boldly during her childhood and at school in Coventry. She now found herself with a sick-room for her world—the brave dreams vanished—all life resuming itself in one task—the task of watching a strong and beloved relative pass slowly and reluctantly down into the shadow.

The modern girl would probably have resented this task, or eluded it, and gone in for the "living of her own life." Rachel took another course. She equipped herself to undertake this new work of nursing and companionship with all the efficiency of which she was capable. She attended lectures, studied every detail of sick-nursing. In the end her efficiency astounded the doctors, who bore testimony that never before had mere nursing achieved so much. Grandmother recovered from one "mortal" illness after another. She lived to be eighty-one, and her life was a happy, and even an exhilarating experience to the end. A new chapter in life was opened for grandmother in the days that are usually assigned to resignation, acquiescence and decay.

My sister's youth was passed in the sick-room. She tried to find pleasure in the intercourse that was open to her; doubtless she tried also to find a solution to the question that haunts youth: "What am I here finally to do?" With enterprise, ambition and unlimited courage, she waited and saw the years pass. She had a sister—far away—

but *she* was alone. It seemed as if nothing happened or could happen *to her.* . . .

She came and went, dressed always in somber black, but attracting, as was natural, a great deal of admiration. The less she desired it, the more she awakened interest and attention; the inner waking [to a vague sense of future mission] was followed by no external change. She was still in the position of one who is waiting for a signal that does not come. She lived for her patient; the sick-room was still her world. No voice spoke. No hand beckoned. Such patient suspense and waiting would be impossible for the modern girl. To most people it will seem to be very painful, dull, intolerable. She had work to do; and beyond it there was no real call as yet and no clear prospect or indication. . . .

She wrote later, at the close of long vigils and days: "Death is staring me always in the face." She had eyes to see it too—unflinching eyes. . . . Our grandmother was very ill—mortally ill—dying. . . . Rachel had to experience all that one feels in accompanying a well-loved and fully conscious friend through suffering to the gates of death. The courage and calm did not lessen the trial—or veil it. It was there stark and bare. Grandmother, young, strong in spirit. Nothing failing but the hull, the physical body. A wonderful quality of love and gratitude burned in all her words and looks, as she looked at the girl who had been long a stranger to her, and bade her farewell.

Grandmother died in July 1888. Four months later Rachel wrote in her diary of a strange experience she had at the moment of death. "I knew that she lives," she wrote; "I learned it most surely and vividly in the moment of her passing."

Rachel, left alone now, refused to be dependent on our uncles. . . . She must make her own way—must face the world alone, and she was not at all dismayed as yet by the fact that she had very small means, and no technical training for any trade or profession whatsoever.

In Margaret McMillan, *The Life of Rachel McMillan* (1928)

DUTIES TO BROTHERS (1839)
Sarah Stickney Ellis
(See p. 124.)

At the same time Sarah Lewis was advising women on their spiritual mission in the home, Sarah Stickney Ellis (1810–1872) was achieving even greater popularity with her prosaic but lengthy volumes Women

of England, Daughters of England, Wives of England, and Mothers
of England. *Mrs. Ellis stressed submissiveness and empathetic concern for the needs of others, yet there was also a hint of shrewd self-
interest in her bland exhortations to keep men happily dependent on
the daily ministrations of their sisters or wives.*

Brothers and sisters are so associated in English homes, as materially
to promote each other's happiness, by the habits of kindness and
consideration which they cultivate; and when a strong friendship can
be formed between such parties, it is perhaps one of the most faithful
and disinterested of any which the aspect of human life presents. . . .
Women, however, must be watchful and studious to establish this
intimate connection, and to keep entire the golden cord by which
they are thus bound. Affection does not come by relationship alone;
and never yet was the affection of man fully and lastingly engaged by
woman, without some means being adopted on her part to increase
or preserve his happiness. The childish and most unsatisfactory fondness that means nothing but "I love you," goes but a little way to
reach the heart of man; but let his home be made more comfortable,
let his peculiarities of habit and temper be studiously consulted, and
social and familiar gratifications provided for his daily use; and, unless
he is ungrateful beyond the common average of mankind, he will be
sure to regard the source from whence his comforts flow with extreme complacency, and not unfrequently with affection.

On the other hand, let the sister possess all that ardor of attachment which young ladies are apt to believe they feel, let her hang
about his neck at parting, and bathe his face with her tears; if she
has not taken the trouble to rise and prepare his early meal, but has
allowed him to depend upon the servant, or to prepare it for himself;
it is very questionable whether that brother could be made to believe
in her affection; and certainly he would be far from feeling its value.
If again, they read some interesting volume together, if she lends her
willing sympathy, and blends her feelings with his, entering into all
the trains of thought and recollection which two congenial minds are
capable of awakening in each other; and if, after the book is closed,
he goes up to his chamber late on the Saturday night, and finds his
linen unaired, buttonless, and unattended to, with the gloves he had
ten times asked to have mended, remaining untouched, where he had
left them; he soon loses the impression of the social hour he had been
spending, and wishes that, instead of an idle sister, he had a faithful
and industrious wife. . . .

I do not mean that sisters ought to be the servants of their brothers, or that they should not, where domestics abound, leave the practical part of these duties to them. . . . There are, however, a few simple rules, by which I should suppose women would be willing to be guided. No woman in the enjoyment of health should allow her brother to prepare his own meals at any time of the day, if it were possible for her to do it for him. No woman should allow her brother to put on linen in a state of dilapidation, to wear gloves or stockings in want of mending, or to return home without finding a neat parlor, a place to sit down without asking for it, and a cheerful invitation to partake of necessary refreshment.

In Sarah Stickney Ellis, *Women of England* (1839)

HERO-WORSHIP OF A BROTHER (1869)
George Eliot

George Eliot (Mary Ann Evans, 1819–1880) wrote of her love for her older brother, Isaac, in the sonnet sequence "Brother and Sister" from which the following three sonnets are taken, and in her novel The Mill on the Floss (1860). *Isaac refused to see her after 1854 when she decided to live with the already married George Lewes.*

(I)

I cannot choose but think upon the time
When our two lives grew like two buds that kiss
At lightest thrill from the bee's swinging chime,
Because the one so near the other is.

He was the elder and a little man
Of forty inches, bound to show no dread,
And I the girl that puppy-like now ran,
Now lagged behind my brother's larger tread.

I held him wise, and when he talked to me
Of snakes and birds, and which God loved the best,
I thought his knowledge marked the boundary
Where men grew blind, though angels knew the rest.

If he said "Hush!" I tried to hold my breath;
Wherever he said "Come!" I stepped in faith.

(X)

His sorrow was my sorrow, and his joy
Sent little leaps and laughs all through my frame;
My doll seemed lifeless and no girlish toy
Had any reason when my brother came.

I knelt with him at marbles, marked his fling
Cut the ringed stem and make the apple drop,
Or watched him winding close the spiral string
That looped the orbits of the humming top.

Grasped by such fellowship my vagrant thought
Ceased with dream-fruit dream-wishes to fulfil;
My aëry-picturing fantasy was taught
Subjection to the harder, truer skill

    That seeks with deeds to grave a thought-tracked line,
    And by "What is," "What will be" to define.

(XI)

School parted us; we never found again
That childish world where our two spirits mingled
Like scents from varying roses that remain
One sweetness, nor can everymore be singled.

Yet the twin habit of that early time
Lingered for long about the heart and tongue:
We had been natives of one happy clime,
And its dear accent to our utterance clung.

Till the dire years whose awful name is Change
Had grasped our souls still yearning in divorce
And pitiless shaped them in two forms that range
Two elements which sever their life's course.

    But were another childhood-world my share,
    I would be born a little sister there.

SISTERLY SACRIFICE (ca. 1805)
Ellen "Nelly" Weeton
(See p. 204.)

Like George Eliot, Nelly Weeton (1775[?]–ca. 1850) grew up ido-
lizing her brother and suffered when he left home to get an education.

Weeton's physical and emotional sacrifices for her brother's future were not uncommon. In poor families with genteel aspirations, the daughters were expected to contribute whatever they could toward the education of at least the oldest son.

Weeton's father was an English sea captain who was killed in the American Revolution, leaving her mother a small pension. She supported Nelly and her brother by keeping a village school. Nelly Weeton was a compulsive letter writer and journal keeper. Her writing, unpublished in her lifetime, is full of passion and complaint. After supporting herself as a governess, she married a man who turned out to be a brutal husband. Her brother was instrumental in arranging this marriage yet ineffectual in protecting her from her husband's violence.

Closely as I was confined by my own studies, assisting my mother to teach and do the work of the house, and in sewing for hire, yet a thought of dissatisfaction never entered my mind. I went through all with continual alacrity; my mother praised me, and my brother loved me, and it was my delight to please them. The affection my brother and I had for each other was noticed by all my mother's acquaintances as being uncommonly strong. My brother's appeared more ardent; but mine for him was more deep, sincere, lasting, as alas! subsequent events have proved. . . .

When, at the age of fourteen, my brother was [apprenticed to a lawyer in Preston], what an affliction it was to me! I thought it was like interring him; for I was entirely bereft of the companion of my girlish days; the promotor of mirth and frolic; the stimulator of my studies. For some weeks after he was gone, I visited each place where he used to be seen, with the most melancholy ideas. . . . Many an hour have I sat alone in the room we called his, thinking over the transactions, the pleasing pastimes of days that were gone. I revered and loved my mother, but I loved my brother a great deal better. I used to console myself with the idea that when he was established in business, I should, as we had from almost infancy promised each other, again live with him. . . .

The whole business of the house rested upon me when my mother's asthmatic complaint prevented her assisting; and I had to attend nine hours a day to the school, to cook, to clean, to sew, and to nurse my poor unfortunate mother, whose patience and fortitude were most wonderful, for she had deprived herself of the comforts,

and even many of the necessaries of life, to support my brother at
Preston. And I suffered with her, for I could not bear to eat a kind of
food which she thought too costly for herself, although she urged me
to do so; and consequently, bread and potatoes were our principal
diet. Butter, cream, sugar, and pastry, as well as butcher's meat, were
rarities but seldom used. She thought my brother would repay us
when old enough for all these deprivations. But it was a vain expectation, for like all his sex, when he was grown up, he considered what
had been done for him was his right; that he owed no gratitude to us,
for we were but *female* relatives, and had only done our duty. And
obligations which were too great to be forgotten, he has had the
ingratitude to deny. Strange that so tender-hearted a boy should become so selfish a man. . . .

When my mother died, I was literally left alone—the only inhabi-
tant of the house she bequeathed me. Her income was much too small
to support my brother and myself; therefore, according to her dying
request, I continued the school for my own support, whilst the income
of an estate at Sunderland was appropriated to my brother's use until
he was of age, and for two years after. [It was then all to go to Nelly
by her mother's wish.] . . .

My brother did all he could to cheer me, writing so affectionately,
and showing me every attention in his power, making me frequently
little presents, borrowing books for me to read, that the fatigues and
deprivations I underwent on his account were borne with cheerfulness, or when I almost sunk under them, still the hopes that we
should live together again and that the period was now very quickly
drawing on, supported and encouraged me to further exertion. I lost
several of my genteel acquaintances owing to the shabbiness of my
dress; they were ashamed to be seen with me! I could afford no better;
I could barely procure necessaries. It was a mortification to me, and
I often wept by myself; but, said I, I do it for my brother's sake, and
he will reward me; we cannot afford both to appear well dressed,
and it is better I should go shabby in a little village like this, than he
should in such a town as Preston. But I did not know that while I
was wanting pence, he was idly spending sixpences and shillings. . . .

At length the period of my brother's clerkship expired. . . .

Having been so little in society for so long a time, that of my
brother quite overpowered me. Often, when we have sat together and
he has chatted to amuse me, has the noise of his conversation, his
cheerfulness, been too much for me. I have burst into violent fits of

crying, and could not help it. I was unused to such happiness; my weakened nerves could not bear it. He has been alarmed and distressed —tender-hearted fellow—has taken so much pains to soothe, been so assiduous to please, that he has made me love him more and more. . . .

He formed an attachment to a young lady, and hastily and imprudently married, neither of them able to command a farthing. . . .

My brother still continued coming on a Saturday, in hopes to do a little business in Holland. He talked of wanting money. I told him of my Mother's request. He stood almost aghast, expecting still to have had a whole share, notwithstanding that for above five years he had had the whole income within ten pounds. I had paid off a debt near fifty pounds; had paid for all his washing; the carriage of his clothes . . . had repaired his linen, and bought him many articles of dress such as pocket handkerchiefs, neck handkerchiefs, stockings, flannel waistcoats, and cambric for ruffles. He thought I had given him all these, without the hope of return. . . .

A married man cannot live without money, so he took his share, one hundred pounds excepted, of which I was to have the interest, promising him to restore it if I married; if not, at my death. I was hurt, but as matters were, there was no help. The law would have given him more, but Justice would have denied him a part of what he had. . . .

I had cause after that for sorrow such as I have not felt before. My brother one Saturday told me that if I lived with them, I must pay thirty guineas a year for board. This was nearly the whole of my income. What must I do for clothes, washing, &c? However, I said nothing. I silently acquiesced. He had just taken a house, and that sum would pay the rent and taxes. I could sew, I thought, for my clothes. Not long after, however, my brother told me that Mrs. Scott and her daughter [his mother-in-law and wife] had concluded it better I should not live with them at all; that such a family was very unpleasant, causing the most unhappy dissensions. This was a stroke I did not expect! Had all my savings, my abstinence from necessary diet, my rising early, my sitting up late, my depriving myself of almost every comfort, come to this! It was almost more than I could bear.

Never shall I forget that day! My heart was almost broken. I had, in the expectation of living with my brother, refused a matrimonial offer from a young man of great abilities and most excellent character. It will be a disappointment to my brother, thought I, if I marry. . . . What a dreary prospect now presented itself. And must I live as long as I do live, thought I, in this solitude—is there to be no hope? For upwards of two years, sure never was a more miserable being! How I did long for death. .... I did finally leave that village, with a resolution never again to return to it unless to live in a different manner to what I had lived.

In Ellen Weeton, *Miss Weeton: Journal of a Governess, 1807–1811*, ed. Edward Hall (Oxford: Oxford University Press, 1936)

SISTERS VS. BROTHERS (1870s)
Emmeline Pankhurst
(See p. 289.)

Emmeline Pankhurst (1858–1928) grew up to be the leader of the militant suffragists and the mother of two suffragist daughters, Christabel and Sylvia.

My childhood was protected by love and a comfortable home. Yet, while still a very young child, I began instinctively to feel that there was something lacking, even in my own home, some incomplete ideal.

This vague feeling of mine began to shape itself into conviction about the time my brothers and I were sent to school. The education of the English boy, then as now, was considered a much more serious matter than the education of the English boy's sister. My parents, especially my father, discussed the question of my brothers' education as a matter of real importance. My education and that of my sister were scarcely discussed at all. Of course we went to a carefully selected girls' school, but beyond the facts that the head mistress was a gentlewoman and that all the pupils were girls of my own class, nobody seemed concerned. A girl's education at that time seemed to have for its prime object the art of "making home attractive"—presumably to migratory male relatives. It used to puzzle me to understand why I was under such a particular obligation to make home attractive to my brothers. We were on excellent terms of friendship, but it was never suggested to them as a duty that they make home attractive to me. Why not? Nobody seemed to know.

In Emmeline Pankhurst, *My Own Story* (1914)

THE TRANSITION TO MARRIAGE

RELATIONS BETWEEN YOUNG MEN
AND WOMEN (1844)

Ann Richelieu Lamb

(*See pp. 28 and 49.*)

It is difficult, in the present degraded state of society, to speak of friendship between persons of opposite sexes; to so low an ebb have matters come, that they can scarcely be on terms of acquaintanceship apart from the tie of matrimony, or bond of relationship. Women are so schooled about catching husbands, that the simplest species of civility from a man is converted into "particular attention," just as might be expected from those, who ever on the watch, are sure to pick up something or other which they can put to use. Thus men are terrified from the presence and society of women, by the vision of an action for "breach of promise," or there rises before them the startling question of some prudent parent, or brother, as to *intentions,* keeping them in a perpetual trepidation, rendering the intercourse between the sexes of the most restrained, artificial, and embarrassing description. This is much to be deplored, for how can young persons ever be the better of each other's society, when such a formidable barrier is raised against it? It cannot be doubted that this almost compulsory banishment of young men from the refining society of young women, is the cause of the demoralization of many of the former, since, when we are deprived of innocent and legitimate enjoyment, we are prone to seek it from sources more questionable. Many young men who have been accustomed to the society of sisters, when compelled to live at a distance from their family, perhaps in cheerless, comfortless lodgings, would most gladly cultivate an acquaintance with those of the other sex, without any thoughts of love being in their heads, were they only permitted to do so. But this is rendered next to impossible by the present artificial usages of civilized life. . . .

Young persons, nay persons from twenty to seventy (so ridiculous have we become), cannot meet a few times, without some love affair being gossiped about, given out as a hint, that if they are not in love they ought to be so, or else it is very imprudent, and such other absurdity; until it has become absolutely dangerous for a Victoria shawl to say, "How d'ye do?" to an Albert surtout. Were women to earn their own livelihood, or succeeded to an equal inheritance of property with men, we should hear less assuredly about falling in love from them. . . .

In Ann Richelieu Lamb, *Can Woman Regenerate Society?* (1844)

A WARNING AGAINST PASSION (1840)
Charlotte Brontë
(See pp. 35, 95, 115, 151, 160, 272, and 273.)

The difficulty of communication between the sexes is made clear in this letter between friends. It reveals the anxieties many women felt over interpreting the gestures of men and over the necessity of remaining sexually passive during the ambiguous period of courtship. In this case, Ellen Nussey was anticipating a proposal, which never came.

My Dearest Nell,

That last letter of thine treated of matters so high and important I cannot delay answering it for a day—Now Nell I am about to write thee a discourse and a piece of advice which thou must take as if it came from thy Grandmother. . . .

I am under difficulties because I don't know Mr. V.— if I did I would give you my opinion roundly in two words. Is the man a fool? is he a knave, a humbug, a hypocrite, a ninny, a noodle? If he is any or all of these things of course there is no sense in trifling with him—cut him short at once—blast his hopes with lightning rapidity and keenness.

Is he something better than this? has he at least common sense—a good disposition, a manageable temper? then Nell consider the matter. You feel a disgust towards him *now*, an utter repugnance—very likely—but be so good as to remember you don't know him—longer and closer intimacy might reconcile you to a wonderful extent. And now I'll tell you a word of truth at which you may be offended or not as you like—From what I know of your character, and I think I know it pretty well, I should say you will never *love before* marriage. After that ceremony is over, and after you have had some months to settle down, and to get accustomed to the creature you have taken for your worse half, you will probably make a most affectionate and happy wife, even if the individual should not prove all you could wish. You will be indulgent towards his little follies and foibles, and will not feel much annoyance at them. This will especially be the case if he should have sense sufficient to allow you to guide him in important matters. Such being the case Nell I hope you will not have the romantic folly to wait for the awakening of what the French call "Une grande *passion*"—My good girl "une grande passion" is "*une* grande *folie.*". . .

Did you not once say to me in all childlike simplicity "I thought, Charlotte, no young ladies should fall in love, till the offer was actually made." I forget what answer I made at the time, but I now reply after due consideration—"Right as a glove—the maxim is just and I hope you will always attend to it—I will even extend and confirm it —no young lady should fall in love till the offer has been made, accepted—the marriage ceremony performed and the first half year of wedded life has passed away—a woman may then begin to love, but with great precaution—very coolly, very moderately—very rationally —if she ever loves so much that a harsh word or a cold look from her husband cuts her to the heart—she is a fool—if she ever loves so much that her husband's word is her law—and that she has got into the habit of watching his looks in order that she may anticipate his wishes she will soon be a neglected fool."

Did I not once tell you of an instance of a Relative of mine [her brother Branwell] who cared for a young lady [Mary Taylor] till he began to suspect that she cared more for him and then instantly conceived a sort of contempt for her? You know to what I allude—never as you value your ears mention the circumstance—but I have two studies—*you* are my study for the success, the credit, and the respectability of a quiet, tranquil character. Mary is my study for the contempt, the remorse, the misconstruction which follow the development of feelings in themselves noble, warm, generous, devoted and profound, but which being too freely revealed—too frankly bestowed —are not estimated at their real value. God bless her—I never hope to see in this world a character more truly noble—she would *die* willingly for one she loved—her intellect and her attainments are of the very highest standards yet I doubt whether Mary will ever marry.

I think I may as well conclude this letter for after all I can give you no advice worth receiving. All I have to say may be comprised in a very brief sentence. On one hand don't accept if you are *certain*

you cannot *tolerate* the man—on the other hand don't refuse because
you cannot adore him.

From Charlotte Brontë to Ellen Nussey, November 20, 1840, in *The Brontës*,
letter no. 106

LETTER TO A YOUNG FIANCEE (1859)
Jane Welsh Carlyle
(See p. 132.)

*Thirty-three years before she wrote this letter, Jane Welsh (1801–
1866) was a young fiancée contemplating marriage to the aspiring
writer Thomas Carlyle. She hesitated for some time because he was
unable to support her in the manner to which she was accustomed
and because she was reluctant to give up her role as a petted daughter, leaving her widowed mother alone. In the end, her love for
Carlyle and awe of his intellect led her to consent to marry. Throughout their marriage she devoted herself to her husband's comfort and
to the nurturance of his genius, often suffering from loneliness because of his demand for creative solitude. Carlyle believed that the
"true destiny of a woman . . . is to wed a man she can love and esteem, and to lead noiselessly under his protection, with all the wisdom,
grace, and heroism that is in her, the life prescribed in consequence."
After his death it was alleged by Jane's friends that Carlyle was impotent as well as emotionally neglectful of his wife.*

And you are actually going to get married! you! already! And you
expect me to congratulate you! or "perhaps not." I admire the judi-
ciousness of that "perhaps not." Frankly, my dear, I wish you all the
happiness in the new life that is opening to you; and you are marrying
under good auspices, since your father approves of the marriage. But
congratulations on such occasions seems to me a tempting of Providence. The triumphal-procession-air which, in our manners and customs, is given to marriage at the outset—that singing of *Te Deum*
before the battle has begun—has, ever since I could reflect, struck me
as somewhat senseless and somewhat impious. If ever one is to pray
—if ever one is to feel grave and anxious—if ever one is to shrink from
vain show and vain babble—surely it is just on the occasion of two
human beings binding themselves to one another, for better and for

worse, till death part them; just on that occasion which it is customary to celebrate only with rejoicings, and congratulations, and *trousseaux*, and white ribbon! Good God!

Will you think me mad if I tell you that when I read your words, "I am going to be married," I all but screamed? Positively, it took away my breath, as if I saw you in the act of taking a flying leap into infinite space. You had looked to me such a happy, happy little girl! your father's only daughter; and he so fond of you, as he evidently was. After you had walked out of our house together that night, and I had gone up to my own room, I sat down there in the dark, and took "a good cry." You had reminded me so vividly of my own youth, when I, also an only daughter—an only child—had a father as fond of me, as proud of me. I wondered if you knew your own happiness. Well! knowing it or not, it has not been enough for you, it would seem. Naturally, youth is so insatiable of happiness, and has such sublimely insane faith in its own power to make happy and be happy.

From Jane Carlyle to Miss Barnes, August 24, 1859, in Mrs. Alexander Ireland, *Life of Jane Welsh Carlyle* (1891)

DECISION TO MARRY (1866)
Annie Besant
(See pp. 146, 294, and 346.)

The decision of Annie Besant (1847–1933) to fulfill her own desire for religious work by marrying a clergyman soon proved to be a mistake. She lost her faith and consequently her husband. When she then made a career for herself as a public orator, activist, and pamphleteer, her husband successfully sued her for custody of their daughter, declaring Annie an unfit mother because of her avowed atheism and advocacy of birth control. Later she converted to theosophy, and lived the last thirty-eight years of her life in India as a prominent religious leader and anticolonialist.

During that autumn I became engaged to the Rev. Frank Besant, giving up with a sigh of regret my dreams of the "religious life," and substituting for them the work which would have to be done as the wife of a priest, laboring ever in the church and among the poor. A queer view, some people may think, for a girl to take of married life,

Annie Besant, 1888

National Museum of Labour History

but it was the natural result of my living the life of the Early Church, of my enthusiasm for religious work. To me a priest was a half-angelic creature, whose whole life was consecrated to heaven; all that was deepest and truest in my nature chafed against my useless days, longed for work, yearned to devote itself, as I had read women saints had done, to the service of the church and the poor, to the battling against sin and misery. "You will have more opportunity for doing good as a clergyman's wife than as anything else," was one of the pleas urged on my reluctance. My ignorance of all that marriage meant was as profound as though I had been a child of four, and my knowledge of the world was absolutely *nil*. My darling mother meant all that was happiest for me when she shielded me from all knowledge of sorrow and of sin, when she guarded me from the smallest idea of the marriage relation, keeping me ignorant as a baby till I left her home a wife. But looking back now on all, I deliberately say that no more fatal blunder can be made than to train a girl to womanhood in ignorance of all life's duties and burdens, and then to let her face them for the first time away from all the old associations, the old helps, the old refuge on the mother's breast. That "perfect innocence" may be very beautiful but it is a perilous possession, and Eve should have the knowledge of good and of evil ere she wanders forth from the paradise of a mother's love. When a word is never spoken to a girl that is not a caress; when necessary rebuke comes in tone of tenderest reproach; when "You have grieved me" has been the heaviest penalty for a youthful fault; when no anxiety has ever been allowed to trouble the young heart—then, when the hothouse flower is transplanted, and rough winds blow upon it, it droops and fades.

In Annie Besant, *Autobiographical Sketches* (1885)

ON HER ELOPEMENT (1846)
Elizabeth Barrett Browning

After spending her youthful years as the petted semi-invalid of her household, Elizabeth Barrett (1806–1861) eloped, at age forty, with fellow poet Robert Browning, six years her junior. Despite the love for her father which she expresses here, he never forgave her or saw her again.

(Letter to Robert Browning)

As to accoutrements, everything has been arranged as simply as possible that way—but still there are necessities—and the letters, the letters! I am paralysed when I think of having to write such words as "Papa, I am married; I hope you will not be too displeased." Ah, poor Papa! You are too sanguine if you expect any such calm from him as an assumption of indifference would imply. To the utmost, he will be angry—he will cast me off as far from him. Well—there is no comfort in such thoughts. How I felt tonight when I saw him at seven o'clock for the first time since Friday, and the event of Saturday [her marriage]! He spoke kindly too, and asked me how I was. Once I heard of his saying of me that I was "the purest woman he ever knew"—which made me smile at the moment, or laugh I believe, outright, because I understood perfectly what he mean by *that* —viz—that I had not troubled him with the iniquity of love affairs, or any impropriety of seeming to think about being married. But now the whole sex will go down with me to the perdition of faith in any of us. See the effect of my wickedness!—"Those women!"

But we will submit, dearest. I will put myself under his feet, to be forgiven a little, enough to be taken up again into his arms. I love him—he is my father—he has good and high qualities after all: he is my father *above* all. And *you*, because you are so generous and tender to me, will let me, you say, and help me to try to win back the alienated affection—for which, I thank you and bless you—I did not thank you enough this morning. Surely I may say to him, too, "With the exception of this act, I have submitted to the least of your wishes all my life long. Set the life against the act, and forgive me, for the sake of the daughter you once loved." Surely I may say *that*, and then remind him of the long suffering I have suffered—and entreat him to pardon the happiness which has come at last.

And *he* will wish in return, that I had died years ago! For the storm will come and endure. And at last, perhaps, he will forgive us—it is my hope—

Your very own BA

From Elizabeth Barrett Browning to Robert Browning, September 14, 1846, in *The Love-Letters of Robert Browning and Elizabeth Barrett*, ed. V. E. Stack (London: Heinemann, 1969)

A PROPOSAL AND COURTSHIP (1852, 1854)
Charlotte Brontë
(*See pp. 35, 95, 109, 151, 160, 272, and 273.*)

When Arthur Nicholls, her father's curate, proposed to Charlotte Brontë she was thirty-six years old, a famous novelist, and had spent most of her life in her isolated Yorkshire parsonage home with her ailing and demanding father. The extreme confinement of her life, which her literary success hardly altered, dictated the terms both of her refusal and her eventual acceptance of Nicholls's proposal. Six years before, Brontë had dismissed the idea of such a marriage, saying of her father's curates, "They regard me as an old maid, and I regard them, one and all, as highly uninteresting, narrow and unattractive specimens of the coarser sex"; and in her novel Shirley (1849), she caricatured her future husband as a religious bigot. Nevertheless, the marriage seems to have been happy though tragically brief. Less than a year after her marriage, Charlotte Brontë died of hyperemesis gravidarum, a complication of early pregnancy characterized by excessive vomiting.

(Charlotte Brontë to Ellen Nussey, December 15, 1852)

I know not whether you have ever observed [Mr. Nicholls] specially when staying here, your perception is generally quick enough, too quick I have sometimes thought, yet as you never said anything, I restrained my own dim misgivings, which could not claim the sure guide of vision. What Papa has seen or guessed I will not inquire though I may conjecture. He has minutely noticed all Mr. Nicholls's low spirits, all his threats of expatriation, all his symptoms of impaired health, noticed them with little sympathy and much indirect sarcasm. On Monday evening Mr. Nicholls was here to tea. I vaguely felt without clearly seeing, as without seeing, I have felt for some time, the meaning of his constant looks, and strange, feverish restraint. After tea I withdrew to the dining-room as usual. As usual, Mr. Nicholls sat with Papa till between eight and nine o'clock, I then heard him open the parlour door as if going. I expected the clash of the front-door. He stopped in the passage: he tapped: like lightning it flashed on me what was coming. He entered—he stood before me. What his words were you can guess; his manner—you can hardly realise—never can I forget it. Shaking from head to foot, looking deadly pale, speaking low, vehemently yet with difficulty—he made me for the first time feel what it costs a man to declare affection where he doubts response.

The spectacle of one ordinarily so statue-like, thus trembling, stirred, and overcome, gave me a kind of strange shock. He spoke of sufferings he has borne for months, of sufferings he could endure no longer, and craved leave for some hope. I could only entreat him to leave me then and promise a reply on the morrow. I asked him if he had spoken to Papa. He said, he dared not. I think I half led, half put him out of the room. When he was gone I immediately went to Papa, and told him what had taken place. Agitation and anger disproportionate to the occasion ensued; if I had *loved* Mr. Nicholls and had heard such epithets applied to him as were used, it would have transported me past my patience; as it was, my blood boiled with a sense of injustice, but Papa worked himself into a state not to be trifled with, the veins on his temples started up like whipcord, and his eyes became suddenly bloodshot. I made haste to promise that Mr. Nicholls should on the morrow have a distinct refusal.

(Charlotte Brontë to Ellen Nussey, April 11, 1854)

Mr. Nicolls came on Monday, and was here all last week. Matters have progressed thus since July. He renewed his visit in September, but then matters so fell out that I saw little of him. He continued to write. The correspondence pressed on my mind. I grew very miserable in keeping it from Papa. At last sheer pain made me gather courage to break it— I told all. It was very hard and rough work at the time—but the issue after a few days was that I obtained leave to continue the communication. Mr. N[icholls] came in Jan[uary]; he was ten days in the neighbourhood. I saw much of him. I had stipulated with Papa for opportunity to become better acquainted—I had it, and all I learnt inclined me to esteem and if not love—at least affection. Still Papa was very, very hostile—bitterly unjust.

I told Mr. Nicholls the great obstacles that lay in his way. He has persevered. The result of this, his last visit, is, that Papa's consent is gained—that his respect, I believe, is won, for Mr. Nicholls has in all things proved himself disinterested and forbearing. He has shown, too, that while his feelings are exquisitely keen—he can freely forgive. Certainly I must respect him, nor can I withhold from him more than mere cool respect. In fact, dear Ellen, I am engaged.

Mr. Nicholls, in the course of a few months, will return to the curacy of Haworth. I stipulated that I would not leave Papa, and to Papa himself I proposed a plan of residence which should maintain his seclusion and convenience uninvaded and in a pecuniary sense bring him gain instead of loss. What seemed at one time impossible is now arranged, and Papa begins really to take a pleasure in the prospect.

For myself, dear Ellen, while thankful to One who seems to have

guided me through much difficulty, much and deep distress and per-
plexity of mind, I am still very calm, very inexpectant. What I taste
of happiness is of the soberest order. I trust to love my husband—I am
grateful for his tender love to me. I believe him to be an affectionate,
a conscientious, a high-principled man; and if, with all this, I should
yield to regrets, that fine talents, congenial tastes and thoughts are
not added, it seems to me I should be most presumptuous and thank-
less.

Providence offers me this destiny. Doubtless then it is the best for
me. Nor do I shrink from wishing those dear to me one not less
happy. . . .

In *The Brontës*, letters nos. 807, 886

THE INSTITUTION OF MARRIAGE

MARRIED WOMEN AND THE LAW (1854)
Barbara Leigh Smith Bodichon
(See p. 267.)

When Barbara Leigh Smith Bodichon (1827–1891) published her
pamphlet summarizing the legal position of women, she set the stage
for the first large-scale effort at feminist political organizing in England. Twenty-six thousand signatures were gathered by Barbara
Bodichon and Bessie Rayner Parkes, on a petition for the rights of
wives to financial independence. Although the Married Women's
Property Bill of 1857 was defeated, the Divorce Act of that year provided separated, divorced, and deserted women with some property
rights. The first successful Married Women's Property Act (1870) was
severely gutted by the House of Lords, who feared that giving women
control over their money would end wifely obedience. It was not
until 1882 that a comprehensive act was passed. In fact, reform came
slowly for all the legal debilities outlined by Bodichon. It was not
until 1886 that women could sue their husbands for maintenance; not
until 1891 that husbands were denied "conjugal rights" to their wives'
bodies without their wives' consent; not until 1923 that the grounds

British Library

"A *Wedding Breakfast*," *from* Cassells Family Magazine, *1876*

for divorce were made the same for women as for men; and not until 1925 that mothers were given equal rights and powers with fathers over their children.

Barbara Bodichon, quoting Judge Hurlbut, summed up the legal situation of women in marriage that persisted for most of the nineteenth century: "In short, a woman is courted and wedded as an angel, and yet denied the dignity of a rational and moral being ever after."

A man and wife are one person in law; the wife loses all her rights as a single woman, and her existence is entirely absorbed in that of her husband. He is civilly responsible for her acts; she lives under his protection or cover, and her condition is called coverture.

A woman's body belongs to her husband; she is in his custody, and he can enforce his right by a writ of *habeas corpus*.

What was her personal property before marriage, such as money in hand, money at the bank, jewels, household goods, clothes, &c., becomes absolutely her husband's, and he may assign or dispose of them at his pleasure whether he and his wife live together or not.

A wife's *chattels real* (i.e., estates held during a term of years, or the next presentation to a church living, &c.) become her husband's....

Neither the Courts of Common Law nor Equity have any direct power to oblige a man to support his wife....

Money earned by a married woman belongs absolutely to her husband; that and all sources of income, excepting those mentioned above, are included in the term personal property.

By the particular permission of her husband she can make a will of her personal property, for by such a permission he gives up his right. But he may revoke his permission at any time before *probate*....

The legal custody of children belongs to the father. During the life-time of a sane father, the mother has no rights over her children, except a limited power over infants, and the father may take them from her and dispose of them as he thinks fit.

If there be a legal separation of the parents, and there be neither agreement nor order of Court, giving the custody of the children to either parent, then the *right to the custody of the children* (except for the nutriment of infants) belongs legally to the father.

A married woman cannot sue or be sued for contracts—nor can she enter into contracts except as the agent of her husband; that is to say, her word alone is not binding in law, and persons giving a wife credit have no remedy against her....

A wife cannot bring actions unless the husband's name is joined.

As the wife acts under the command and control of her husband, she is excused from punishment for certain offences, such as theft, burglary, housebreaking, &c., if committed in his presence and under his influence. A wife cannot be found guilty of concealing her felon husband or of concealing a felon jointly with her husband. She cannot be found guilty of stealing from her husband or of setting his house on fire, as they are one person in law. A husband and wife cannot be found guilty of conspiracy, as that offence cannot be committed unless there are two persons.

In Barbara Leigh Smith Bodichon, A *Brief Summary in Plain Language of the Most Important Laws Concerning Women* (1854)

"WIFE TORTURE IN ENGLAND" (1878)
Frances Power Cobbe
(See pp. 92, 162, 198, and 261.)

Frances Power Cobbe wrote this article as part of the successful campaign for the Matrimonial Causes Act of 1878, which enabled abused wives to obtain separation orders to keep their husbands away from them. The laws of England and their interpretation by the courts encouraged physical punishment of wives as deriving from a husband's responsibility for his wife's actions. In common law a man had the right "to give his wife moderate correction . . . by domestic chastisement" just as he could his children or apprentices. Common law also recognized his right to restrain his wife physically "to prevent her going into society of which he disapproves, or otherwise disobeying his rightful authority."

The assault on a wife by her husband seems to be surrounded by a certain halo of jocularity which invites people to smile whenever they hear of a case of it (terminating anywhere short of actual murder), and causes the mention of the subject to conduce rather than otherwise to the hilarity of a dinner party. The occult fun thus connected with wife-beating forms by no means indeed the least curious part of the subject. Certainly in view of the state of things revealed by our criminal statistics there is something ominous in the circumstance that "Punch" should have been our national English street-drama for more than two centuries. . . . [In which] it is . . . remarkable that so much of the enjoyment should concentrate about the thwacking of poor Judy, and the flinging of the baby out of the window. . . .

Probably the sense that they must carry with them a good deal of tacit sympathy on the part of other men has something to do in encouraging wife-beaters, just as the fatal notion of the good fellowship of drink has made thousands of sots. . . .

The general depreciation of women *as a sex* is bad enough, but in the matter we are considering, the special depreciation of *wives* is more directly responsible for the outrages they endure. The notion that a man's wife is his PROPERTY . . . is the fatal root of incalculable evil and misery. Every brutal-minded man, and many a man who in other relations of life is not brutal, entertains more or less vaguely the notion that his wife is his *thing*, and is ready to ask with indignation (as we read again and again in the police reports), of any one who interferes with his treatment of her, "May I not do what I will *with my own?*" It is even sometimes pleaded on behalf of poor men, that they possess *nothing else* but their wives, and that, consequently, it seems doubly hard to meddle with the exercise of their power in that narrow sphere. . . .

[N]ot only is an offence against a wife condoned as of inferior guilt, but any offence of the wife against her husband is regarded as a sort of *Petty Treason*. . . . Should she be guilty of "nagging" or scolding, or of being a slattern, or of getting intoxicated, she finds usually a short shrift and no favour—and even humane persons talk of her offence as constituting if not a justification for her murder, yet an explanation of it. She is, in short, liable to capital punishment without judge or jury for transgressions which in the case of a man would never be punished at all, or be expiated by a fine of five shillings.

[Here is an example], as reported in the *Manchester Courier*, February 5th, so instructive in its details of the motives for wife-murder, the sort of woman who is murdered, the man who kills, and the sentiment of juries as to what constitutes "provocation" on the part of a wife, that I shall extract it at length:

MANSLAUGHTER AT DUKINFIELD

Thomas Harlow, 39, striker, Dukinfield, was indicted for the manslaughter of his wife, Ellen Harlow, 45 years old, at Dukinfield, on 30th November, 1877. The prisoner was committed by the magistrates on the charge of wilful murder, but the grand jury reduced the indictment to that of manslaughter. Mr. Marshall prosecuted; and the prisoner, who was undefended by counsel, states, in his plea, that he had no intention of killing his wife when he struck her.

The prisoner, who was employed in and about Dukinfield, lived with his wife and three children in Waterloo Street, in that town. On the morning of the 30th November the deceased went out hawking as usual, and returned shortly after twelve o'clock. During the time she was away the prisoner remained in the house sitting by the fire, and for the most part drinking beer. When she returned she busied herself in preparing dinner, and the prisoner went out for a short time.

In the afternoon the prisoner laid himself down, and slept for two or three hours. About five o'clock the deceased, and a lodger named Margaret Daley, and several others, were sitting in the house, when the prisoner came in and asked his wife for twopence. She replied that she had not twopence, and that she had had trouble enough with being out hawking all day in the rain and hungry. He then began to abuse her, and asked her for something to eat. She gave him some potatoes and bacon; after eating the greater part of which he again began to abuse her. He once more asked her for twopence, and Margaret Daley, seeing there was likely to be a disturbance, gave him the twopence, and told him he had better get a pint of beer. Instead of getting beer, however, he sent a little girl to purchase a quantity of coal, and then recommenced abusing his wife. Shortly afterwards he was heard to exclaim, "There will be a life less to-night, and I will take it." At this time the persons who were sitting in the house when the prisoner came in went out, leaving Harlow, his wife, and their son Thomas, and Daley together. The prisoner had some further altercation with his wife, which ended with him striking her a violent blow under the right ear, felling her to the floor. She died in a few minutes afterwards, the cause of death being concussion of the brain. The prisoner subsequently gave himself into custody, and made a statement attributing his conduct to the provocation his wife had given him.

The jury found the prisoner guilty, and recommended him to mercy *on account of the provocation* he received. Sentence was deferred.

In *Contemporary Review*, April 1878

A RENUNCIATION OF THE RIGHTS OF HUSBANDS (1851)
John Stuart Mill
(See p. 31.)

John Stuart Mill (1806–1873) was the first member of Parliament to propose women's suffrage.

Being about, if I am so happy as to obtain her consent, to enter into the marriage relation with the only woman I have ever known, with whom I would have entered into that state; and the whole character of the marriage relation as constituted by law being such as both she and I entirely and conscientiously disapprove, for this among other reasons, that it confers upon one of the parties to the contract, legal power and control over the person, property, and freedom of action of the other party, independent of her own wishes and will; I, having no means of legally divesting myself of these odious powers (as I most assuredly would do if an engagement to that effect could be made legally binding on me) feel it my duty to put on record a formal protest against the existing laws of marriage, in so far as conferring such powers; and a solemn promise never in any case or under any circumstances to use them. And in the event of marriage between Mrs. Taylor and me I declare it to be my will and intention, and the condition of the engagement between us, that she retains in all respects whatever the same absolute freedom of action and disposal of herself and of all that does or may at any time belong to her, as if no such marriage had taken place; and I absolutely disclaim and repudiate all pretension to have acquired any rights whatever by virtue of such marriage.

[6 March 1851, J. S. Mill]

In *The Letters of John Stuart Mill*, Hugh S. R. Eliot, ed. (London: Longman's, Green & Co., 1910)

CHARACTERISTICS OF HUSBANDS (1843)
Sarah Stickney Ellis
(See p. 100.)

Much of Mrs. Ellis's writing was addressed to the discrepancies between ideal and actual domestic life. Here, she obliquely informs her readers how to satisfy the demands of wifely obedience despite one's knowledge of one's husband's faults.

Were all men excellent, without inconsistencies, and without defects, there would be no need for words of caution or advice addressed to the weaker sex, but especially to wives, for each would have perpetually before her, a perfect model of true excellence, from which she would be ashamed to differ, and by which she would be taught at once to admire and imitate whatever is more worthy of esteem. With gratitude we ought to acknowledge our belief, that . . . in the character of a noble, enlightened, and truly good man, there is a power and a sublimity, so nearly approaching what we believe to be the nature and capacity of angels, that as no feeling can exceed, so no language can describe, the degree of admiration and respect which the contemplation of such a character must excite. To be permitted to dwell within the influence of such a man, must be a privilege of the highest order; to listen to his conversation, must be a perpetual feast; but to be permitted into his heart—to share his counsels, and to be the chosen companion of his joys and sorrows!—it is difficult to say whether humility or gratitude should preponderate in the feelings of the woman thus distinguished and thus blest.

If all men were of this description, these pages might be given to the winds. We must suppose, however, for the sake of meeting every case, and especially the most difficult, that there are men occasionally found who are not, strictly speaking, noble, nor highly enlightened, nor altogether good. That such men are as much disposed as their superiors to enter into the married state, is also a fact of public notoriety, and it is to the women who venture upon uniting themselves to such men for life, that I would be understood chiefly to address myself. . . .

All women should, therefore, be prepared for discovering faults in men, as they are for beholding spots in the sun, or clouds in the summer sky. . . .

Much allowance should be made . . . for the peculiar mode of education by which men are trained for the world. From their early childhood, girls are accustomed to fill an inferior place, to give up, to fall back, and to be as nothing in comparison with their brothers; while boys, on the other hand, have to suffer all the disadvantages in after life, of having had their precocious selfishness encouraged, from the time when they first began to feel the dignity of superior power, and the triumph of occupying a superior place.

The young and inexperienced woman, who has but recently been made the subject of man's attentions, and the object of his choice, will probably be disposed to dispute this point with me, and to argue that one man at least is free from selfishness; because she sees, or rather *hears* her lover willing to give up everything for her. But let no woman trust to such obsequiousness, for generally speaking, those who are the most extravagant in their professions, and the most servile in their adulation before marriage, are the most unreasonable and requiring afterwards. . . .

As it is the natural characteristic of woman's love in its most refined, as well as its most practical development, to be perpetually doing something for the good or the happiness of the object of her affection, it is but reasonable that man's personal comfort should be studiously attended to; and in this, the complacence and satisfaction which most men evince on finding themselves placed at table before a favorite dish, situated beside a clean hearth, or accommodated with an empty sofa, is of itself a sufficient reward for any sacrifice such indulgence may have cost. In proofs of affection like these, there is something tangible which speaks home to the senses—something which man can understand without an effort: and he will sit down to eat, or compose himself to rest, with more hearty goodwill towards the wife who has been thoughtful about these things, than if she had been all day busily employed in writing a treatise on morals for his special benefit.

Again, man's dignity, as well as his comfort, must be ministered unto. . . . I have said, that whether well or ill, a husband is entitled to respect; and it is perhaps when ill, more than at any other time, that men are impressed with a sense of their own importance. It is, therefore, an act of kindness, as well as of justice, and a concession easily made, to endeavor to keep up this idea by all those little acts of delicate attention which at once do good to the body, and sustain the mind. Illness is to men a sufficient trial and humiliation of itself. . . . A sensible and kind-hearted woman, therefore, will never inflict upon the man she loves, when thus circumstanced, the additional punishment of feeling that it is possible for him to be forgotten or neglected.

But chiefly in poverty, or when laboring under depressed circumstances, it is the part of a true wife to exhibit by the most delicate, but most profound respect, how highly she is capable of valuing her husband, independently of all those adventitious circumstances, according to which he has been valued by the world. It is here that the dignity of man is most apt to give way—here that his stout heart fails him—and here then it must be woman's part to build him up. Not, as many are too apt to suppose, merely to comfort him by her endearments, but actually to raise him in his own esteem, to restore to him his estimate of his moral worth, and to convince him that it is beyond the power of circumstances to degrade an upright and an honest man. . . .

I will not ask how often, after this exhibit of his weakness, after regaining his post of honor, and being received again a competitor for distinction, he has forgotten the witness of his humiliation; but I believe it is only as a wife, a mother, or a sister, that woman can be this friend to man, with safety to herself, and with certainty that he will not afterwards rather avoid than seek her, from the feeling that she has beheld him shorn of his dignity, and is consequently able to remind him of the humiliating past. For the wife it might also be a dangerous experiment even in her fondest and most un-guarded moments, to make any allusion to scenes and circumstances of this description; especially to presume upon having necessarily assumed at such times the stronger and more important part. When her husband chooses to be dignified again, and is capable of main-taining that dignity, she must adapt herself to the happy change, and fall back into comparative insignificance, just as if circumstances had never given her a momentary superiority over him.

In Sarah Stickney Ellis, *The Wives of England* (1843)

THE PERFECT IDEAL
OF AN ENGLISH WIFE (1875)
Dr. William Acton
(See pp. 394, 427, and 432.)

Throughout the nineteenth century, medical doctors like William Acton (1814–1875) increasingly offered professional judgments on matters of sexual arrangements and general social behavior. Acton's minimizing of women's sexual desires, like Mrs. Ellis's exaggeration of men's needs for domestic comfort and respect, represents a widely consulted expression of a cultural norm, but not necessarily a descrip-tion of the general experience of marriage. Women's denial of their own sexuality, moreover, could be a useful tactic for avoiding the dangers and discomforts of childbearing. But though Acton placed so little importance on women's sexual needs, he nevertheless blamed those wives who refused to have sexual relations in order to avoid conception, for damaging their husband's health.

I am ready to maintain that there are many females who never feel any sexual excitement whatever. Others, again, immediately after each period, do become to a limited degree, capable of experiencing it; but this capacity is temporary, and may entirely cease until the next menstrual period. Many of the best mothers, wives, and managers of households, know little of or are careless about sexual indulgences. Love of home, of children, and of domestic duties are the only passions they feel.

As a general rule, a modest woman seldom desires any sexual gratification for herself. She submits to her husband's embraces, but principally to gratify him; and, were it not for the desire of maternity, would far rather be relieved from his attentions. No nervous or feeble young man need, therefore, be deterred from marriage by any exaggerated notion of the arduous duties required from him. Let him be well assured, on my authority backed by the opinion of many, that the married woman has no wish to be placed on the footing of a mistress.

One instance may better illustrate the real state of the case than much description.

In ——, 185-, a barrister about thirty years of age, came to me on account of a sexual debility. On cross-examination I found he had been married a twelvemonth, that an attempt at connection had taken place but once since the commencement of the year, and that even then there was some doubt as to the completion of the act. He brought his wife with him, as she was, he said, desirous of having some conversation with me.

I found the lady a refined but highly sensitive person. . . . She neither blushed nor faltered in telling her story, and I regret that my words must fail to convey the delicacy with which her avowal was made.

Her husband and herself, she said, have been acquainted from childhood, had grown up together, became mutually attached, and married. She had reason to consider him debilitated, but—as she was fully convinced—from no indiscreet acts on his part. She believed it was his natural condition. She was dotingly attached to him, and would not have determined to consult me, but that she wished for his sake, to have a family, as it would, she hoped, conduce to their mutual happiness. She assured me that she felt no sexual passions whatever; that if she was capable of them they were dormant. Her passion for her husband was of a Platonic kind, and far from wishing to stimulate his frigid feelings, she doubted whether it would be right or not. She loved him as he was, and would not desire him to be otherwise except for the hope of having a family.

I believe this lady is a perfect ideal of an English wife and mother, kind, considerate, self-sacrificing, and sensible, so pure-hearted as to be utterly ignorant of and averse to any sensual indulgence, but so unselfishly attached to the man she loves, as to be willing to give up her own wishes and feelings for his sake.

In William Acton, *The Functions and Disorders of the Reproductive Organs, in Childhood, Adult Age, and Advanced Life, Considered in Their Physiological, Social, and Moral Relations* (1875)

CURING "INSANITY" THROUGH CLITORIDECTOMY (1866)
Isaac Baker Brown

Isaac Baker Brown was a gynecologist who ran a fifty-bed private clinic. He claimed to have been successful during his peak years of activity (1866–1867) in curing antisocial behavior of various kinds by practicing the surgical removal of the clitoris. His career came to an abrupt end when he was expelled from the Obstetrical Society for neglecting to inform his patients or their families of the nature of the operation. He was by no means the only practitioner of clitoridectomies in nineteenth-century England, but his coercive practices and ultimate disgrace were extreme enough to render the operation unpopular in England. However, the basic assumption that woman's sexual physiology was potentially treacherous to her mental health shaped medical opinion on many women's issues, such as the controversy over higher education (see pp. 220–225).

SYMPTOMS AND PROGRESS OF DISEASE

Every medical practitioner must have met with a certain class of cases which has set at defiance every effort at diagnosis, baffled every treatment, and belied every prognosis. He has experienced great anxiety and annoyance, and felt how unsatisfactory was his treatment to the friends of his patient: and this, not so much because he was ignorant of the cause, as that he was unable to offer any hope of relief.

The period when such illness attacks the patient is about the age of puberty, and from that time to almost every age the following train of symptoms may be observed, some being more and less marked than others in the various cases.

The patient becomes restless and excited, or melancholy and retiring, listless and indifferent to the social influences of domestic
life. She will be fanciful in her food, sometimes express even a distaste for it, and apparently (as her friends will say) live upon nothing.
She will always be ailing, and complaining of different affections. At
first, perhaps, dyspepsia and sickness will be observed; then pain in
the head and down the spine; pain, more or less constant, in the
lower part of the back, or on either side in the lumbar region. There
will be wasting of the face and muscles generally; the skin sometimes dry and harsh, at other times cold and clammy. The pupil will
be sometimes firmly contracted, but generally much dilated. This
latter symptom, together with a hard cord-like pulse, and a constantly
moist palm, are, my son informs me, considered by Mr. Moore,
Colonial Surgeon of South Australia, pathognomonic of this condition. There will be quivering of the eyelids, and an inability to look
one straight in the face. On inquiring further, there is found to be
disturbance or irregularity in the uterine functions, there being either
complete cessation of the catamenia, or too frequent periods, generally attended with pain; constant leucerrhoea [white discharge]
also frequently existing. Often a great disposition for novelties is exhibited, the patient desiring to escape from home, fond of becoming
a nurse in hospitals, "sister of charity," or other pursuits of the like
nature, according to station and opportunities. To these symptoms in
the single female will be added, in the married, distaste for marital
intercourse, and very frequently either sterility or a tendency to abort
in the early months of pregnancy.

These physical evidences of derangement, if left unchecked, gradually lead to more serious consequences. The patient either becomes a
confirmed invalid, always ailing, and confined to bed or sofa, or, on
the other hand, will become subject to catalepsy, epilepsy, idiocy, or
insanity. In any case, and more especially when the disease progresses
as far as these latter stages, it will almost universally be found that
there are serious exacerbations at each menstrual period.

CASE XIX

A young lady, age 20, came under my care in 1863, having for the
last two years suffered from almost constant menorrhagia, during
which time she had suffered great irregularities of temper, been dis-
obedient to her mother's wishes, and had sleepless nights, restless desires for society, and was constantly seeking admiration; all these
symptoms culminating in a monomania that every gentleman she

admired was in love with her, and she insisted on always sending her visiting card to her favoured one for the time being. In her quieter moments she would spend much time in serious reading. On being consulted, I quickly discovered that all these symptoms arose from peripheral excitement [masturbation], and that there existed no organic disease to cease the menorrhagia. The usual plan of treatment [clitoridectomy] was followed with the most rapid and marked success. She went the full interval between the ensuing menstrual periods, and the secretion was normal in quantity. All her delusions disappeared, and after three or four months of careful watching, with change of air, she was perfectly normal in every respect. A year afterward she married, and ten months later gave birth to a healthy son. She is now again pregnant.

CASE XLVIII

In 1863, Mrs. S. M., married, mother of three children, age 30, came under my care, because she had been suffering for more than a year from menorrhagia, which had gradually affected her mind, causing her to have a great distaste for her husband; so much so, that he and his friends were induced seriously to contemplate a separation. On the first examination, her face indicated mental disturbance, eyes restless, pupils dilated, and manner generally excitable. She told me that she could not sleep at night, complained of constant weary uneasiness of her womb, pain in her back, great pain on defecation, constant desire to micturate. She said she was glad to be away from home, as she made everyone around her unhappy. Believed that she would be a permanently insane patient, and never expected to return to her family again.

On more minute examination, I found irritable clitoris and labia, a painful fissure of the rectum, which, on inquiry, was found to be caused by frequent introduction of her finger, with a view to peripheral irritation. At her own request she had long been separated à mensâ from her husband, on account of her great distaste for him and cohabitation with him.

I pursued the usual surgical treatment, which was followed by uninterrupted success, and after two months treatment, she returned to her husband, resumed cohabitation, and stated that all her distaste had disappeared; soon became pregnant, resumed her place at the head of the table, and became a happy and healthy wife and mother. She was in due time safely delivered, and has ever since remained in perfect health.

Remarks: From observations of this case, one feels compelled to say, may not it be typical of many others where there is a judicial separation of husband and wife, with all the attendant domestic miseries, and where, if medical and surgical treatment were brought to bear, all such unhappy measures would be obviated?

In Isaac Baker Brown, *On the Curability of Certain Forms of Insanity, Epilepsy, and Hysteria in Females* (1866)

THE EXPERIENCE OF MARRIAGE

THE CARE OF A LIVING AUTHOR (1843)
Jane Welsh Carlyle
(See p. 111.)

My dear Jane [Aiken],
    Carlyle returned from his travels very bilious and continues very bilious up to this hour. The amount of bile that he does bring home to me, in these cases, is something "awfully grand!" Even through that deteriorating medium he could not but be struck with a "certain admiration" at the immensity of needlework I had accomplished in his absence, in the shape of chair-covers, sofa-covers, window curtains, &c., &c., and all the other manifest improvements into which I had put my whole genius and industry, and so little money as was hardly to be conceived! For three days his satisfaction over the rehabilitated house lasted; on the fourth, the young lady next door took a fit of practising on her accursed pianoforte, which he had quite forgotten seemingly, and he started up disenchanted in his new library, and informed heaven and earth in a peremptory manner that "there he could neither think nor live," that the carpenter must be brought back and "steps taken to make him a quiet place somewhere—perhaps best of all on the roof of the house." Then followed interminable consultations with the said carpenter, yielding, for some days, only plans (wild ones) and estimates. The roof on the house could be made all that a living author of irritable nerves could desire: silent as a tomb, lighted from above; but it would cost us one hundred twenty pounds! Impossible, seeing that we may be turned out of the house any year! so one had to reduce one's schemes to the

altering of rooms that already were. By taking down a partition and instituting a fire-place where no fire-place could have been fancied capable of existing, it is expected that some bearable approximation to that ideal room in the clouds will be realised. But my astonishment and despair on finding myself after three months of what they call here "regular mess," just when I had got every trace of the workpeople cleared away, and had said to myself, "Soul, take thine ease, or at all events thy swing, for thou hast carpets nailed down and furniture rubbed for many days!" just when I was beginning to lead the dreaming, reading, dawdling existence which best suits me, and alone suits me in cold weather, to find myself in the thick of a new "mess": the carpets, which I had nailed down so well with my own hands, tumbled up again, dirt, lime, whitewash, oil, paint, hard at work as before, and a prospect of new cleanings, new sewings, new arrangements stretching away into eternity for anything I see!

From Jane Welsh Carlyle to Mrs. Jane Aiken, October 1843, in *The Life of Jane Welsh Carlyle* (1891)

A VICTIM OF THE RIGHTS
OF HUSBANDS (ca. 1835/1854)
Caroline Norton

Caroline Norton (1808–1877), the granddaughter of Richard Brinsley Sheridan, was a celebrated beauty. She wrote stories and poems, but is most remembered for her unfortunate marriage and for the tracts (excerpted here) that she wrote against her husband and the marriage laws. At nineteen, she married George Norton, a man of considerably less intellect than herself. With her great social charm, she hosted leading politicians of the day, including the aging Lord Melbourne, who was a close friend. It was a cause of contention in the marriage that Caroline could not use her influence with Lord Melbourne to advance her husband's civil service career as much as he wished her to. When they finally separated, he attempted to win a money settlement from Melbourne by suing him for adultery, which was most likely an untrue accusation. Melbourne would not buy Norton off, and at the trial the jury quickly decided there was no proof of adultery. However, Caroline Norton lost all around. Humiliated by her legal position as a woman, which made it impossible for her to appear in her own defense at the trial, she had to endure the shame of imputed immorality—and then to discover that the restitution of her public virtue meant that there was no chance of a legal divorce. Worst of all, Norton manipulated his wife by withholding permission to see the children. Because of her political connections Caroline Norton succeeded in having the Infant Custody Act passed in 1839; but this was a limited victory, since it merely established visitation privileges and a procedure for women to legally solicit custody of children under seven.

Caroline Norton's appeals for reform of her individual situation and of the general legal injustices done to women were based on her sense of the need of poor helpless women for the chivalrous protection of their male legislators. She carefully distinguished her position from the "wild and stupid theories advanced by a few women of 'equal rights' and 'equal intelligence.' . . . I, for one, (I, with millions more) believe in the natural superiority of man, as I do in the existence of a god." But she proved with every sentence she wrote (and probably with every word she uttered in her domestic life) that she felt herself to be much the superior of her own husband. In its own way, Norton's legal-biographical writing belongs to the tradition of feminist confessions that runs from Mary Wollstonecraft to contemporary feminists, in which biographical material is made the basis of an argument for social reform.

The treatment I received as a Wife would be incredible if, fortunately (or unfortunately), there were not witnesses who can prove it on oath. . . .

We had been married about two months, when, one evening, after we had all withdrawn to our apartments, we were discussing some opinion [Mr. Norton] had expressed; I said (very uncivilly), that "I thought I had never heard so silly or ridiculous a conclusion." This remark was punished by a sudden and violent kick; the blow reached my side; it caused great pain for many days, and being afraid to remain with him, I sat up the whole night in another apartment.

Four or five months afterwards, when we were settled in London, we had returned home from a ball; I had then no personal dispute with Mr. Norton, but he indulged in bitter and coarse remarks respecting a young relative of mine, who, though married, continued to dance—a practice, Mr. Norton said, no husband ought to permit.

I defended the lady spoken of, and then stood silently looking out of the window at the quiet light of dawn, by way of contrast. Mr. Norton desired I would "cease my contemplations," and retire to rest, as he had already done; and this mandate producing no result, he suddenly sprang from the bed, seized me by the nape of the neck, and dashed me down on the floor. The sound of my fall woke my sister and brother-in-law, who slept in a room below, and they ran up to my door. Mr. Norton locked it, and stood over me, declaring no one should enter. I could not speak—I only moaned. My brother-in-law burst the door open and carried me downstairs. I had a swelling on my head for many days afterwards. . . .

Early [one] summer, the quarrel, which divided him from [my affections] for ever, took place. On this occasion I left Mr. Norton, and withdrew to the house of my brother-in-law; and my husband desiring my return, my brother sent a friend to arrange conditions for that return, in writing, stating that till that was done he refused to enter into any correspondence whatever with Mr. Norton, nor was it to be thought that any brother would permit his sister to receive the treatment I did. I was warned and earnestly advised *not* to go back, after all that had occurred; and if I had taken that advice—if I had more resolution and less credulity—I should not now be summing up the evidence of seventeen years of torment, sorrow, and shame. But it would not have suited Mr. Norton so to let me escape. He gave the written pledge of good treatment to the friend my brother had sent. He said he was willing to "make any sacrifice, provided I returned to my home." . . . He adjured me not to "crush" him, and he ended his letter with the words, "I go on my knees to you! Have pity—have compassion on me!" I answered him: I pitied him: I went back to him. . . .

After my return, he treated me as he had done before. As to the conditions, they had been broken before I had been two days in my home: and during a very severe illness which followed the agitation and misery to which I had been exposed, and in which I prematurely lost my infant, he behaved with the utmost harshness and neglect, leaving me to be nursed by my brother, and refusing to be answerable for the expenses incurred. . . .

[Quarrels continued over her family's rejection of him and over her friend Lord Melbourne's refusal to help him advance professionally.]

We [she and her husband] spent the evening together at a party

at Lord Harrington's and returned home together. The dispute was
then renewed, whether under the circumstances [her family refused
to invite Mr. Norton] I should go to my brother's. Mr. Norton's last
words were—"Well, the children shall not, that I have determined";
and as he entered the house he desired the servant to unpack the
carriage (which had been prepared for starting), and to take the
children's things out, for that they were not going. He then went up
to the nursery, and repeated the order to the nurse. It was admitted
at the trial that the sole observation I made on this occasion, when
the nurse asked me "what she was to do?" was, that *"Mr. Norton's
orders must be obeyed."* I neither braved him with useless words,
nor complained. I waited till the morning, and then went to my sister's, to consult with her what was to be done.

While I was with my sister, my children were kidnapped and
taken possession of by Miss Vaughan [a friend of Mr. Norton's who
encouraged him to quarrel with his wife]; as I doubt not had been
agreed upon the day before. . . .

After the [adultery] trial was over, I consulted whether a divorce
"by reason of cruelty" might not be pleaded for me; and I laid before my lawyers the many instances of violence, injustice, and ill-
usage, of which the trial was but the crowning example. I was then
told that no divorce *I* could obtain would break my marriage; that I
could not plead cruelty *which I had forgiven*; that by returning to
Mr. Norton I had *"condoned"* all I complained of. I learnt, too, the
LAW as to my children—that the right was with the father; that
neither my innocence nor his guilt could alter it; that not even his
giving them into the hands of a mistress, would give me any claim
to their custody. The eldest was but six years old, the second four,
the youngest two and a half, when we were parted. I wrote, therefore, and *petitioned* the father and husband in whose power I was,
for leave to see them—for leave to keep them, till they were a little
older. Mr. Norton's answer was, that I should not have them; that
if I wanted to see them, I might have an interview with them at
the chambers of his attorney. . . .

What I suffered on my children's account, none will ever know
or measure. "The heart knoweth its own bitterness," and God knew
mine! The days and nights of tears and anguish, that grew into the
struggle of years—it is even *now* a pain to me to look back upon:
even *now*, the hot agony of resentment and grief rises in my mind,
when I think of the needless tyranny I endured in this respect. Mr.

Norton held my children as hostages; he felt that while he had them, he still had a power over me that nothing could control. Baffled in the matter of the trial and damages, he had still the power to do more than punish—to torture—the wife who had been so anxious to part from him. I never saw them; I seldom knew where they were. Once, when I wrote to ask after them in illness, my letter to the nurse (which contained no syllable of offence, or beyond the subject of my inquiry) was turned inside out, and franked back to me. . . .

[To Lady Menzies] my husband's sister . . . on payment of so much a head, my three children were consigned; and removed to Scotland, where neither their father nor I could be with them. There, with one whom I knew to be haughty and intemperate, those children were left, who had hitherto been so gently and tenderly treated; and the eldest of whom was delicate in health, sensitive in disposition, and just recovering from illness. The first step she made in their education, was to flog this very child (a child of six years old) for merely receiving and reading a letter from me (I being in England and he in Scotland) to "impress on his memory" that he was not to receive letters from me. Having occasion to correct one still younger, she stripped it naked, tied it to the bed-post, and chastised it with a riding-whip. . . .

These boys having been the gleam of happiness and compensation in my home, it was not to be supposed I would give them up without a struggle, because it was so "written in the bond" of English law. Ceaselessly, restlessly, perseveringly, I strove; and, fortunately for me, other cases of hardship had already drawn attention to the necessity of some reform on this subject. . . . A new "Infant Custody Bill" was brought forward by the learned Serjeant [Talfourd] and passed, after a struggle of three years [in 1839], by a majority of four to one. . . .

Mr. Norton yielded—simply so far as the law would have compelled him, and as was necessary to save himself from the threatened and certain exposure which my appeal under the new law would have entailed. I saw my children in the most formal and comfortless manner. . . .

His cruel carelessness was afterwards proved, on a most miserable occasion. My youngest child, then a boy of eight years old, left without care or overlooking, rode out with a brother but little older than himself, was thrown, carried to the house of a country neighbour, and died there of lock jaw, consequent on the accident. Mr. Norton

allowed the child to lie ill for a week—indeed to be at death's door—
before he sent to inform me. Sir Fitzroy and Lady Kelly were staying
with Mr. Norton in the country. Lady Kelly (who was an utter
stranger to me) met me at the railway station. I said—"I am here—
is my boy better?" "No," she said—"he is not better—he is dead."
And I found, instead of my child, a corpse already coffined.

Mr. Norton asked my forgiveness then, as he had asked it often
before; he sent his elder child to plead for him—for well he knew
what my children were to me; he humbled himself, and grieved for
an hour, till he changed into pity the horror and repugnance I had
expressed at the idea of seeing him—and then he buried our child,
and forgot both his sorrow and his penitence.

In Caroline Norton, *English Laws for Women in the Nineteenth Century*
(1854)

HUSBANDLY COMFORT (1850s)
Josephine Butler
(See pp. 218, 295, 317, 428, 435, and 436.)

*Josephine Butler (1828–1906) was the outspoken leader of the cam-
paign against state-regulated prostitution. In this memoir of her husband, educational reformer George Butler, she describes how he
helped her to find her commitment to her work amid the male-biased
world of Oxford.*

In the frequent social gatherings in our drawing-room in the evenings there was much talk, sometimes serious and weighty, sometimes
light, interesting, critical, witty, and brilliant, ranging over many
subjects. It was then that I sat silent, the only woman in the company, and listened, sometimes with a sore heart; for these men would
speak of things which I had already resolved deeply in my own mind,
things of which I was convinced, which I knew, though I had no
dialectics at command with which to defend their truth. . . .

A book was published at that time by Mrs. Gaskell [*Ruth* (1853)
about the rehabilitation of an unmarried mother], and was much
discussed. This led to expressions of judgment which seemed to me
false—fatally false. A moral lapse in a woman was spoken of as an
immensely worse thing than in a man; there was no comparison to

be formed between them. A pure woman, it was reiterated, should be absolutely ignorant of a certain class of evils in the world, albeit those evils bore with murderous cruelty on other women. One young man seriously declared that he would not allow his own mother to read such a book as that under discussion—a book which seemed to me to have a very wholesome tendency, though dealing with a painful subject. Silence was thought to be the great duty on all such subjects. On one occasion, when I was distressed by a bitter case of wrong inflicted on a very young girl, I ventured to speak to one of the wisest men—so esteemed—in the University, in the hope that he would suggest some means, not of helping her, but of bringing to a sense of his crime the man who had wronged her. The Sage, speaking kindly however, sternly advocated silence and inaction: "It could only do harm to open up in any way such a question as this; it was dangerous to arouse a sleeping lion." I left him in some amazement and discouragement. . . .

Again, some painting of Raphael was being discussed and criticised. I said I found the face insipid. "Insipid! of course it must be," said a distinguished college tutor; "a woman's face when engaged in prayer could never wear any other expression than that of insipidity." "What!" I asked, "when one converses with a man of high intelligence and noble soul, if there be any answering chord in one's own mind, does one's expression immediately become insipid? Does it not rather beam with increased intelligence and exalted thought? And how much more if one converses face to face with the highest Intelligence of all! Then every faculty of the mind and emotion of the soul is called to its highest exercise." No one made any remark, and the silence seemed to rebuke my audacity. The first speaker merely accentuated his idea of prayer as a kind of sentimental, dreamy devoutness of feeling. . . .

My motive in writing these recollections is to tell what *he* was— my husband—and to show how, besides all that he was in himself and all the work he did, which was wholly and especially his own, he was of a character to be able from the first to correct the judgment and soothe the spirit of the companion of his life when "the waters had come in even unto her soul." I wish to show, also, that he was even more to me in later life than a wise and noble supporter and helper in the work which may have been called more especially my own. He had a part in the creation of it, in the formation of the first impulses towards it. . . . But for him I should have been much more perplexed than I was. The idea of justice to women, of equality between the sexes, and of equality of responsibility of all human beings to the Moral Law, seems to have been instinctive in him. He never needed convincing. He had his convictions already from the first—straight, just, and clear. I did not at that time speak much; but whenever I spoke to him the clouds lifted.

It may seem a little strange to say so, but, if I recall it truly, what helped me most of all at that time was, not so much any arguments he may have used in favour of an equal standard, but the correctness with which he measured the men and the judgments around him. I think there was even a little element of disdain in his appreciation of the one-sided judgments of some of his male friends. He used to say, "I am sorry for So-and-so," which sounded to me rather like saying, "I am sorry for Solomon," my ideas of the wisdom of learned men being perhaps a little exaggerated. He would tell me that I ought to pity them: "They know no better, poor fellows." This was a new light to me. I had thought of Oxford as the home of learning and of intellect. I thought the good and gifted men we daily met must be in some degree authorities on spiritual and moral questions. It had not occurred to me to think of them as "poor fellows!"

That blessed gift of common sense which he possessed in so large a degree came to the rescue, to restore for me the balance of a mind too heavily weighted with sad thoughts of life's perplexing prob-lems. And then in the evenings, when our friends had gone, we read together the words of Life, and were able to bring many earthly notions and theories to the test of what the Holy One and the Just said and did. Compared with the accepted axioms of the day, and indeed of centuries past, in regard to certain vital questions, the sayings and actions of Jesus were, we confessed to one another, revolutionary . . . and we prayed together that a holy revolution might come about, and that the Kingdom of God might be established on the earth. And I said to myself: "And it is a man who speaks to me thus—an intelligent, a gifted man, a learned man too, few more learned than he, and a man who ever speaks the truth from his heart."

In Josephine E. Butler, *Recollections of George Butler* (1892)

MOTHERHOOD

HOW TO AVOID CONCEPTION (1826)
Richard Carlile

It was hard for a woman to get information about birth control in nineteenth-century England, and the known birth-control strategies were very unreliable. Coitus interruptus, the vaginal sponge, douching, and an erroneously calculated form of the rhythm method were the methods in use. Condoms were not widely available or reliable until after the process for the vulcanization of rubber was invented in 1843. But both sponges and condoms were too costly for most working-class people to use regularly. Abortion was a statutory crime after 1803, although it continued to be practiced with the help of doctors for those who could pay high prices, or otherwise through drugs and home remedies (such as ergot, aloes, lead preparations, purgatives, and knitting needles), which varied widely in safety and effectiveness. Despite official suppression of birth-control information as indecent and corrupting to the morals of women, radicals and social reformers— among them Francis Place, Richard Carlile (1790–1843), Robert Owen, and Annie Besant—attempted to give poor women in particular information on how to limit their families. Carlile's pamphlet Every Woman's Book, or What Is Love? *(1826), excerpted here, was written in Newgate Prison, where he was serving time for publishing Thomas Paine's essays.*

If methods can be pointed out by which all the enjoyments of wedded life may be partaken of without the apprehension of too large a *family*, and all its bitter consequences, he surely who points them out, must be a benefactor of mankind. Such at any rate are the motives which govern the writer of this address.

The means of prevention are simple, harmless, and might, but for false delicacy, have been communicated generally. They have long been practised in several parts of the Continent, and experience has proved, that the greatest possible benefits have resulted; the people in these parts, being in all respects better off, better instructed, more cheerful, and more independent, than those in other parts, where the practises have not prevailed to a sufficient extent.

The methods are two, of which the one to be first mentioned

seems most likely to succeed in this country as it depends upon the female. It has been resorted to by some of our most eminent physicians, and is confidently recommended by first rate accoucheurs, in cases where pregnancy has been found injurious to the health of delicate women. It consists in a piece of sponge, being placed in the vagina previous to coition, and afterwards withdrawn by means of a double twisted thread, or bobbin, attached to it. No injurious consequences can in any way result from its use, neither does it diminish the enjoyment of either party. The sponge should, as a matter of preference, be used rather damp, and, when convenient, a little warm. It is almost superfluous to add, that there may be more pieces than one, and that they should be washed after being used.

The other method resorted to, when from carelessness or other causes the sponge is not at hand, is for the husband to withdraw, previous to emission, so that none of the semen enter the vagina of his wife. But a little practise and care in the use of the sponge will render all other precautions unnecessary.

ON CHILDBEARING AND MOTHERHOOD (1858–1859)
Queen Victoria

Queen Victoria (1819–1901) lived one of the more dramatically contradictory lives of the period that bears her name. After a sheltered girlhood with little more education than most women of her time, she assumed the throne in 1837. Her marriage to Prince Albert relieved her of the burdens of political decisions, but she always felt pained by the contradictions between wifely submission and queenly prerogatives. She thought of Albert as her guardian angel and protector, relied upon his judgment, and was violently inconsolable for years after his death. A strong opponent of women's rights, which she looked upon as a kind of "mad, wicked folly," she was the very emblem of maternal sanctity. Yet, as these letters to her daughter reveal, Victoria felt little exultation in woman's motherly self-sacrifice. Her resentment of women's physical sufferings led her to be among the first to use chloroform for anesthesia in childbirth, which she did in 1853 and 1857 with her eighth and ninth deliveries, thus making the practice respectable for other women.

March 24, 1858
Now to reply to your observation that you find a married woman

BBC Hulton Picture Library

*Queen Victoria with the Princess Royal and the future King Edward VII,
from the painting by Sir Edwin Landseer*

has much more liberty than an unmarried one; in one sense of the
word she has—but what I meant was—in a physical point of view—
and if you have hereafter (as I had constantly for the first two years
of my marriage)—aches—and sufferings and miseries and plagues—
which you must struggle against—and enjoyments etc. to give up—
constant precautions to take, you will feel the yoke of a married
woman! Without that—certainly it is unbounded happiness—if one

has a husband one worships! It is a foretaste of heaven. And you have a husband who adores you, and is, I perceive, ready to meet every wish and desire of yours. I had nine times for eight months to bear with those above-named enemies and real misery (besides many duties) and I own it tried me sorely; one feels so pinned down— one's wings clipped—in fact, at the best (and few were or are better than I was) only half oneself—particularly the first and second time. This I call the "shadow side" as much as being torn away from one's loved home, parents and brothers and sisters. And therefore—I think our sex a most unenviable one.

June 15, 1858

What you say of the pride of giving life to an immortal soul is very fine, dear, but I own I cannot enter into that: I think much more of our being like a cow or a dog at such moments; when our poor nature becomes so very animal and unecstatic—but for you, dear, if you are sensible and reasonable not in ecstasy nor spending your day with nurses and wet nurses, which is the ruin of many a refined and intellectual young lady, without adding to her real maternal duties, a child will be a great resource. Above all, dear, do remember never to lose the modesty of a young girl towards others (without being prude): though you are married don't become a matron at once to whom everything can be said, and who minds saying nothing herself. I remained particular to a degree; indeed feel so now and often feel shocked at the confidences of other married ladies. I fear abroad they are very indelicate about these things. Think of me who at that first time, very unreasonable and perfectly furious as I was to be caught, having to have drawing-rooms and levées and made to sit down—and be stared at and take every sort of precaution.

[On January 27 the princess bore a son, after a difficult and dangerous labor.]

January 29, 1859

God be praised for all his mercies, and for bringing you safely through this awful time! Our joy, our gratitude knows no bounds.

My precious darling, you suffered much more than I ever did— and how I wish I could have lightened them for you! . . . You will and must feel so thankful all is over! But don't be alarmed for the future, it never can be so bad again!

April 20, 1859

I really think I shall never let your sisters marry—certainly not to be so constantly away and see so little of their parents—as till now, you have done, contrary to all that I was originally promised and told. I am so glad to see that you so entirely enter into all my feelings as a mother. Yes, dearest, it is an awful moment to have to give one's innocent child up to a man, be he ever so kind and good—and to think of all that she must go through! I can't say what I suffered, what I felt—what struggles I had to go through—(indeed I have not quite got over it yet) and that last night when we took you to your room, and you cried so much. I said to Papa as we came back "after all, it is like taking a poor lamb to be sacrificed." You now know—what I meant, dear. I know that God has willed it so and that these are the trials which we poor women must go through: no father, no man can feel this! Papa never would enter into it at all! As in fact he seldom can into my very violent feelings. It really makes me shudder when I look around at all your sweet, happy, unconscious sisters—and think that I must give them up too—one by one!! Our dear Alice, has seen and heard more (of course not what no one ever can know before they marry and before they have had children) than you did, from your marriage—and quite enough to give her a horror rather of marrying.

May 1, 1859

I always thought the Princess was so fond of babies, and much more so than I am: I like them better than I did, if they are nice and pretty, and my grandchild, I should delight in. Abstractedly, I have no tendre for them till they have become a little human: an ugly baby is a very nasty object—and the prettiest is frightful when undressed—till about four months: in short as long as they have their big body and little limbs and that terrible froglike action. But from four months, they become prettier and prettier. And I repeat it— your child would delight me at any age.

In *Dearest Child: Letters Between Queen Victoria and the Princess Royal (1858–1861)*, ed. Roger Fulford (London: Evans Brothers, 1964)

HER DAUGHTER'S ILLNESS (1871)
Annie Besant
(See pp. 112, 294, and 346.)

The near death of her beloved daughter Mabel was a spiritual landmark for Annie Besant. Yet, despite her anguish and loss of faith, Besant was fortunate in her daughter's recovery. As Mabel's haphazard treatment makes clear, there was little that nineteenth-century medicine could do to combat infectious diseases, which were particularly dangerous to very young children.

In the spring of 1871 both my children were taken ill with whooping-cough. The boy, Digby, vigorous and merry, fought his way through it with no danger, and comparatively little suffering; Mabel, the baby, had been delicate since her birth; there had been some little difficulty in getting her to breathe after she was born, and a slight tendency afterwards to lung-delicacy. She was very young for so trying a disease as whooping-cough, and after a while bronchitis set in, and was followed by congestion of the lungs. For weeks she lay in hourly peril of death; we arranged a screen round the fire like a tent, and kept it full of steam to ease the panting breath, and there I sat all through those weary weeks with her on my lap, day and night. The doctor said that recovery was impossible, and that in one of the fits of coughing she must die; the most distressing thing was that at last the giving of a drop or two of milk brought on the terrible convulsive choking, and it seemed cruel to torture the apparently dying child. At length, one morning when the doctor was there, he said that she could not last through the day; I had sent for him hurriedly, for her body had swollen up rapidly, and I did not know what had happened; the pleura of one lung had become perforated, and the air escaping into the cavity of the chest had caused the swelling; while he was there, one of the fits of coughing came on, and it seemed as though it would be the last; the doctor took a small bottle of chloroform out of his pocket, and putting a drop on a handkerchief, held it near the child's face, till the drug soothed the convulsive struggle. "It can't do any harm at this stage," he said, "and it checks the suffering." He went away, saying that he would return in the afternoon, but he feared he would never see the child alive again. . . .

That chance thought of his about the chloroform, verily, I believe, saved the child's life. Whenever one of the convulsive fits was coming on I used it, and so not only prevented to a great extent the violence of the attacks, but also the profound exhaustion that followed them, when the baby would lie as though almost dead, a mere flicker of breath at the top of the throat showing that she still lived. At last, though more than once we had thought her dead, a change took place for the better, and the child began slowly to mend. For years, however, that struggle for life left its traces on her, not only in serious lung-delicacy, but also in a form of epileptic fits. In her play she would suddenly stop, and become fixed for about a minute, and then go on again as though nothing had occurred. On her mother a more permanent trace was left.

Not unnaturally, when the child was out of danger, I collapsed from sheer exhaustion, and I lay in bed for a week. But an important change of mind dated from those silent weeks with a dying child on my knees. There had grown in my mind a feeling of angry resentment against the God who had been for weeks, as I thought, torturing my helpless baby. For some months a stubborn antagonism to the Providence who ordained the sufferings of life had been steadily increasing in me, and this sullen challenge, "Is God good?" found voice in my heart during those silent nights and days. My mother's sufferings, and much personal unhappiness, had been intensifying the feeling, and as I watched my baby in its agony, and felt so helpless to relieve, more than once the indignant cry broke from my lips: "How canst thou torture a baby so? What has she done that she should suffer so? Why dost thou not kill her at once, and let her be at peace?" More than once I cried aloud: "O God, take the child, but do not torment her." All my personal belief in God, all my intense faith in his constant direction of affairs, all my habit of continual prayer and of realisation of his presence, were against me now. To me he was not an abstract idea, but a living reality, and all my mother-heart rose up in rebellion against this person in whom I believed, and whose individual finger I saw in my baby's agony.

In Annie Besant, *Autobiographical Sketches* (1885)

MOTHER'S FEARS (1841)
Elizabeth Gaskell
(See p. 89.)

(See p. 89.)

Elizabeth Gaskell's marriage was marked by frequent separation from her husband, since they both led active professional lives. When he was home he read all her letters before she sent them, and she took advantage of his absences to relieve her mind of anxieties or to make special confidences to her friends. In this letter, probably written to her husband's sister, she expresses her concern over her husband's limitations as a father and faces the common anxiety—and not uncommon fate—of the period that she might not live to see her children raised.

My dearest Nancy,

I am sitting all alone, and not feeling over & above well; and it would be such a comfort to have you here to open my mind to—but that not being among the possibilities, I am going to write you a long private letter; unburdening my mind a bit. And yet it is nothing, so don't prepare yourself for any wonderful mystery. . . . I am so so glad to say Marianne is better; she has jelly & strengthening medicine each twice a day, and is to have broth & eggs whenever she can particularly fancy them, and seems much less languid—though still I fear she is not strong. . . . We have Mr. Partington of course & he was very encouraging this morning and she certainly *is* better—but one can't help having "Mother's fears"; and William, I dare say kindly, won't allow me ever to talk to him about anxieties, while it would be SUCH A RELIEF often. So don't allude too much to what I've been saying in your answer. William is at a minister's meeting tonight. . . .

I have of course had Marianne more with me during this delicacy of hers, and I am more and more anxious about her—not exactly her health; but I see hers is a peculiar character—*very* dependent on those around her—almost as much so as Meta is *in*dependent & in this point I look to Meta to strengthen her. But I am more & more convinced that love & sympathy are very *very* much required by Marianne. The want of them would make Marianne an unhappy character, probably sullen and deceitful—while the sunshine of love & tenderness would do everything for her. She is very conscientious, and very tender-hearted—Now Anne, will you remember this? It is difficult to have the right trust in God almost, when thinking about one's children—and you know I have no sister or near relation whom I could entreat to watch over any peculiarity in their disposition. Now you know that dear William feeling most kindly towards his children, is yet most reserved in *expressions* of either affection or sympathy—and in case of my death, we all know the probability of widowers marrying again—would you promise, dearest Anne, to remember Marianne's peculiarity of character, and as much as circumstances would permit, watch over her & cherish her. The feeling, the conviction that you were aware of my wishes and would act upon them would be *such* a comfort to me. Meta is remarkably independent, & will strengthen Marianne, if she is spared. Now don't go & fancy I am low-spirited &c &c. As for death I have I think remarkably little constitutional dread of it—I often fear I do not look forward to it with sufficient awe, considering the futurity which *must* follow—and I do often pray for trust in God, complete trust in him—with regard to what becomes of my children. Still let me open my heart sometimes to you dear Anne, with reliance upon your sympathy and secrecy.

From Elizabeth Gaskell to Anne Robson[?], December 23, 1841, in *The Letters of Mrs. Gaskell,* letter no. 16

SISTERS AND FRIENDS

THE BIRTH OF HER FAVORITE SISTER (1811)
Harriet Martineau
(See pp. 96, 161, 216, 291, 330, and 364.)

Harriet Martineau was much blamed as a child for her difficult temperament, and she often felt oppressed by the frequent quarrels among her siblings. Her warmest and most lasting family relationship was with this sister, who was born when Martineau was nine years old.

In November came the news which I had been told to expect. My sister Rachel had been with us in the country for a fortnight; and we knew that there was to be a baby at home before we went back; and I remember pressing so earnestly, by letter, to know the baby's name as to get a rebuff. I was told to wait till there was a baby. At last, the carrier brought us a letter one evening which told us that we had a little sister. . . . Homesick before, I now grew downright ill with longing. I was sure that all old troubles were wholly my fault, and fully resolved that there should be no more. Now, as so often afterwards (as often as I left home), I was destined to disappointment. I scarcely felt myself at home before the well-remembered bickerings began—not with me, but from the boys being troublesome, James being naughty; and our eldest sister angry and scolding. I then and there resolved that I would look for my happiness to the new little sister, and that she should never want for the tenderness which I had never found. This resolution turned out more of a prophecy than such decisions, born of a momentary emotion, usually do. That child was henceforth a new life to me. I did lavish love and tenderness on her; and I could almost say that she has never caused me a moment's pain but by her own sorrows. There has been much suffering in her life; and in it I have suffered with her: but such sympathetic pain is bliss in comparison with such feelings as she has *not* excited in me during our close friendship of above forty years. When I first saw her it was as she was lifted out of her crib, at a fortnight old, asleep, to be shown to my late hostess, who had brought Rachel and me home. The passionate fondness I felt for her from that moment has been unlike any thing else I have felt in life. . . .

In *Harriet Martineau's Autobiography*, ed. Maria Weston Chapman (1877)

THE DECORUMS OF FRIENDSHIP (1861)
Isabella Beeton
(See pp. 83, 93, and 335.)

Mrs. Beeton was careful to advise her readers on the means of limiting their intimacies with other women. Her notion of an appropriate female friendship was one that served the purposes of the household rather than the personal needs of the mistress herself.

The choice of acquaintances is very important to the happiness of a mistress and her family. A gossiping acquaintance, who indulges in the scandal and ridicule of her neighbours, should be avoided as a pestilence. . . . If the duties of a family do not sufficiently occupy the time of a mistress, society should be formed of such a kind as will tend to the actual interchange of general and interesting information. . . . Friendships should not be hastily formed, nor the heart given, at once, to every new-comer. . . . Hospitality is a most excellent virtue; but care must be taken that the love of company, for its own sake, does not become a prevailing passion. . . . With respect to the continuance of friendship . . . it may be found necessary, in some cases, for a mistress to relinquish, on assuming the responsibility of a household, many of those commenced in the earlier part of her life. . . .

In conversation, trifling occurrences, such as small disappointments, petty annoyances, and other every-day incidents, should never be mentioned to your friends. The extreme injudiciousness of repeating these will be at once apparent, when we reflect upon the unsatisfactory discussions which they too frequently occasion, and on the load of advice which they are the cause of being tendered, and which is, too often, of a kind neither to be useful nor agreeable. . . . If the mistress be a wife, never let an account of her husband's failings pass her lips. . . .

In paying visits of friendship . . . if a lady be pressed by her friend to remove her shawl and bonnet, it can be done if it will not interfere with subsequent arrangements. . . . During these visits, the manners should be easy and cheerful, and the subjects of conversation such as may be readily terminated. Serious discussions or arguments are to be altogether avoided.

In Isabella Beeton, *Beeton's Book of Household Management* (1861)

RECORDS OF FRIENDSHIP (1836–1845)
Charlotte Brontë, Ellen Nussey, Mary Taylor
(See pp. 35, 58, 95, 109, 115, 160, 272, and 273.)

Charlotte Brontë met Ellen Nussey and Mary Taylor at Miss Wooler's boarding school when they were all in their early teens. Despite her shyness and awkwardness in play, Brontë made friends with these two girls and kept their friendship all her life. Nussey and Taylor came from large Yorkshire wool merchant families, and had considerably more money and resources than Brontë, who as the daughter of a very poor clergyman in the isolated town of Haworth relied upon her friends as her sole source of human warmth and stimulation outside of her immediate household. Ellen Nussey was a conventional Victorian woman—quiet, loyal, and unoriginal—who is now remembered for hoarding all of Charlotte's letters. Mary Taylor, coming from a lively radical family, was extraordinarily adventurous and defiant of the constraints upon women. Unfortunately for us, she burned Charlotte's letters while Charlotte was still alive, because she considered them dangerous for reasons we are left to puzzle over.

In her late teens and early twenties, Charlotte longed for Ellen's conventional piety and resignation to the restrictions of her life. In later years, which brought the deaths of her brother Branwell and her sisters Emily and Anne, she relied on Ellen as on another sister to help her bear her grief. With Mary Taylor, Brontë shared her intellectual and artistic concerns. She was spurred on by Mary's example to go to school in Brussels, the one great adventure of her twenties. Though often shocked by Mary's radical politics and by her willingness to act unconventionally, Charlotte respected her intelligence and honesty just as she respected Ellen's loyal dutifulness. The intensity of her feelings for both of her friends and the directness with which she expressed her love and admiration were not uncommon for women of her time.

Charlotte found it difficult to leave home and relied upon her friends to shake her out of the monotony of life at Haworth—to take her to the sea, to urge her to travel and learn, to distract her from family problems. When Mary Taylor set out for New Zealand with her brother in 1845, Charlotte felt "as if a great planet fell out of the sky." The meeting described in Mary's reminiscence is the last one they ever had, since Charlotte died while Mary was still in Wellington. Even from the other side of the world, the energetic Mary Taylor continued to try to convert Charlotte into a believer in work for women, and to urge her to live a more active life. When she heard of Brontë's acquiescence in her father's opposition to her marriage, she wrote indignantly to Ellen Nussey, pointing up the differences between Charlotte's two closest friends:

You talk wonderful nonsense about Charlotte Brontë in your letter. What do you mean about "bearing her position so long, and enduring to the end?" and still better, "bearing our lot, whatever it is." If it's Charlotte's lot to be married, shouldn't she bear that too? or does your strange morality mean that she should refuse to ameliorate her lot when it lies in her power? How would she be inconsistent with herself in marrying? Because she considered her own pleasure? If this is so new for her to do, it is high time she began to make it more common. It is an outrageous exaction to expect her to give up her choice in a matter so important, and I think her to blame in having been hitherto so yielding that her friends can think of making such an impudent demand.

(Charlotte Brontë to Ellen Nussey, 1836)

Weary with a day's hard work, during which an unusual degree of stupidity has been displayed by my promising pupils, I am sitting down to write a few hurried lines to my dear Ellen. Excuse me if I say nothing but nonsense, for my mind is exhausted and dispirited. It is a stormy evening, and the wind is uttering a continual moaning sound that makes me feel very melancholy. At such times, in such moods as these, Ellen, it is my nature to seek repose in some calm, tranquil idea, and I have now summoned up your image to give me rest. There you sit upright and still in your black dress and white scarf, your pale, marble-like face, looking so serene and kind—just like reality. I wish you would speak to me. If we should be separated—if it should be our lot to live at a great distance, and never to see each other again—in old age I should conjure up the memory of my youthful days, and what a melancholy pleasure I should feel in dwelling on the recollection of my early friend Ellen Nussey. . . .

It is from religion you derive your chief charm, and may its influence always preserve you as pure, as unassuming, and as benevolent in thought and deed as you are now. What am I compared to you? I feel my own utter worthlessness when I make the comparison. I am a very coarse, commonplace wretch, Ellen. I have some qualities which make me very miserable, some feelings that you can have no participation in, that few, very few people in the world can at all understand. I don't pride myself on these peculiarities, I strive to conceal and suppress them as much as I can, but they burst out sometimes, and then those who see the explosion despise me, and I hate myself for days afterwards.

(Charlotte Brontë to Ellen Nussey, 1836)

I feel in a strange state of mind still gloomy but not despairing. I keep trying to do right, checking wrong feelings, repressing wrong thoughts—but still—every instant I find myself going astray—I have

Charlotte Brontë, from the portrait by George Richmond

a constant tendency to scorn people who are far better than I am. . . . I abhor myself—I despise myself—if the Doctrine of Calvin be true I am already an outcast—you cannot imagine how hard, rebellious and intractable all my feelings are—When I begin to study on the subject I almost grow blasphemous, atheistical in my sentiments, don't desert me—don't be horrified at me, you know what I am—I wish I could see you my darling, I have lavished the warmest affec-

Ellen Nussey, as drawn by her friend Charlotte Brontë

tions of a very hot, tenacious heart upon you—if you grow cold—it's over. . . .

(*Charlotte Brontë to Ellen Nussey, 1836*)

I wish exceedingly that I could come to see you before Christmas, but it is impossible—however I trust ere another three weeks elapse I shall again have my comforter beside me, under the roof of my own dear quiet home—if I could always live with you and daily read the bible with you, if your lips and mine could at the same time drink the same draught from the same pure fountain of mercy, I hope, I trust, I might one day become better, far better, than my evil wandering thoughts, my corrupt heart, cold to the spirit, and warm to the flesh will now permit me to be. . . .

(*Charlotte Brontë to Ellen Nussey, August 14, 1839*)

[*In August 1839, when she was twenty-three years old, Charlotte attempted to go on a pleasure excursion with her friend Ellen to gain her first view of the sea.*]

I have in vain packed my box, and prepared everything for our anticipated journey. It so happens that I can get no conveyance this week or the next. . . . Papa decidedly objects to my going by the coach, and walking to Birstall, though I am sure I could manage it. Aunt exclaims against the weather, and the roads, and the four winds of heaven; so I am in a fix, and, what is worse, so are *you* . . . for I rather imagine there is small chance of my ever going at all. The elders of the house have never cordially acquiesced in the measure; and now that impediments seem to start up at every step opposition grows more open. Papa, indeed, would willingly indulge me, but this very kindness of his makes me doubt whether I ought to draw upon it; so, though I could battle out aunt's discontent, I yield to Papa's indulgence. He does not say so, but I know he would rather I stayed at home. . . . Reckon on me no more . . . perhaps I ought, in the beginning, to have had prudence sufficient to shut my eyes against such a prospect of pleasure, so as to deny myself the hope of it.

(*Ellen Nussey's memoir of the trip to the sea*)

Charlotte's first visit to the sea-coast deserves a little more notice than her letters give of the circumstances. It was an event eagerly coveted, but hard to attain. Mr. Brontë and Miss Branwell had all manners of doubts and fears and cautions to express, and Charlotte was sinking into despair. There seemed only one chance of securing her the pleasure; her friend [Ellen Nussey herself] must fetch her. . . . This step proved to be the very best thing possible, the surprise was so good in its effects, there was nothing to combat—everybody rose into high good humours, Branwell was grandiloquent, he declared "it was a brave defeat, that the doubters were fairly taken aback." You have only to *will* a thing to *get* it, so Charlotte's luggage was speedily prepared, and almost before the horse was rested there was a quiet but triumphant starting; the brother and sisters at home were not less happy than Charlotte herself in her now secured pleasure. It was the first of real freedom to be enjoyed either by herself or her friend. . . .

[The day after their arrival] they walked to the sea, and as soon as they were near enough for Charlotte to see it in its expanse, she was quite overpowered, she could not speak till she had shed some tears— she signed to her friend to leave her and walk on; this she did for a few steps, knowing full well what Charlotte was passing through, and the stern efforts she was making to subdue her emotions—her friend turned to her as soon as she thought she might without inflicting pain; her eyes were red and swollen, she was still trembling, but submitted to be led onwards where the view was less impressive; for the remainder of the day she was very quiet, subdued, and exhausted.

(*Charlotte Brontë to Ellen Nussey, August 7, 1841*)

[*Working as a governess in a private family at age twenty-five, Brontë was stirred by Mary Taylor's experiences as a student and traveler on the Continent.*]

This is Saturday evening. I have put the children to bed and now I am going to sit down and answer your letter. I am again by myself— . . . for Mr. and Mrs. White are staying with a Mrs. Duncan of Brook-Hall near Tadcaster . . . [relieving] me from the heavy duty of endeavouring to seem always easy, cheerful and conversible with those whose ideas and feelings are nearly as incomprehensible to *me*, as probably mine (if I shewed them unreservedly) would be to them. . . .

Mary is returning immediately to the Continent with her brother John . . . to take a month's tour and recreation. . . . Mary's letter spoke of some of the pictures and cathedrals she had seen—pictures the most exquisite—and cathedrals the most venerable—I hardly know what swelled to my throat as I read her letter—such a vehement impatience of restraint and steady work. Such a strong wish for wings—wings such as wealth can furnish—such an urgent thirst to see—to know—to learn—something internal seemed to expand boldly for a minute—I was tantalized with the consciousness of faculties unexercised—then all collapsed and I despaired.

My dear Nell—I would hardly make that confession to any one

but yourself—and to you rather in a letter than "viva voce"—these rebellious and absurd emotions were only momentary, I quelled them in five minutes—I hope they will not revive—for they were acutely painful. . . .

(Mary Taylor says goodbye, 1845)

[With Mary's help Charlotte arranged for her sister Emily and herself to study languages in Brussels. After her return in 1844 she plunged into a deep depression. Instead of looking for work with her valuable new training, she stayed home with her invalid father and indulged her unrequited passion for her Brussels professor, M. Heger. Mary Taylor, about to leave for New Zealand, tried to stir her friend to action.]

When I last saw Charlotte . . . she told me she had quite decided to stay at home. She owned she did not like it. Her health was weak. She said she would like any change . . . and she thought that there must be some possibility for some people of having a life of more variety and more communication with human kind, but she saw none for her. I told her very warmly that she ought not to stay at home; that to spend the next five years at home, in solitude and weak health, would ruin her; that she would never recover it. Such a dark shadow came over her face when I said, "Think of what you'll be five years hence!" that I stopped, and said, "Don't cry, Charlotte!" She did not cry, but went on walking up and down the room, and said in a little while, "But I intend to stay, Polly."

(One of Mary Taylor's last letters
to Charlotte Brontë, April 1850)

I have set up shop! I am delighted with it as a whole—that is, it is as pleasant or as little disagreeable as you can expect an employment to be that you earn your living by. The best of it is that your labour has some return and you are not forced to work on hopelessly without result. . . . I have seen some extracts from Shirley in which you talk of women working. And this first duty, this great necessity you seem to think some women may indulge in—if they give up marriage and don't make themselves too disagreeable to the other sex. You are a coward and a traitor. A woman who works is by that alone better than one who does not and a woman who does not happen to be rich and who still earns no money and does not wish to do so, is guilty of a great fault—almost a crime—a dereliction of duty which leads rapidly and almost certainly to all manner of degradation. It is very wrong of you to *plead* for toleration for workers on the ground of their being in peculiar circumstances and few in number or singular in disposition. Work or degradation is the lot of all except the very small number born to wealth. . . .

As to when I'm coming home you may well ask. I have wished for 15 years to begin to earn my own living. Last April I began to try. It is too soon yet to say with what success. I am woefully ignorant, terribly wanting in tact and obstinately lazy, and almost too old to mend. Luckily there is no other chance for me; so I must work. Ellen [her cousin] takes to it kindly. It gratifies a deep ardent wish of hers as of mine and she is habitually industrious. For *her*, 10 years younger, our shop will be a blessing. She may possibly secure an independence—and skill to keep it and use it before the prime of life is past.

In *The Brontës*, letters no. 46, 48, 53, 81, 119, and vol. I, p. 188; Joan Stevens, *Mary Taylor, Friend of Charlotte Brontë: Letters from New Zealand and Elsewhere* (New Zealand and Oxford: Auckland University Press and Oxford University Press, 1974), Appendix B, p. 161, and letter no. 20

SINGLE WOMEN

THE WORTH OF OLD MAIDS (1889)
Maria Grey

Being single often meant an increase in rather than a release from household and family responsibilities as this praise of "old maids" makes clear. Mrs. Grey (1816–1906), a reformer of girls' secondary education, worked in close partnership with her unmarried sister, Emily Shirreff.

I know no class of the community whose service to it is nobler or more valuable than that of the so-called "old maids"; the unmarried daughters in whom fathers and mothers find the comfort and staff of their declining years; the elder sisters who take the lost mother's place with the younger children, with the brothers especially; the maiden aunts who step into every gap in the household, and are called upon with a trust which is never deceived, for help of heart, hand, head, and purse in every family difficulty. Such a maiden aunt of mine, who spent her long and good substance in service like this, said to me one day in my girlhood: "My dear, if you don't marry, you will find that you have on your shoulders half a dozen husbands, and as many families of children."

In Maria Grey, *Last Words to Girls* (1889)

EVEN A LONE WOMAN CAN BE HAPPY (1846)
Charlotte Brontë
(See pp. 35, 95, 109, 115, 151, 272, and 273.)

Brontë was nearly thirty years old when she wrote to her old school-teacher and lifelong friend Miss Wooler.

I am glad you like Bromsgrove, though I daresay there are few places you would *not* like with Mrs. Moore for a companion. I always feel a peculiar satisfaction when I hear of your enjoying yourself, because it proves to me that there is really such a thing as retributive justice even in this world; you worked hard, you denied yourself all pleasure, almost all relaxation in your youth and the prime of your life—now you are free—and that while you have still, I hope, many years of vigour and health, in which you can enjoy freedom—Besides I have another and very egotistical motive for being pleased—it seems that even "a lone woman" can be happy, as well as cherished wives and proud mothers—I am glad of that—I speculate much on the existence of unmarried and never-to-be-married women nowadays, and I have already got to the point of considering that there is no more respectable character on this earth than an unmarried woman who makes her own way through life quietly, perseveringly—without support of husband or brother, and who, having attained the age of 45 or upwards—retains in her possession a well-regulated mind—a disposition to enjoy simple pleasures—fortitude to support inevitable pains, sympathy with the sufferings of others, and willingness to relieve want as far as her means extend.

From Charlotte Brontë to Miss Wooler, January 30, 1846, in *The Brontës*, letter no. 224

THANKFUL FOR NOT HAVING MARRIED (1877)
Harriet Martineau
(See pp. 96, 149, 216, 291, 330, and 364.)

This passage in her autobiography follows the spare description of Martineau's brief engagement to a man who suddenly went insane and died.

I am, in truth, very thankful for not having married at all. I have never since been tempted, nor have suffered any thing at all in relation to that matter which is held to be all-important to women—love and marriage. Nothing, I mean, beyond occasional annoyance, presently disposed of. Every literary woman, no doubt, has plenty of importunity of that sort to deal with; but freedom of mind and coolness of manner dispose of it very easily: and since the time I have been speaking of, my mind has been wholly free from all idea of love-affairs. My subsequent literary life in London was clear from all difficulty and embarrassment—no doubt because I was evidently too busy, and too full of interests of other kinds to feel any awkwardness—to say nothing of my being then thirty years of age; an age at which, if ever, a woman is certainly qualified to take care of herself. I can easily conceive how I might have been tempted—how some deep springs in my nature might have been touched, then as earlier; but, as a matter of fact, they never were; and I consider the immunity a great blessing, under the liabilities of a moral condition such as mine was in the olden time.

If I had had a husband dependent on me for his happiness, the responsibility would have made me wretched. I had not faith enough in myself to endure avoidable responsibility. If my husband had *not* depended on me for his happiness, I should have been jealous. So also with children. The care would have so overpowered the joy—the love would have so exceeded the ordinary chances of life—the fear on my part would have so impaired the freedom on theirs, that I rejoice not to have been involved in a relation for which I was, or believed myself unfit. The veneration in which I hold domestic life has always shown me that that life was not for those whose self-respect had been early broken down, or had never grown. . . .

When I see what conjugal love is, the extremely rare cases in which it is seen in its perfection, I feel that there is a power of attachment in me that has never been touched. When I am among little children, it frightens me to think what my idolatry of my own children would have been. But, through it all, I have ever been thankful to be alone. My strong will, combined with anxiety of conscience, makes me fit only to live alone; and my taste and liking are for living alone. The older I have grown, the more serious and irremediable have seemed to me the evils and disadvantages of married life, as it exists among us at this time: and I am provided with what it is the bane of single life in ordinary cases to want—substantial, laborious, and serious occupation. My business in life has been to think and learn, and to speak out with absolute freedom what I have thought and learned. The freedom is itself a positive and never-failing enjoyment to me, after the bondage of my early life. My work and I have been fitted to each other, as is proved by the success of my work and my own happiness in it. The simplicity and independence of this vocation first suited my infirm and ill-developed nature, and then sufficed for my needs, together with family ties and domestic duties, such as I have been blessed with, and as every woman's heart requires. Thus, I am not only entirely satisfied with my lot, but think it the very best for me—under my constitution and circumstances: and I long ago came to the conclusion that, without meddling with the case of wives and mothers, I am probably the happiest single woman in England.

In *Harriet Martineau's Autobiography*, ed. Maria Weston Chapman (1877)

A PRODUCTIVE LIFE WITHOUT A HUSBAND (1894)
Frances Power Cobbe
(See pp. 92, 121, 198, and 261.)

My brothers were all older than I; the eldest eleven, the youngest five years older; and my mother, when I was born, was in her forty-seventh year; a circumstance which perhaps makes it remarkable that the physical energy and high animal spirits of which I have just made mention came to me in so large a share. My old friend Harriet St. Leger . . . who knew us all well, said to me one day laughing: "You know *you* are your Father's *Son!*" Had I been a man, and had possessed my brother's facilities for entering Parliament or any pro-

BBC Hulton Picture Library

Frances Power Cobbe, 1894

fession, I have sometimes dreamed I could have made my mark and done some masculine service to my fellow-creatures. But the woman's destiny which God allotted to me has been, I do not question, the best and happiest for me; nor have I ever seriously wished it had been otherwise, albeit I have gone through life without that interest which has been styled "woman's whole existence." Perhaps if this book [her autobiography] be found to have any value it will partly consist in the evidence it must afford of how pleasant and interesting, and withal, I hope, not altogether useless a life is open to a woman, though no man has ever desired to share it, nor has she seen the man she would have wished to ask her to do so. The days which many maidens, my contemporaries and acquaintances—

"Lost in wooing,
In watching and pursuing,"

(or in being pursued, which comes to the same thing) were spent by me, free from all such distractions, in study and in the performance of happy and healthful filial and housewifely duties. Destiny, too, was kind to me, likewise, by relieving me from care respecting the other great object of human anxiety—to wit, Money. . . . Thus it has happened that in early womanhood and middle life I enjoyed a degree of real *leisure* of mind possessed by few; and to it, I think, must be chiefly attributed anything which in my doings may have worn the semblance of exceptional ability. I had good, sound working brains to start with, and much fewer hindrances than the majority of women in improving and employing them. *Voilà tout.*

In Frances Power Cobbe, *Life of Frances Power Cobbe* (1894)

A CLIMB IN THE ROCKY MOUNTAINS (1873)
Isabella Bird Bishop

Isabella Bird Bishop (1831–1904) was forty-two years old when she joined up with Mountain Jim Nugent to climb to the summit of Long's Peak. She had been a sickly girl. Operated on for a spinal tumor when she was eighteen, she spent most of her youth languishing in a Victorian woman's malaise, characterized by vague achiness and listlessness, which was relieved only by two trips to America. When she was forty, with both parents dead, she commenced her life as a serious adventurer and writer of travel books. Setting off for the antipodes she sampled Australia, New Zealand, Hawaii, and then the Rocky Mountains, as she recounts here. Mountain Jim died the next year, shot by an old enemy, much to Isabella's grief.

Although she always became ill on her return home, Isabella was fit again as soon as she set off for Japan or the Malayan jungles. After her beloved sister Henrietta's death, she married Dr. John Bishop. However, when he died five years later, she took off again at age fifty-seven for more adventures, mostly in Asia. In 1901, she made her last journey, a thousand miles on horseback through Morocco. Though her life intermittently contained the charitable works and the confinement to home characteristic of other clergymen's daughters, Isabella Bird Bishop was a devoted renegade from domestic responsibilities and the most daring solitary woman explorer of her time.

I was roped to Jim, but it was of no use, my feet were paralysed and slipped on the bare rock, and he said it was useless to try to go that way, and we retraced our steps. I wanted to return to the "Notch," knowing that my incompetence would detain the party, and one of the young men said almost plainly that a woman was a dangerous encumbrance, but the trapper replied shortly that if it were not to take a lady up he would not go at all. He went on to explore, and reported that further progress on the correct line of ascent was blocked by ice; and then for two hours we descended, lowering ourselves by our hands from rock to rock along a boulder-strewn sweep of 4000 feet, patched with ice and snow, and perilous from rolling stones. My fatigue, giddiness, and pain from bruised ankles, and arms half pulled out of their sockets, were so great that I should never have gone half-way had not Jim, *nolens volens* [willy-nilly] dragged me along with a patience and skill, and withal a determination that I should ascend the Peak, which never failed. After descending about 2000 feet to avoid the ice, we got into a deep ravine with inaccessible sides, partly filled with ice and snow and partly with large and small fragments of rock, which were constantly giving way, rendering the footing very insecure. That part to me was two hours of painful and unwilling submission to the inevitable; of trembling, slipping, straining, of smooth ice appearing when it was least expected, and of weak entreaties to be left behind while the others went on. Jim always said that there was no danger, that there was only a short bit ahead, and that I should go up even if he carried me! . . .

[Having reached the summit, it] was not possible to remain long. One of the young men was seriously alarmed by bleeding from the lungs, and the intense dryness of the day and the rarefaction of the air, at a height of nearly 15,000 feet, made respiration very painful. There is always water on the Peak, but it was frozen hard as a rock, and the sucking of ice and snow increases thirst. We all suffered severely from want of water, and the gasping for breath made our mouths and tongues so dry that articulation was difficult, and the speech of all unnatural. . . .

It was something at last to stand upon a storm-rent crown of this lonely sentinel of the Rocky Range, on one of the mightiest of the vertebrae of the backbone of the North American continent, and to see the waters start for both oceans. Uplifted above love and hate and storms of passion, calm amidst the eternal silences, fanned by zephyrs and bathed in living blue, peace rested for that one bright day on the Peak. . . .

We placed our names, with the date of ascent, in a tin within a crevice, and descended to the Ledge, sitting on the smooth granite, getting our feet into cracks and against projections, and letting ourselves down by our hands, Jim going before me, so that I might steady my feet against his powerful shoulders. I was no longer giddy, and faced the precipice of 3500 feet without a shiver. . . . I had various falls, and once hung by my frock, which caught on a rock, and Jim severed it with his hunting-knife, upon which I fell into a crevice full of soft snow. . . . For the last 200 feet the boulders were of enormous size, and the steepness fearful. Sometimes I drew myself up on hands and knees, sometimes crawled; sometimes Jim pulled me up by my arms or a lariat, and sometimes I stood on his shoulders, or he made steps for me of his feet and hands, but at six we stood on the Notch in the splendour of the sinking sun, all colour deepening, all peaks glorifying, all shadows purpling, all peril past. . . .

In Isabella Bird Bishop A *Lady's Life in the Rocky Mountains* (1879)

TWO

Domestic Life in Poverty

Although most women lived far below the economic level of the middle-class domestic angel, it is hard to find first-person accounts of poor women's domestic lives. Most records of the poor come to us filtered through the sensibilities and prejudices of middle-class reporters and bureaucrats. Somewhat more reliable are the accounts of a socialist woman like Maud Pember Reeves, who wanted to understand working-class women in their own terms. But even she only touched on one of the more secure groups of poor families. Those women who did write down their own stories were no doubt exceptional in having the leisure, the education, or the longevity to do so. Most of them lived at the end of the century, when education was more general and many belonged to the Women's Co-operative Movement, an organization associated with cooperative retail stores for working people, which fostered self-help and actively solicited writing. Furthermore, even where we get a first-person report, we have to make allowance for a woman's self-consciousness in writing about or discussing her life in a public forum ruled by middle-class values.

For working-class women, the feminine virtues of self-sacrifice and clever household management were practiced within a context of precarious family survival. The husband usually determined how much of his wages he wished to keep for his own pocket money and how much he would give for the support of the family. It was then the wife's job to budget however much money he allowed her. It was also up to her to care for the physical well-being of the family. The emotional strain of serving as a buffer between inadequate and chancy resources and the needs of the family was intense.

The physical strain was also considerable. Ordinary housework was extremely difficult due to crowded housing; inconvenient, shared plumbing; and smoky, inadequate cooking facilities. Infant mortality was as high as one in four among the poorest segments of the population; childbirth, which was rarely attended by a trained midwife or doctor, was rendered more risky by the ravages of malnutrition. The extra labor and pain of nursing a sickly child or an injured or chronically ailing husband was a commonplace of poor women's lives. Women had little recourse against abusive or neglectful husbands or against desertion by the father of an illegitimate child. Even healthy and reliable husbands could not help but be subject to the low wages and precarious employment that marked working men's occupations. Because women usually could earn only half of a man's wages, the sickness, desertion, or death of the husband could plunge a family into the direst poverty.

It was difficult for women to pay the rent, feed their families, and keep money in reserve for inevitable periods of reduced income or for occasional "emergency" purchases of clothing or medicine. Most of their strategies for getting by involved substituting their own labor or discomfort for cash. They did a great deal of household sewing, salvaging old garments, and adapting them to new uses. They stinted their own physical needs, going without sleep, saving meat for the men of the house, rarely buying themselves shoes, warm clothing, or a new dress. They also supplemented the men's wages by taking in work at home in the form of lodgers, matchboxes to be assembled, slopwork sewing (see Part IV), babysitting, or laundry.

Some wives regularly helped with their husband's occupation. A woman married to a fish peddler might fry up the merchandise for him to take into the streets; a carpenter's wife might put the finishing touches of silk lining onto a lap desk or box. People relied heavily on pawn shops as a source of ready money or regular short-term loans. Sunday clothes were often pawned and redeemed by the week; and other household items, such as tables, beds, blankets, plates, and silverware, were sacrificed as the need arose. Small tradesmen extended credit in return for the captive trade of neighborhood residents at slightly higher prices. People also set aside small weekly sums in "clubs" for the purchase of clothing or—grim reality—as insurance against the frequent expense of children's funerals.

Families lived close to their relatives if they could, and neighbors looked after one another. Because of the closeness of housing and the sharing of toilet and water facilities, neighbors were usually on fairly intimate terms. People pooled their resources, sharing clothing,

Homeworkers assembling match boxes, ca. 1900

National Museum of Labour History

food, pots, beds, babysitting, space, and sometimes even coming up with rent money or food when illness incapacitated their neighbors. In the childbearing years (which could mean about one third of a woman's life) and in old age, women were particularly dependent upon their neighbors for help, and women's domestic work was almost always part of this group effort to survive.

As a result, working-class women were generally less solitary and more self-reliant than more privileged women. Yet, ironically, the dependency, confinement, and powerlessness felt by middle-class women were often experienced in the lower classes in an exaggerated form. In contrast with the informality of neighborly aid, the more privatized middle-class ethic of respectability and ceremonial home life came into these strenuous, painful lives as an added oppression. Those seeking self-respect through "respectability" expended much labor in hiding the miseries of poverty. There might be too few petticoats to keep them warm, but their outer dress was faultlessly scrubbed and mended. There might be little food on the table, but the cloth was fresh and the dishes turned about on the shelves so the cracks would not show. Pictures were hung; children were instructed to watch their language; drink was avoided or hidden; the rowdy pleasures of neighborly street life were shunned; tired bodies were taken to church on Sunday. The respectability ethic was increasingly urged upon the poor in the last third of the century, the blame being placed on the wife and mother if the impoverished home were disorderly or the family underfed. It was women's labor that was supposed to create the appearance of comfort, to obliterate the gap in personal amenities between middle-class and working-class life (see pp. 14–15). Poor women were thus often judged by the same standards of angelic, sheltered femininity as middle-class and upper-class women. Yet their demanding lives mocked the ceremonial idleness of the idealized household angel just as their monotonous, starchy, insufficient meals mocked the imperial plenitude of Mrs. Beeton's menus.

THE HOUSING OF THE POOR (1913)
Maud Pember Reeves
(See p. 183.)

Maud Pember Reeves (d. 1953) was a feminist, social reformer, and organizer of the Fabian Women's Group. Between 1909 and 1913 this group visited women in the Lambeth section of London to learn how they coped with daily family life on a low income. Although Lambeth women were far from the bottom of the working class—their husbands were employed and earning about a pound a week, which placed them among the more fortunate workers—Reeves's study made clear that contrary to popular middle-class opinion, working-class mothers did not need education in more enlightened methods of child care and sanitation. They needed more money.

The ordinary housing for 8s. a week consists generally of three rooms out of a four-roomed house where the responsible tenant pays 10s. or 11s. for the whole, and sublets one small room for 2s. to 3s.; or of three or four rooms out of a five- or six-roomed house where the whole rent might be 14s. or 15s., and a couple of rooms may be sublet at 6s. or 7s. Some of the older four-roomed houses are built on a terrible plan. The passage from the front door runs along one side of the house straight out at the back. Two tiny rooms open off it, a front one and a back one. Between these two rooms, at right angles to the passage, ascends a steep flight of stairs. Because of the narrowness of

Residents of Providence Street, London, 1909

the house, the stairs have no landing at the top but continue as stairs until they meet the wall. Where the landing should be . . . two doors leading into a front bedroom and a back stand opposite one another, and open directly on to the steps themselves. Coming out of a bedroom with a child in their arms, obscuring their own light from the door behind them, many a man and woman in Lambeth has trodden on the edge of a step and fallen down the stairs to the ground below. There is no hand-rail, nothing but the smooth wall on each side.

Where two families share a six-roomed house, the landlady of the two probably chooses the ground floor, with command over the yard and washing arrangements. The upstairs people contract with her for the use of the copper [a large washing tub with a fire beneath it] and yard on one day of the week. The downstairs woman hates having the upstairs woman washing in her scullery [back-kitchen, used for washing and dirty work], and the upstairs woman hates washing there. Differences which result in "not speaking" often begin over the copper. Each woman scrubs the stairs in turn—another fruitful source of difficulty. Some of these houses are frankly arranged for two families, although the landlord only recognizes one tenant. In such cases, though there is but one copper, there will be a stove in an upstairs room. In some houses the upstairs people have to manage with an open grate and a hob [iron frame with a place to put a kettle in a fireplace], and nearly all of them have to carry water upstairs and carry it down again when dirty. . . .

In another family, where there are four children in one room and only a very small washtub, the children get a bath on Saturday or Sunday. The mother manages to get hers when the two elder children are at school. The father, who can never afford a twopenny bath, gets a "washdown" sometimes after the children have gone to sleep at night. "A bath it ain't, not fer grown-up people," explained his wife; "it's just a bit at a time like." Some families use the copper when it is built in the kitchen or a well-built scullery. But it is more trouble to empty, and often belongs to the other people's part of the house. All of these bathing arrangements imply a great deal of hard work for the mother of the family. Where the rooms are upstairs and water is not laid on . . . the work is excessive.

The equipment for cooking is as unsatisfactory as are the arrangements for sleeping or bathing. One kettle, one frying-pan, and two saucepans, both burnt, are often the complete outfit. . . . Once a week, for the Sunday dinner, the plunge is taken. Homes where there is no oven send out to the bakehouse on that occasion. The rest of the week is managed on cold food, or the hard-worked saucepan and frying-pan are brought into play. The certainty of an economical stove or fireplace is out of the reach of the poor. They are often obliged to use old-fashioned and broken ranges and grates which devour coal with as little benefit to the user as possible. . . .

Table appointments are never sufficient. The children hardly sit down to any meal but dinner, and even then they sometimes stand round the table for lack of chairs. Some women have a piece of oil-cloth on the table; some spread a newspaper. So many plates are put round, each containing a dinner. The eating takes no time at all. A drink of water out of a tea-cup which is filled for each child in turn finishes the repast.

Equipment for cleaning is one of the elastic items on a budget. A Lambeth mother would like to spend 5d. on soap, 1d. on soda, 1d. on blue and starch. She is obliged in many cases to compress the expenditure to 3d. or 5d. all told. She sometimes has to make 2d. do.

There is the remains of a broom sometimes. Generally there is only one bucket and a cloth, which latter, probably, is the quite hopelessly worn out shirt or pinafore of a member of the family. . . .

Two pennyworth of soap may have to wash the clothes, scrub the floors, and wash the people of a family, for a week. It is difficult to realise the soap famine in such a household. Soda, being cheap, is made to do a great deal. It sometimes appears in the children's weekly bath; it often washes their hair. A woman who had been using her one piece of soap to scrub the floor next brought it into play when she bathed the baby, with the unfortunate result of a long scratch on the baby from a cinder in the soap. She sighed when the visitor noticed the scratch, and said: "I sometimes think I'd like a little oven best, but now it do seem as if I'd rather 'ave two bits of soap." The visitor helpfully suggested cutting the one piece in two, but the mother shook her experienced head, and said: "It wouldn't last not 'arf as long."

In Maud Pember Reeves, *Round About a Pound a Week* (1913)

THE DIET OF THE POOR (1901)
B. Seebohm Rowntree

When Seebohm Rowntree (1871–1954) studied the dietary habits of poor families in York, he discovered that on the whole, inmates of prisons and workhouses (who were notoriously underfed) ate better than the working poor. Rowntree divided the poor into categories by income, but he noted how precarious relative advantages were. The birth of children or the temporary unemployment of the male breadwinner could send any of Rowntree's families plummeting into the lowest income group. Widows living alone or supporting young families were commonly among the very poorest.

Mrs. Smith

Mrs. Smith, an excellent housewife, with a steady husband and three children at home, gave the following account of how she managed. Her house is scrupulously clean and tidy. Mr. Smith is in regular work and earns 20s. per week. He keeps 2s. a week for himself, and hands over 18s. to his wife. Out of his two shillings Mr. Smith spends 1d. per day on beer, 3d. a week on tobacco, puts 3d. into the chil-

dren's savings-box, and clothes himself on the remainder. One new
dress, Mrs. Smith tells us, will last for years. For everyday wear she
buys some old dress at a jumble sale for a few shillings. Old garments,
cast off by some wealthier family, are sometimes bought from the
ragman . . . and made up into clothes for the children. Mrs. Smith
said that she once bought a pair of old curtains from the ragman for
3d. She cut out the worn parts and then made curtains and short
blinds from the remainder sufficient for all the windows in her house.
She regularly pays 6d. a week for sick clubs, 4d. for life insurance, and
3d. per week into the clothing club held in connection with her
church.

It was obvious that with such a normal expenditure there was no
appreciable sum available for "extras." "Then how do you do, Mrs.
Smith," my investigator asked, "when you have to meet any extraordinary expenditure, such as a new dress, or a pair of boots?" "Well,
as a rule," was the answer, "we 'ave to get it out of the food money
and go short; but I never let Smith suffer—'e 'as to go to work, and
must be kept up, yer know! And then Smith 'as ollers been very good
to me. When I want a new pair of shoes, or anythink, 'e 'elps me
out of 'is pocket money, and we haven't to pinch the food so much."

BUDGET No. 6

OFFICE CLEANER. WAGES IRREGULAR

(AVERAGE FOR FOUR WEEKS: 11s. 9d. PER WEEK)

This family consists of a mother, aged 63, and a daughter, aged 20.
Mrs. K. cleans offices, and is at work by 5:30 a.m. except on Fridays,
when she commences at about 4:30 a.m. She earns 6s. per week. Her
daughter is pale and delicate. She is employed in a confectionery
factory, but keeps irregular hours, and consequently does not earn
more than 5s. or 6s. per week. The mother looks fairly well-nourished.
She was a cook in a good family before she married, but has been a
widow for eight years.

Mother and daughter live in one room, for which they pay 1s. 8d.
per week rent. It is three storeys up, and is approached by a crooked,
narrow, wooden staircase which is unventilated, and almost pitch
dark. The room when reached is, however, both clean and comfortable. The large double bed covered with a worn though clean patch-
work quilt occupies a good deal of the floor space. In addition to this
there are a couple of chairs and a small round table. Some old-
fashioned wooden travelling trunks are placed one upon another,

and covered with white cloths, and apparently take the place of chests of drawers. The walls are whitewashed and decorated with unframed prints and pictures. There is a small open grate with an oven, in which Mrs. K. bakes her bread. The grate is beautifully clean, and the hearth nicely whitened. By the side of the grate is a small cupboard; the food is kept on the top shelves, and the coal at the bottom. The floor is covered with odd pieces of oilcloth and a hearthrug. Very little sunshine penetrates to this room, as it is situated in a narrow street with high buildings on the opposite side. All the water has to be carried from the basement of the building up the dark and crooked flight of stairs, and all the dirty water has to be carried down again to the drain in the basement.

The mother gets her breakfast before going out to her work in the early morning. It generally consists of bread, butter, and a cup of tea. The daughter gets up later and has her breakfast before going to work, taking her tea from the pot which her mother had left standing on the hob. The mother's cleaning is finished by 9 a.m. She then returns home and does her own house-work, washing, etc., and often does a bit of sewing for her grandchildren. . . .

An examination of this family's diet shows that the supply of protein is 25 percent and the energy value 23 percent below standard requirements.

BUDGET NO. 12
LABOURER. WAGES 21S.

This household consists of a father, aged 23, mother, aged 23, and four children, ranging in age from a boy of 6 to a baby 11 months old. The father is a small, lightly built man, and does not appear to be very strong. The mother is a bright woman, but is at present much handicapped by her young family, and is suffering from neuralgia and bad headaches. The children look puny and undeveloped, and have not much appetite.

The house contains three rooms. The front door opens into a tiny hall about 4 feet square. The stairs to the bedrooms and the door to the living-room lead out of it. The living-room contains an open fireplace with an oven for baking bread, and is well provided with cupboards in the walls. The furniture is fairly comfortable. The father had been out of work for several months before he obtained his present situation, and the family are still suffering from the privations they then endured. They are also labouring under a debt contracted

MENU OF MEALS PROVIDED DURING WEEK ENDING JUNE 21, 1901

	Breakfast.	Dinner.	Tea.	Supper.
Friday	Bread, butter, tea.	Bacon, eggs, bread, tea.	Bread, butter, currant square.	Bread, butter, tea.
Saturday	Bacon, bread, tea.	Meat pie, potatoes, tea.	Bread, butter, onions, lettuce.	Fish, bread, cocoa.
Sunday	Bread, butter, eggs, tea.	Roast beef, potatoes, Yorkshire pudding, peas.	Bread, butter, jam.	Potatoes, peas, cold meat.
Monday	Bread, butter, tea.	Cold meat, potatoes.	Bread, butter, tea.	Bread, butter, onions.
Tuesday	Bread, butter, bacon, tea.	Mashed potatoes.	Hot cakes, butter, tea.	Bread, cheese, tea.
Wednesday				
Thursday	Bread, butter, tea.	Bacon, sausages, bread, tea.	Cakes, butter, tea.	Bread, butter, tea.

during this period, and are paying off "back rent." In addition to this, Mrs. T. is paying for a wringing machine [a hand-cranked set of rollers for wringing water out of clothes after washing] in weekly instalments, thus the margin of income available for ordinary current expenditure is seriously reduced. Mrs. T.'s mother is very kind to her, and helps her, and a brother living away from York sends her things now and again.

The meals are fairly regular, but sometimes Mr. T. has to take his breakfast with him to work. As is usual with poor families, the husband comes off better as regards food than the rest of the family, for although Mrs. T. and the children have no meat for breakfast, her husband, she explained, "must have a bit of bacon to take with him for his breakfast, or else all the others would talk so."

Mrs. T. buys in the principal stock of food on Saturday, but has to get odd things during the week. She always buys her meat late on Saturday night, when she gets it cheaper, and she gets vegetables and fish in the same way. She makes her own bread and cakes, but complains of being "dead sick of bread and butter—nothing but bread and butter, until I hate the sight of it."

An examination of the diet of this family shows that the protein is 25 percent and the fuel value 14 percent below standard requirements.

In B. Seebohm Rowntree, *Poverty: A Study of Town Life* (1901)

MOTHER'S CHORES ON WASH-DAY (ca. 1900)

Grace Foakes
(See pp. 179 and 252.)

This London housewife's struggle to wash her family's clothes is representative of the weekly exertions of other women of her time with the cumbersome copper tub, which was usually located at a distance from the source of water.

Monday was always wash-day. After sending us off to school, Mother would collect all the dirty washing and sort it into groups. First came the sheets and pillow-slips, then the shirts and towels, petticoats, dresses, teacloths and handkerchiefs and—last of all—the coarse aprons and stockings and my father's socks. A zinc bath was placed on the kitchen table, the copper was lit and heated with wood picked up from the foreshore. When the water was hot it was baled out into buckets with a small bowl with a wooden handle—Mother called this the "copper bowl." Enough water was carried in buckets until the bath was half full. She added a handful of soda to soften the water and then the washing commenced.

My mother, a coarse apron made from a sack round her and a square of mackintosh pinned over her chest, rubbed each piece with "Sunlight" soap, giving an extra rub to the very dirty parts. Not being very tall, she had to stand on a wooden box so that she could reach the rubbing board. After the whites were washed, they were put into the copper to boil together with more soda. They were continually stirred with the copper-stick and kept boiling for half an hour. The whole place smelt of boiling washing and steam. After this, they were lifted out on to the wrong side of the copper's wooden lid and left to drain, for the water had to be saved ready for the next boil. The washing was then put through the wringer to extract the rest of the water. The wringing had to be left until the rest of the washing was done as, having only one bath, she could not rinse the clothes until it was empty. Mother struggled to the sink with the bath of dirty washing water and emptied it. Then it was filled with cold water and placed under the wringer. The washing was rinsed once and put through the wooden rollers. If the weather was fine, it would be hung out to dry. . . .

If it was a wet day, then the washing had to be dried in the kitchen. . . . The ceiling was not very high and most of the time the washing was dangling on our heads. The place was damp and smelly, with steam running down windows and walls. Sometimes in bad weather the washing took two or three days to dry. . . .

On each packet of "Sunlight" soap there were the words "Why does a woman look older sooner than a man?" It went on to explain the merits of the soap, but it was small wonder that women *did* look old at forty. This one day alone was truly an exhausting one, for not only was the washing done but the children had to be cared for, the meals prepared and a thousand and one other things done before the day was over.

In Grace Foakes, *My Part of the River* (1974)

DAUGHTER'S CHORES ON WASH-DAY (1860s)
Mrs. Layton
(See pp. 187 and 308.)

Because they were expected to contribute to family survival by doing chores and running errands (if not actually working for wages), poor children learned to combine work and play as Mrs. Layton remembers here. The writer was born in 1855 in a poor section of London, the seventh of fourteen children.

My fourth sister and I always stayed away from school on washing day to mind the babies. In the summer it was real sport, because so many people did their washing on the same day, and everybody had large families and generally kept the elder girls, and sometimes boys, at home to mind the little ones. We used to plan to go out all to-gether with our babies and prams into Victoria Park. Very few people had prams of their own, but could hire them at 1d. an hour to hold one baby, or 1½d. an hour to hold two. Several mothers would pay a few pence for the hire of a pram and the children used to manage between them how they were to be used. I need hardly say each pram was used to its full seating capacity. The single pram had always to accommodate two and the double pram three or more, and we always kept them the full length of time for which we had paid. We would picnic on bread and treacle under the trees in the Park, and return home in the evening a troop of tired but happy children.

In *Life As We Have Known It,* ed. Margaret Llewelyn Davies (London: Hogarth Press, 1931).

CLEANING THE DOORSTEP (ca. 1900)
Grace Foakes
(See pp. 177 and 252.)

This reminiscence of early-twentieth-century housekeeping in one of the poorest neighborhoods in London pays tribute to a very popular ritual of respectability: cleaning the front step.

The majority of poor women were clean, patient and hardworking, bringing up families under the worst kinds of conditions. They cleaned their windows each week, and their curtains were taken down and washed every fortnight. They got so black that you soaked them in salted water before you washed them. When this water was poured away it was as black as soot. The air was full of smoke and grime from many factories and ships, and from the coal fires which everyone used, but each fortnight those curtains went up clean.

Then there were the doorsteps. Each front door had a wooden doorstep, which was scrubbed white each morning. The pavement outside the house was swept and then the woman of the house, kneeling down with a bucket of hot water and some whitening, proceeded to wash the pavement immediately in front of her door, making a half-circle which she would afterwards whiten with the whitening. Thus each house you passed had its half-circle of white pavement and its white-scrubbed doorstep. When the front door opened, in many cases one would see lace curtains draped just half-way down the passage or hall, as it is now called. This looked nice, and also prevented people seeing into the room beyond, which in nearly every case was the living-room-cum-everything. No matter how poor or how little a family had, this outward appearance had to be kept up at all costs.

In Grace Foakes, *My Part of the River* (1974)

Semi-vagrant girl rocking her baby, from Grundy's English Views,
no. 428, ca. 1857

AN UNMARRIED MOTHER'S STORY (1845)
London Foundling Hospital Records

Unmarried mothers found it difficult to support and care for their
children. The New Poor Law of 1834, in an attempt to promote female chastity, had deprived a mother of the right to bring the puta-
tive father of her child to court to induce him to marry her or to
provide weekly support payments. Even after 1844, when the law was
reversed, women had a hard time tracking down a man in an increasingly urban and mobile population; nor could they count on having

community pressure on their side as they had once had in the world of village life. If a woman was lucky, she could enlist the aid of family or friends to care for her child while she tried to earn a living. However, she would often be obliged to pay a neighbor or "dry nurse" to take care of the child. Even at the lowest rates, the cost of buying care for a baby was more than the salary of the average maidservant. Mortality rates, in general about 15 percent in the first year of life, were estimated at least twice as high for illegitimate children. Although we cannot be sure of the reliability of these figures or of the extent to which they reflect active or passive infanticide (as some observers charged), it is certainly true that a woman would have had a very tough time earning a living and caring for her baby.

The London Foundling Hospital, an orphanage, accepted children of only those mothers who had "previously borne a good character for Virtue, Sobriety, and Honesty." As a result, most of the women applying to have their children accepted there tried to prove that they had no previous illegitimate children, little experience of intercourse, and had conceived the child either through belief in a promise of marriage, rape, or (not infrequently) both.

The following is an official report of the hospital's investigation of Ann Thain, twenty-four years old and the mother of a baby girl by one Isaac Parting, a chronometer maker.

Your Enquirer is informed by Mrs. Thain that the Petitioner is her daughter being the eldest of seven children—that until the Petitioner went to Miss Hopper of No. 10 Bedford Place, Commercial Road, to improve herself in the business of a Dressmaker and Milliner she was always at home and conducted herself in an unexceptionable manner. That about three years ago an acquaintance commenced between the Petitioner and Isaac Parting, whom the Petitioner introduced to her (Mrs. Thain) and subsequently asked her consent to pay his addresses to the Petitioner which was granted and which courtship was carried on until the Petitioner's pregnancy was discovered. That she (Mrs. Thain) then took private lodging for the Petitioner with the view of hiding her shame, which has been accomplished, her own father and other Members of the Family being ignorant of what has taken place. That since proceedings were taken against Parting before the Magistrate he has contrived to elude every search after him and has not contributed anything toward the support of the child. That should the Petitioner be relieved of the child she will go to Service, and that she would swear the child is her *first*.

Your Enquirer is informed by Miss Hopper of No. 10 Bedford Place, Commercial Road (who appears to be a very respectable woman) that the Petitioner was with her about twelve months as an improver in the business of a Dressmaker and Milliner and conducted herself, as far as her observations went, in such a way that she had not a word to say against her. That during that time Isaac Parting visited her frequently, and that both his manner and his words indicated an honourable courtship, which she (Miss Hopper) fully expected would have ended in Marriage.

The Petitioner has placed in the hands of your Enquirer several love letters addressed to her by Isaac Parting which are of a character likely to mislead a young person.

Dear Ann
If I may take the liberty of addressing you in that way I trust you are well and hope that you escaped the scolding which you expected to receive from your mother for being out so late. I send you a few lines which I have wrote and trust that you will not be in any way offended at them. Do write as soon as you possibly can but not in the same style as you wrote before.
Goodbye.

I remain yours etc.
Isaac Parting

To Ann
Do not chide me
I would not give you pain
But turn again those looks on me
And love me once again
Yes let me gaze upon that form
That to my heart is dear
And yet expect again those words
That I do love to hear
For oh indeed my heart it beats
With love for none but you
Then trust me and believe me Ann
I could not be untrue . . .

From London Foundling Hospital Records, Petition of Ann Esther Thain (1845)

MOTHERS' DAYS (1913)
Maud Pember Reeves
(See p. 170.)

(See p. 170.)

Mrs. P. is under thirty, and, when she has time to look it, rather pretty. Her eldest child is only ten. The tightest economy reigns in that little house, partly because Mr. P. is a careful man and very delicate, and partly because Mrs. P. is terrified of debt. It was she who discovered the plan of buying seven cracked eggs for 3d. As she said, it might lose you a little of the egg, but you could smell it first, which was a convenience. She is clean, but untidy, very gentle in her manner, and easily shocked. . . . Her mother rents one of her rooms, and, much beloved, is always there to advise in an unscientific, inarticulate, but soothing way when there is a difficulty. The children are fair and delicate, and are kept clean by their tired little mother, who plaintively declared that she preferred boys to girls, because you could cut their hair off and keep their heads clean without trouble, and also because their nether garments were less easily torn. . . .

The next case is that of Mrs. O. who has but two children alive, both very young. Two rooms have to be looked after, and extremely well looked after, for Mr. O. is the gentleman who keeps 5s. a week out of 25s., and expects 4s. 4d. a week spent on his own extra food. He likes the place nice, and cannot see that his wife need ever go out except for the purpose of buying the family food. He believes that women are prone to extravagance in dress, and does not encourage Mrs. O. in any such nonsense. When it was necessary that she should come once a fortnight to the weighing centre, to have the baby weighed, the price of a pair of boots had to be saved out of several weeks' food, much to the annoyance of Mr. O., who could not understand why any of his family should ever leave the two rooms where they live.

Her day runs as follows:

7:00 Get up and get husband's breakfast; nurse baby while he has it.
7:30 He goes to work. Get little girl dressed, get her breakfast, and have it with her.
8:00 Wash up.
8:30 Get baby's bath and wash and dress him.
9:00 Nurse him and put him to sleep.

9:30 Do beds and sweep bedroom, and carry up water.

11:00 Start to make little girl a frock till baby wakes; nurse him when he does.

12:15 Get dinner for self and child ready (husband had dinner away from home).

1:00 Have dinner.

1:30 Nurse baby and clear away and wash up dinner things. Sweep and scrub floor and passage, clean grate; every other week do stairs.

2:30 Wash self and little girl, and take children out till four.

4:00 Get tea and nurse baby.

4:30 Clear away, and get husband's tea; wait for him till he comes in; very uncertain, between five and seven o'clock; go on making frock till he does.

6:00 Put children to bed.

6:30 Wash up husband's tea things, if he has finished. As soon as he has finished, he changes and goes out.

8:00 Go up The Walk for shopping for next day, leaving children in bed.

9:00 Mend husband's clothes, and go on with frock till ten.

10:00 Nurse baby and make both children comfortable for the night.

11:00 If husband has come in, go to bed.

This is not a hard day as things go in Lambeth. The noticeable thing about it is its loneliness. Mrs. O. knows nothing of her neighbours, and, until the visitor insisted on the children's getting out every afternoon, and agitated for the boots, Mrs. O. never took them out. She did her shopping at night in order that her old slippers might not be seen. She sat indoors and mended and made clothes in her neat room, while her pale little girl amused herself as best she could and the baby lay on the bed. The husband merely ate and slept at home. He was a particularly respectable and steady man, who kept his clothes neat and his person scrupulously clean. His wife ministered to him in every way she could, but saw nothing of him. He took no interest in the little daughter, but was proud of the boy, and it was by means of the boy's need for fresh air that he was persuaded to allow his wife to save for her boots. For her he did not consider them necessary, as he was in favour of women staying at home and minding the house.

The last "day" is that of the woman who has eight children under thirteen. The fact that her husband works at night enables the family

National Museum of Labour History

Mother and child at home, ca. 1900

to sleep seven in one room—the mother and five children by night and the husband by day; in the other bedroom three older children sleep in a single bed. This woman is tall and would be good-looking if her figure were not much misshapen. She has quantities of well-washed hair, and good teeth; but her face is that of a woman of fifty. She is thirty-eight. . . . She seems always to be hearing a baby wake, or correcting a child of two, or attending to the soiled face of the little girl of three and a half, who is so much smaller than her younger brother. She once went for a fortnight's change to the seaside. The visitor asked her, when she came back, what she had most enjoyed. She thought for a considerable time, and then made the following statement: "I on'y 'ad two babies along of me, an' wen I come in me dinner was cooked for me."

There is no doubt that if Mrs. B. were stronger she would not need to nurse her baby quite so often. He is small and hungry, and will soon need to be weaned if his mother is to work as hard as she does on ordinary days; with extra exertion on washing-days, and extra noise and interruption in holiday-time.

Mr. B., printer's labourer; wage 30s.; allows 28s. [for the family budget]; night worker. Eight children; eldest, a girl of twelve years; youngest, three months.

6:45 Nurses baby.

7:00 Rises, calls children, lights fire and puts on kettle, washes and dresses elder four children. Girl of twelve can do for herself. Boy of ten can do all but his ears.

8:00 Gets breakfast; bread and butter and tea for children.

8:15 Gives children breakfast; gets them off to school by 8:45.

8:45 Nurses baby.

9:00 Fetches down the three babies, washes and dresses them; gives the two bigger their breakfast.

9:30 Husband comes home; cooks him rasher or haddock.

10:00 Gives him his breakfast, and goes upstairs to tidy her room for husband to sleep in; makes her bed for him, which has been airing since seven o'clock. Turns out and airs beds in other room, taking two elder babies with her.

10:30 Clears away and washes up all the breakfast things.

11:00 Nurses baby and puts all three to sleep.

11:15 Goes out to buy dinner.

11:30 Prepares dinner.

12:10 Children all home again; goes on with dinner.

1:00 Lays and serves dinner.

1:30 Washes hands and faces of five children, and sends them off to school.

1:45 Nurses baby, and sits down till 2:30.

2:30 Washes up and begins cleaning. Sweeps kitchen, scullery, and passage, scrubs them, cleans grate; three babies to mind all the time.

4:10 Children all home again; gets their tea, nurses baby.

4:30 Clears away, and begins to cook husband's dinner.

5:00 Husband wakes; gives him dinner; sits down while she cuts his food for him to take to work, keeping babies and children as quiet as she can.

6:00 Nurses baby.

6:30 He starts for work. She makes children's beds, turns out his, airs his room, and makes his bed up for herself and three children to sleep in at night. All water used in bedrooms has to be carried upstairs, and when used, carried down.

7:30 Washes and puts to bed two babies.

8:00 Nurses baby.

8:15 Washes and puts to bed elder children.

8:45 Mends clothes.

10:00 Nurses baby and puts him to bed.

10:30 Goes to bed; nurses baby twice in the night.

In Maud Pember Reeves, *Round About a Pound a Week* (1913)

MARRIAGE AND MOTHERHOOD (ca. 1880)
Mrs. Layton
(See pp. 178 and 308.)

Mrs. Layton later had a career as a midwife and was an energetic worker for women's causes with the Women's Co-operative Guild.

It was at a mission hall, where I went when I found the church too stiff and conservative, that I met my husband. We were both keenly interested in social problems. . . . I was engaged for three years before we were in a position to settle down, and then when everything was fixed up, rooms taken, furniture bought, arrangements made for the wedding to take place, the piano-making firm my husband worked for went bankrupt and he was thrown out of work. We decided not to put off the wedding, hoping he would soon find other work, and we were married on December 2nd, 1882, he being twenty-seven and I twenty-six years of age.

For eight months my husband tramped from early morn till late at night looking for work, and during all that time he did small jobs which brought in three pounds in all. The little money I had saved had dwindled down to a few pounds. I had tried to help the situation by first going out to work and then by doing washing at home. I turned my hand to anything that would honestly bring in money. My health was becoming impaired with work and worry and I was expecting a baby which made it very hard for me. But I made the best of what every one of my friends called a bad job, and like Mr. Micawber was always hoping for something to turn up. It did at last, just a month before my baby was born. My husband got a job on the Midland Railway as carriage cleaner at St. Pancras. He worked on nights, twelve hours a night, six nights a week, at the large wage of 19s. a week. It was very dirty work, but we were thankful for that amount of money, for I was beginning to wonder how my confinement was to be paid for when I had to give up work. I was also very anxious about the health of the coming baby. I knew enough about maternity to know that I had not sufficient food to nourish myself and child, and then I felt the great responsibility of bringing a new life into the world. I used to worry myself a great deal and wonder whether I should make a good mother. But I prayed that I might make a worthy mother and that the child might be strong and healthy, and that I should be able to bring it up well.

My baby, a boy, was born on September 3rd, 1883. I had rather a bad time as I had to be delivered with forceps and had nothing to lull the pain, so had to feel all that was going on. The baby was small and puny and very cross. I had no one with me after the morning and had to depend on the neighbours. My husband did what he could, but he had to sleep in the daytime and I was always all alone at night. I was up at the seventh day, but I took care to do no more than I could help. When my baby was three months old my husband lost his job, and was out of work again. When he came home and told me I did not know what to do. I was weak and my baby was cross and poorly. I had never given in with all the previous troubles but now I could not help giving way. I had never parted with any of my clothes or furniture by pawning, as I had been advised to many times by kindly folk who thought they were suggesting a good thing for hard times . . . but now I could see my things going, for I could not work with a young baby even as I had done before he was born. However, it was not so bad as I had anticipated, for a man who lived in the same house told my husband to go after a job at St. Pancras Station . . . as porter on the bank, which meant loading and unloading trucks, all night work at 17s. a week. My rent was 7s. a week, club 8d. a week, and I was obliged to pay 1s. 3d. a week for fares for my husband to ride one way to his work. We lived six miles from St. Pancras and it was impossible for him to walk both ways and work the long hours which constituted a night's work. The long hours and heavy work told on him, and when winter set in he was taken ill and was ill for a long time. Then I had only 12s. a week club money. From that time

London docker and wife, 1889

till he died, I am sure he had an average six months' illness every year. I was very poor but no one outside my door ever knew how often I was hungry or how I had to scheme to get my husband nourishment.

My baby grew into a strong, sturdy little fellow, full of mischief. It was a great treat to look after him and help to earn the living. At the same time it meant taking him out in the daytime and working after my husband had gone to work at night. Many times till 4 o'clock in the morning in bitter cold weather I have been washing, and have just been able to get two hours' sleep before the child woke up, which he did about 6 o'clock. My second child, a boy, was born three years later. By that time my husband's wages had risen to £1 1s. a week, and he worked nearer home which was a little better for me. My baby was delicate from birth and was ill for some months before he died. I was insufficiently nourished during pregnancy and nearly lost my

life through want of nourishment and attention at my confinement
and lying-in period. I think if it had not been for a good neighbour I
should have gone under.

In *Life As We Have Known It* (1931)

THE TOLL OF MOTHERHOOD (ca. 1900)
Anonymous

*This is one of several hundred stories solicited by the Women's Co-
operative Guild in a lobbying effort on behalf of state benefits for
mothers. This life story, one of the more hopeful in the collection,
captures the mixture of joy and misery that motherhood entailed for
women struggling by on too little money.*

I was married at twenty-eight in utter ignorance of the things that
most vitally affect a wife and mother. My mother, a dear, pious soul,
thought ignorance was innocence, and the only thing I remember her
saying on the subject of childbirth was, "God never sends a babe
without bread to feed it." Dame Experience long ago knocked the
bottom out of that argument for me. My husband was a man earning
32s. a week—a conscientious, good man, but utterly undomesticated.
A year after our marriage the first baby was born, naturally and with
little pain or trouble. I had every care, and motherhood stirred the
depths of my nature. The rapture of a babe in my arms drawing nourishment from me crowned me with glory and sanctity and honour.

Alas! the doctor who attended me suffered from eczema of a very
bad type in his hands. The disease attacked me, and in twenty-four
hours I was covered from head to foot . . . finally leaving me partially
and sometimes totally crippled in my hands. Fifteen months later a
second baby came—a dear little girl, and again I was in fairly good
condition physically and financially, but had incurred heavy doctor's
bills and attendance bills, due to my incapacity for work owing to
eczema. Both the children were delicate, and dietary expenses ran
high. Believing that true thrift is wise expenditure, we spent our all
trying to build up for them sound, healthy bodies, and [were] ill-
prepared financially and physically to meet the birth of a third baby
sixteen months later. Motherhood ceased to be a crown of glory, and
became a fearsome thing to be shunned and feared.

The only way to meet our increased expenditure was by dropping an endowment policy, and losing all our little, hard-earned savings. I confess without shame that when well-meaning friends said: "You cannot afford another baby; take this drug," I took their strong concoctions to purge me of the little life that might be mine. They failed, as such things generally do, and the third baby came. Many a time I have sat in Daddy's big chair, a baby two and a half years old at my back, one sixteen months and one one month on my knees, and cried for very weariness and hopelessness. I fed them all as long as I could, but I was too harassed, domestic duties too heavy, and the income too limited to furnish me with a rich nourishing milk. . . .

Nine months later I was again pregnant, and the second child fell ill. "She cannot live," the doctors said, but I loved . . . I watched by her couch three weeks, snatching her sleeping moments to fulfill the household task. The strain was fearful, and one night I felt I must sleep or die—I didn't much care which; and I lay down by her side, and slept, and slept, and slept, forgetful of temperatures, nourishment or anything else. . . . [The daughter lived to be a "delicate but bright and intelligent child."] A miscarriage followed in consequence of the strain, and doctor's bills grew like mushrooms. The physical pain from the eczema, and working with raw and bleeding hands, threatened me with madness.

Two years later a fourth baby came. Varicose veins developed. I thought they were a necessary complement to childbirth. He was a giant of a boy and heavy to carry, and I just dragged about the housework, washing and cleaning until the time of his birth; but I looked forward to that nine days in bed longingly; to be still and rest was a luxury of luxuries. Economics became a greater strain than ever now that I had four children to care for. Dimly conscious of the evils of sweating [employment of needleworkers at low pay for long hours], instead of buying cheap ready-made clothes, I fashioned all their little garments and became a sweated worker myself.

The utter monotony of life, the lack of tone and culture, the drudgery and gradual lowering of the standard of living consequent upon the rising cost of living, and increased responsibilities, was converting me into a soulless drudge and nagging scold. I felt the comradeship between myself and husband was breaking up. He could not enter into my domestic, I would not enter into his intellectual pursuits, and again I had to fight or go under. I could give no time to mental culture and I bought Stead's penny editions of literary masters, and used to put them on a shelf in front of me washing-day, fastened back their pages with a clothes-peg, and learned pages of Whittier, Lowell, and Longfellow, as I mechanically rubbed the dirty clothes, and thus wrought my education. This served a useful purpose; my children used to be sent off to sleep by reciting what I had learned during the day. My mental outlook was widened, and once again I stood a comrade and helpmeet by my husband's side, and my children all have a love for good literature.

Three years later a fifth baby came. I was ill and tired, but my husband fell ill a month prior to his birth, and I was up day and night. Our doctor was, and is, one of the kindest men I have ever met. I said: "Doctor, I cannot afford you for myself, but will you come if I need?" "I hope you won't need me, but I'll come." I dare not let my husband in his precarious condition hear a cry of pain from me, and travail pain cannot always be stifled; and here again the doctor helped me by giving me a sleeping draught to administer him as soon as I felt the pains of childbirth. Hence he slept in one room while I travailed in the other, and brought forth the loveliest boy that ever gladdened a mother's heart.

So here I am a woman of forty-one years, blessed with a lovely family of healthy children, faced with a big deficit, varicose veins, and an occasional loss of the use of my hands. . . . I would like nice clothes (I've had three new dresses in fourteen years), but I must not have them yet. I'd like to develop mentally, but I must stifle that part of my nature until I have made good the ills of the past, and I am doing it slowly and surely, and my heart grows lighter, and will grow lighter still when I know that the burden is lifted from the mothers of our race.

In *Maternity: Letters from Working Women*, ed. Margaret Llewelyn Davies (London: G. Bell & Sons, 1915)

Part III

WOMAN'S
MIND

Female education for most of the nineteenth century was determined by women's confinement to the domestic world. Upper-class and middle-class women were educated to be drawing-room ornaments; poor women were trained to be drudges. The standards of female attainment were set to suit women's economic dependency on men. Autonomy of mind or individuality of interests was discouraged as unwomanly or futile, the pervasive ideal of womanly self-sacrifice extending even to a woman's opinions. The perfect wife and mother was to recognize her own intellectual weakness and sweetly rely on her husband's judgments.

It was in this discouraging environment that women with intellectual ambitions, excluded from most serious institutions of higher learning and forced to work amid the limitless distractions of home, struggled to educate themselves. By the 1860s, such lonely, individual struggles led to the formation of a determined movement demanding secondary and higher education for girls and women. Education came to be seen not only as the key to wider employment opportunities, but also as the symbol of woman's right to the fullest possible use of her mind. Women who could learn what men learned felt entitled to assume male occupations and privileges, and most importantly to judge for themselves what was in their own interests and in the general interests of society. It is therefore not hard to understand why education should have been one of the earliest and most successful targets of the women's movement; why it should have met with such passionate opposition; and why the challenge to sexual segregation in schooling provoked a wide-ranging reassessment of ideas of male and female capacities.

The establishment of new educational institutions for women was one of the chief gains of nineteenth-century feminism. It did not, however, extend to the working class—the majority of the population—who received only elementary education, which in the last decade of the century increasingly stressed the importance of domestic work. Ironically, just as middle-class women were using their new educational structures to break down the restrictions of home, poor women were being socialized by their new state-supported board schools into greater approximations of domestic angelhood.

ONE

Ornamental Education and Its Victims

A "gentleman's education" in the nineteenth century was considered the proper preparation either for a life of achievement in the professions or for enjoying a comfortable inherited income. It started with private tutors in Latin, Greek, and mathematics, continued with boarding school from age eight in an atmosphere of competitive play and male camaraderie, and ended with university studies. The sisters of such gentlemen were educated quite differently. Kept at home with a governess until they were fourteen, they were then usually sent off for a year or two to finishing school, where they learned a smattering of foreign languages, singing, drawing, dancing, and "the use of the globes." By the time they were sixteen, their education was over and they were left to keep up their piano playing and to read light French literature on their own. Such an education might be laborious in its emphasis on rote learning, but it could never produce a serious mastery of any skill or branch of knowledge. In fact, its shallowness was intentional, and considered appropriate to women's limited powers and subservient condition.

Those women with higher educational goals needed both luck and heroic persistence to obtain anything close to the opportunities that were given to talented or untalented boys as a matter of course. Nelly Weeton's futile attempts to keep up her outlawed literary efforts by constantly erasing her slate as she wrote are an emblem of the hopelessness of many women's efforts within the social limits of the time (see p. 204).

THE PURPOSES OF ORNAMENTAL EDUCATION (1797)
Thomas Gisborne

Thomas Gisborne (1758–1846), whose Duties of the Female Sex (1797) offered parents advice on how to bring up moral and accomplished daughters, was pleased with "the fact that people no longer believed that she who was completely versed in the science of pickling and preserving and in the mysteries of cross stitch and embroidery [and] thoroughly mistress of the family receipt-book and her needle . . . [had] reached the measure of female perfection." Though he applauded the advance of general literacy among privileged women, Gisborne carefully defined the proper uses of the newly fashionable ornamental education.

Let the pupil . . . be thoroughly impressed with a conviction of the real end and use of all such [ornamental] attainments; namely, that they are designed, in the first place, to supply her hours of leisure with innocent and amusing occupations; occupations which may prevent the languor and the snares of idleness, render home attractive, refresh the wearied faculties, and contribute to preserve the mind in a state of placid cheerfulness, which is the most favourable to sentiments of benevolence to mankind and of gratitude to God; and in the next place, to enable her to communicate a kindred pleasure, with all its beneficial effects, to her family and friends, to all with whom she is now, or may hereafter, be intimately connected.

A FASHIONABLE FINISHING SCHOOL (1830s)
Frances Power Cobbe
(See pp. 92, 121, 162, and 261.)

The boarding school Frances Power Cobbe describes here was one of the most respected such establishments in the 1830s. Located in fashionable Brighton, it was also, according to Cobbe, outrageously expensive, the nominal fee of £120 to £130 per annum representing scarcely a fourth of the potential charges for "extras" like music and French. Cobbe's bill was £1,000 for two years' schooling, a sum comparable at that time to the cost of three years at Cambridge or Oxford

An "accomplished" young lady

for young men. Cobbe's experience left her an early and devoted advocate of university education for women. In 1862, she presented the idea to the National Association for the Promotion of Social Science. Though her request was met with "universal ridicule" by the press, it marked the beginning of the campaign that led to the opening of universities to women on an equal basis with men.

The din of our large double schoolrooms was something frightful. Sitting in either of them, four pianos might be heard going at once in rooms above and around us, while at numerous tables scattered about the rooms there were girls reading aloud to the governesses and reciting lessons in English, French, German, and Italian. This hideous clatter continued the entire day till we went to bed at night, there being no time whatever allowed for recreation, unless the dreary hour of walking with our teachers (when we recited our verbs) could be so described by a fantastic imagination. In the midst of the uproar we were obliged to write our exercises, to compose our themes, and to commit to memory whole pages of prose.

On Saturday afternoons, instead of play, there was a terrible ordeal generally known as the "Judgment Day." The two schoolmistresses sat side by side, solemn and stern, at the head of the long table. Behind them sat all the governesses as Assessors. On the table were the books wherein our evil deeds of the week were recorded; and round the room against the wall, seated on stools of penitential discomfort, we sat . . . expecting our sentences according to our ill-deserts. It must be explained that the fiendish ingenuity of some teacher had invented for our torment a system of imaginary "cards," which we were supposed to "lose" (though we never gained any) whenever we had not finished all our various lessons and practisings every night before bed-time, or whenever we had been given the mark for "stooping," or had been impertinent, or had been "turned" in our lessons, or had been marked "P" by the music master, or had been convicted of "dis-order" (e.g., having our long shoe-strings untied), or, lastly, had told lies! . . . I have seen . . . no less than nine young ladies obliged to sit for hours in the angles of the three rooms, like naughty babies, with their faces to the wall; half of them being quite of marriageable age and all dressed, as was *de rigueur* with us every day, in full evening attire of silk or muslin, with gloves and kid slippers. . . . Those who escaped the fell destiny of the corner were allowed, if they chose, to write to their parents, but our letters were perforce committed at night to the schoolmistress to seal, and were not, as may be imagined, exactly the natural outpouring of our sentiments as regarded those ladies and their school.

On the whole, looking back after the long interval, it seems to me that the young creatures there assembled were full of capabilities for widely extended usefulness and influence. . . . But all this fine human material was deplorably wasted. Nobody dreamed that any one of us could in later life be more or less than an "Ornament of Society." That a pupil in that school should ever become an artist, or authoress, would have been looked upon by Miss Runeiman and Miss Roberts as a deplorable dereliction. . . . Everything was taught us in the inverse ratio of its true importance. At the bottom of the scales were

BBC Hulton Picture Library

Caricature of early-nineteenth-century schools of deportment for girls. The artist, Edward Burney, is ridiculing the practicing of graceful attitudes and the use of absurd and uncomfortable devices to encourage good posture.

Morals and Religion, and at the top were Music and Dancing; miserably poor music, too, of the Italian school then in vogue, and generally performed in a showy and tasteless manner on harp or piano. . . . The waste of money involved in all this, the piles of useless music, and songs never to be sung, for which our parents had to pay, and the loss of priceless time for ourselves, were truly deplorable; and the result of course in many cases (as in my own) complete failure. . . .

Next to music in importance in our curriculum came dancing. The famous old Madame Michaud and her husband both attended us constantly, and we danced to their direction in our large play-room . . . till we had learned not only all the dances in use in England in that anti-polka epoch, but almost every national dance in Europe, the Minuet, the Gavotte, the Cachucha, the Bolero, the Mazurka, and the Tarantella. To see that stout old lady in her heavy green velvet dress, with furbelow a foot deep of sable, going through the latter cheerful performance for our example, was a sight not to be forgotten. Beside the dancing we had "calisthenic" lessons every week from a "Capitaine" Somebody, who put us through manifold exercises with poles and dumbbells. How much better a few country scrambles would have been than all these calisthenics it is needless to say, but our dismal walks were confined to parading the esplanade and neighbouring terraces. . . .

Beyond all this, our English studies embraced one long, awful lesson each week to be repeated to the schoolmistress herself by a class, in History one week, in Geography the week following. Our first class, I remember, had once to commit to memory—Heaven alone knows how—no less than thirteen pages of Woodhouselee's "Universal History"! . . .

Each morning we were bound publicly to repeat a text out of certain little books, called "Daily Bread," left in our bedrooms, and always scanned in frantic haste while "doing-up" our hair at the glass, or gabbled aloud by one damsel so occupied while her room-fellow (there were never more than two in each bed-chamber) was splashing about behind the screen in her bath.

It is almost needless to add, in concluding these reminiscences, that the heterogeneous studies pursued in this helter-skelter fashion were of the smallest possible utility in later life; each acquirement being of the shallowest and most imperfect kind, and all real education worthy of the name having to be begun on our return home, after we had been pronounced "finished." Meanwhile the strain on our mental powers of getting through daily, for six months at a time, this mass of ill-arranged and miscellaneous lessons, was extremely great and trying. . . .

If true education be the instilling into the mind, not so much Knowledge, as the desire for Knowledge, mine at school certainly proved a notable failure. I was brought home (no girl could travel in those days alone) from Brighton by a coach called the Red Rover. . . . My convoy-brother naturally mounted the box, and left me to enjoy the interior all day by myself; and the reflections of those solitary hours of first emancipation remain with me as lively as if they had taken place yesterday. "What a delightful thing it is," so ran my thoughts, "to have done with study! Now I may really enjoy myself! I know as much as any girl in our school, and since it is the best school in England, I *must* know all that it can ever be necessary for a lady to know. I will not trouble my head ever again with learning anything; but read novels and amuse myself for the rest of my life."

This noble resolve lasted, I fancy, a few months, and then depth

below depth of my ignorance revealed itself very unpleasantly! I tried
to supply first one deficiency and then another till, after a year or two,
I began to educate myself in earnest.

In Frances Power Cobbe, *Autobiography* (1894)

LESSONS FOR LADIES (1867)
M. A. Johnston

*Miss Johnston's book of exercises and others like it were widely used
by governesses and teachers. The pupil would prepare a lesson by
memorizing the answers to varied sets of questions like those below.
The governess herself would be unlikely to know more about a subject than the information provided in the terse answers, which were
often memorized by the students in improper order with comic results. According to Miss Johnston, "the frequent change of subject
[produces] greater readiness of mind and [tends] to sustain the interest of the pupil."*

Lesson 1.

1. Mention Wordsworth's chief works, and the characteristics of his
   poetry.
2. Whence the quotations "Coming events cast their shadows before"—"What's in a name," &c.—"My poverty, but not my will,
   consents"?
3. Who are the authors of "The Task," "Scots wha hae wi' Wallace
   bled," "The Revolt of Islam," "The Corsair," "The Dunciad,"
   "Christabel," "The Angel in the House," and "Hiawatha"?
4. Mention the three famous Greek contemporaries, during the first
   Persian war, with their characters and achievements.
5. Who always ended his speeches in the senate, with "Delenda est
   Carthago"?
6. Who founded L'Académie Française?
Theme: Compare the Revolution in England in the reign of Charles I
with that in France in the reign of Louis XVI.

Lesson 2.

1. Whose are the expressions, "L'Etat c'est moi," "Après moi le
   déluge," and "Qui ne sait pas dissimuler ne sait pas régner"?

2. What do quadrumana and pachydermata signify, and how are
   these families represented in Europe?
3. Name the last three Laureates, and their chief works.
4. Some account of the Escurial.
5. Who was Deucalion?
6. When was the Bank of England established?
Theme: Modern Inventions.

Lesson 3.

1. Name the chief places of historic interest in England.
2. Which is the planet nearest the sun, and which the most distant?
   Name their diameters, and the time they take to revolve round
   the sun.
3. Chief characters of the reign of Augustus Caesar?
4. An account of the education of the Spartan youth, with the defects
   and virtues produced by the system.
5. Mention the chief generals of Napoleon I.
6. How many orders of architecture are there?
Theme: Pride.

In M. A. Johnston, *The Ladies' College and School Examiner* (1867)

DISCOURAGEMENT OF A YOUNG WRITER (1809)
Ellen "Nelly" Weeton
(See p. 103.)

Whether I should have made any figure in literature or no, is not for
me to decide; but surely no one's ardour was ever more damaged than
mine. My mother and my brother shewed the strongest disapproba-
tion of every little production I shewed them, yet notwithstanding
the little encouragement I met with, I could not forbear composing
sometimes. At eleven years old, I wrote a play. As this was my first
production, except a letter now and then and an immense heap of
prose Enigmas, my mother had not reflected on the consequences
that might possibly follow a little encouragement or approbation, and
permitted me to dedicate three whole weeks to the writing of my
play. How busy was I! How delighted! The 5th of November was to
be a festival to the girls under my mother's tuition, and this day was
fixed upon to act this play. I wrote each their part out separately,
that each might study it at home. The day, the grand day, at length
arrived; the play was acted. . . . It went off, according to our ideas,

very well, and for many a day after afforded a subject for conversation as we sat at our work in the school. . . . From that time my mother continually checked any propensity I shewed to writing or composing; representing to me what a useless being I should prove if I were allowed to give up my time to writing or reading, when domestic duties were likely to have so frequent a call upon me. "It is very likely, my dear girl," she would often say, "that you will have to earn your own livelihood, at least in a great measure; and a *wretched* subsistence do they obtain who have it to earn by their literary abilities! Or should you become a wife, think in what a ragged, neglected state your family would be if you gave up much of your time to books." This kind of conversation certainly made a deep impression on me; indeed, it was too frequently repeated to allow a possibility of my forgetting it; and too many living instances were pointed out to my notice, to permit me to be blind to the injurious consequences of females dedicating their time to the increase of literary knowledge. Yet that impression had little apparent influence; for what I before did openly because my mother seemed pleased with it, I now practised by stealth, till she found it necessary positively to prohibit the use of pen and ink, or slate pencil, except whilst receiving instruction from her or the writing master. My brother was made a spy upon my actions, and by way of deterring me from disobeying my mother, would often threaten to tell her when he had seen me writing upon the wall with a pin, which sometimes I did when I had no other resources. . . . [A]s it was almost impossible to be out of either his sight or hers, I had little opportunity of indulging a propensity that was so strong, except during the hour of the writing master's attendance. He was not so watchful, and I could finish more than my expected share of arithmetical or grammatical exercises, and have some time to spare; but alas! I was obliged to rub off my slate, almost as soon as written, what I had transcribed there, lest my mother should come to examine when the writing master was gone. . . .

In Ellen Weeton, *Miss Weeton: Journal of a Governess, 1807–1811*, ed. Edward Hall (1936)

EDUCATION OF A WOMAN OF SCIENCE (1791–1813)
Mary Somerville

Growing up in Scotland at the end of the eighteenth century, Mary Fairfax Somerville (1780–1872) enjoyed a high degree of physical freedom. In her native seashore town of Burntisland, she cultivated an observant eye for nature, an education which was more useful to her than all her formal lessons in deportment, dancing, and pastry making. Although she was fifty-one years old when she first received serious attention as a scientific writer, by midcentury she was regularly referred to as the most remarkable woman of her time, living proof that women could excel at the male pursuits of mathematics and scientific investigation. Somerville's work as a mathematical astronomer and expositor of science influenced the teaching and practice of the physical sciences in England and America, and helped establish the standard for modern scientific writing. Her name led the first petition presented to Parliament in support of women's suffrage. Oxford's Somerville College for women, founded in 1879, was named for her.

Although her account of her roundabout self-education makes clear that her socialization as a woman was a handicap to her, midcentury feminists like her friend Frances Power Cobbe rejoiced in Somerville's domestic skills, her pleasure in mothering, and her warm second marriage. They considered her the proof of her friend Sydney Smith's contention that "a woman's love for her children hardly depends upon her ignorance of Greek, nor need we apprehend that she will forsake an infant for a quadratic equation." Somerville bore six children, three of whom died in childhood.

In her daughter's words, Mary's first husband, Captain Samuel Grief, who died in 1807 after three years of marriage, "possessed in full the prejudice against learned women which was common at that time." Only after her marriage to the sophisticated army officer William Somerville in 1812 did she at last meet "with one who entirely sympathized with her, and warmly entered into all her ideas, encouraging her zeal for study to the utmost." Her second husband "frankly and willingly acknowledged her superiority to himself [and took] honest pride and gratification . . . in the fame and honours she attained."

[A]t ten years old I was sent to a boarding-school, kept by a Miss Primrose, at Musselburgh, where I was utterly wretched. . . . A few days after my arrival, although perfectly straight and well-made, I was enclosed in stiff stays with a steel busk in front, while, above my frock, bands drew my shoulders back till the shoulder-blades met. Then a steel rod, with a semi-circle which went under the chin, was clasped to the steel busk in my stays. In this constrained state I, and most of the younger girls, had to prepare our lessons. The chief thing I had to do was to learn by heart a page of Johnson's dictionary, not only to spell the words, give their parts of speech and meaning, but as an exercise of memory to remember their order of succession. Besides I had to learn the first principles of writing, and the rudiments of French and English grammar. The method of teaching was extremely tedious and inefficient. . . .

Soon after my return home [about a year later] I received a note from a lady in the neighbourhood, inquiring for my mother, who had been ill. This note greatly distressed me, for . . . I could neither compose an answer nor spell the words. . . . The school at Musselburgh was expensive, and I was reproached with having cost so much money in vain. My mother said she would have been content if I had only learnt to write well and keep accounts, which was all that a woman was expected to know. . . .

My mother did not prevent me from reading, but my aunt Janet, who came to live in Burntisland after her father's death, greatly disapproved of my conduct. She was an old maid who could be very agreeable and witty, but she had all the prejudices of the time with regard to women's duties, and said to my mother, "I wonder you let Mary waste her time in reading, she never *shews* (sews) more than if she were a man." Whereupon I was sent to the village school to learn plain needlework. I do not remember how long it was after this that an old lady sent some very fine linen to be made into shirts for her brother, and desired that one should be made entirely by me. This shirt was so well worked that I was relieved from attending the school, but the house linen was given into my charge to make and to mend. . . .

We had two small globes, and my mother allowed me to learn the use of them from Mr. Reed, the village schoolmaster, who came to teach me for a few weeks in the winter evenings. Besides the ordinary branches, Mr. Reed taught Latin and navigation, but these were out of the question for me. At the village school the boys often learnt Latin, but it was thought sufficient for the girls to be able to read the Bible; very few even learnt writing.

My bedroom had a window to the south, and a small closet near had one to the north. At these I spent many hours, studying the stars by the aid of the celestial globe. . . .

I was often invited with my mother to the tea-parties given either by widows or maiden ladies who resided at Burntisland. . . . I there became acquainted with a Miss Ogilvie, much younger than the rest, who asked me to go and see fancy works she was doing, and at which she was very clever. I went next day, and after admiring her work, and being told how it was done, she showed me a monthly magazine with coloured plates of ladies' dresses, charades, and puzzles. At the end of a page I read what appeared to me to be simply an arithmetical question; but on turning the page I was surprised to see strange-looking lines mixed with letters, chiefly X's and Y's, and asked "What is that?" "Oh," said Miss Ogilvie, "it is a kind of arithmetic: they call it Algebra; but I can tell you nothing about it." And we talked about other things; but on going home I thought I would look if any of our books could tell me what was meant by Algebra.

In Robertson's "Navigation" I flattered myself that I had got precisely what I wanted; but I soon found that I was mistaken. I perceived, however, that astronomy did not consist in star-gazing, and as I persevered in studying the book for a time, I certainly got a dim view of several subjects which were useful to me afterwards. Unfortunately not one of our acquaintances or relations knew anything of science or natural history; nor, had they done so, should I have had courage to ask any of them a question, for I should have been laughed at. I was often very sad and forlorn; not a hand held out to help me. . . .

Nasmyth, an exceedingly good landscape painter, had opened an academy for ladies in Edinburgh, a proof of the gradual improvement which was taking place in the education of the higher classes; my mother very willingly allowed me to attend it. . . . Mr. Nasmyth, besides being a very good artist, was clever, well-informed, and had a great deal of conversation. One day I happened to be near him while he was talking to the Ladies Douglas about perspective. He said, "You should study Euclid's Elements of Geometry; the foundation not only of perspective, but of astronomy and all mechanical science." Here, in the most unexpected manner, I got the information I wanted, for I at once saw that it would help me to understand some parts of Robertson's "Navigation"; but as to going to a bookseller and asking for Euclid the thing was impossible! Besides I did not yet know anything definite about Algebra, so no more could be done at that time; but I never lost sight of an object which had interested me from the first. . . .

On returning to Burntisland, I played on the piano as diligently as ever, and painted several hours every day. At this time, however, a

Mr. Craw came to live with us as tutor to my youngest brother, Henry. He had been educated for the kirk [church], was a fair Greek and Latin scholar, but, unfortunately for me, was no mathematician. He was a simple, good-natured kind of man, and I ventured to ask him about algebra and geometry, and begged him, the first time he went to Edinburgh, to buy me something elementary on these subjects, so he soon brought me "Euclid" and Bonnycastle's "Algebra," which were the books used in the schools at that time. Now I had got what I so long and earnestly desired. I asked Mr. Craw to hear me demonstrate a few problems in the first book of "Euclid," and then I continued the study alone with courage and assiduity, knowing I was on the right road. . . .

I had to take part in the household affairs, and to make and mend my own clothes. I rose early, played on the piano, and painted during the time I could spare in the daylight hours, but I sat up very late reading Euclid. The servants, however, told my mother "It was no wonder the stock of candles was soon exhausted, for Miss Mary sat up reading till a very late hour"; whereupon an order was given to take away my candle as soon as I was in bed. I had, however, already gone through the first six books of Euclid, and now I was thrown on my memory, which I exercised by beginning at the first book, and demonstrating in my mind a certain number of problems every night, till I could nearly go through the whole. My father came home for a short time, and, somehow or other, finding out what I was about, said to my mother, "Peg, we must put a stop to this, or we shall have Mary in a strait jacket one of these days. There was X., who went raving mad about the longitude!" . . .

I was very much out of health after my [first] husband's death, and chiefly occupied with my children, especially with the one I was nursing; but as I did not go into society, I rose early, and, having plenty of time, I resumed my mathematical studies. . . . I became acquainted with Mr. Wallace, editor of a mathematical journal. . . . I had solved some of the problems contained in it and sent them to him, which led to a correspondence, as Mr. Wallace sent me his own solutions in return. Mine were sometimes right and sometimes wrong, and it occasionally happened that we solved the same problem by different methods. At last I succeeded in solving a prize problem! . . . I was awarded a silver medal cast on purpose with my name, which pleased me exceedingly.

Mr. Wallace was elected Professor of Mathematics in the University of Edinburgh, and was very kind to me. When I told him that I earnestly desired to go through a regular course of mathematical and astronomical science, even including the highest branches, he gave me a list of the requisite books. . . . I was thirty-three years of age when I bought this excellent little library. I could hardly believe that I possessed such a treasure when I looked back on the day that I first saw the mysterious word "Algebra," and the long course of years in which I had persevered almost without hope. It taught me never to despair. I had now the means, and pursued my studies with increased assiduity; concealment was no longer possible, nor was it attempted. I was considered eccentric and foolish, and my conduct was highly disapproved of by many, especially by some members of my own family. . . . They expected me to entertain and keep a gay house for them, and in that they were disappointed.

In *Personal Recollections from Early Life to Old Age of Mary Somerville*, ed. Martha Somerville (1873)

TWO

The Debate on Education

The reforms in the education of women, which were urged and in large part accomplished in the nineteenth century, posed a basic challenge to the social and even biological understanding of the differences between the sexes. The debate on education began as a debate on the purposes of women's lives: what should women be trained to be? The initial answers were that they were to be ornaments to the home, at best companions to men, and at very best mothers. As Sarah Ellis put it, "the first thing of importance is to be content to be inferior to men, inferior in mental power in the same proportion that you are inferior in bodily strength." Moreover, it was not just conservatives like Ellis, Sewell, and Landels who thought that learning was irreconcilable with womanliness. Feminists like Martineau and Butler found they could not easily assimilate their new goals of autonomy and independent thought for women into their belief in women's domesticity, passivity, and powers of nurturance. Even a pioneering feminist like Dr. Elizabeth Garrett Anderson found it difficult to overcome her sense of womanly modesty to address publicly the question of menstrual disorders in her reply to Maudsley's attack on women's intellectual capabilities.

Beneath the cultural and ideological debate were deeper economic and psychological issues. Women needed access to the new schooling in order to become self-supporting (see Part IV). At the same time, their entry into formerly male domains raised primitive fears of the eradication of sexual differences. It now seemed possible that women might not only cease to be conventionally submissive, dependent, and self-sacrificing, but that they might also refuse to love and marry men and to bear and rear children. The magnitude of the fears evoked by women's educational progress is a significant measure of the widespread social importance of the change.

SUBDUED, PASSIVE AUTOMATONS (1843)
Marion Reid

Mrs. Reid's early feminist-suffragist tract was written partly as a refutation of Sarah Lewis's Woman's Mission (see Part I). Although she argued that women should be educated in order to make better mothers, she had a stronger sense of women's need for intellectual autonomy than many of her contemporaries.

If, instead of looking at the amount of actual instruction provided for the young, we look to the spirit which pervades that instruction, we shall find the education of young women as defective in [spirit] as it is deficient in [instruction]. A proper education may be stated shortly to be that training which assists the mind to look into itself, which enables it to see its own powers and to use them effectively. Now, the education of girls, whatever facts it may teach them, does not, we think, tend to expand and develop their minds, but to cramp and confine them. Far from being encouraged to use their own faculties, any symptom of independent thought is quickly repressed. The consequence, as might be expected, is, that the majority of girls are subdued into mere automatons—their very excellences are not made their own, by being powerfully grasped by their own minds; they are rather the physical effect of example and habit, than the result of the exercise of their own moral and intellectual nature. Hence, many women pass a considerable portion of their lives with great apparent propriety, paying even more than due submission to the guardian—be he husband, brother, or father—who happens to have charge of the grown baby. Yet if any strong passion, such as love, jealousy, or hatred, takes possession of her mind, she will allow it to burst forth with such fury, as manifestly to show that her former good conduct was quite mechanical, and proceeded from no firm principle rooted in her mind. Nay, we have observed in every such case, that the more submissive and subservient a woman has been before such an outburst of passion, the more perfectly does she show a want of all self-control when it is required. The effect of the common system of female education is to produce a mechanical performance of duty, converting women into mere machines; so that all the good they do is towards others, their own minds all the while lying barren and unfruitful. For our part, we would rather see a few errors in routine, if accompanied with the true self-improving spirit, than the most faultless exterior of mechanical performance of duty, convinced that, in any emergency out of the usual routine, the first would stand fast and the last would utterly fail.

We confess we feel strongly the evil of the tendency of female education to produce a mere automaton—a subdued, passive tool, which the elements of society fashion outwardly, but which has no inward power to seize upon those elements and convert them into means of growth, both moral and intellectual.

In Mrs. Hugo Reid, A *Plea for Women* (1843)

AGAINST HIGHER EDUCATION FOR WOMEN (1868)
Sarah Sewell

Sarah Sewell, an antifeminist and antisuffragist writer, believed that finishing schools, like the one Frances Power Cobbe attended, destroyed the "genuine simplicity and purity of morals learned at home," substituting "a smattering of a number of showy accomplishments, which they exercise to get a lover." She was equally opposed to any higher standard of education for women, as indicated by the passage below, which sums up a popular Victorian argument against higher education for women.

The education of girls need not be of the same extended, classical, and commercial character as that of boys; they want more an education of the heart and feelings, and especially of firm, fixed, moral principles. They should be made conversant with history, geography, figures, the poets, and general literature, with a sure groundwork of religion and obedience. The profoundly educated women rarely make good wives or mothers. The pride of knowledge does not amalgamate well with the every-day matter of fact rearing of children, and women who have stored their minds with Latin and Greek seldom have much knowledge of pies and puddings, nor do they enjoy the hard and uninteresting work of attending to the wants of little children; and those women, poor things, who have lost their most attractive charm of womanliness, and are seen on the public platforms, usurping the exclusive duties of men, are seldom seen in their nurseries; though they may become notorious themselves, their children rarely do them credit, and the energy they throw away upon the equalising bubble, would be much better expended in a more womanly and motherly manner, in looking after their husbands' comforts, the training of their children, and the good of the household at large.

In Sarah Sewell, *Women and the Times We Live In* (1868)

THE MENTAL CAPACITY OF
MEN AND WOMEN (1870)
William Landels

William Landels (1823–1899), a Baptist clergyman who favored the Married Women's Property Act, and even women's suffrage (providing elections could be run more decorously), was nevertheless an exponent of the popular belief in the intrinsic weakness of women's intellect relative to men's.

Man excels in imagination, woman in fancy. Man has the profounder reflection, woman the quicker discernment. Man surpasses woman in reasoning power, and in the judgments which are necessarily founded on, and which require therefore to grasp, a lengthened process of argument; woman surpasses man in intuitive perception and tact. Man can handle facts better than she, and grasp principles; she can deal better with persons. She sees at a glance the conclusion at which man arrives by a slow process. . . . He reflects profoundly on facts and principles, laboriously manipulating them, and marshalling and remarshalling, that he may arrive safely at generalisations which he can turn to practical account; she, on the other hand, using her quick perception, brings it immediately to bear on the details of practical life, and, without stopping to reason about them, uses her fine tact in applying to others the things which she knows.

Man's profounder study may lead to greater results in politics, or law, or physics, or engineering, or science, or art; but woman's more sprightly and vivacious movements render her the most charming and agreeable companion, the best fitted to enliven the intercourse of home, and to exert the most potent influence on human feelings and character. Thus her mental and bodily capacity point both in the same direction, and mark her out for the same sphere. The body which unfits her for the rough competition and jostling which belongs to public life, is not matched to a mind which requires to move in that public sphere. . . .

In William Landels, *Woman: Her Position and Power* (1870)

STRONG-MINDEDNESS (1866)
Charlotte Carmichael Stopes

The accusation of "strong-mindedness" was one of the most effective social weapons used against women seeking to be educated or intellectually assertive. Debating and discussion societies, such as the one described here, provided one opportunity for women to build up their confidence. But as Charlotte Carmichael Stopes's (1841–1929) memoir makes clear, even with collective support it took an effort for individual women to overcome internalized prohibitions against "unwomanly" behavior.

Stopes herself overcame her early lack of confidence to become a noted writer on Shakespearean questions. She was the mother of the well-known sex reformer and birth-control advocate, Marie Stopes.

[For years I had] heard of discussion Societies of brothers and male friends, of students in that much-hungered-for University, under whose portals no women could enter as undergraduates. When I was ready for it I was, however, taken to a real Literary Society. The Misses Mair had formed one among their class fellows and friends in Abercromby Place, Edinburgh, the house of their mother . . . and a friend introduced me as a member. This was different from other societies of the kind, in having, as the fundamental reason for its existence, the editing of its own Magazine. But it looked forward to include debates, and the very day I joined the members *discussed* a *Discussion*. We were invited to give our opinion if such an exercise would be desirable. I remember replying: "Yes, I think the discussion the most important part of any Society. We can write in any magazine, but we can only learn to speak among ourselves." That was early in 1866.

At the next meeting we had a debate on the subject "Ought women to be strong-minded." There was a paper on each side, well-written, timidly read, duly supported, but discussion flagged. It was

evidently handicapped by some strong things said against "unwomanly strong-minded women." Suddenly I heard my name called, with
a mild reproach that I had not seemed very ready to take the opportunity of learning to speak. I had taught myself that when anything
unpleasant had to be done, it was better to get it over than to think
about it. So I rose at once. If I relate what followed, it is only for the
benefit of beginners. . . . A tearing traffic seemed to have started
through the quiet street, salvoes of artillery resounded from the castle,
and an earthquake shook the foundations of the rock-built house in
which we met. My own sensations matched my surroundings, my
ears rang, my head swam, my knees trembled, my back ached, my
heart stood still, and then tried to beat down its bounds, and a lump
stuck in my throat larger than ever Adam's apple grew. I spasmodi-
cally gasped, "Ought women to be *weak-minded?*" and then my
parched tongue absolutely refused to move further, all the ideas that
had been coursing through my brain five minutes before had vanished,
and I sat down in shame and confusion. It took half-an-hour before
the storm and tremor ceased, and my heart beat normally.

In *Englishwoman's Review*, July 1902

REASONS FOR FEMALE EDUCATION (1823–1861)
Harriet Martineau
(See pp. 96, 149, 161, 291, 330, and 364.)

*The first selection that follows is from an essay Harriet Martineau
published anonymously at age twenty-one; the second is from a protest she made four decades later against the timid reformism of the
directors of Queen's College (see p. 312). Together they illustrate the
way the attitude of educational reformers changed as women's education grew in strength and popularity.*

I wish to imply . . . not that great stores of information are as necessary to women as to men, but that as much care should be taken of
the formation of their minds. . . .
    It must be allowed by all, that one of woman's first duties is to
qualify herself for being a companion to her husband, or to those
with whom her lot in life is cast. She was formed to be a domestic
companion, and such a one as shall give to home its charms, as

shall furnish such entertainment that her husband need not be driven abroad for amusement. This is one of the first duties required from a woman. . . . If [her] thoughts are continually occupied by the vanities of the world, if that time which is not required for the fulfillment of household duties, is spent in folly, or even in harmless trifles in which the husband has no interest, how are the powers of pleasing to be perpetuated, how is she to find interesting subjects for social converse? Surely these desirable objects are best promoted by the hours of leisure being devoted to the acquirement of useful knowledge, such knowledge as may excite the reflective powers, enlarge and steady the mind, and raise it, nearly at least, to the level of the other sex. Thus there may be companionship between the sexes, and surely no woman who aspires to and labours for this end can be accused of neglecting her peculiar duties. But for this object to be completely gained, the work must be begun early. . . .

If we consider woman as the guardian and instructress of infancy, her claims to cultivation of mind become doubly urgent. It is evident that if the soul of the teacher is narrow and contracted, that of the pupil cannot be enlarged. . . . It has been frequently and justly observed, that almost all men, remarkable for talents or virtue, have had excellent mothers, to the early influence of whose noble qualities, the future superiority of their children was mainly to be ascribed. If this be true, what might not be hoped from the labours of a race of enlightened mothers. . . .

Let woman then be taught that . . . her proper sphere is *home*— that there she is to provide, not only for the bodily comfort of man, but that she is to enter also into community of mind with him; . . . that she is to be the participator in his happiness, the consoler of his sorrows, the support of his weakness, and his friend under all circumstances. For this purpose she must exert her own faculties, store her mind, strengthen her reason, and so far enrich her natural powers by cultivation, as to be capable of performing the important duties which fall to her lot. . . . Like our attendant planet, let her, while she is the constant companion of man, borrow sufficient light from the sun of knowledge to cheer him in his hours of darkness, and he will find that the progress she makes towards this great luminary will not interfere with the companionship she owes to him.

Harriet Martineau, "On Female Education," *Monthly Repository*, February 1823

[T]he majority of the friends of female education . . . think they have said everything when they have recommended good intellectual training as fitting women to be "mothers of heroes," "companions to men," and so on. No great deal will be done for female improvement while this sort of sentiment is supposed to be the loftiest and most liberal. Girls will never make a single effort, in any length of school years, for such an object as being companions to men, and mothers of heroes. If they work, and finally justify the pains taken for them in establishing such colleges as these, it will be for the same reasons that boys work well and come out worthy of their schooling, because they like their studies, and enjoy the sense of moral and mental development which is so strong in school and college years; and because their training is well adapted to educe, develope, and strengthen their powers and render them as wise and good as their natures, years, and circumstances permit. Till it is proposed, in educating girls, to make them, in themselves and for their own sakes, as good specimens of the human being as the conditions of the case may allow, very little will be effected by any expenditure of time, pains, and money.

As quoted in *Englishwoman's Review*, April 1876

WOMANLINESS, MANLINESS, AND EDUCATION (1868)

Josephine Butler

(See pp. 138, 295, 317, 428, 435, and 436.)

Josephine Butler was a strong proponent of higher education for women and an early supporter of Newnham College, Cambridge. Butler's major life achievement, her campaign against the double standard of sexual conduct as it was expressed in state attempts to regulate prostitution, derived from the same deeply felt sense of "a common standard of excellence for men and women" that she expresses here.

There are two classes of advocates of the improvement of the education and condition of women. The one class urge everything from the domestic point of view. They argue in favour of all which is likely to make women better mothers, or better companions for men, but they seem incapable of judging of a woman as a human being by herself, and superstitiously afraid of anything which might strengthen her to stand alone, prepared, singlehanded, to serve her God and her country. When it is urged upon them that the women who do and must stand alone are counted by millions, they are perplexed, but only fall back on expressions of fear lest a masculine race of women should be produced, if we admit any theories respecting them apart from conjugal and maternal relationships.

On the other hand, there are advocates who speak with some slight contempt of maternity, in whose advocacy there appears to me little evidence of depth of thought, or tenderness, or wisdom, and which bespeaks a dry, hard, unimaginative conception of human life. They appear to have no higher ideal for a woman than that of a *man* who has been "tripos'ed" [won university honors], and is going to "get on in the world," either in the way of making money or acquiring fame. They speak of women as if it were a compliment to them, or in any way true, to say that they are like men. . . .

The first class of advocates do not know how deeply the maternal character is rooted in almost all women, married or unmarried. . . . Every good quality, every virtue which we regard as distinctively womanly will, under conditions of greater freedom, develop more freely, like plants brought out into the light from a cellar in which they languished, dwarfed and blanched, without sun or air. . . . It will always be in her nature to foster, to cherish, to take the part of the weak, to train, to guide, to have a care for individuals, to discern the small seeds of a great future, to warm and cherish those seeds into fulness of life. "I serve," will always be one of her favourite mottos, even should the utmost freedom be accorded her in the choice of vocation; for she, more readily perhaps than men do, recognises the wisdom and majesty of Him who said—"I am among you as he that serveth." . . .

The second kind of advocacy of the rights of women, of which I spoke, may be said to be simply a reaction against the first. It is chiefly held by a few women of superior intellect who feel keenly the disadvantages of their class; their feebleness, through want of education, against public opinion, which is taken advantage of by base people; their inability, through want of representation, to defend their weaker members; and the dwarfing of the faculties of the ablest and best among them. These women have associated little with men, or, at best, know very little of their inner life, and do not therefore see, as clearly as they see their own loss, the equal loss that it is to men, and the injury it involves to their characters to live dissociated from women: they therefore look forth from their isolation with some-

thing of an excusable envy on the freer and happier lot, which includes, they believe, a greater power to do good, and imagine that
the only hope for themselves is to push into the ranks of men, to
demand the same education, the same opportunities, in order that
they may compete with them on their own ground. They have lost
the conception of the noblest development possible for both men
and women; for assuredly that which men, for the most part, aim at,
is not the noblest, and yet that is what such women appear to wish
to imitate. . . . When St. Chrysostom preached in Constantinople,
that "men ought to be pure, and women courageous," he was treated
as a dangerous innovator, a perverter of the facts of nature, a changer
of customs. I hope that many such innovators will arise, who will
show forth in practise the possibility of the attainment of a common
standard of excellence for man and woman, not by usurpation on
either hand, nor by servile imitation, but by the action of each upon
each, by mutual teaching and help.

In Josephine Butler, "The Education and Employment of Women," *Woman's
World*, July 1868 (also published as pamphlet, 1868)

"SEX AND MIND IN EDUCATION" (1874)
Dr. Henry Maudsley

*Dr. Henry Maudsley (1835–1918) brought the discussion of women's
natural disabilities out of the medical journals and into the realm of
public debate with this controversial article, which relied upon the
widespread contemporary medical view of menstruation as a disability.
Maudsley was a prominent psychiatric physician who operated his
own private mental hospital for women.*

It is quite evident that many of those who are foremost in their zeal
for raising the education and social status of woman, have not given
proper consideration to the nature of her organization, and to the demands which its special functions make upon its strength. . . . Before
sanctioning the proposal to subject woman to a system of mental
training which has been framed and adapted for men, . . . it is needful
to consider whether this can be done without serious injury to her
health and strength. It is not enough to point to exceptional instances
of women who have undergone such a training, and have proved their

capacities when tried by the same standard as men; without doubt there are women who can, and will, so distinguish themselves if stimulus be applied and opportunity given; the question is, whether they may not do it at a cost which is too large a demand upon the resources of their nature. Is it well for them to contend on equal terms with men for the goal of man's ambition?

Let it be considered that the period of the real educational strain will commence about the time when, by the development of the sexual system, a great revolution takes place in the body and mind, and an extraordinary expenditure of vital energy is made, and will continue through those years after puberty when, by the establishment of periodical functions, a regularly recurring demand is made upon the resources of a constitution that is going through the final stages of its growth and development. The energy of a human body being a definite and not inexhaustible quantity, can it bear, without injury, an excessive mental drain as well as the natural physical drain which is so great at that time? Or, will the profit of the one be to the detriment of the other? . . .

Nor is it a sufficient reply to this argument to allege, as is sometimes done, that there are many women who have not the opportunity of getting married, or who do not aspire to bear children; for whether they care to be mothers or not, they cannot dispense with those physiological functions of their nature that have reference to that aim, however much they might wish it, and they cannot disregard them in the labour of life without injury to their health. They cannot choose but to be women; cannot rebel successfully against the tyranny of their organization, the complete development and function whereof must take place after its kind. . . .

It will have to be considered whether women can scorn delights, and live laborious days of intellectual exercise and production, without injury to their functions as the conceivers, mothers, and nurses of children. For it would be an ill thing, if it should so happen, that we got the advantages of a quantity of female intellectual work at the price of a puny, enfeebled, and sickly race. . . .

In the second place, a proper regard to the mental nature of women means attention given to those qualities of mind which correlate the physical differences of her sex. Men are manifestly not so fitted mentally to be the educators of children during the early years of their infancy and childhood; they would be almost as much out of place in going systematically to work to nurse babies as they would be in attempting to suckle them. On the other hand, women are manifestly endowed with qualities of mind which specially fit them to stimulate and foster the first growths of intelligence in children, while the intimate and special sympathies which a mother has with her child as a being which, though individually separate, is still almost a part of her nature, give her an influence and responsibilities which are specially her own. . . .

A small volume, entitled "Sex in Education," which has been published recently by Dr. Edward Clarke of Boston, formerly a Professor in Harvard College, contains a somewhat startling description of the baneful effects upon female health which have been produced by an excessive educational strain. . . . The girl enters upon the hard work of school or college at the age of fifteen or thereabouts, when the function of her sex has perhaps been fairly established; ambitious to stand high in class, she pursues her studies with diligence, perseverence, constancy, allowing herself no days of relaxation or rest out of the schooldays, paying no attention to the periodical tides of her organization, unheeding a drain "that would make the stroke oar of the University crew falter." For a time all seems to go well with her studies; she triumphs over male and female competitors, gains the front rank, and is stimulated to continued exertions in order to hold it. But in the long run nature, which cannot be ignored or defied with impunity, asserts its power; excessive losses occur; health fails, she becomes the victim of aches and pains, is unable to go on with her work, and compelled to seek medical advice. Restored to health by rest from work, a holiday at the sea-side, and suitable treatment, she goes back to her studies, to begin again the same course of unheeding work, until she has completed the curriculum, and leaves college a good scholar but a delicate and ailing woman, whose future life is one of more or less suffering. . . . [I]f she is subsequently married, she is unfit for the best discharge of maternal functions, and is apt to suffer from a variety of troublesome and serious disorders in connection with them. In some cases the brain and the nervous system testify to the exhaustive efforts of undue labour, nervous and even mental disorders declaring themselves.

In *Fortnightly Review*, April 1874

"SEX AND MIND IN EDUCATION: A REPLY" (1874)
Dr. Elizabeth Garrett Anderson

Elizabeth Garrett (1836–1917) left school at fifteen, but felt unsatisfied with the life of a comfortably well off, idle young girl. In March 1859, she heard a speech by the American Elizabeth Blackwell, the world's first woman doctor. Garrett immediately decided that she would try to become the first English woman doctor. Though she found all the schools and hospitals closed to her, she managed to begin training as a nurse at Middlesex Hospital and to gain admission to lectures and even to the dissection room. When she placed first in an exam, however, the male medical students protested her presence and had her thrown out. Garrett then applied for matriculation at London University. Despite the formidable organizing efforts of her friend and close supporter Emily Davies, she was turned down. Instead, she qualified for licensing as a doctor through the Society of Apothecaries—a back door into medical practice that was hastily shut behind her. Garrett eventually received her M.D. from the University of Paris in 1870. The next year she married the steamship merchant James Anderson, with whom she subsequently had two children and an apparently happy family life. Mrs. Garrett Anderson, as she preferred to be called, enjoyed a successful practice among women and children. In 1872, she founded the New Hospital for Women, which was renamed the Elizabeth Garrett Anderson Hospital after her death.

When we are told that in the labour of life women cannot disregard their special physiological functions without danger to health, it is difficult to understand what is meant, considering that in adult life healthy women do as a rule disregard them almost completely. It is, we are convinced, a great exaggeration to imply that women of average health are periodically incapacitated from serious work by the facts of their organization. Among poor women, where all the available strength is spent upon manual labour, the daily work goes on without intermission, and, as a rule, without ill effects. For example, do domestic servants, either as young girls or in mature life, show by experience that a marked change in the amount of work expected from them must be made at these times unless their health is to be injured? It is well known that they do not. . . .

If we had no opportunity of measuring the attainments of ordinary young men, or if they really were the intellectual athletes Dr. Maudsley's warnings would lead us to suppose them to be, the question, "Is it well for women to contend on equal terms with men for the goal of man's ambition?" might be as full of solemnity to us as it is to Dr. Maudsley. As it is, it sounds almost ironical. Hitherto most of the women who have "contended with men for the goal of man's ambition" have had no chance of being any the worse for being allowed to do so on equal terms. They have had all the benefit of being heavily handicapped. Over and above their assumed physical and mental inferiority, they have had to start in the race without a great part of the training men have enjoyed, or they have gained what training they could in an atmosphere of hostility, to remain in which has taxed their strength and endurance far more than any amount of actual mental work could tax it. Would, for instance, the ladies who for five years have been trying to get a medical education at Edinburgh [see p. 311] find their task increased, or immeasurably lightened, by being allowed to contend "on equal terms with men" for that goal? . . .

Even were the dangers of continuous mental work as great as Dr. Maudsley thinks they are, the dangers of a life adapted to develop only the specially and consciously feminine side of the girl's nature would be much greater. From the purely physiological point of view, it is difficult to believe that study much more serious than that usually pursued by young men could do a girl's health as much harm as a life directly calculated to over-stimulate the emotional and sexual instincts, and to weaken the guiding and controlling forces which these instincts so imperatively need. The stimulus found in novel-reading, in the theatre and ball-room, the excitement which attends a premature entry into society, the competition of vanity and frivolity, these involve far more real dangers to the health of young women than the competition for knowledge, or for scientific or literary honours, ever has done, or is ever likely to do. And even if, in the absence of real culture, dissipation be avoided, there is another danger still more difficult to escape, of which the evil physical results are scarcely less grave, and this is dulness. . . .There is no tonic in the pharmacopoeia to be compared with happiness, and happiness worth calling such is not known where the days drag along filled with make-believe occupations and dreary sham amusements. Thousands of young women, strong and blooming at eighteen, become gradually languid and feeble under the depressing influence of dulness, not only in the special functions of womanhood, but in the entire cycle of the processes of nutrition and innervation, till in a few years they are morbid and self-absorbed, or even hysterical. If they had had upon leaving school some solid intellectual work which demanded real thought and excited general interest, and if this interest had been helped by the stimulus of an examination, in which distinction would have been a legitimate source of pride, the number of such cases would probably be indefinitely smaller than it is now. . . . Moreover, by entering society at a somewhat less immature age, a young woman is more able to take an intelligent part in it; is prepared to get more real pleasure from the companionship it affords, and, suffering less from *ennui*, she is less apt to make a hasty and foolish marriage. From the physiological point of view . . . [a] change in the arrangements of young women's lives which tends to discourage very early marriages will probably do more for their health and for the health of their children than any other change could do.

In *Fortnightly Review*, May 1874

THREE

The New Institutions

The revolution in female education began quietly in the late 1840s, with the establishment of the first two serious colleges for women. Queen's College, formed by members of the Governesses' Benevolent Institution, attempted to certify women as governesses to raise their potential earning power and to introduce some measure of professional standards in the single most important occupation open to gentlewomen. Bedford College, established by the wealthy widow Elizabeth Reid, served ladies as well but was more ambitious in its scope. It eventually won affiliation with London University, while Queen's College declined into a secondary school. The differences between these two institutions reflect the two major approaches to women's higher education. Some reformers believed that women should receive separate, specialized education, while others were intent upon offering the same subjects and judging them by the same standards as men.

Emily Davies was the most important and effective champion of the latter view. After doing pioneer work in organizing for passage of the Married Women's Property Laws and the extension of the suffrage to women, she turned her attention in the early 1860s to the cause of higher education for women. In 1863, she arranged for girl students to be admitted for the first time to the Cambridge Local Examinations, a standardized national examination for secondary-school students. There were few schools in England at the time that could adequately prepare a girl for such an examination. The finest two—North London Collegiate School and Ladies College, Cheltenham—were run by Frances Mary Buss and Dorothea Beale, both graduates of Queen's College. Miss Buss, who supplied a large proportion of the first students to be examined, was forced to upgrade the mathematical instruction at her school as a result of the students' dismal showing in that field. Miss Beale, however, declined to let her students participate in the first tests, feeling that girls should be educated and tested separately from boys.

In 1864, Emily Davies persuaded the Schools Inquiry Commission, headed by Lord Taunton, to look into the state of girls' secondary schools. The final report summed up the situation in much the way the feminist reformers saw it:

> We find, as a rule, a very small amount of professional skill, an inferior set of school-books, a vast deal of dry, uninteresting task work, rules put into the memory with no explanation of their principles, no system of examination worthy of the name, a very false estimate of the relative value of the several kinds of acquirements, a reference to effect rather than to solid worth, a tending to fill or to adorn rather than to strengthen the mind.

The Schools Inquiry Commission Report endorsed the local examinations and the upgrading of girls' schools to the level of those run by Miss Buss and Miss Beale. It also recommended that endowment money be made available to girls' schools as it was to boys' schools. In 1871, two sisters with a long-time interest in women's education, Maria Grey and Emily Shirreff, founded the National Union for the Education of Girls, which, through the Girls Public Day School Company, set up over thirty secondary schools based on Miss Buss's model.

The advancement of secondary education provided the basis for extending university education to women. Here Emily Davies made her most significant contribution by establishing at Hitchin in 1869 a women's institution, which originally had five students but which grew to become Girton College, Cambridge. She regarded Newnham College, founded at Cambridge in 1871 by Henry Sidgwick, Anna Jemima Clough, and others, as "the serpent which is gnawing at our vitals," because the Newnham group was ready to accept a separate, special women's examination that excluded Greek and Latin. In women's education, Emily Davies believed that "different means lower."

Latin, Greek, and higher mathematics were then considered the most difficult of all studies and, therefore, the most manly. They carried with them the aura of secret masculine mysteries, and it was even argued that physical prowess was required to master them. Initiation into classical languages was the traditional sign of a gentleman, a means of establishing class differences among men. As a result, the admission of women to such studies meant the passing of a barrier with social as well as economic implications. Given such extreme sexual stereotyping of curriculum, Davies's unwavering insistence upon a single standard of instruction was a powerful strategy. As women routinely began to pass the same examinations as men, it was harder for opponents to argue for the innate inferiority of the female intellect. Gains came slowly, and often as the direct result of a particular student's success. The pressure on the pioneering students was thus extreme, but so was the sense of exhilaration at pushing open new doors for women.

Male undergraduates did not welcome women "competitors" (as they called them) with open arms. As late as 1897, Cambridge students rioted on the occasion of an unsuccessful vote to admit women to the same degrees as men. Yet the old sense of mystification between the sexes could not easily survive their common participation in the privileges and pursuits of university life. A new comaraderie marked the breakdown of the marriage-market mentality, of sexual prudery, and of mutual ignorance, all of which went to make up the social embarrassment between the sexes so often lamented at mid-century.

ON A SINGLE STRAND OF EDUCATION
FOR MEN AND WOMEN (1868)
Emily Davies

Emily Davies (1830–1921) began her feminist life as an active proponent of suffrage. In June 1866, along with Elizabeth Garrett Anderson, she carried the first suffrage petition to Parliament. Like many other women of her time, Davies was introduced to reform work through male relatives, in her case her brother Llewelyn, who came into contact with the Christian socialist educational reformer Frederick Maurice, a founder of the Governesses' Benevolent Institution and of Queen's College for women. From the first, Davies was a fine organizer and a master of political tact. Once devoted to educational reform, she was careful not to associate herself publicly with other feminist causes so as to avoid arousing the anger of those who feared

Demonstration at Cambridge against granting degrees to women, 1897.
An effigy of a woman on a bicycle is hanging above the crowd.

education would make women wild, strong-minded, and recalcitrant family members. Students at Girton College often disagreed with her and rebelled against the strict rules of decorum she established (including, for instance, a ban on college theatricals). But her attention was always on the establishment of an enduring institution, equal to the best of the University Colleges for men, and only secondarily on the interests and needs of the immediate student body. She lived to see Cambridge award "titular" degrees to women in 1921.

This early essay was written just after the victory Davies achieved in having the Cambridge Local Examinations extended to women.

Among the controversies to which the movement for improving the education of women has given rise, there is one which presses for settlement. The question has arisen and must be answered—Is the improved education which, it is hoped, is about to be brought within

reach of women, to be identical with that of men, or is it to be as
good as possible, but in some way or other specifically feminine? The
form in which the question practically first presents itself is—What
shall be the standards of examination? . . .

Probably only women who have laboured under [a double educational standard] can understand the weight of discouragement produced by being perpetually told that, as women, nothing much is
ever to be expected of them, and it is not worth their while to exert
themselves—that they can write lively letters, full of graphic description and homely touches, but that anything like original research or
profound learning is not for them to think of—that whatever they
do they must not interest themselves, except in a second-hand and
shallow way, in the pursuits of men, for in such pursuits they must
always expect to fail. Women who have lived in the atmosphere produced by such teaching know how it stifles and chills; how hard it is
to work courageously through it. Every effort to improve the education of women which assumes that they may, without reprehensible
ambition, study the same subjects as their brothers and be measured
by the same standards, does something towards lifting them out of
the state of listless despair of themselves into which so many fall.
Supposing that the percentage of success attained by women should
be considerably less than that of men, the sense of discouragement
thus engendered would be as nothing compared with the general
self-distrust produced by having it taken for granted that they are
by nature disqualified to stand the ordinary tests. To make the dis-
covery of individual incompetence may be wholesomely humbling or
stimulating, as the case may be, but no one is the better for being
told, on mere arbitrary authority, that he belongs to a weak and incapable class. And this, whatever may be the intention, is said in
effect by the offer of any test of an exclusively female character.

In Emily Davies, "Special Systems of Education for Women," *The London
Student,* June 1868, reprinted in Emily Davies, *Thoughts on Some Questions
Relating to Women, 1860–1908* (1910)

THE FRANCES MARY BUSS SCHOOL (1871–1875)

Sara Burstall

(See p. 279.)

*Frances Mary Buss (1827–1894) began her teaching career at the age
of fourteen in her mother's proprietary school, which grew into the*

North London Collegiate School under her leadership. Buss turned down opportunities for marriage in order to support her family through the school. She educated two of her brothers as clergymen in this way. But Buss was mainly motivated by an intense desire to alleviate "the terrible sufferings of the women of my own class for want of a good elementary training . . . to lighten ever so little, the misery of women brought up to be married and taken care of, but left alone in the world destitute."

Like Emily Davies, she believed in a single standard of education and insisted her graduates attend Girton for its rigorous adherence to this practice. Buss could be quite sentimental. She liked to kiss her girls goodbye every day, and she wept with embarrassment when called to testify before the Taunton Commission. (The commissioners were favorably impressed with such womanly delicacy and kindly called Emily Davies into the room to provide Buss with the necessary moral support.) Yet she was also a shrewd behind-the-scenes organizer. In 1870, she founded the Camden School, which provided relatively inexpensive education for lower-middle-class girls. Some pupils, like Sara Burstall (1859–1939) (later in life an educational administrator), went from the limited curriculum of the Camden School to the North London Collegiate School and then to Girton, with the help of scholarships.

> After many years, on looking back from the middle turn of life's way at the events of the past . . . we may see here and there, in the grey throng, some figure glowing with a faint radiance. . . . And by this glow we may recognise the faces of our true adventures. . . .
>
> CONRAD: *The Mirror of the Sea*

Such an adventure was my entrance at the Camden School for girls in September, 1871, and my coming under the influence of that great pioneer headmistress, Frances Mary Buss, which was destined to shape my whole life, as it has that of many others. But her figure glows with no faint radiance, even through the grey mist of years. She had an extraordinary personality, characterised by a will of intense potency, deep emotion, and an almost faultless intuition for the right way to take through difficulties. . . . She had the statesman's far-seeing thought, the general's eye for a situation, the mother's unconquerable instinct to fight for her young, the leader's power to inspire self-sacrifice. Her whole life from early girlhood—and she began to teach at fourteen—to premature old age—for she died at sixty-eight, worn out by her efforts—was devoted to reforming the education of women.

My going to the Camden School was an adventure in another sense, coming about by an accident, and a girlish impulse of mine. I was always a great newspaper reader, and running through the columns of the *Daily Telegraph* in July, 1871, the paper we then took, I came upon an account of the Distribution of [the Camden School] Prizes by the Lord Mayor of London. . . . I was immensely impressed, having a great idea of the dignity and grandeur of the Lord Mayor, and I said to my father, "Oh, Papa, do let me go to that school, and some day I may receive a prize from the Lord Mayor!" The school was within walking distance, and the fees were within my father's means; so I became a pupil in September, 1871, more than sixty years ago.

Our curriculum at the Camden School included: Divinity, well taught in the old ways; first-rate arithmetic, followed by good book-keeping for those who wished, but not in 1874 including algebra or geometry; excellent English, thorough and attractive, with speech-training and the study of poetry; history in the thin and meagre text-books of the time, and geography. . . . To French much time and attention was given, both to grammar and to speech. For this latter we had a strange old Frenchwoman, Mlle. Cuvillier . . . and if we chose we could and did learn to speak from her, and in any case we had to treat her with respect. We had science lectures from men: I remember vividly those given about 1871–72 by Miss Buss's father, R. W. Buss, an artist who had illustrated the first numbers of "Pickwick." I can see now the water rising in the bell glass as he demonstrated the proportion of nitrogen in air by burning phosphorus. . . .

Our hours were from 9 to 12:30 in the morning, with a short afternoon session, 2:30 to 3:30, generally needlework, drawing or some easier subject. In the long midday break those girls who did not go home had an hour's preparation. School dinner was provided, but it was of course an extra expense, and unappetising, as school dinners (alas!) so often are, and most of us brought food from home. . . . After the school meal we were encouraged to run about and play in the garden space behind the houses, even though we were no longer children, which was quite a liberal idea for those times. Physical education indeed was not neglected. We had simple calisthenic lessons most days for short periods, with marching. Swimming was encouraged, the local swimming-bath, through Miss Buss's efforts, being reserved for girls and women on Saturday mornings. Most of us did a good deal of walking to and from school, and it was considered correct to have dancing lessons, and most families provided the extra fees. In the 'seventies, well-to-do women rode, practised archery, and played croquet, but games in the modern sense for schoolgirls would have been considered outrageous. The pioneers had to go very gently; perhaps that is why they succeeded so well. . . .

In my last year a dozen of us had special afternoon lessons in Latin, which enabled us to take Latin later on in the Senior Cambridge [local exam], and on entering the North London, we could— because the Camden had taught us so well—drop arithmetic altogether and much of our English, and give more time to the new subjects. Looking back, I am amazed that they did such good work with us; with low fees, and no grants of course, and no endowment, the classes were large, and the staff limited. Some were only student teachers receiving training and an honorarium. But there was never a better example of the truth of the proverb about an army of stags with a lion for a leader. We had a first-rate Head Mistress, Miss Emma J. Elford, who worked under Miss Buss's superintendence, and along her lines. She pervaded the whole place, and she taught arithmetic and English *well*. The order and the tone were good too, and we were happy and well cared for. I loved the Camden School, and am proud and glad to bear witness to what it did for us in the very beginning of the reform movement. . . .

In Sara A. Burstall, *Retrospect and Prospect: Sixty Years of Women's Education* (1933)

A BUTTONHOLE (1881)
M. Vivian Hughes
(See p. 280.)

M. Vivian Hughes (d. 1956) obtained an exceptionally good education in early girlhood. She therefore presents a less admiring (and later) view of Buss's school, emphasizing its quaint and sometimes ridiculous rules.

An afternoon was fixed for me to attend, and taking the train from Highbury to Camden Town I found my way to the school—a formidable-looking building. Seeing some steps labelled "Pupils' Entrance" I went down them, told the first person I saw the reason of my appearance and was ushered into a room in the basement. Here I was provided with paper, pens, and ink, and various sets of questions which I could take in any order.

Keyed up as I was for something stiff, these papers seemed to me pifflingly easy. As for an explanation of the tides, I knew much more about them than men of science do to-day, and drew beautiful diagrams to show how the water was piled up, in Biblical style, with no visible means of support. A blank map of Africa was to be filled in with "all you know," and I was still busily inserting rivers and mountains, towns and capes, when all the papers were collected. I had floored them all, even the arithmetic, and sat back in a slightly supercilious mood. The very large and motherly official (addressed as Miss Begbie) who swam towards me looked a little surprised as she gathered up my stack of answers, and was almost deferential as she said, "Now, dear, just make a buttonhole before you go."

This was a quite unexpected blow. I confessed that I hadn't the faintest idea how to set about it, and thought that buttonholes just "came." Up went Miss Begbie's hands in shocked surprise.

"What! A girl of sixteen not know how to make a buttonhole!"

"Can't I come to the school then?" I asked in dismay.

"Well, possibly, dear. We shall see. But you must go home, learn to make a buttonhole, and come again this day week to make it."

Mother was watching at the window for my return, and as she opened the door I exclaimed, "I've failed." How heartily she laughed when she heard of my disgrace. "A buttonhole! Why, I'll teach you to make one in five minutes." So indeed she did, and I practised the trick so assiduously all the week that even now I can make a buttonhole with the best. Meanwhile Mother made me a little case to hold needles, cotton, scissors, and thimble, to take with me, "to look businesslike." On the appointed day I appeared, was given a piece of calico, made my buttonhole, and went home. It seemed absurd to take the railway journey just for that, but it was a rule of the school that no girl should enter who couldn't make a buttonhole.

In M. Vivian Hughes, A London Girl of the Eighties (1936)

FAINTING FITS AT SCHOOL (1889)

F. Cecily Steadman

Dorothea Beale (1831–1906) ran the Ladies College, Cheltenham, with the same personal force as Frances Mary Buss ran the North London Collegiate School. Both of them were looked upon by some as strong-minded, sexless anomalies, as witness this anonymous popular rhyme:

> Miss Buss and Miss Beale
> Cupid's darts do not feel
> How different from us
> Miss Beale and Miss Buss.

This memory of Beale's regime indicates some of the difficulties early reformers had in resocializing girls to a new standard of behavior.

There was, however, a minor ailment that gave some trouble, and that was the addiction of some girls to slight fainting fits. This was, I think, partly the consequence of measures taken in the hope of securing an eighteen-inch waist, and partly a legacy from the days when swooning was considered the mark of a refined and delicate sensibility, and when, according to contemporary novels, properly brought up young ladies were able, it seemed, to go off at will. Whatever the cause, some young people certainly contrived to accomplish a good deal of unconsciousness, and even to make it correspond to a surprising degree with unpopular homework. But Mrs. Smith found a plan that unerringly distinguished between the child who was really ill and the minx who was shamming for ulterior motives. She would walk to the door and call out to the Matron,

"Harris! Harris! Bring me a large can of cold water to pour over Miss Edith!"

Shammers always recovered before the arrival of the can, and were then given a dose of Gregory's Powder [a laxative].

At College it was usually at Prayers that fainting was attempted, if ever at all, but on the whole house fainting was preferred, for Miss Beale had a way of stopping just as one began to droop, and saying sharply,

"Miss Jones! control yourself and stand properly."

Thereupon Miss Jones *did* control herself. Afterwards Miss Beale would say that no one was expected to attend Prayers if she felt unable to do so, those who undertook responsibility must show themselves equal to it, and stay to the end. She watched carefully over the health of the College, and was especially vigilant over that of girls working hard under pressure of financial difficulties or of home cares. . . . All was done, however, in such a way as to brace rather than enervate, for pampering in any form was utterly alien to her. . . .

In F. Cecily Steadman, *In the Days of Miss Beale: A Study of Her Work and Influence* (1930)

A GIRTON PIONEER (1869–1873)
Louise Lumsden

Louise Lumsden (1840–1935) was remembered by generations of students as one of the three gallant ladies, "Woodhead, Cook, and Lumsden, the Girton pioneers" (sung to the tune of the "British Grenadiers"), to take the first tripos (honors) exams opened to women. In 1922, she returned to Cambridge to officially receive the degree she earned but could not be awarded fifty years earlier.

The College, Hitchin, was just large enough to hold a few students, the Mistress, Mrs. Manning, and her daughter. . . . There were five students the first term, and after Christmas our numbers were increased to six by the arrival of Miss Rachel Cook from St. Andrews. . . . The Mistress's sitting-room and the library, where lectures were given and which was also our common room, were on the ground floor, and the dining-room was in the basement, a bare ugly room with two tables, at one of which we students sat, while the Mistress and her friends sat at the "High table" alongside. It was at first expected that we should sit in a formal row down one side of our table, lest we should be guilty of the discourtesy of turning our backs upon the "High." But this was too much and we rebelled, quietly ignored the rule and insisted upon comfortably facing each other. So academically formal was the order imposed from the first at Hitchin, small as our numbers were. But the bareness and formality of the dining-room mattered little; what did matter was that we shared it with black beetles—gruesome crawling creatures, by no means pleasant table companions.

Four lecturers came to Hitchin in the first term, Messrs. Seeley, Hort, Clark and Stuart, and we had one lecture every day which everybody attended, the length of this lecture being fixed neither by our capacities of taking in knowledge, nor by the convenience of the lecturer, but by the hours of railway trains. . . . We had two Latin lectures a week, two Mathematical, one English and one Divinity. Now seeing that we had none of us any school training in Classics or Mathematics, and that some of us at any rate had, vigorously encouraged thereto by Miss Davies, decided to attempt the regular undergraduate course, and to deserve, at least, a Cambridge degree, whether we ever got one or not, it might naturally be imagined that we would waste no time over non-essentials, but would concentrate upon the work which had to be got through in the limited time assigned by University regulations. But we did nothing of the sort; on the contrary, the course of study provided for us—no doubt with excellent intentions—was highly discursive. Mr. Clark indeed took a practical view of our position—and by this, as well as by his most interesting and stimulating teaching, he earned our warmest gratitude—taking up only Little-go [first examination for the B.A.] subjects, Terence in the first term, Herodotus in the second and third. But Mr. Seeley discoursed pleasantly upon "Lycidas," and set us to write original verse, a delightful occupation, but one can hardly call it practically useful, while Mr. Hort selected the Acts of the Apostles as his theme, St. Luke's Gospel being actually the book required for the Little-go. . . .

This plain statement of the oddity of our lecture arrangements at Hitchin fitly introduces the great Tripos question, which, by the end of the first term, had become acute. In the interval between the Entrance Examination and the opening of the College . . . I had studied a copy of the Cambridge Calendar, lent to me by Miss Davies, and I rose from this study with the settled determination to attempt the Classical Tripos. Gradually most of my fellow students formed similar resolutions. Miss Cook and Miss Townshend decided for the Classical, Miss Woodhead for the Mathematical Tripos. . . . Now, to get more essential teaching and to drop all non-essential work became a pressing necessity. But an unlooked for difficulty arose.

The Committee [which governed Hitchin College] was displeased. I think the truth was that, never having seen us students, they forgot that we were not mere schoolgirls, altogether destitute of culture, and besides, the ladies of the Committee at any rate, knowing nothing themselves about University examinations, imagined that it was possible to take a tripos lightly by the way, without giving our whole time to the preparation. . . . To them we seemed simply ungrateful for the good things offered to us, careless of culture, mere imitators of men. It was difficult even for our lecturers to grasp our position. They were most kind. Never let it be supposed that we were any thing but grateful to such men as Mr. Seeley and Mr. Hort for their willingness to spend time upon a handful of obscure young women. Still, the fact remained that Mr. Seeley and Mr. Hort had to be shunted and the Committee had to be shocked.

The second and third years at Hitchin found things greatly improved. Other lecturers had been placed on the staff. . . . We had outgrown the house, and an iron building had been put up, to which some of us migrated, I among the number, to my regret when I discovered that life in the "tin house," as we called it, was a misery. If it rained the rattle on the roof was maddening, if the sun shone we were baked as in an oven, and the rooms were so small that Miss Woodhead, a tall, athletic young woman, declared that in her doll's house sitting-room, without rising from her chair, by merely reaching out a long arm [she] could either poke the fire or open the door. . . .

[Encouraged by Woodhead's taking a Second in the Mathematical Tripos earlier in the term, Cook and Lumsden made the journey to Cambridge, chaperoned by Emily Davies, to take the Classics exam. The questions were to be brought to them separately and unofficially but at the same time as the regular male students received them.]

How well I remember the first morning at the University Arms. We settled down in our sitting-room, pen in hand, expectant of the paper, while Miss Davies knitted away steadily by the fire—I can hear the click of her needles still! But minute after minute slipped away and still, until a whole hour had gone by, no paper came.

Miss Davies said nothing, but she must have despaired, for she knew, though she had considerately hidden it from us, that some of the examiners were dead against admitting us to the examination at all. For my part I grew desperate—had the examiners at the eleventh hour refused the paper? When at last the messenger came, he had, it appeared, been sent first to a wrong address. My nerves were all in a quiver and work was almost impossible. Miss Cook took it with superior calm—I do not think she cared so intensely as I did about the whole adventure. That morning was far the worst bit of the week, and it settled my class, a Third, while Miss Cook took a Second. There were certainly moments of depression when we sat on the bridge behind King's and thought as we looked down upon the slowly sliding Cam that, had the water not been so muddy, one plunge might have ended all! . . . The kindness of friends and two very pleasant dinner-parties cheered us, however, and the ordeal came to an end at last. I was visiting friends when the news that we had passed came to Hitchin, so I cannot relate what happened there as an eye-witness. But I have been told that the students in their triumph climbed to the roof of "the College" and set the fire bell a-tolling, to proclaim the news to all the world, and that the good folks of Hitchin were properly amazed and no doubt disgusted by the noise.

In Louise Lumsden, *Yellow Leaves: Memories of a Long Life* (1933)

MEMOIR OF GIRTON (1882–1885)
Helena Swanwick
(See p. 72.)

By the time Helena Sickert (later Swanwick) arrived at Girton, it had moved from its seclusion at Hitchin to its permanent home closer to the rest of the university. However, the same isolation and sense of being on trial was still a part of the Girton experience.

My last term at school was greatly disturbed by anxiety as to what was to happen to me next. The Head had inspired in me an intense desire to go to Girton College and I particularly wanted to study Economics. I was determined to qualify myself to earn my own living, not at all relishing the idea of living as a dependent at home, with a strong mother quite competent to run the household without help. I did not quite see how my independence was to be accomplished, but I have never looked very far ahead in my life, taking opportunities as they came. My mother saw no necessity for me to go to college and wished me to live as a "daughter at home." In this my father, though personally indifferent, supported her. I was given to understand that there would be no money to pay for a university course.

My hopes went up and down. Miss Jones told me that a benefactor of the school had promised a scholarship to the girl in my year whom the headmistress should select, and that she had selected me.

But when I told my mother, she dashed my hopes by saying that the scholarship would by no means cover the annual cost, and it was out of the question that any more should be spent on me. As the fees at Notting Hill had been only £15 a year, I did not think that my four years' schooling had been very expensive; but clearly, if there was not enough money, that settled it. By an extraordinary piece of good luck, my godmother, Mrs. Nichols, of Holmwood Park, Dorking, whom I ever after thought of as my fairy godmother, at this time paid my mother one of her rare visits and heard about my dilemma. Without any hesitation, she undertook to make up the balance of my expenses, and in the Michaelmas Term 1882 I entered Girton College. I was eighteen, but still very unevenly educated, and exceedingly undeveloped in mind and character. At a students' supper-party, when I, in turn with other freshers, was asked what tripos I was taking, and replied, "Moral Sciences" [philosophy], a third-year student cried, "What! That babe?" . . .

Miss Bernard, who was still Mistress in my first year, had a talk with me, but she knew nothing whatever about the Moral Sciences [philosophy] and I was too ignorant to discover this. When my Little-Go had been polished off, she examined the lecture list and remarked that Dr. Venn and Dr. James Ward were very distinguished lecturers and I would probably find them interesting. Dr. Venn was lecturing on "The Logic of Chance" and Dr. Ward was giving his highly original and difficult course on Psychology.

I faithfully attended these classes as recommended; of Dr. Venn's I think I understood nothing whatever, whereas of Dr. Ward's I may have understood one sentence in ten. My philosophical vocabulary was still so childish that I used to take notes phonetically, and I can remember puzzling over the question as to what on earth "discreet" points could be. Dr. Ward became aware of the chaotic state of my mind and once startled me horribly by opening his lecture with the remark: "Miss Sickert, you won't understand a word of what I am going to say to-day." And I didn't. But I rather wish now that I had had the nerve to get up and go out.

I look back with amazement at my serenity under these circumstances. I ought, after a few weeks, to have felt exasperated at being offered only such indigestible food, and to have made a row about it. I expect I should have secured some helpful advice if I had done this. But I was still in the receptive mood of the good girl who takes what is given her. It was such a miracle to be at college at all and I was

Artist's notion of a Newnham Hall study, from the Graphic, *1877*

far too shy to hold up the class for explanation which the others appeared not to require. The idea of waylaying these great men with questions, even if I could have formulated them, never occurred to me. . . .

On the other hand, the social life of the college was to me so intoxicating that it was more than enough for me. I was too excited to eat or sleep properly. To begin with, I now had a study as well as a bedroom to myself. My mother had brought me to Girton on the first day and we were shown round by an old student. . . . When the door of my study was opened and I saw my own fire, my own desk, my own easy chair and reading-lamp—nay, even my own kettle—I was speechless with delight. Imagine my dismay when my mother turned to me with open arms and tears in her eyes, saying, "You can come home again with me, Nell, if you like!" It was horrible. That which had enraptured me had struck her as so unutterably dismal that she was prepared to rescue me at all costs. I hardly knew how decently to disguise my real feelings. . . .

To have a study of my own and to be told that, if I chose to put "Engaged" on my door, no one would so much as knock was in itself so great a privilege as to hinder me from sleep. I did not know till then how much I had suffered from the incessant interruptions of my

home life. I could have worked quite easily in a mere noise. I never
found it at all difficult to do prep. in a crowded schoolroom. What
disturbed my mind were the claims my mother made on my attention, her appeals to my emotions and her resentment at my interest
in matters outside the family circle. . . .

Our college rules were imposed partly from without. One of these
was the insistence upon a chaperone for all women-students attending lectures in Trinity. . . . It was an unfortunate rule for me. In my
first year, I was the only Girton student attending Dr. Ward's lectures, and my chaperone was an incurably unpunctual person; a de-
cayed gentlewoman with the poorest sort of twittering manners. I
was expected not to go in alone to the lecture, but to wait in the
porch of Trinity Chapel, to be the butt and mockery of a certain
type of undergraduate, until my silly guardian chose to turn up, out
of breath and apologetic. I would not go in without her, for fear of
getting her into trouble, for I think her small fee was of importance
to her. . . .

There can be no doubt that all this prudery on the part of authority retarded the growth of respect and comradeship in the
male undergraduates. . . . The rules about male visitors had absurd
results. We might receive them in the public "reception room" (a
dismal little hole about twelve feet square) or in our studies, provided we left the door open and did not sit down. An extremely
loquacious young acquaintance of mine once kept me standing by
the fire, with the door open, for two hours, after which I told him
that I was too exhausted to endure more; a good example of my social helplessness. . . .

It seems queer to me that none of the authorities appreciated the
effect of all this mincing prudery on the undergraduates of both
sexes. Into the old monastic life of the university had been introduced
women. Not "Woman," the legendary snare and lure of the devil,
but real individual women, with qualities and capacities and ambitions and difficulties quite unconnected with sex. The marriage of
Fellows was still a comparatively new thing, and perambulators in
the quads were still matters of comment. We felt acutely that we
were on trial, on sufferance even, and while this made us circumspect
and docile in an exaggerated degree, I cannot deny that it perpetuated
and strengthened in some of us the revolt against the indignities to
which women were submitted merely on account of their sex.

In Helena Swanwick, *I Have Been Young* (1935)

WOMEN AT OXFORD (1883)
Lillian Faithfull

Oxford followed Cambridge's example in establishing colleges for women. Faithfull (d. 1952) attended Somerville College, named for Mary Somerville and founded in 1879. Lillian Faithfull (d. 1952) succeeded Dorothea Beale as principal of Ladies College, Cheltenham.

But, to return to those early Oxford days. We worked very hard and played hard. We were very conscious of the fact that we had to establish traditions, and everything was new and delightful. After organised studies in school, it was an immense pleasure to be free to arrange one's work as one pleased. What an enormous change it was after "doing lessons" to be "reading a subject" and, after considerable control, how surprising to receive the minimum of direction in one's work and be left firmly to oneself. One can hardly exaggerate the delight of getting beyond elementary work and coming to grips for the first time with a subject, and investigating a special field of knowledge, however small it may be. The continual association with specialists and real authorities on the subject one has decided to study dignifies and changes one's entire conception of intellectual work. . . . Nor could one be insensible to the concentration of all those around one on the things eminently worth having in life; a new standard of values was gently pressing on one day by day. College life was in those days, and is probably at all times, wonderfully free from pettiness and personal gossip, or anything approaching snobbishness. To women, more than to men, the delight of having three years in which it was right to be selfishly absorbed in intellectual pursuits was unspeakable, for claims great and small are apt to beset women in life at a very early age. And, in addition to this, there was the appeal made by the beauty of Oxford, and the pride in having a part, however small, in University life. Truly

> Bliss was it in that dawn to be alive,
> But to be young was very heaven.*

The fact that we were no less ambitious for the reputation of the College than for our own made it a matter of course to work hard,

---

* William Wordsworth, *The Prelude*, Book XI

and failures or successes counted much with so small a body. Some
of the proudest moments of those days live in one's mind—the day
when the men's examinations were open to women—the year in
which a woman gained a First in *Literae Humaniores*. Quite simply,
without fuss or flourish of trumpets, women vindicated their right
to a share in the riches of the University; quite simply their work and
ability was standardised in the schools and there was no need to continue to assert what had once been proved.

Did the pioneers, as they thought of equipping women for professions, dream of the changes to be wrought in the social life of
England—the transformation in the relationships of men and women
which dates from the end of the nineteenth century? I think not. Up
to that time girls met men only in their own homes under careful
supervision of parents, and any intimacy or evidence of more than
ordinary friendship might provoke an inquiry as to the intentions of
the possible suitor, which either precipitated an engagement or ended
the visits. But when men and women worked side by side in labora-
tories and lecture-rooms a new comradeship began, which had its
foundation in community of interests as often as in admiration, and
might and did grow into a friendship such as of man with man or
woman with woman. Men were no longer debarred from women's
comradeship. And if they could work together they could also play
together, go to theatres together. Intercourse became more natural
and more easy. . . .

I think there can be little doubt that indirectly the higher education of women discouraged marriage in as far as it gave to women an
alternative which had none of the dullness or limitations of home life,
and much of the variety and opportunity for initiative and energy
which would not normally be found in domesticity. And for men,
the desire for women's companionship could be satisfied in great
measure without undertaking the increasing financial burdens of
married life. On the other hand, it may be urged that the marriages
which did take place among the professional class were often more
satisfactory, being founded on greater knowledge and truer sympathy,
and that professional life encouraged and brought in its train a much
more rational and closer association of men and women. The novel
excitement and independence of life offered to us great attractions.
We were fired with the sentiment of the explorer: new seas were to be
charted by women; new avenues of usefulness were before us; and,
with something of the arrogance of Bacon, we cried, "We have taken

all knowledge to be our province." Even school teaching was regarded with respect, not dismay. Its living wage, its opportunities for promotion, its possibilities of putting into practice all kinds of reforms and of infecting others with our own enthusiasm, made most of us eager to get posts and content to keep them for years.

In Lillian Faithfull, *In the House of My Pilgrimage* (1924)

FOUR

Working-Class Education

One of the most important elements of nineteenth-century liberal thought was a belief in the power of education. After the extension of the suffrage to part of the male working class, general education seemed a matter of national interest. Unlike American myths and experience, however, the establishment of free, compulsory, universal elementary education (which came about in degrees between 1870 and 1918) did not bring with it the promise of upward mobility in class or earning power. Indeed, education for the working class was purposely limited to "elementary" education—that is, reading, writing, and some arithmetic—in order to prevent the poor from forming expectations above their station in life. Elementary school was thought of as an instrument of socialization, meant to make workers more industrious, content, and respectable in their static situation at the bottom of the heap. Though boys were given some training for future industrial employment, girls' education was meant, in the words of one early reformer, to fit them to be improved "servants of the rich" and "wives of the poor."*

Before the establishment of state-supported schools, elementary education had been difficult for the poor to obtain. In the first half of the century, children were expected to be at work (see Part IV). Those who did attempt to gain a basic education had to pay fees to the overcrowded church-run schools in whose chaotically conducted classes students rarely had the opportunity to write on paper and girls were mostly taught to sew. Some urban children without the money for fees, the requisite clean clothing, or the freedom to attend school during the day might attend the rougher Ragged Schools.

---

* Mrs. Austin, *Two Lectures on Girls' Schools and the Training of Working Women* (1857), p. 12.

Learning domestic chores at a London elementary school, 1907.

which often met in the evenings and were aimed at reducing delin-
quency. Frances Power Cobbe, who worked in Mary Carpenter's
Ragged School for girls in Bristol, said of such places:

> They were specially designed to *civilize* the children; to *tame*
> them enough to induce them, for example, to sit reasonably
> still on a bench for half an hour at a time; to wash their
> hands and faces; to comb their hair; to forbear from shout-
> ing, singing, . . . making faces . . . ; after which preliminaries
> they began to acquire the art of learning lessons.*

Girls at Ragged Schools were scrupulously policed for bad language
or signs of sexual knowledge, and expelled for fear of moral contami-

---

* *Life*, p. 269–70

nation. Industrial schools—those run for the poor by charity or manufacturing interests—were similarly concerned with socialization and
sexual tracking. A visitor to one of the more progressive of such
schools, run by the educational reformer James Kay-Shuttleworth, at
Norwood in the 1840s, described the scene this way:

> We saw the boys making clothes and shoes, others working as
> carpenters, tinsmiths and blacksmiths, and a large body of
> little fellows, dressed as sailors, climbed rigging, drilled as
> soldiers, and practised at great guns. The girls wash, iron,
> mangle, cook, learn to make clothes and to knit.†

The girls at this school were essentially servants to the institution.

The education of poor girls for domestic service was an unquestioned practice throughout the century. Significantly enough, the
first government investigation led by a woman—Mrs. Senior's 1874
report on the conditions of workhouse schools for girls—criticized
the institutions for training the young girls so poorly that they turned
out to be bad servants. On the other hand, Mrs. Senior was little
concerned with their ability to read or write. One rough measure
of the inadequacy and unavailability of instruction for the poor was
the number of people who were unable to sign their names on their
wedding days and marked the registry books with crosses. In 1851,
the Registrar General reported that 30.8 percent of grooms and 45.3
percent of brides were illiterate (figures that may have been somewhat distorted by bridal reluctance to show up a less accomplished
groom). The rate of female illiteracy was reduced as the century
wore on, but men always received more education than women.

The schools established after the institution of compulsory education followed these earlier models. In London in the 1870s, girls
spent up to a quarter of their time on needlework. Teachers were
strict disciplinarians and considered themselves the bearers of higher
standards of conduct (neatness, obedience, industriousness) as well
as knowledge. Classes in cities could number as many as sixty or
more students. Teaching was often by rote recitation, and most
children left by age fourteen, with girls attending less regularly than
boys because of the expectation that they be helpful at home. Cookery
classes became popular after 1880, and general housekeeping—often

---

* Letter from Lady McNeill to Miss Ferrier, June 19, 1841, in *Memoir of
Susan Ferrier*, quoted in *Englishwoman's Review*, January 1907

oriented to service in the homes of the rich—was a regular part of girls' training by the end of the century. The tendency to blame the ill health and squalor of the poor upon bad housekeeping led to increased pressure on the school system to produce future wives and mothers with properly middle-class notions of cleanliness, nutrition, and general household management.

The following memoirs of schooling make clear the contradictions faced by young girls with normal youthful curiosity and energy entering such institutions. They demonstrate the physical hardships that women had to endure in order to receive even a scanty education and the pervasive class prejudices that prevented the poor from benefitting from the extention of higher education to middle-class and upper-class women.

A SCHOOL IN THE FENS (1880s)
Kate Mary Edwards

Kate Mary Edwards attended a family-run, one-room rural school, the only one available despite the fact that elementary education was by then under state supervision.

Soon after we moved house and went to live about three miles from the school. . . . We were just inside the distance limit, so I had to go, but the journeys were terrible then, specially in winter. . . . Walking is allus bad along the fen droves, up to your hocks in mud in the winter time and in dry dust in the summer. Even the high way had ruts in it you could lay down and hide in, and the only difference was that it had been "gravelled" with great granite stones the size of a tea cup. They were all left loose on the road to bed down as best they might, and we did the best we could walking over them by keeping one behind the other up the smoother tracks made by the cart-wheels. . . . We did suffer on them journeys, specially with cold in the winter. Most of us had a good coat, and the girls had a clean print hood, starched and stiff, every Monday morning. . . . We wanted something to keep us warm, because we coul'n't hurry no faster than the droves and the stones on the road 'ould let us, nor no faster than the pace the littlest ones of our gang could keep up. None of our clothes kept the wet out, and no stuff 'ill keep out a black-frost wind blowing across the fen. But worst of all were our sore feet. The boots we had were all made of strong, stiff leather to last a long while and to stand up to the stony road. They got stiffer and heavier through being wet and dried quick over night, standing on the hearth, and they chafed our heels raw. . . . The little children 'ould start to cry with their feet afore they'd gone a quarter of a mile, and the slower they walked, the colder they got. Most of us 'ould be crying about something afore we got to school, sobbing quietly or grizzling or wailing or roaring out loud, according to the sort o' children we were. . . .

When we arrived at school, after starting out as soon as ever it were daylight, in the winter, we were already exhausted and frez to the marrow or else sopping wet through, but there were no comfort there for us. Nobody had a change o' clothes or shoes, and there were no means of getting warm or dry. The school had two rooms, "the schoolroom" (the main big room) and "the classroom" (a smaller one for the babies). Both of them had a tiny fire place at one end, but no warmth from it ever reached us where we sat and we never got near the tiny fire. At dinner times the biggest children fit for the places near the fire as soon as the teachers had gone out and left us by ourselves, so the little 'uns and the weakest ones and the shy ones never got near it at all. We were never looked after at all in the dinner times, so nobody knowed or cared whether we ever felt the fire or not, though I remember envying one little girl I used to play with. She were a farmer's child, and I should think the teacher must a-give orders as she were to have a special place near the fire, because it were allus left for her. She were the only one of us as had proper sandwiches with meat in them for her dockey [lunch], and she used to bring a long knitting needle with her and hang a sandwich on the end of it and toast it in front of the fire and make all our mouths water so that our own bit o' "bread and seam" [lard] di'n't taste as good as it ought to a-done.

School in them days was a place where you "learnt your lessons," and teachers di'n't do nothing only "teach." It warn't part o' their job to look after the child'en in any other way. . . .

The school were run by a family called Rigby. Old Daddy Rigby were the schoolmaster, and his family helped him. . . . Of course we hated 'em all, every one of 'em. Teachers in them days were cruel to the children in any case, because they thought that were the only way to make 'em learn anything, and for all I know it may be so. But looking back on the Rigby's, it seems to me that they must have despised us all as poor, ignorant creatures of a different sort from theirselves, and treated us more like animals than child'en.

We were very poor, but my mother . . . loved to do things as well as she could . . . and so we were kept as neat and clean and tidy and pretty as any o' the farmers' children. Perhaps that was why the Rigby women singled my sister and me out. Not for any favouritism, but for special duties. One morning after I'd answered to my name on the register and said prayers, Miss Mary called me out and took me through the door into the school house. There she set me to work, washing up the breakfast things and dusting until morning school were over. Next morning, it were the same again, only it were doing the vegetables and cleaning the shoes, and some days I went back in the afternoons as well. At the end of the week, she gave me my pay, a quarter of an orange peel! This went on for weeks and months. Then one night at home we were all sitting round the table at home "making pothooks" on our slates, and writing words, and Mother said "I don't know why it is Kate don't seem to improve as much in her schooling as you others do," and my sister, who was younger than me but a lot perkier, said, " 'Tain't likely she'll get on, 'cos she's never at school." Mother began to ask questions, and soon found the truth out. But as far as I know, it never made no difference. Perhaps she di'n't complain, because she'd know we should be the ones that 'ould suffer. I still went on going to the school house, and got promoted to doing the bedrooms out before I left. After that my sister were took on, but she were different from me and had a lot more pluck. She woul'n't do just as she were told as meek as I did, and she knowed she ought to a-bin in school doing her lessons. . . .

In Sybil Marshall, *Fenland Chronicle: Recollections of William Henry and Kate Mary Edwards Collected and Edited by Their Daughter* (Cambridge, England: Cambridge University Press, 1967)

A LONDON SCHOOLING (ca. 1900)

Grace Foakes

(See pp. 177 and 179.)

Grace Foakes attended a London board school—a modern, free, compulsory elementary school supervised by the London School Board.

The girls' school was upstairs. The stairs were very wide and at the top was another cloakroom with wash-basins. Through the double doors were four classrooms: one of medium size at one end; a large room in the middle, which may have been meant for use as a hall, but which was divided down the centre with screens, making it into two classrooms; and at the other end another classroom of medium size. If you were in one of the classrooms where the screens were, it was very difficult to concentrate, as you found yourself listening to what was going on in the class on the other side of the screen. . . .

If you were in the end classroom and wished to be excused, then you had to walk through the two classes in the hall and through the door which led to the stairs, then down the stairs out into the playground. By this time you either had an accident or things were becoming extremely urgent!

Throughout my years at that school, I always kept to the same classroom, teacher and desk. The room held thirty-six desks; with two girls at each desk, seventy-two girls must have been in the one class. The desks did not open and the seats were attached. Each had an inkwell at either end, filled each day by the ink monitor. We were each given a pen with a nib which had to last a week. Books, too, were given out for each subject and collected and put in a cupboard when the lesson finished. We learned spelling, writing, reading, history, geography, arithmetic and nature study. . . .

We would drone our tables out loud until we knew them by heart, and to this day, if I cannot remember six fives, or seven nines, I repeat the table until I come to it. The tables were lessons never forgotten. My teacher was Mrs. Hamlyn. She was tall, thin and terrifying. If we misbehaved she would bring us out to the front of the class, stand behind us, fold our arms over our chest, and lean over us. Then, pushing our sleeves up, she slapped us as hard as she could until our arms burned with the sting. We had a punishment book, kept by the Governess (Headmistress). If you were really naughty, you were sent to the Governess for the cane and to have your name put in red ink in the punishment book. This went against you when you left school, as each of us was given our "character" (reference) when we left school. Without a good "character" you could not get a job, as it was always asked for when applying for one. I still have my "character." It is one of my treasures, of which I am rather proud. . . .

In winter there was a very large coal fire lit before we came into class. In front of it was a large, iron fire-guard. The fire was lovely to look at but didn't seem to warm the classroom. My seat at the back of the class was always cold. I had so many chilblains on my fingers that sometimes I could not hold the pen. Not being able to afford gloves for us, my mother sewed up the legs of worn-out socks and threaded them through with elastic to keep them on. This was quite all right for going to school, but one cannot write with sewn-up socks on one's hands; and so, once at school, I had to go cold.

Most of us girls were very poorly shod, some coming to school with no boots or stockings at all. Those of us who did have them were lucky. Even so, most boots were made with cardboard soles which wore out very quickly, especially in wet weather. . . .

[W]e were not allowed to walk about as children do today, and we were not permitted to talk or ask questions. If you disobeyed, you sat with your hands on your head until told to take them off. . . .

We were taught hemming, sew and fell, top-sewing and gathering. Pieces of material were given to each girl and we would have to gather the material in, then stroke the gathers until they all were in a perfectly straight line. I could never see the sense of this, and as we never got any further than the piece of material I'm afraid I never tried very hard. We had no sewing-machines and were never encouraged to make a garment, and so there seemed to be a general dislike of the subject.

As we grew older, we were sent for one half-day a week to a central school for a course of either housewifery, laundry or cooking. We could not choose the course, it was chosen for us. At the laundry we were taught how to wash clothes, iron with a flat iron, goffer [fold ruffles or frills] with a goffering iron, to starch and to smooth with a smoothing iron. . . . If we did the housewifery course, we were taught to sweep, dust, polish, make beds and bathe a life-size doll. We had great fun on this course, for it was held in a house set aside for the purpose, and with only one teacher in charge we were quick to take advantage when she went to inspect some other part of the house. We jumped on the bed, threw pillows, drowned the doll and swept dirt under the mats. This was the highlight of the week, the one lesson that we never minded going to.

In Grace Foakes, *My Part of the River* (1974)

"GETTING ON IN LIFE" (1871)
London School Board

Readers used in London Board Schools like Grace Foakes's were heavily moralistic in tone and attempted to teach working-class boys and girls socially acceptable behavior. Reading directed toward girls stressed domestic skills. For example, a textbook for beginning readers portrays a girl whose neglectful behavior toward her baby brother results in his burning himself; and a girl whose mother will not give her dinner until she obediently mends her clothes, a skill likely to help her get a job as a servant. Two stories for more advanced third-standard readers describe the calamities brought on by a lazy girl who claims to have "no time for housework," and by a too-ambitious student who all but kills her mother by selfishly pursuing her schoolwork when she should be doing household chores. The selection that follows is from a fifth-standard reader.

Amongst girls . . . there are great mistakes made by their longing to "better themselves," as they say. And in one sense it is quite right that they should have such a wish. But first let them be sure that it *is* bettering themselves to change merely for higher wages, or to go into a higher family. When the girl who is only fitted for housework thinks that because she has been well educated at school, she ought to be a lady's maid, when the lady's maids wish to be governesses, depend upon it they are not getting on in life. Whatever is the position you would naturally fill, try to do your very best in it. If you are a housemaid, it is "getting on" if your rooms look cleaner and fresher, your fire-irons brighter, your steps whiter, your whole house neater than other people's. And this not merely once a year, when you are cleaning up, as it is called. Every day of your life, every room should be thoroughly attended to. If to doing your work so well, you add a nice respectful way of speaking to your mistress, and good temper amongst your fellow-servants, and a contented disposition, not looking out for a change that you may "better yourself" (falsely so called), I will promise you that your mistress will value and respect you and that every year you stay, you will in reality "be getting on in life." . . .

It is more common than it used to be, to find strong, hearty grown-up girls unwilling to leave home, or to go to service. They think they shall "get on in life" by spending their time in dress and gossiping with their neighbours. If their parents are not very poor, they allow them to do this, not considering that unless they will be able to leave them money enough to keep themselves eventually, they are doing their children the greatest injury—in fact, they are keeping them back in life. If they do not go to service early they never make good servants. Service, like other trades, is one that must be learnt young, if you wish to excel. The idleness of a home life is a bad preparation for the difficulties that await you. To be a valued servant in a respectable, kind family, is a position no one need disdain. If servants behave well, and remain in their places, they become friends rather than servants, and are treated accordingly. But when girls are always making difficulties about their work, and threatening "to leave this day month" unless everything is arranged to their fancy, can one wonder that so many of them die, friendless and moneyless, in the workhouse?

I think that by watching children at school one can pretty well tell who will hereafter "get on." Not the cleverest child, nor the forwardest, but the one who, like the Duke of Wellington, does his duty, the boy or girl whose mind is in the work set before him, who does not require to be told the same thing twice over, who does not feel it beneath him to fag on at one rule in arithmetic, or at one reading lesson, till he thoroughly knows it. But the girl who gets angry if told her needlework is so bad that she must be taught how to hold her needle properly, or the boy who declines learning the multiplication table perfectly, because he thinks he is old enough to do sums in proportion, will not only fail to get on in life, but will probably go backwards, till they find they can scarcely maintain themselves by the hardest and lowest drudgery.

In *Fifth Standard*, School Managers Series of Reading Books, ed. Rev. A. R. Grant (1871)

Part IV

WOMAN'S
WORK

T hose who believed in the cult of the domestic angel looked upon women as necessarily having nothing to do with work. Yet, in the 1850s, several essays written by feminists forced the reading public to think of women's work in new terms. Feminists like Barbara Leigh Smith Bodichon, Jessie Boucherett, Josephine Butler, Frances Power Cobbe, Anna Jameson, and Bessie Rayner Parkes called for middle-class women to be released from domestic idleness, confinement, and impoverishment, and allowed to share in the productive work of the world. At the same time, in her analysis of the 1851 census data—the same census that revealed women's "redundancy" (see p. 48)—Harriet Martineau destroyed the popular fiction that most women were supported by men. She reported that "three out of six million of adult Englishwomen work for subsistence; and two out of three in independence."

Just the same, the belief in the naturalness of the domestic dependency of women continued to influence attitudes toward women's work throughout the century. Moreover, ideological battles over the suitability of female employment were reinforced by economic competition between the sexes. From the eighteenth century on, women had been complaining that men were taking over traditionally female occupations, from midwifery to shopkeeping and hairdressing, while the new jobs that industrialization created for women often represented an invasion of unskilled labor into a formerly higher-paying, skilled male occupation. Manufacturers relied on women and children in order to cut costs, thereby driving men out of work and creating an antagonism among organized male workers toward women as harbingers of unemployment and underpayment. In the china-painting trade, for instance, men succeeded in banning women from using maulsticks (handrests), thus preventing them from doing the more detailed and better-paid work. Resentment of women's competition and restriction of their work to low-paying jobs extended to the new professions and clerical occupations, which opened up to women at the end of the century; medical students rioted rather than allow women to join their ranks; and post office employees were paid and promoted on separate scales according to sex. In general, women were paid half the wages paid to men and were often segregated into jobs that offered the least advancement and security.

As in the case of education, "reform" took different directions for middle-class and working-class women. In 1889, reformer Maria Grey noticed the result of the feminist re-evaluation of middle-class women's work life:

> Within these few years a vast and sweeping change has taken place, of unprecedented rapidity, causing a reaction from this doctrine of idleness and dependence as essential to ladyhood toward the opposite extreme, of work and independence as essential to honorable womanhood; work, meaning paid work, and independence, meaning life apart from the home life, and free from the duties and constraining order of home.*

Yet, at exactly the same moment, through the related processes of protective legislation and mass socialization, working-class women were urged to take on "respectable" values, which included a strong prohibition against earning money outside the home. Because the expansion of middle-class occupations was accompanied by the demeaning of working women's labor, the image of the woman worker that emerged from the more than half-century of active public debate and change did not include a positive vision of women in the jobs that most women did for money. There were few voices to extol the strength, vitality, and endurance of the mill worker, charwoman, or seamstress. Women's work might be applauded as a plucky excursion into the domain of male prestige or a noble self-sacrificing venture into public service, but the nineteenth century closed without the energy of the majority of women workers finding any real means of public expression.

* *Last Words to Girls: On Life in School and After School* (1889), pp. 239–40

PROLOGUE

THE TWO CLASSES OF WOMEN (1876)
Frances Power Cobbe
(See pp. 92, 121, 162, and 198.)

Melodramatic stereotypes of women as either parasites or victims, such as the ones Frances Power Cobbe uses here, gave expression to the widespread Victorian uneasiness at female poverty and marginality without shedding light on the underlying economic situation. Although Cobbe is arguing in favor of women's suffrage, such stereotypes also reinforced the popular belief that dependency or suffering were the only alternatives open to women. Moreover, the portrayal of working-class women as helpless victims encouraged the protective response that what women really needed was to be forced back into the supposed shelter of domestic life.

On one side I see women who are lapped in every luxury which the hands of loving fathers and husbands can give them. The wind of heaven never visits their cheeks too roughly; they never know any of the great realities of life. Life is from beginning to end one long, sweet holiday. The never hear rough words, never toil, never know hunger, never know any of the rougher part of life; and I am sorry to say that, though some of these are among the most excellent and unselfish of human beings, and live in palace homes as holily and as truly for God as ever a nun lived in her cell, yet others are not so. They are spoiled by the indulgences which their vanity, their luxuriousness, their selfishness receive every hour of the day; they are heartless, they are silly, they are frivolous; their nobler facilities lie dormant; they live for stupid, silly fashion, and lead the lives of butterflies in a world of toil. . . . These exquisite ladies pass over the muddy places of mortal life, like Queen Elizabeth treading on Raleigh's cloak. . . . I suppose there are from ten to twenty thousand—or let us be liberal, and say 40,000—of these very happy women. And then I see on the other side, not ten or twenty thousand, but several hundred thousand women—perhaps there are a million or so—who are very poor, struggling sorrowfully, painfully, often failing under

PIN MONEY.   NEEDLE MONEY.

Punch's *view of the two classes of women, 1861*

pressure of want of employment, or of grinding oppression and cruelty from those whose duty it is to protect and cherish them. With all the difficulties which both men and women undergo in the poorer classes, and with all the double troubles, the double weakness, the double difficulties, which under every circumstance beset the path of women—they have to fight a far harder battle than ever falls to the lot of man. And when I look at these women's faces, I seem to see in them stories of years of sordid toil, of petty cares, of pleasure-less lives, of blighted expectations, of wrong and oppression—borne as if those things were natural to them. I say unhesitatingly that there is wrong, grievous wrong somewhere.

From a suffrage speech by Frances Power Cobbe, quoted in *Victoria Magazine,* July 1876

ONE

Occupations for Ladies

At midcentury it became apparent that there was too little work available for middle-class women. The only jobs open to such women were extentions of their domestic activities: governessing, teaching, companioning, and philanthropy. Women of lesser gentility might gain a middle-class income by keeping a shop, lodging house, or restaurant, usually with their husbands, and offering to the general public the services done by women family members or servants at home. At the lower end of the gentility scale, women had even fewer opportunities. The work of a shop assistant, for instance, would have been higher in status though not necessarily less arduous than that of a factory hand because the higher-priced shops employed well-dressed clerks; but as with office work, such jobs were considered the province of men until the 1870s.

The second half of the century saw the expansion of genteel work for women and the shift from domestic occupations to professional and commercial work. This process began with those persons who sought to advance the employment situation of women by enhancing the prestige and professional standards of the ministering professions. Such advances were sometimes aided by sentimental images that were molded to traditional expectations of women: the powerless, lonely governess; the self-sacrificing, angelic nurse; and the motherly prison matron all captured the popular imagination and brought financial and moral support to women entering serious professional life. At the same time, however, women encountered strong resistance to their engaging in traditionally male professional activities, such as speaking in public, running for office, talking freely about "delicate" matters, or administering institutions.

Women benefitted from changing economic circumstances, such

as the expansion of the retail trade and the growth of commercial and government office work, which was related to England's burgeoning role as an imperial and industrial nation. Hence, the post office and particularly the telegraph system were among the first to employ women—although at lower pay and in lower-status jobs than men. By the end of the century, the number of women clerical workers had grown from the handful trained by the Society for Promoting the Employment of Women into an "army" of typists, clerks, telegraphers, and bookkeepers. For women born into or aspiring toward the middle class and for ambitious women needing to earn their own money or pursue their own interests, the opening of the new professions and clerical occupations offered an opportunity to retain the sanction of respectability without remaining within the emotional and economic constrictions of home. Yet, despite these considerable gains, teaching, although an underpaid profession, remained virtually the only field open to large numbers of "respectable" women.

ATTITUDES

WOMEN AS PROFESSIONALS (1826)
"Mrs. B—"

The London Cooperative Magazine and Monthly Herald *advocated equality of the sexes in general as part of its cooperative ideal. This specific plea for equality in women's professional employment was a very early and, at that time, radical foreshadowing of what was to become an important issue in the struggle for working women's rights. It is also an early expression of the common feminist hope that women would improve the human responsiveness of any professions they entered.*

> *A few observations in reply to a question made by a female friend: "whether Mrs. B— thinks that her sex would be more happy in endeavouring to become lawyers, physicians, judges, bishops, &c.; or where does she hope to draw the line?"*

Yes, Mrs. B— does think that women would become happier, wiser, and better, not only by endeavouring to become of all those professions above mentioned, but by absolutely becoming them; and Mrs. B— thinks the happiness of her sex alone would not be the full result of the change in public customs, but that of *the whole species* would be augmented in an incalculable degree.

With respect to law, Mrs. B—'s opinion is, that it can and ought to be made extremely simple, and certainly understood by *every individual* of our *race*. . . . Were laws simplified and the judges multiplied, so as to bring *justice* within every person's reach, the services of the whole tribe of lawyers and attornies might be usefully dispensed with. Why justice should be less mildly and skilfully distributed by a woman of superior mental power than by a man of similar powers, I cannot conceive. Nor can I conceive how human happiness can be promoted by setting the brand of incapacity and degradation on one half the human race, by their *exclusion*, tho' possessing appropriate talent and freely elected, from the judicial office.

With respect to our becoming physicians, I think it is the profession of all others to which nature prompts women, to which their organization appears peculiarly fitted; a physician should be a gentle, patient, watchful, an *ever present friend*, all humanity will call out send us a clever, a good woman: the very *sight* of her will cheer our drooping frames. Were the trade of curing and bringing on diseases superseded, as it might be and ought to be, by the art of preserving health, by a delightful regimen, the banishment of injurious occupations, and other known means, disease would be comparatively rare and easy of cure, and physicians would be chiefly occupied in attending to the birth of infants and after treatment. For whom so well as women, is this department of medicine suited? in a rational state of society, women would be perhaps more engaged in the medical department than men.

With respect to bishops my opinions are peculiar, I doubt not; but, as you asked them, I will candidly answer, I should wish to see every human being his own bishop. . . . When cannot other sects follow the rational example of the quakers, and permit any individual amongst them, man or woman, properly qualified, to exhort and instruct? are the quakers the worst sect in existence? Art their women the least amiable or modest? Alas! It is not women, but men, that have need to learn the very meaning of the word modesty.

With respect to the navy and army, which I presume are included in your &c. I hope one of the first and most beneficial effects of my sex's influence will be the total annihilation of war, in every shape in which it may attempt to shew its hydra head. . . . Strength and fortitude being the qualities wanting in war, there is no need of insulting *exclusions* preventing any amazons amongst women who should be so disposed, from their engaging in war, than there now is to prevent them from becoming ploughmen and blacksmiths. Under a system of free exertion, every individual, man or woman, would naturally fall into that line of action which would be best adapted to the talents, natural and acquired, of the individual, and which would therefore be the most agreeable and the most productive under a system of equality and justice. The tendency of women would probably be to the greater cultivation of intellectual pursuits, of men to those requiring superior strength. Or rather, perhaps, physical pursuits requiring most strength, would be chiefly followed by men, those requiring least strength would be chiefly followed by women; and intellectual, as well as social pursuits, would be equally pursued by both.

MARGARET B.

In *The London Cooperative Magazine and Monthly Herald*, May 1826

A LADY MUST NOT WORK (1853)
Margaretta Grey

Margaretta Grey (d. 1858), the progressive-thinking aunt of Josephine Butler, was known for dressing as a boy in order to gain admittance to Parliament to observe her cousin, the Whig Prime Minister Earl Grey.

The shame at earning money persisted in the early days of reform. Even Sophia Jex-Blake (see p. 311) refused a salary as a mathematics lecturer at Queen's College because her father considered payment improper.

It appears to me that, with an increase of wealth unequally distributed, and a pressure of population, there has sprung up among us a spurious refinement, that cramps the energy and circumscribes the usefulness of women in the upper classes of society. A lady, to be such, must be a mere lady, and nothing else. She must not work for profit, or engage in any occupation that money can command, lest she invade the rights of the working classes, who live by their labour.

Men in want of employment have pressed their way into nearly all the shopping and retail businesses that in my early years were managed, in whole or in part by women. The conventional barrier that pronounces it ungenteel to be behind a counter, or serving the public in any mercantile capacity, is greatly extended. The same in household economy. Servants must be up to their several offices, which is very well; but ladies, dismissed from the dairy, the confectionary, the store-room, the still-room, the poultry-yard, the kitchen-garden, and the orchard, have hardly yet found themselves a sphere equally useful and important in the pursuits of trade and art to which to apply their too abundant leisure.

In Josephine Butler, *Memoir of John Grey of Dilston* (1894)

WOMEN AND WORK (1856)
Barbara Leigh Smith Bodichon
(See p. 118.)

Barbara Leigh Smith Bodichon was one of the most energetic and influential feminists of her generation. Her work was disparate and interrupted by her marriage to a French doctor, with whom she lived half of each year in Algeria. As a result, until recently she had been remembered primarily for her friendship with George Eliot, who used Bodichon as the model for her heroine Romola in the novel of that name.

Barbara Leigh Smith Bodichon was born into a radical Unitarian family. Her father, an ardent supporter of the Reform Bill of 1832 and of Corn Law Repeal, believed in educating his daughters as well as his sons, and in making them independent. She therefore received an annuity of £300 at her majority, an income that she made use of throughout her life for feminist causes as well as for her own independence. In addition to her work for suffrage and reform of the laws for married women, she helped found the Englishwomen's Journal, the first feminist magazine in England, and was a major supporter of Girton College.

Her marriage to Dr. Eugène Bodichon in 1857, when she was thirty and he forty-six, proved remarkably unconventional. Although she considered her husband very handsome, English friends found him repulsively alien because he had dark skin, sometimes dressed in Arab or French peasant clothes, and refused to learn English. The couple were apart for four months of each year.

Despite the disruption of spending winters in Algeria, Bodichon still enjoyed many close female friendships. It was to her that the older George Eliot turned for advice about whether she should live with the already married George Lewes. Bodichon comforted and inspired other women, took pleasure in their children and their accomplishments, and was particularly supportive of the early Girton women. She had a firm faith in the eventual emancipation of women, working always in the hope of seeing things she considered inevitable accomplished within her lifetime. She was not at her best as a pamphleteer, but some of her inspirational energy is apparent in this essay from 1856.

Cries are heard on every hand that women are conspiring, that women are discontented, that women are idle, that women are overworked, and that women are out of their sphere. God only knows what is the sphere of any human being. . . .

One great corresponding cry rises from a suffering multitude of women saying, "We want work." . . .

God sent all human beings into the world for the purpose of forwarding, to the utmost of their power, the progress of the world. We must each leave the world a little better than we found it. . . .

No human being has the right to be idle. . . . Whatever comes under our hands should be bettered by the touch of our fingers. The land we own we should drain and make more fertile for ever. The children who are in our power should be educated. . . . If an old pot comes to us to mend, we must mend it as best we can. *And we must train ourselves to do our work well.* . . . Women must, as children of God, be trained to do some work in the world. Women may not take a man as a god: they must not hold their first duty to be towards any human being. . . .

To think a woman is more feminine because she is frivolous, ignorant, weak, and sickly, is absurd; the larger-natured a woman is, the more decidedly feminine she will be; the stronger she is, the more strongly feminine. You do not call a lioness unfeminine, though she is different in size and strength from the domestic cat, or mouse.

If men think they shall lose anything charming by not having ignorant, dependent women about them, they are quite wrong. The vivacity of women will not be injured by their serious work. None play so heartily as those who work heartily. The playfulness of women which makes them so sympathetic to children, is deep in their nature; and greater development of their whole natures will only increase this and all their natural gifts. . . .

Never since the world began have women stood face to face with God. Individual women have done so, but not women in general. They are beginning to do it now; the principle that Jesus Christ laid down is beginning to be admitted. Young women begin to ask at the age of sixteen or seventeen, "What am I created for? Of what use am I to be in the world?" According to the answer is often the destiny of the creature.

Mothers! the responsibility lies with you: what do you say in answer? I fear it is almost always something to this purport: "You must marry some day. Women were made for men. Your use is to bear children; to keep your home comfortable for your husband. In marriage is the only respectable life for woman."

If a girl has a religious or an inquiring mind, she will be much dissatisfied with this answer, and say, "But if no one ask me to marry whom I can love? or suppose I do not want to marry? Suppose my husband dies? or, what am I to do all the years I have to wait for a husband? Is there nothing I can do for anybody?" . . .

There is nothing in the world so sad, so pitiful to see, as a young woman, who has been handsome, full of youthful joy, animal spirits and good nature, fading at thirty or thirty-five. Becoming old too soon, getting meagre, dried up, sallow, pettish, peevish, the one possible chance of life getting very uncertain, and the mind so continually fixed on that one hope that it becomes gradually a monomania. . . . We do not mean to say work will take the place of love in life; that is impossible; does it with men? But we ardently desire that women should not make *love their profession*.

Love is not the end of life. It is nothing to be sought for; it should come. If we work, love may meet us in life; if not, we have something still, beyond all price.

Oh young girls! waiting listlessly for some one to come and marry you; wasting the glorious spring time of your lives sowing nothing but vanity, what a barren autumn will come to you! You are trying hard to make yourselves agreeable and attractive by dress and frivolity, and all this time your noblest parts lie sleeping. Arouse yourselves! Awake! Be the best that God has made you. Do not be contented to be charming and fascinating; be noble, be useful, be wise.

In Barbara Leigh Smith Bodichon, *Women and Work* (1856)

"WANTED: MORE WOMEN" (1876)
Englishwoman's Review

While some feminists like Barbara Leigh Smith Bodichon wished women to live up to male ideals of industriousness, others saw the widening of opportunities for women as a chance for them to bring their maternal values into the public arena.

"An ounce of mother is worth a pound of clergy," says an old Spanish proverb, and we would add without derogation to organized civilisation, it is worth an hundred-weight of Boards, Committees, and Police. Our English social economy teems with elaborately arranged systems, but they want the vitalising warmth of woman's work, and still more, of woman's control—the *mother* influence and the benefit that would accrue to society by their more general adoption of public duties.

Yes, we want both men and women to carry on the public work of the world: the State, which is only an aggregate of families can no more do with only masculine government than can an individual family. The household which is only ruled over by women wants breadth of interest and activity; the household which is only ruled over by men wants tenderness and consideration for diversities of temperament and powers. So it is with the State: the laws made by men, be they ever so good, cannot be made to fit comfortably a world which contains so many sick, poor, and little ones, without the help of women's insight and adaptability to special requirements. A regimental outfitter makes his coats after one size and pattern; a dressmaker fits and shapes her garment to suit individual curves. There is something of this difference in men and women's work. We need more women, not only on the School Boards, but on Workhouse Committees, in jails, on Boards of Health and Town Councils, on juries, in science, and in law. When we hear it said there is a redundancy of women in England, it means of women who cannot set their hands and brains to any particular work, who are the drones of society: there is not a redundancy, but a scarcity of women who will put aside the comfort and ease of private life for the public responsibility of being useful. Fortunately, the number is increasing of those who recognize that there is more womanliness in being "motherly" to the sick, ignorant, and suffering, than in remaining silent, and unoccupied within the four walls of a house, be it ever so secluded and comfortable.

In *Englishwoman's Review*, December 1876

TEACHING

In England in 1850, there were an estimated twenty-one thousand governesses and many more would-be governesses in need of work. Wages ranged from as low as £10 a year up to an unusual £100 for an educated woman in an outstanding school. Most governesses struggled along on £20 to £30 a year plus room and board. Although that put them well above women factory workers, it was still below what men were making as tutors, teachers, or clerks. Because governessing or teaching of some kind was virtually the only occupation open to genteel young women, many girls took the work without any interest in teaching and even with a loathing of children.

Little education was required for a governess. She was primarily engaged to impart a veneer of learning and genteel manners to her charges, and to act as a babysitter. As Lady Eastlake makes clear, the governess was caught between classes in a rigidly class-structured society. Too low for the family, too high for the servants, she was isolated and sometimes universally despised. Governesses worked all day, often taking care of the children's baths and meals as well as their lessons; doing family mending in odd moments; and sharing a bedroom and sometimes a bed with the children at night. Often employers discouraged affection between their children and the governesses who tended them. Yet the long hours and confinement made it impossible for a governess to find other intimates. She had as little chance of saving money as did any other servant, and the same low level of job security. When her services were no longer needed, she was out of work and home without a pension; and if she did not receive a good reference from her employers, she might not find a new position. The life of a governess in a private household was isolated without being private, and demanding without being secure. No wonder then that Florence Nightingale and others noticed that many governesses ended their days in hospitals or insane asylums, just as domestic servants often died in the workhouse.

The boom in elementary and secondary education described in Part III eventually rendered governessing obsolete. The new secondary schools required an equally new, professional woman teacher and headmistress with formal training, a clear curriculum, and a public place of work. The elementary schools provided opportunities for better-off working-class girls to progress from an apprenticeship at age thirteen to training school and finally a salaried teaching post. Women teachers remained underpaid as well as discriminated against by an age bar that denied promotion to headmistress after thirty-five. However, by the end of the century, teaching was professional work for women, with clear standards of certification and pay, free from the suffocation and social indignities of domestic service.

DIARY OF A YOUNG TEACHER (1836)
Charlotte Brontë
(See pp. 35, 95, 109, 115, 151, 160, and 273.)

In 1835, Charlotte Brontë, age nineteen, began working as a teacher in the small proprietary school where she received her own formal education. During the few moments of solitude and privacy she could find, she kept a diary. Obsessed with her private saga of "Angria," an imaginary kingdom inhabited by passionate characters she had created with her brother Branwell, Brontë found the boredom and confinement of the school physically painful.

Friday August 11th . . . I had been toiling for nearly an hour with Miss Lister, Miss Marriott, & Ellen Cook striving to teach them the distinction between an article and a substantive. The parsing lesson was completed, a dead silence had succeeded it in the school-room & I sat sinking from irritation & weariness into a kind of lethargy. The thought came over me: am I to spend all the best part of my life in this wretched bondage, forcibly suppressing my rage at the idleness, the apathy, and the hyperbolical & most asinine stupidity of those fat-headed oafs, and on compulsion assuming an air of kindness, patience, & assiduity? Must I from day to day sit chained to this chair, prisoned within these four bare-walls, while these glorious summer suns are burning in heaven & the year is revolving in its richest glow & declaring at the close of every summer day [that] the time I am losing will never come again? Stung to the heart with this reflection, I started up mechanically & walked to the window—a sweet August morning was smiling without. The dew was not yet dried off the field, the early shadows were stretching cool & dim from the hay-stack, & the roots of the grand old oaks & thorns scattered along the sunk fence. All was still except the murmur of the scrubs about me over their tasks. I flung up the sash, an uncertain sound of inexpressible sweetness came on a dying gale from the south. . . . It was the bells of Huddersfield Parish Church. I shut the window & went back to my seat. I felt as if I could have written gloriously—I longed to write. . . . If I had had time to indulge it I felt that the vague sensations of that moment would have settled down into some narrative better at least than anything I ever produced before. But just then a dolt came up with a lesson. I thought I should have vomited.

In the afternoon Miss B— L— . . . nearly killed me between the violence of the irritation her horrid wilfulness excited & the labour it took to subdue it to a moderate appearance of calmness. My fingers trembled as if I had had twenty-four hours tooth-ache, & my spirits felt worn down to a degree of desperate despondency. Miss Wooler tried to make me talk at tea time and was exceedingly kind to me but I could not have roused if she had offered me worlds. After tea we took a long weary walk . . . Miss L— & Miss M—t had been boring me with their vulgar familiar trash all the time we were out. If those girls knew how I loathe their company they would not seek mine so much as they do. The sun had set nearly a quarter of an hour before we returned and it was getting dusk. The ladies went into the school-room to do their exercises & I crept into the bedroom to be alone for the first time that day. Delicious was the separation I experienced as I laid down on the spare bed & resigned myself to the luxury of twilight & solitude. The stream of Thought, checked all day came flowing free & calm along its channel.

In Charlotte Brontë, *Roe Head Journal*, "All this day" Bonnell Collection 98(8), Brontë Parsonage Museum

ON THE REQUIREMENTS OF A GOVERNESS (1848)
Charlotte Brontë
(See pp. 35, 95, 109, 115, 151, 160, and 272.)

Brontë wrote this letter of advice to her editor W. S. Williams, who was thinking of training one of his daughters to be a governess.

Some remarks in your last letter on teaching commanded my attention. I suppose you never were engaged in tuition yourself; but if you had been, you could not have more exactly hit on the great qualification—I had almost said the *one* qualification—necessary to the task: the faculty, not merely of *acquiring* but of imparting knowledge—the power of influencing young minds—that natural fondness for, that innate sympathy with, children, which, you say, Mrs. Williams is so happy as to possess. . . . If the faculty be absent, the life of a teacher will be a struggle from beginning to end. No matter how amiable the disposition, how strong the sense of duty, how active the desire to please; no matter how brilliant and varied the accomplishments; if the governess has not the power to win her young charge, the secret to instil gently and surely her own knowledge into the growing mind intrusted to her, she will have a wearing, wasting existence of it. . . . As a school-teacher she may succeed; but as a resident governess she will never (except under peculiar and exceptional circumstances) be happy. Her deficiency will harass her not so much in school-time as in play-hours; the moments that would be rest and recreation to the governess who understood and could adapt herself to children, will be almost torture to her who has not that power. Many a time, when her charge turns unruly on her hands, when the responsibility which she would wish to discharge faithfully and perfectly, becomes unmanageable to her, she will wish herself a housemaid or kitchen girl, rather than a baited, trampled, desolate, distracted governess.

The Governesses' Institution may be an excellent thing in some points of view, but it is both absurd and cruel to attempt to raise still higher the standards of acquirements. Already governesses are not half nor a quarter paid for what they teach, nor in most instances is half or a quarter of their attainments required by their pupils. The young teacher's chief anxiety, when she sets out in life, always is to know a great deal; her chief fear that she should not know enough. Brief experience will, in most instances, show her that this anxiety has been misdirected. She will rarely be found too ignorant for her pupils; the demand on her knowledge will not often be larger than she can answer. But on her patience—on her self-control, the requirement will be enormous; on her animal spirits (and woe be to her if these fail!) the pressure will be immense. . . .

It is true the world demands a brilliant list of accomplishments. For £20 per annum, it expects in one woman the attainments of sev-

"The Family Governess"

eral professors—but the demand is insensate, and I think should rather be resisted than complied with. If I might plead with you in behalf of your daughters, I should say, "Do not let them waste their young lives in trying to attain manifold accomplishments. Let them try rather to possess thoroughly, fully, one or two talents; then let them endeavour to lay in a stock of health, strength, cheerfulness.

Let them labour to attain self-control, endurance, fortitude, firmness; if possible, let them learn from their mother something of the precious art she possesses—these things, together with sound principles, will be their best supports, their best aids through a governess's life.

From Charlotte Brontë to W. S. Williams, May 12, 1848, in *The Brontës*, letter no. 368

ON GOVERNESSES (1848)
Lady Eastlake

In this essay, Lady Eastlake (writing anonymously) both consciously and unconsciously portrayed the class snobbery that increased the governess's unhappiness. Lady Eastlake's class allegiance was stronger than her empathy with other women. She was, for instance, offended by Charlotte Brontë's Jane Eyre because she felt the novel emphasized Jane's dissatisfactions as a governess and her lack of gratitude to her employers.

The Governesses' Benevolent Institution, founded in 1843, helped governesses save money and find employment, and provided them with money in unemployment and a place to live in old age.

. . . If these times puzzle us how to meet the claims and wants of the lower classes of our dependants, they puzzle and shame us too in the case of that highest dependant of all, the governess—who is not only entitled to our gratitude and respect by her position, but, in nine cases out of ten, by the circumstances which reduced her to it. For the case of the governess is so much the harder than that of any other class of the community, in that they are not only quite as liable to all the vicissitudes of life, but are absolutely supplied by them. There may be, and are, exceptions to this rule, but the real definition of a governess, in the English sense, is a being who is our equal in birth, manners, and education, but our inferior in worldly wealth. Take a lady, in every meaning of the word, born and bred, and let her father pass through the gazette [go bankrupt], and she wants nothing more to suit our highest *beau idéal* of a guide and instructress to our children. . . .

Man cannot live by the head alone, far less woman. A governess has no equals, and therefore can have no sympathy. She is a burden

and restraint in society, as all must be who are placed ostensibly at
the same table and yet are forbidden to help themselves or to be
helped to the same viands. She is a bore to most ladies by the same
rule, and a reproach too—for her dull, fagging, bread-and-water life
is perpetually putting their pampered listlessness to shame. The servants invariably detest her, for she is a dependant like themselves, and
yet, for all that, as much their superior in other respects as the family
they both serve. Her pupils may love her, and she may take the deepest interest in them, but they cannot be her friends. She must, to all
intents and purposes, live alone, or she transgresses that invisible but
rigid line which alone establishes the distance between herself and
her employers. . . .

Nor have we brought [these evils] forward with any view, or hope,
or even with any wish to see them remedied, for in the inherent constitution of English habits, feelings, and prejudices, there is no possibility that they should be. . . . We shall ever prefer to place those
immediately about our children who have been born and bred with
somewhat of the same refinement as ourselves. We must ever keep
them in a sort of isolation, for it is the only means for maintaining
that distance which the reserve of English manners and the decorum
of English families exact. . . . But there *is* one thing, the absence of
which need not be added to the other drawbacks of her lot; which
would go far to compensate to her for the misfortunes which reduced
her to this mode of life, and for the trials attendant upon it—for
the years of chilly solitude through which the heart is kept shivering
upon a diet that can never sufficiently warm it, and that in the longing season of youth—for the nothing less than maternal cares and
solicitudes for which she reaps no maternal reward—for a life spent in
harness from morning till night, and from one year's end to another—
for the old age and incapacity creeping on and threatening to deprive her even of that mode of existence which habit has made endurable—there is something that would compensate for all this, and
that is *better pay*. . . .

It may be quite true that she is glad to get even [£20 a year]; and
if so, it is very deplorable: but this has no relation to the services
exacted and the assistance given; and these should be more especially
the standard where the plaintiff, as in the case of the governess,
possesses no means of resistance. Workmen may rebel, and tradesmen
may combine, not to let you have their labour under a certain rate;
but the governess has no refuge—no escape; she is a needy *lady*, whose
services are of far too precious a kind to have any stated market

value, and is therefore left to the mercy, or what they call the *means*, of the family that engages her. . . .

While we therefore applaud heartily the efforts for their comfort and relief which have been made within the last few years, in the establishment of the Governesses' Benevolent Institution, we look with sorrow, and almost with horror, at the disclosures which those efforts have brought to light. There is no document which more painfully exposes the peculiar tyranny of our present state of civilisation than those pages in the Report of this Society containing the list of candidates for the few and small annuities which the Institution is as yet in the condition to give. We know of nothing, in truth or fiction, more affecting than the sad and simple annals of these afflicted and destitute ladies, many of them with their aristocratic names, who, having passed through that course of servitude which, as we have shown, is peculiarly and inevitably deprived of most of those endearing sympathies which gladden this life, are now left in their old age or sickness without even the absolute necessaries for existence. . . . Conversant with several languages—skilled in many accomplishments—crammed with every possible fact in history, geography, and the use of the globes—and scarcely the daily bread to put into her mouth! . . . We give a few specimens—omitting the surnames, as not required here:

Miss Catherine ——, aged sixty-three. Became a governess on the insolvency of her father. The support of an aged father and afflicted mother prevented her laying by for herself. Her mother, dependent upon her for twenty-six years, died of cancer. Present income less than 5s. a week. . . .

Miss Margaret ——, aged seventy-one. Fifty years a governess, having been left an orphan at three years old, and the uncle who meant to provide for her being lost at sea. Assisted her relations as far as possible from her salaries. She is now very feeble, and her health failing fast. Her entire support is an annuity of fourteen guineas.

Miss Dorothea ——, aged fifty-four. Father a surgeon in the army, governess, chiefly in Scotch families, for thirty years; was the chief support of her mother and the younger members of her family from 1811 to 1838, when her mother died, leaving her with failing health through over exertion. . . .

In Lady Eastlake, "*Vanity Fair, Jane Eyre,* and the Governesses' Benevolent Institution," *Quarterly Review,* December 1848

EARNING A LIVING (1882)

Sara Burstall

(See p. 230.)

I began my professional career in June, 1882, as assistant mistress in the North London Collegiate School in the new building in Camden Road, at what was for those times an exceedingly good salary, £120 per annum. Economic independence is, after all, one of the requisites to a full and happy life: "To learn and labour truly to get mine own living," as the Church Catechism says, is not only a duty but a basis for better things. The joy and satisfaction of the modern woman's economic independence is sometimes not stressed as it should be in the many discussions on feminism. One aspect of it, in particular, the power to help those who are dear to us, our family and our friends, is often not known, for naturally neither we nor they talk very much about it. But it is there, and is an important element in the struggle to get the ban removed on married women in professions, and in the demand for proper pay. I can claim to have had a wide experience among my own profession, and I have never known a woman teacher who had "no dependants": those I have known have been called to help by their earnings someone among kinsfolk or friends, either permanently or for a period. It simply is not true to say that women teachers have no dependants: the support of the elderly mother, the delicate brother or sister, the education of younger members of the family come almost naturally on the spinster's income. The men of the family have their wives and children to keep.

Apart however from income, we teachers have the additional work which is happy in itself, whether we get any pay for it or not. Indeed the first time I cashed my cheque, I thought the shining sovereigns passed across the counter were magical, for I should have been glad to do the work for nothing.

In Sara A. Burstall, *Retrospect and Prospect: Sixty Years of Women's Education* (1933)

"MY FIRST POST" (1886)
M. Vivian Hughes
(See p. 233.)

What appalled me was not the number of subjects assigned to me, but the elder [boarding students]. I met these girls at supper on my arrival, and barely slept for fear of facing them in class on the morrow. Big girls they were, in long skirts and with their hair done up, looking older than I did, or felt, and apparently far more women of the world. . . . Few animals are more awe-inspiring than a group of English schoolgirls who are taking your measure. I had had no opportunity for preparing a lesson, so it was with assumed nonchalance that I asked: "What country are you to be taking next?"

"Italy," was the lack-lustre reply.

"Oh, then we shall want a map," said I as casually as I could, but thanking my stars for that map of the Mediterranean I had practised for the matriculation. With careless ease I turned to the board and executed the western half of my masterpiece. When I looked round the class had come to life, and amazement sat on the previously disdainful faces.

"Did you do that out of your head?" exclaimed one girl.

At this I spread out my hands, to show that there was no book or atlas near me, and said, "No deception, ladies and gentlemen." When a laugh greeted this my nervousness had entirely gone, and we all set out to fill up the map, as by a kind of dentistry I extracted a few of the "natural features" from the class. . . .

I had taken my first fence, but there was another to be taken that I had not even suspected. During those first few days one after another of the elder boarders would come up to me at any odd time of the day to ask me the meaning of something—anthropomorphic, bicentenary, protoplasm, and other long words. I gave the meaning briefly, but one day it was "upanishad."

"I have no idea what that means," said I, "fetch the book where you came across it, and we shall be able to give a guess at it from the context."

The expectant group looked uncomfortable, and then confessed that they hadn't got any book, but had picked it out of the dictionary. Then they told me that my predecessor had always explained a

London teachers in 1906

word if she knew it, but if she didn't she would not admit her ignorance but would say, "Don't bother me about a mere word, look it up in the dictionary, dear." This sport lost its zest as soon as I admitted ignorance, and we laughed together at the absurdity of pretending to know everything.

After this we were friends, and sincerer friends than those few elder girls I have never had. . . .

While all lessons with the elder classes were sheer pleasure, those with the younger ones gave me more difficulty. Soon it became clear that "giving lessons" as we had done in the Training College, when each one was an adventure, was a different matter from teaching day after day the same children in subjects that were already dull to them. . . . The hour-long lessons were a trial with the younger ones, for I hadn't learnt the technique of making the pupils do all the work. But this soundest of principles was discovered by me in the following way. The period of the week most dreaded by me was an hour and a quarter, at the close of Friday, assigned to reading. At first it was greeted by the pupils cordially, for my predecessor had allowed them to "read round" and when once the turn of each was past she engaged in her own affairs. But I dodged them, and they had no peace. The only available Reader was more than stale, and already decorated with pipes in the mouths of the persons illustrated. "Oh, don't let's have this one," was the inevitable murmur whichever one I chose. Silent reading, even if there had been any books for it, would have been considered laziness on my part by the headmistress, who was a martinet. She had scolded me up and down for having dismissed this dreadful class five minutes before time. An *hour* of horribly bad reading, with an undercurrent of insubordination, was bad enough, but it was that extra quarter of an hour that drove me to desperation. Surely heavenly inspiration is not confined to solemn matters, or else whence came my idea?

"Have you girls got any books at home?" said I.

"Yes, a lot," was the rather indignant reply from several.

"Next Friday, then, I want each of you to bring to school any book you like, and read a bit out of it to us all."

Questions rained on me—Did I mean it? Would poetry do? How long must it be? Must it be a school-book? May it be really *anything* we like? May it be funny? . . .

"It doesn't really matter whether it's long or short, comic or tragic, poetry or prose, grown-up or childish. But there are three things you must remember. First, it must be something that will interest us. Secondly, you must practise it at home, reading it aloud to your mother or in an empty room, till you can do it really well. And lastly, you must keep it a dead secret from the rest of the class, because we all want to have a little surprise over each reading; now rehearse the three points to remember: interesting—well prepared—secret."

It was as though a magician had waved a wand over the class. Friday afternoon became the star turn of the week. The children were seen coming to school with volumes of all sizes wrapped up in newspaper for purposes of protection and concealment, and when the turn came to read there was a solemn unveiling of a fat Shakespeare, or a wedding-present-looking Tennyson, or a tattered copy of *Alice*. I had prepared a chapter of *Uncle Remus* to read to them if the supply of matter failed. But it never did. There was such eagerness to read that I had to put names into a box and draw out by hazard. I enjoyed myself as much as they did, for they chose quite good stuff and rendered it in entirely their own fashion; and of course I was secretly glorying in the vast improvement in the reading without the slightest effort on my part.

In M. Vivian Hughes, *A London Girl of the Eighties* (1936)

PUBLIC WORK

Philanthropy was long considered the proper work of privileged women. Acts of "Christian charity," such as visiting the cottages of the poor, offering remedies to the sick, or running a school for village children, were all acceptable voluntary occupations for clergymen's daughters or women who lived on country estates. However, as an industrializing society turned the care of the poor into a state-run enterprise, some women began to move into the new institutions bringing the same ministering, motherly spirit to the workhouse that they had formerly been expected to take into the homes of their poor neighbors or tenants. Religious feeling, within or outside the Anglican Church, often provided the strongest motivation for women's philanthropic work. Quaker minister Elizabeth Fry set the pattern for this new style of philanthropy when she set up her prayer meetings and sewing circles in Newgate Prison and urged other women to follow her example.

Fry's work revealed an important contradiction that persisted in most women's philanthropic and public service. Like many women, Fry wanted to enter institutions in which women were under the authority of men in order to offer them the care of their own sex. Yet, as these selections show, her efforts were often of most use to the administrators of the prison in establishing greater order and helping to create a more docile prison population. There were, however, a few feminist philanthropists, like Emily Faithfull and Jessie Boucherett, who used their organizational skills to set up woman-run institutions that were meant to provide jobs and training for other women.

Many of the women represented in other sections of this anthology did serious reform or institutional work, which derived from these somewhat amateurish early efforts at philanthropy. Fry and Faithfull, among others, pioneered activities that women then joined in ever-increasing numbers and with ever-greater professionalism. The National Association for the Promotion of Social Science served as an umbrella organization for many newly developing feminist and philanthropic groups, from the Society for Promoting the Employment of Women to the Workhouse Visiting Society.

By the last decades of the century, feminists were even being elected to municipal offices—among them Emily Davies and Elizabeth Garrett Anderson, who were two of the first female school-board members. Emmeline Pankhurst, elected poor-law guardian in the 1890s, worked to make the local workhouse more responsive to the needs of the poor rather than forcing the inmates to adapt to the institution. Pankhurst's experiences marked a turning point in her career as a challenger of traditional male structures, and are generally representative of the change in women's attitudes and strategies from the pious volunteerism of the early century.

Throughout this period, women were finding their public voices, risking ridicule and even violence in order to take their place in public life. The last three selections in this section record the excitement and dangers of individual transitions from silence to public expression.

"ON VISITING PRISONS" (1827)
Elizabeth Fry

Elizabeth Fry (1780–1845) began her charitable work with the ordinary activities of visiting the poor, relieving the sick, and keeping school. A devout Quaker, she married at twenty and had ten children. She struggled against her desire to become a minister until she was called upon to speak at her father's funeral when she was twenty-nine. Her natural ability as a gripping public speaker then made her choice inevitable. In 1813, she became involved with the reform of conditions for women in Newgate Prison. At the time there were three hundred women and their children in the prison, the convicted and untried kept together, all of them lacking in clothing, unsupplied with beds or bedding, but given access to alcohol. The conditions were notoriously dangerous and unruly. Fry brought clothes to the prisoners, set up a school, and instituted a system comprising matrons, monitors, severe clothing, moral supervision, mandatory needlework, and chapel, which brought order and routine to the prisoners' lives.

She gave readings from the Scriptures that were famous for their pathos and emotional force. Her personality was calming and compelling, and her sincerity was apparent to all who knew her. Yet the encounter between Fry's follower "Sophia de C." and the pregnant felon under sentence of death suggests the female philanthropist's inevitable conflict between her sympathy for her fellow women and her ties to the power structure in which these women were caught.

No person will deny the importance attached to the character and conduct of a woman . . . when she is filling the station of a daughter, a sister, a wife, a mother, or a mistress of a family. But it is a dangerous error to suppose that the duties of females end here. Their gentleness, their natural sympathy with the afflicted, their quickness of discernment, their openness to religious impressions, are points of character (not unusually to be found in our sex) which evidently qualify them, within their own peculiar province, for a far more extensive field of usefulness. . . .

Much may be accomplished by the *union of forces*. If, in every parish or district, such ladies as desire to make the best use of their time would occasionally meet together, in order to consider the condition of their neighbourhood, and would then divide themselves and allot the labours of Christian love to the several parties respectively, according to their suitability for different objects, the employment of but a small portion of their time would enable them to effect more extensive good than could previously have been thought possible; and, instead of being incapacitated for their domestic duties, they would often return to these duties, refreshed in spirit, and stimulated to perform them with increased cheerfulness, propriety, and diligence.

To revert, for a short time, to the subject of our own public institutions, although I feel it a delicate matter so earnestly to insist on the point, I must now express my conviction, that few persons are aware of the *degree* in which the female departments of them stand in need of the superintending care of judicious ladies. So great are the abuses which exist in some of these establishments, that *modest* women dare not run the risk to which they would be exposed, did they attempt to derive from them the relief which they require. I would have this subject occupy the serious consideration of the benevolent part of the community. All reflecting persons will surely unite in the sentiment, that the female, placed in the prison for her crimes, in the hospital for her sickness, in the asylum for her insanity, or in the workhouse for her poverty, possesses no light or common claim on the pity and attention of those of her own sex, who, through the bounty of a kind Providence, are able *"to do good, and to communicate."*

May the attention of *women* be more and more directed to these labors of love; and may the time quickly arrive, when there shall not exist, in this realm, a single public institution of the kind, in which the degraded or afflicted females who may happen to be its inmates shall not enjoy the *efficacious superintendence* of the pious and benevolent of THEIR OWN SEX!

In Elizabeth Fry, *Observations on the Visiting, Superintending, and Government of Female Prisoners, 1819–1827* (1827)

THE EFFECTS OF MRS. FRY'S SYSTEM (1813)
Anonymous Gentleman

In their memoir of their mother, Elizabeth Fry's daughters offer this first-hand account of the effects of Fry's system at Newgate, written by a gentleman who visited just a fortnight after the rules were adopted.

I went, and requested permission to see Mrs. Fry, which was shortly obtained, and I was conducted by a turnkey to the entrance of the women's wards. On my approach, no loud or dissonant sounds or angry voices indicated that I was about to enter a place, which, I was credibly assured, had long had for one of its titles, that of "Hell above ground." The court-yard, into which I was admitted, instead of being peopled with beings scarcely human, blaspheming, fighting, tearing each other's hair, or gaming with a filthy pack of cards, for the very clothes they wore, which often did not suffice even for decency, presented a scene where stillness and propriety reigned. I was conducted by a decently-dressed person, the newly appointed yard's-woman, to the door of a ward, where, at the head of a long table, sat a lady belonging to the Society of Friends. She was reading aloud to about sixteen women prisoners, who were engaged in needle-work around it. Each wore a clean looking blue apron and bib; with a ticket, having a number on it, suspended from her neck by a red tape. They all rose on my entrance, curtsied respectfully, and then, at a signal given, resumed their seats and employments. Instead of a scowl, leer, or ill-suppressed laugh, I observed upon their countenances an air of self-respect and gravity, a sort of consciousness of their improved character, and the altered position in which they were placed. I afterwards visited the other wards, which were the counterparts of the first.

In *Memoir of the Life of Elizabeth Fry, with Extracts from Her Journal and Letters, Edited by Her Two Daughters* (Philadelphia: H. Longstreth, 1847)

A VISIT TO NEWGATE (1817)
Sophia de C.

Fifth Month 1st, 1817. After nearly a sleepless night, spent in anticipation of the scenes of the morrow, I called on Dorcas Coventry, who had promised to introduce me to inspect the important labours which the Ladies of the Prison Committee had engaged in, for the reformation of the women in Newgate, for some time past. . . . Most of the prisoners were collected in a room newly appropriated for the purpose to hear a portion of the Sacred Scriptures read to them, either by the matron, or by one of the Ladies' Committee; which last is far preferable. They assemble when the bell rings, as near nine o'clock as possible, following their monitors or wards-women, to the forms which are placed in order to receive them. I think I can never forget the impression made upon my feelings at this sight. Women from every part of Great Britain; of every age and condition, below the lower middle rank, were assembled in mute silence, except when the interrupted breathing of their suckling infants informed us of the unhealthy state of these innocent partakers in their parents' punishment. The matron read; I could not refrain from tears; the women wept also; several were under the sentence of death. Swain, for forging, who had just received her respite, sat next to me; and on my left hand, sat Lawrence, alias Woodman, surrounded by her four children, and only waiting the birth of another, which she hourly expects, to pay the forfeit of her life; as her husband had done for the same crime, a short time before.

Such various, such acute, and such new feelings passed through my mind, that I could hardly support the reflection, that what I saw was only to be compared to an atom in the abyss of vice, and consequently, misery in this vast metropolis. The hope of doing the least lasting good, seemed to vanish; and to leave me in fearful apathy. . . .

23rd. I found poor Woodman lying-in, in the common ward, where she had been suddenly taken ill; herself and little girl were each doing very well. She was awaiting her execution, at the end of the month. What can be said of such sights as these.

24th. I read to Woodman, who is not in the state of mind we could wish for her, indeed, so unnatural is her situation, that one can hardly tell how or in what manner to meet her case. She seems afraid to love her baby, and the very health which is being restored to her, produces irritation of mind.

In *Memoir of the Life of Elizabeth Fry, with Extracts from Her Journal and Letters, Edited by Her Two Daughers* (1847)

THE VICTORIA PRESS (1860)
Emily Faithfull

Emily Faithfull (1835–1894) was one of the original members of the Society for Promoting the Employment of Women. At her urging, the Society helped establish the Victoria Press in order to introduce women into the trade of printing. Compositing was considered work appropriate to women by the Society's committee members, because it required "chiefly a quick eye, a ready hand, and steady application" and involved "no exposure to weather, no hard labour." Although printing did not become an important woman's occupation, the number of female printers increased from 419 in 1861 to 741 in 1871, a fact that was credited in part to Faithfull's efforts. The Victoria Press undertook much feminist publishing, including the Englishwoman's Journal (1858–1864) and Victoria Magazine (1863–1870). Emily Faithfull was also a novelist, an energetic essayist, and a public speaker.

We ventured to call it the Victoria Press, after the Sovereign to whose influence English women owe so large a debt of gratitude, and in the hope also that the name would prove a happy augury of victory. . . . The Society for Promoting the Employment of Women apprenticed five girls to me at premiums of £10 each; others were apprenticed by relatives and friends, and we soon found ourselves in the thick of the struggle, for such I do not hesitate to call it. Work came in immediately, from the earliest day. In April we commenced our first book, and began practically to test all the difficulties of the trade. . . .

In the month of April, when work was coming in freely, I was fortunate enough to secure a skilled hand from Limerick. She had been trained as a printer by her father, and had worked under him for twelve years. At his death she had carried on the office, which she was after some time obliged to relinquish, owing to domestic circumstances. Seeing in a country newspaper that an opening for female compositors had occurred in London, she determined on taking the long journey from Ireland to seek employment in a business for which she was well competent. She came straight to my office, bringing with her a letter from the editor of a Limerick paper, who assured me that I should find her a great assistance in my enterprise. I engaged her there and then; she came to work the very next day, and has proved herself most valuable. . . .

The hours of work are from nine till one, and from two till six. Those who live near, go home to dinner between one and two; others have the use of a room in the house, some bringing their own dinners ready cooked, and some preparing it on the spot. When they work overtime, as is occasionally unavoidable, for which of course they receive extra pay per hour, they have tea at half past five, so as to break the time.

It is too early yet to judge of the effect of this employment upon the health of women, even under careful sanitary arrangements; but I may state that one of my compositors, whom I hesitated to receive on account of the extreme delicacy of her health, . . . has, since she undertook her new occupation, become quite strong, and her visits to her doctor have entirely ceased.

In Emily Faithfull, "The Victoria Press," *Transactions of the National Association for the Promotion of Social Sciences* (1860)

WORK AS A POOR LAW GUARDIAN (1894)
Emmeline Pankhurst
(See p. 107.)

And now began a new, and, as I look back on it, an absorbingly interesting stage of my career. . . . [O]ur leaders in the Liberal Party had advised the women to prove their fitness for the Parliamentary franchise by serving in municipal offices, especially the unsalaried offices. A large number of women had availed themselves of this advice, and were serving on Boards of Guardians, on school boards, and in other capacities. My children now being old enough for me to leave them with competent nurses, I was free to join these ranks. A year after my return to Manchester I became a candidate for the Board of Poor Law Guardians. . . .

The Board of Poor Law Guardians disburses for the poor the money coming from the Poor Rates (taxes), and some additional moneys allowed by the local government board, the president of which is a cabinet minister. . . . The Board of Guardians has control of the institution we call the workhouse, . . . which [is] all kinds of institutions in one. We had, in my workhouse, a hospital with nine hundred beds, a school with several hundred children, a farm, and many workshops.

When I came into office I found that the law in our district, Chorlton, was being very harshly administered. The old board had been made up of the kind of men who are known as rate savers. They were guardians, not of the poor but of the rates, and, as I soon discovered, not very astute guardians even of money. For instance, although the inmates were being very poorly fed, a frightful waste of food was apparent. Each inmate was given each day a certain weight of food, and bread formed so much of this ration that hardly anyone consumed all of his portion. In the farm department pigs were kept on purpose to consume this surplus of bread, and as pigs do not thrive on a solid diet of stale bread the animals fetched in the market a much lower price than properly fed farm pigs. I suggested that, instead of giving a solid weight of bread in one lump, the loaf be cut in slices and buttered with margarine, each person being allowed to eat all that he cared to eat. The rest of the board objected, saying that our poor charges were very jealous of their rights, and would suspect in such an innovation an attempt to deprive them of a part of their ration. This was easily overcome by the suggestion that we consult the inmates before we made the change. Of course the poor people consented, and with the bread that we saved we made puddings with milk and currants, to be fed to the old people of the workhouse. These old folks I found sitting on backless forms, or benches. They had no privacy, no possessions, not even a locker. The old women were without pockets in their gowns, so they were obliged to keep any poor treasures they had in their bosoms. Soon after I took office we gave the old people comfortable Windsor chairs to sit in, and in a number of ways we managed to make their existence more endurable.

These, after all, were minor benefits. But it does gratify me when I look back and remember what we were able to do for the children of the Manchester workhouse. The first time I went into the place I was horrified to see little girls seven and eight years old on their knees scrubbing the cold stones of the long corridors. These little girls were clad, summer and winter, in thin cotton frocks, low in the neck and short sleeved. At night they wore nothing at all, night dresses being considered too good for paupers. The fact that bronchitis was epidemic among them most of the time had not suggested to the guardians any change in the fashion of their clothes. There was a school for the children, but the teaching was of the lowest order. They were forlorn enough, these poor innocents, when I first met them. In five years' time we had changed the face of the earth for them. We had bought land in the country and had built a cottage system home for the children, and we had established for them a modern school with trained teachers. We had even secured for them a gymnasium and a swimming-bath.

The trouble is, as I soon perceived after taking office, the law cannot, in existing circumstances, do all the work, even for children, that it was intended to do. We shall have to have new laws, and it soon became apparent to me that we can never hope to get them until women have the vote. . . . I thought I had been a suffragist before I became a Poor Law Guardian, but now I began to think about the vote in women's hands not only as a right but as a desperate necessity.

In Emmeline Pankhurst, *My Own Story* (1914)

HER FIRST ARTICLE (1821)

Harriet Martineau
(See pp. 96, 149, 161, 216, 330, and 364.)

At this time . . . was my first appearance in print. . . . My brother James, then my idolized companion, discovered how wretched I was when he left me for his college, after the vacation; and he told me that I must not permit myself to be so miserable. He advised me

to take refuge, on each occasion, in a new pursuit; and on that particular occasion, in an attempt at authorship. . . . What James desired, I always did, as of course; and after he had left me to my
widowhood soon after six o'clock, one bright September morning, I
was at my desk before seven, beginning a letter to the Editor of the
"Monthly Repository." . . . It was on Female Writers on Practical
Divinity. I wrote away, in my abominable scrawl of those days, on
foolscap paper, feeling mightily like a fool all the time. I told no
one, and carried my expensive packet to the post-office myself, to
pay the postage. I took the letter V for my signature—I cannot at all
remember why. The time was very near the end of the month: I
had no definite expectation that I should ever hear any thing of my
paper; and certainly did not suppose it could be in the forthcoming
number.

That number was sent in before service-time on a Sunday morning. My heart may have been beating when I laid hands on it; but
it thumped prodigiously when I saw my article there, and, in the
Notices to Correspondents, a request to hear more from V. of Norwich. There is certainly something entirely peculiar in the sensation
of seeing oneself in print for the first time:—the lines burn themselves in upon the brain in a way of which black ink is incapable, in
any other mode. So I felt that day, when I went about with my secret.

I have said what my eldest brother was to us, in what reverence
we held him. He was just married, and he and his bride asked me to
return from chapel with them to tea. After tea he said, "Come now,
we have had plenty of talk; I will read you something," and he held
out his hand for the new "Repository." After glancing at it, he exclaimed, "They have got a new hand here. Listen." After a paragraph,
he repeated, "Ah! this is a new hand; they have had nothing so
good as this for a long while." (It would be impossible to convey
to any who do not know the "Monthly Repository" of that day, how
very small a compliment this was.) I was silent, of course. At the
end of the first column, he exclaimed about the style, looking at
me in some wonder at my being as still as a mouse. Next (and well I
remember his tone, and thrill to it still) his words were—"What a
fine sentence that is! Why, do you not think so?" I mumbled out,
sillily enough, that it did not seem any thing particular. "Then," he
said, "you were not listening. I will read it again. There now!" As
he still got nothing out of me, he turned round upon me, as we sat
side by side on the sofa, with "Harriet, what is the matter with you?

BBC Hulton Picture Library

Harriet Martineau

I never knew you so slow to praise any thing before." I replied, in utter confusion, "I never could baffle any body. The truth is, that paper is mine." He made no reply, read on in silence, and spoke no more till I was on my feet to come away. He then laid his hand on my shoulder, and said gravely (calling me "dear" for the first time) "Now, dear, leave it to other women to make shirts and darn stockings; and do you devote yourself to this." I went home in a sort of dream, so that the squares of the pavement seemed to float before my eyes. That evening made me an authoress.

In *Harriet Martineau's Autobiography*, ed. Maria Weston Chapman (1877)

HER FIRST LECTURE (1873)
Annie Besant
(See pp. 112, 146, and 346.)

In the autumn following her delivery of this "first lecture," Annie Besant left her husband. She became a striking figure as a public lecturer, with a red tam-o'-shanter pulled over her wild, short-cut red hair, and a short skirt and loose blouse offset by a bright-red tie.

In that spring of 1873, I delivered my first lecture. It was delivered to no one, queer as that may sound to my readers. And indeed, it was queer altogether. I was learning to play the organ, and was in the habit of practising in the church by myself, without a blower. One day, being securely locked in, I thought I would like to try how "it felt" to speak from the pulpit. Some vague fancies were stirring in me, that I could speak if I had the chance; very vague they were, for the notion that I might ever speak on the platform had never dawned on me; only the longing to find outlet in words was in me; the feeling that I had something to say, and the yearning to say it. So, queer as it may seem, I ascended the pulpit in the big, empty, lonely church, and there and then I delivered my first lecture! I shall never forget the feeling of power and of delight which came upon me as my voice rolled down the aisles, and the passion in me broke into balanced sentences, and never paused for rhythmical expression, while I felt that all I wanted was to see the church full of upturned faces, instead of the emptiness of the silent pews. And as though in a dream the solitude became peopled, and I saw the listening faces and the eager eyes, and as the sentences came unbidden from my lips, and my own tones echoed back to me from the pillars of the ancient church, I knew of a verity that the gift of speech was mine, and that if ever—and it seemed then so impossible—if ever the chance came to me of public work, that at least this power of melodious utterance should win hearing for any message I had to bring.

But that knowledge remained a secret all to my own self for

many a long month, for I quickly felt ashamed of that foolish speech-
ifying in an empty church, and I only recall it now because, in trying to trace out one's mental growth, it is only fair to notice the first
silly striving after that expression in spoken words, which, later, has
become to me one of the deepest delights of life.

In Annie Besant, *Autobiographical Sketches* (1885)

SPEECH AT PONTEFRACT (1872)
Josephine Butler
(See pp. 138, 218, 317, 428, 435, and 436.)

*Josephine Butler's campaign against state regulation of prostitution
led her into the rough arena of nineteenth-century election battles.
This gang of thugs who tried to scare her out of town counted on
public sentiment against any woman who would openly discuss prostitution. But, partly as a result of the attack, Butler succeeded in bringing about the defeat of the pro-Contagious Diseases Act candidate.*

We had been obliged to go all over the town before we found anyone bold enough to grant us a place to meet in. At last we found a
large hay-loft over an empty room on the outskirts of the town. We
could only ascend to it by means of a kind of ladder, leading through
a trap-door in the floor. However, the place was large enough to hold
a good meeting, and was soon filled. Mr. Stuart . . . found the floor
strewn with cayenne pepper in order to make it impossible for us to
speak, and there were some bundles of straw in the empty room
below. He got a poor woman to help him, and with buckets of water
they managed to drench the floor and sweep together the cayenne
pepper. Still, when we arrived, it was very unpleasant for eyes and
throat. We began our meeting with prayer, and the women were listening to our words with increasing determination never to forsake
the good cause, when a smell of burning was perceived, smoke began to curl up through the floor, and a threatening noise was heard
below at the door. The bundles of straw beneath had been set on
fire, and the smoke much annoyed us. Then, to our horror, looking
down the room to the trap-door entrance, we saw appearing head
after head of men with countenances full of fury; man after man
came in, until they crowded the place. There was no possible exit

for us, the windows being too high above the ground, and we women were gathered into one end of the room like a flock of sheep surrounded by wolves. . . .

It is difficult to describe in words what followed. It was a time which required strong faith and calm courage. Mrs. Wilson and I stood in front of the company of women, side by side. She whispered in my ear, "Now is the time to trust in God; do not let us fear"; and a comforting sense of the Divine presence came to us both. It was not personal violence that we feared so much as the mental pain inflicted by the rage, profanity and obscenity of the men, of their words and their threats. Their language was hideous. They shook their fists in our faces, with volleys of oaths. This continued for some time, and we had no defence or means of escape. Their chief rage was directed against Mrs. Wilson and me. We understood by their language that certain among them had a personal and vested interest in the evil thing we were opposing [prostitution]. . . . The new teaching and revolt of women had stirred up the very depths of hell. We said nothing, for our voices could not have been heard. We simply stood shoulder to shoulder—Mrs. Wilson and I—and waited and endured; and it seemed all the time as if some strong angel were present; for when these men's hands were literally upon us, they were held back by an unseen power.

There was among our audience a young Yorkshire woman, strong and stalwart, with bare muscular arms, and a shawl over her head. She dashed forward, fought her way through the crowd of men, and, running as fast as she could, she found Mr. Stuart on the outskirts of Mr. Childers' meeting, and cried to him, "Come! Run! They are killing the ladies." He did run, and came up the ladder stairs into the midst of the crowd. As soon, however, as they perceived that he was our defender, they turned upon him. A strong man seized him in his arms; another opened the window; and they were apparently about to throw him headlong out. Some of us ran forward between him and the window, thus giving him time to slip from between the man's arms on to the floor, and glide away to the side where we were. . . .

Our case seemed now to become desperate. Mrs. Wilson and I whispered to each other in the midst of the din, "Let us ask God to help us, and then make a rush for the entrance." Two or three working women placed themselves in front of us, and we pushed our way, I scarcely know how, to the stairs. It was only myself and one or two other ladies that the men really cared to insult and terrify, so if we could get away we felt sure the rest would be safe. I made a dash forward, and took one leap from the trap-door to the ground-floor below. Being light, I came down safely. I found Mrs. Wilson with me very soon in the street. Once in the open street, these cowards did not dare to offer us violence. We went straight back to our own hotel, and there we had a magnificent women's meeting. Such a revulsion of feeling came over the inhabitants of Pontefract when they heard of this disgraceful scene that they flocked to hear us, many of the women weeping. We were advised to turn the lights low, and close the windows, on account of the mob; but the hotel was literally crowded with women, and we scarcely needed to speak; events had spoken for us, and all honest hearts were won.

In Josephine Butler, *Personal Reminiscences of a Great Crusade* (1896)

THE MEDICAL PROFESSIONS

Three medical professions opened to women in the nineteenth century—nursing, midwifery, and doctoring—but it was only in nursing, the one most subject to the supervision and authority of male doctors, that women were widely accepted. The practice of midwifery, once the province of women, had been wrested from them by male practitioners in the seventeenth and eighteenth centuries. Only with considerable difficulty was it partially taken back during this period; and the training and licensing of female physicians was bitterly opposed by the male medical establishment every step of the way.

Florence Nightingale and the Professionalization of Nursing

Born into a wealthy, upper-class, liberal family, Florence Nightingale (1820–1910) was brought up to be satisfied by ordinary domestic occupations combined with the stimulation of frequent travel and the company of some of the most influential and progressive men in England. However, from the time she was seventeen, she felt herself to be called by God to some unnamed greater work. At twenty-five, she understood that the work set out for her was nursing; but the thought of a young lady undertaking such menial, indecent, and revolting work "terrified" her mother, and Florence was forced to abandon her project for six more years. Her devotion to her family caused her to try to reconcile herself to their demands and to win them over to her own sense of mission. She spent countless hours in the family drawing room, wondering (as she later reported) if the clock would ever reach ten, fearing that she was sentenced to spend her life in such enforced stultification. Still, she clung to the idea of doing some great work in the world, and even turned down marriage to Richard Monckton Milnes, of whom she wrote:

> I have an intellectual nature which requires satisfaction and that would find it in him. I have a passionate nature which requires satisfaction and that would find it in him. I have a moral, an active nature which requires satisfaction and that would not find it in his life. . . . I could be satisfied to spend a life with him in combining our different powers in some great object. I could not satisfy this nature by spending a life with him in making society and arranging domestic things.*

In 1851, she finally decided to enter the Institute of Protestant Deaconesses at Kaiserswerth near Dusseldorf, where she was to receive her only formal training as a nurse. On the evening of her departure, her overly dependent sister, Parthenope, developed hysterics and fought with her so bitterly that Florence fainted. When she returned home a few months later, her mother and sister treated her like a person who had just committed a crime. Nonetheless, her Kaiserswerth training proved terribly important for her morale though not for her technical knowledge. She later commented that at Kaiserswerth, "the nursing was nil, the hygiene horrible. . . . But never have I met with a higher tone, a purer devotion."

Hospitals in the nineteenth century were generally places of abominable filth and stench. Nursing duties were minimal, and the low-paid, untrained nurses were reputed to sustain themselves by relying on drink. They were also often accused of loose sexual behavior with their male charges. The only organized nursing was done

---

* Cecil Woodham-Smith, *Florence Nightingale, 1820–1910* (London: Constable, 1950), p. 77

by Catholic nuns or by their few Protestant equivalents, like the Deaconesses. In this context, Florence Nightingale's notion of nursing as a lay profession combining the devotion of the Deaconesses with attention to matters of sanitation was actually revolutionary.

In 1853, she undertook the administration of the Hospital for Invalid Gentlewomen and proved herself to be a forceful manager who knew how to turn compassion into action. The Crimean War broke out in January 1854, and by autumn *The Times* was printing accounts of the terrible neglect of the English wounded. In October, at the request of the government, Florence Nightingale set out with thirty-eight other women to tend the sick. All the nurses were ill-trained. They included twenty-four nuns or Anglican sisters, most of whom tended to ignore the physical needs of their patients and to look down upon the fourteen hospital nurses who were hardier but more difficult to discipline.

Once in the Crimea, Nightingale found conditions at the army hospital in Scutari a nightmare. The men were lying close together in rooms rank with excrement, in clothes stiff with dirt and gore, without blankets or decent food. War wounds accounted for only one sixth of their deaths; typhus, cholera, dysentery, and other diseases accounted for most of the rest.

The doctors and military personnel, suspecting Nightingale of interfering with their authority, welcomed neither her nor her nurses. In the end, however, the fact that she had access to funds raised by *The Times* for her own use made her indispensable and forced the doctors to work with her. Under her direction, sanitary conditions in the hospital improved tremendously. Her mode of management was one of quiet resolve combined with an irresistible force of moral authority. When orderlies neglected to empty overflowing receptacles of excrement, Nightingale would quietly take up a stand amid the filth until the job was done.

In 1856, she returned to England as a national heroine. She was celebrated and praised by the queen, Parliament, the press, and the mass of English people. By 1860, £59,000 had been raised to found the Nightingale School and Home for Nurses associated with St. Thomas's Hospital. In August 1857, Nightingale suffered a health collapse, which marked the beginning for her of a half-century of invalidism. Although she never directly administered her school or the other related projects involving newly trained nurses, she did influence policy throughout her life, always advocating high standards of disci-

plined, professional achievement and always contemptuous of mere
do-goodism.

The glorification of Florence Nightingale as a self-sacrificing,
ministering angel, the "Lady with the Lamp" spreading comfort as
she passed among the wounded, was essential to the establishment
of the nursing profession. Yet it was, in many ways, a distortion of
her actual character. She succeeded not through selflessness but
through courageous and stubborn self-assertion. Nor did she think
of herself as particularly womanly. In fact, she held a low opinion
of women. Nightingale considered herself neither a "Woman's Missionary" nor a feminist; and, as she told Harriet Martineau, she was
"brutally indifferent to the wrongs or rights of my sex."

It was no doubt bitter family experience that convinced Florence
Nightingale that other women were demanding and selfish, and that
although they wished to be loved, they were not capable of loving
others. Even after her internationally celebrated achievements in the
Crimea, she had difficulty keeping her mother and sister at bay. She
relied on her invalidism to separate herself from them and to release
her from family obligations. Had she been able to maintain her health
and to ally herself with feminists like her relative Barbara Leigh Smith
Bodichon, she might have developed a less morbid and pessimistic
attitude toward her own accomplishments and toward the dedication
of the women who followed her into the profession of nursing.

BALLAD TO FLORENCE NIGHTINGALE (ca. 1856)
Anonymous

This is the most popular of the many broadsheet ballads sung about
Florence Nightingale's service in the Crimea.

On a dark lonely night on the Crimea's dread shore
There had been bloodshed and strife on the morning before;
The dead and the dying lay bleeding around,
Some crying for help—there was none to be found.
Now God in His mercy He pitied their cries,
And the soldiers so cheerful in the morning do arise.
  So forward, my lads, may your hearts never fail
  You are cheered by the presence of a sweet Nightingale.

Now God sent this woman to succour the brave;
Some thousands she saved from an untimely grave.
Her eyes beam with pleasure, she's beauteous and good,
The wants of the wounded are by her understood.
With fever some brought in, with life almost gone,
Some with dismantled limbs, some to fragments are torn.
   But they keep up their spirits, their hearts never fail,
   They are cheered by the presence of a sweet Nightingale.

Her heart it means good, for no bounty she'll take,
She'd lay down her life for the poor soldier's sake;
She prays for the dying, she gives peace to the brave,
She feels that a soldier has a soul to be saved.
The wounded they love her as it has been seen,
She's the soldiers' preserver, they call her their Queen.
   May God give her strength, and her heart never fail,
   One of Heaven's best gifts is Miss Nightingale.

The wives of the wounded, how thankful are they!
Their husbands are cared for by night and by day.
Whatever her country, this gift God has given,
And the soldiers they say she's an Angel from Heaven.
All praise to this woman, and deny it who can
That woman was sent as a comfort to man:
   Let's hope that no more against them you'll rail,
   Treat them well, and they'll prove like Miss Nightingale.

In Sir Edward Cook, *The Life of Florence Nightingale* (1913)

THE FAULTS OF WOMEN (1861)
Florence Nightingale
(See pp. 90, 303, and 304.)

[Y]ou say, "women are more sympathetic than men." Now if I were
to write a book out of my experience, I should begin *Women have no
sympathy.* Yours is the tradition. Mine is the conviction of experience.
I have never found one woman who has altered her life by one iota
for me or my opinions. Now look at my experience of men. A statesman [Sidney Herbert], past middle age, absorbed in politics for a
quarter of a century, out of sympathy with me, remodels his whole
life and policy—learns a science the driest, the most technical, the

Idealized painting of "The Lady with the Lamp" by Henrietta Rae

most difficult, that of administration, as far as it concerns the lives of men—not, as I learnt it, in the field from stirring experience, but by writing dry regulations in a London room by my sofa with me. . . . Another (Alexander, whom I made Director-General) does very nearly the same thing. . . . Clough, a poet born if ever there was one, takes to nursing administration in the same way, for me. I only mention three whose whole lives were remodelled by sympathy for me. But I could mention very many others . . . who in a lesser degree have altered their work by my opinion.

Now just look at the degree in which women have sympathy—

as far as my experience is concerned. And my experience of women is almost as large as Europe. And it is so intimate too. I have lived and slept in the same bed with English Countesses and Prussian Bauerinnen. No Roman Catholic Supérieure has ever had charge of women of the different creeds that I have had. No woman has excited "passions" among women more than I have. Yet . . . my doctrines have taken no hold among women. Not one of my Crimean following learnt anything from me, or gave herself for one moment after she came home to carry out the lesson of that war or of those hospitals. . . . You say somewhere that women have no attention. Yes. And I attribute this to want of sympathy. . . . It makes me mad, the Women's Rights talk about "the want of a field" for them—when I know that I would gladly give £500 a year for a Woman Secretary. And two English Lady Superintendents have told me the same thing. And we can't get *one*. . . . They don't know the names of the Cabinet Ministers. They don't know the offices at the Horse Guards. They don't know who of the men of the day is dead and who is alive. They don't know which of the Churches has Bishops and which not. Now I'm sure I did not know these things. When I went to the Crimea I did not know a Colonel from a Corporal. But there are such things as Army Lists and Almanacs. Yet I never could find a woman who, out of sympathy, would consult one—for my work. . . . In one sense, I do believe I am "like a man," as Parthe says. But how? *In having sympathy.* I am sure I have nothing else. I am sure I have no genius. I am sure that my contemporaries, Parthe, Hilary, Marianne, Lady Dunsany, were all cleverer than I was, and several of them more unselfish. But not one had a bit of sympathy. . . . Women crave *for being loved*, not for loving. They scream out at you for sympathy all day long, but they are incapable of giving *any* in return, for they cannot remember your affairs long enough to do so.

From Florence Nightingale to Mme. Mohl, December 13, 1861, in *The Life of Florence Nightingale* (1913)

ADVICE TO YOUNG WOMEN (1868)
Florence Nightingale
(See pp. 90, 301, and 304.)

I have no peculiar gifts. And I can honestly assure any young lady, if she will but try to walk, she will soon be able to run the "appointed course." But then she must first learn to walk, and so when she runs she must run with patience. (Most people don't even try to walk.)

1. But I would also say to all young ladies who are called to any particular vocation, qualify yourselves for it as a man does for his work. Don't think you can undertake it otherwise. . . . And

2. If you are called to man's work, do not exact a woman's privileges—the privilege of inaccuracy, of weakness—ye muddleheads. Submit yourselves to the rules of businesss, as men do, by which alone you can make God's business succeed. . . .

3. But to all women I would say, look upon your work, whether it be an accustomed or an unaccustomed work, as upon a trust confided to you. This will keep you alike from discouragement and presumption, from idleness and from overtaxing yourself. Where God leads the way, He has bound Himself to help you to go the way.

From Florence Nightingale to Lemuel Moss, September 13, 1868, in *Englishwoman's Review*, January 1869

ADVICE TO NURSING STUDENTS (1873–1876)
Florence Nightingale
(See pp. 90, 301, and 303.)

The world, more especially the Hospital world, is in such a hurry, is moving so fast, that it is too easy to slide into bad habits before we are aware. And it is easier still to let our year's training slip away without forming any real plan of training ourselves.

For, after all, all that any training is to do for us is: to teach us how to train ourselves, how to observe for ourselves, how to think out things for ourselves. Don't let us allow the first week, the second week, the third week to pass by—I will not say in idleness, but in bustle. Begin, for instance, at once making notes of your cases. From the first moment you see a case, you can observe it. Nay, it is one of the first things a Nurse is strictly called upon to do: to observe her sick. . . .

But give but one-quarter of an hour a *day* to jot down, even in words which no one can understand but yourself, the progress or change of two or three individual cases, not to forget or confuse them. . . . To those who have not much education, I am sure that our kind Home Sister, or the Special Probationer in the same Ward, or nearest in any way, will give help. The race is not always to the swift, nor the battle to the strong; and "line upon line"—*one* line every day—in the steady, observing, humble Nurse has often won the race over the smarter "genius" in what constitutes real Nursing. But few of us women seriously think of improving our own mind or character *every day*. And this is fatal to our improving in Nursing. . . .

A woman who takes a sentimental view of Nursing (which she calls "ministering" as if she were an angel) is of course worse than useless. . . .

To be a Nurse *is* to be a Nurse: not to be a Nurse only when we are put to the work we like. If we can't work when we are put to the work we don't like—and Patients can't always be fitted to Nurses— that is behaving like a spoilt child, like a naughty girl: not like a Nurse. If we can do the work we don't like from the higher motive till we do like it, that is one test of being a real Nurse. . . . For the Patients want according to their wants, and not according to the Nurse's likes or dislikes. If you wish to be trained to do *all* Nursing well, even what you do not like—trained to perfection in little things—that is Nursing for the sake of Nursing, for the sake of God and of your neighbour. And remember, in little things as in great—No Cross, no Crown.

Nursing is said, most truly said, to be a high calling, an honourable calling. But what does the honour lie in? In working hard during your training to learn and to do all things perfectly. The honour does not lie in putting on Nursing like your uniform, your dress. . . . Honour lies in loving perfection, consistency, and in working hard for it: in being ready to work patiently: ready to say not "How clever I am!" but "I am not yet worthy; and I will live to deserve and work to deserve to be called a Trained Nurse."

In Florence Nightingale, *Florence Nightingale to Her Nurses: A Selection from Miss Nightingale's Addresses to Probationers and Nurses of the Nightingale School at St. Thomas's Hospital* (1915)

"THE DIFFICULTIES OF TRAINED NURSES" (1876)
Victoria Magazine

The wages of a probationer [trainee] at the Birmingham and Midland Counties' Institution . . . are £12 for the first year and £20 for the remaining 2, with board, lodging, and uniform. Probationers must be between 25 and 35. These are the usual terms; but we do not ourselves expect to see nursing widely embraced among women—and especially among gentlewomen—until the terms are improved. A young woman who has to work must begin before 25; a nurse's life is so arduous that the usual computation allows them 12 years of work, after which time they are incapacitated. Is it a career likely to tempt a woman of culture, to commence at 25 upon wages which an incompetent servant maid of 18 will not take, and to end her working life —while still in her prime—upon less wages than a head-nurse or a "plain cook" can demand and easily obtain? . . . Surely a well-trained sick-nurse—when we consider all the needful qualifications—is worth more than a kitchen-maid.

In *Victoria Magazine*, June 1876

Midwifery

Although nursing continued to be an arduous and underpaid occupation, even after Nightingale's reforms, there was another medical route for women: the traditional female attendance at childbirth and postpartum. Educated and skilled women had trained one another as midwives until male practitioners pushed them out of this practice during the seventeenth and eighteenth centuries. As a result, nineteenth-century midwives were untrained and unlicensed. They were used mainly by women too poor to afford doctors. In the last quarter of the century, however, feminists and female practitioners joined together to reclaim this traditionally female profession. After twenty-five years of effort, the Midwives Act of 1902 re-established the profession by setting up clear, modern standards and licensing procedures.

THE NEED FOR THE PROFESSIONALIZATION OF MIDWIFERY (1881)
Englishwoman's Review

A Society with a very useful object has been lately established in London with the title of the "Matrons' Aid," or more properly the "Trained Midwives' Registration Society." The importance of this profession in the hands of women, is sufficiently established by the statement of a Committee which in 1869 was appointed by the Council of the Obstetrical Society to investigate the cause of infant mortality; this Committee stated that out of the 1,250,000 births which annually take place in Great Britain, about 7 out of 10 (and according to another authority 9 out of 10) births were attended by women only. The larger number of these women have received little or no special training; a great many women who have been educated only as monthly nurses [nurses for newly delivered mothers], assume the profession, and if they have good certificates of conduct or capacity from hospitals or physicians, consider themselves exceedingly well qualified for it. Others, it is to be feared, have not even this degree of practical training. At present the only technical instruction obtainable by midwives is that supplied in seven or eight lying-in institutions in London, Edinburgh, and Dublin. These receive midwives for a course of from three to six months, and sometimes grant certificates after an examination. There is no uniform system of training or standard of examination in these institutions, and the number of midwives trained in them annually, hardly exceeds a hundred. The only independent examination and diploma is that granted by the Obstetrical Society of London, 291, Regent Street, but few women comparatively have presented themselves for these examinations. It is difficult we may assume for a large number of women to obtain instruction at all. Under these circumstances it is not strange if the *status* of midwives has sunk into disrepute. . . .

What we should desire to do now is not necessarily to increase the number of women who practise this profession (for an exceedingly large number of women do this already), but to educate them more highly, and so dignify it for themselves and render it less dangerous for the patient. Midwives are employed by the poor in preference to doctors, on account of the extreme cheapness of their terms. In the provinces we are informed the fee is from 4s. to 6s., which includes attendance at birth, washing and dressing the infant, and a visit for the same purpose daily until the fourth day, and afterwards every other day till the eighth. In London the charge for the same duties is 5s. to 7s. So low a scale of charges proves that the average professional skill cannot be high. [Although even] under the present disadvantage, the rate of mortality in cases under the care of women practitioners compares very favorably with that of patients attended by medical men. . . .

The *Lancet* a few years ago (1873) advocated better education of midwives, not on the ground of the womanliness of such an employment for women, or the better chances it would give to both mother and infant, but almost entirely on the ground of the saving in drudgery it would give to medical men. The argument is worth preserving:

> As a matter of fact, a large number of women are attended by midwives, and the practice has a certain sanction from both law and custom. Not only so it is very desirable that medical men should be saved from the drudgery of very cheap midwifery. It is very doubtful, indeed, whether the physical strength of women is equal to the duties of a large obstetric practice. The affirmative view of this question is too readily assumed; but it has to be proved. Be this as it may, a very large midwifery practice is injurious in a high degree to men who have all the other duties of medical practice to do, and it is so especially among the poor, the hygienic condition of whose dwellings terribly enhances the bad effects of loss of sleep and tedious waiting. Sir Robert Christison gave it as the result of his large observation that nothing was more injurious to the health of rural medical men than heavy midwifery duties. Even in the interest of medical men, then, we think it very desirable that women should be educated in the practice of midwifery, and as a matter of prudence and humanity there cannot be any doubt about it.

> . . . One immediate result of raising the education of the practitioners would be that a richer class of women would employ them, till we might hope that in time the profession would return to its original dignity. It is evident that if women of higher social rank and good education would enter upon this calling, they might, by rendering the employment of midwives again popular, really re-open a remunerative employment to women.

In *Englishwoman's Review*, May 1881

A MIDWIFE'S CAREER (1890s)

Mrs. Layton

(See pp. 178 and 187.)

Mrs. Layton's experiences illustrate the confusion of the old system of unlicensed, untrained midwives, and some of the difficulties in the transition to the new one laid out in the Midwives Act of 1902. *It is not surprising that her first clients came to her through fellow members of the co-operative movement, which, in addition to operating co-operative retail stores, was an important base for political organizing among women.*

When my husband was promoted to the position of under-guard, we had to leave Brondesbury and come to Cricklewood to live. Then it was I gave up washing and took up nursing. My husband's wages had now risen to £1 3s. a week, and he had an allotment. I got a nice little flat for 7s. a week, so that I did not live a life of drudgery, but had to do something to help. The chance of nursing came to me through one of the members of our Management Committee [of the local Workers' Co-operative Union], who advised his master [employer] to come for me when his wife was ill, saying, "She is not a nurse but I am sure she will do, and be kind to your wife." I did what I could and satisfied both patient and doctor, who recommended me to others of his patients. My first maternity case came to me in an unexpected manner. One of our [Women's Co-operative] Guild members was expecting her confinement and could not find a nurse. So at last I got a crippled girl I knew to stay in my house while I went into the Guild member's house, and acted as maternity nurse for a fortnight. I did not intend to take up maternity nursing, but after I had started, other Guild members came to me to attend them. I began to like the work, and the doctors were so satisfied with me that I determined to keep on. Then several doctors advised me to go in for midwifery, but I could not go into hospital for training. The fees were a bar to me. I found that the cheapest training I could get would cost anything from £30 to £50, and then I would be away from home for three months. This was quite impossible, for my husband's health needed all the care I could bestow on it to keep him anything like fit for work part of his time. I had no money, only as I earned it week by week, and it was impossible to save. So I had to content myself with being a maternity nurse, but I always hoped I should ultimately become a midwife.

I read and asked questions of the doctors and in this way knew a great deal about the theory of midwifery, and I was gaining experience in the practical part. There were three doctors who were very good to me and were willing to lend me books or to teach me anything. I was taught to deliver with forceps, which midwives are not taught in hospitals. I went to several post-mortems with a doctor. One was the case of a young girl who was pregnant and had poisoned herself. The doctor opened the womb and let me see the dear little baby lying so snugly in its mother, and gave me a lot of information that was real knowledge to me, showing me things in the human body which were both interesting and instructive.

Quite a large number of young married people came to live in Cricklewood, and I had sometimes as many as a hundred cases in a year. The doctors left so much to me and did so little for their fees, that people asked me to take their cases without a doctor. I did not care to do so at first, so I asked a doctor (who, when he thought my husband had not many days to live, had promised him to help me) if he thought I should be right to take cases without a doctor. He told me I was quite all right, and that if at any time I came across a case that I was not sure was quite straightforward, he would come to my assistance. I was very pleased with his offer and did many cases on my own responsibility, and both patients and doctors were satisfied, but I was not. I was called a midwife, but I felt I should have liked a hospital training, and as I earned more money began to save to get the training I longed for. I scraped, and saved, twisted and turned clothes about, even went as far as to turn an overcoat for my husband. I managed to save £30, and got the necessary papers which had to be signed by a doctor. When I went to him, he positively refused to sign it. He said it would be a wicked waste of money, that I knew more than the hospital could teach me, that I could not be spared from the neighbourhood for three months, and advised me to give up the idea. . . .

I don't think I should have taken his advice if I had known that the Midwives Act was coming along. The doctors trained me and sent me up for examination in midwifery. But alas! I failed, as about 130 did at the same examination. The written examination took place at 9 p.m., in a closely packed room. We had two hours to answer the questions, and a fortnight later an oral examination. It was just five minutes past 10 p.m. when I went into the examiners' room; at ten minutes past I came out with a slip of paper to give the Secretary with the word "failed" written on it. I was told I could pay another fee and go through another exam, but I refused to do so. I was always a little nervous when writing or answering questions, and when I had to do both in a room full of doctors, I felt I should not make a better job of another exam. When the Midwives Act became

Elizabeth Garrett Anderson passing her oral examination for the M.D. degree at the University of Paris, 1870

law, I was recommended for a certificate as a *bona fide* midwife.

In Mrs. Layton, "Memories of Sixty Years," in *Life As We Have Known It* (1931)

Women Doctors

The first woman doctor in England was Elizabeth Garrett Anderson, who was forced to receive her degree in Paris (see p. 223). Following her example, other women then brought pressure on British universities to admit them to training. Sophia Jex-Blake (1840–1912) led a small group of such pioneers at the University of Edinburgh. After spending two years there as special students, the women were forbidden to do the necessary clinical work at the university-affiliated infirmary and were subjected to riotous violence from their male fellow students. The speech excerpted here, which Jex-Blake delivered in an attempt to win infirmary privileges, resulted in her being sued for libel by the medical student she obliquely accused of drunkenness. Legal fees from this case and from related efforts to win access to the university ran very high, and the burden of all such legal maneuvering fell on Jex-Blake, who failed her qualifying exams as a result.

In 1874, with Edinburgh still closed against women, she opened her own medical school, the London School of Medicine for Women, with Elizabeth Garrett Anderson and Elizabeth Blackwell on staff. Jex-Blake eventually received a medical degree at Berne, Switzerland, was reexamined in Dublin, and admitted to practice. By 1880, it was possible for women to obtain a medical education and be licensed in Britain, and by 1891 there were 101 women doctors in practice. In April 1895, Dr. Sophia Jex-Blake was an honored guest at the ceremonious final opening to women of the University of Edinburgh Medical School.

Pioneers like Elizabeth Garrett Anderson and Sophia Jex-Blake challenged social taboos on several levels. Because the professionalism and prestige of medicine increased all through the nineteenth century, the men in the practice were strongly resistant to welcoming women. Moreover, the penetration of anatomical secrets was considered indelicate work, fit only for men. The discussion of anatomical matters, especially the dissection of human corpses, was considered highly unsuitable for women to experience, particularly in mixed company. It was no accident, therefore, that opposition to Jex-Blake and her group focused on their admission to anatomy classes along with male students. Yet the same Victorian sense of sexual privacy made women doctors all the more welcome to patients such as Josephine Butler, who were greatly relieved at the opportunity of discussing intimate bodily functions with members of their own sex.

WOMEN'S EDUCATION
AND MALE PROFESSIONS (1857)
Frederick Denison Maurice

Frederick Denison Maurice (1805–1872), a Christian Socialist and educational reformer, was one of the founders of the Governesses' Benevolent Institution and of Queen's College.

You will not wonder, that I should have hailed the suggestion of the ladies whom I consulted, that the proper foundation of a College for Working Women would be a college in which ladies should learn to teach. It was not that I believed they had more need of this learning than we have. I know the opposite assertion to be true. I believe there is immeasurably more aptitude for teaching in women than in men. . . . The woman receives, not from her husband, not from her physician, not from her spiritual adviser, not from the books which she consults—all these may help somewhat, if they do not hinder—but from the Spirit of God Himself, the intuitions into her child's character, the capacity for appreciating its strength and its weakness, the faculty of calling forth the one and sustaining the other, in which lies the mystery of education, apart from which all its rules and measures are utterly vain and ineffectual. . . .

I hope . . . I have guarded myself against the suspicion that I would educate ladies for the kind of tasks which belong to *our* professions. In America some are maintaining that they should take degrees and practise as physicians. I not only do not see my way to such a result; I not only should not wish that any college I was concerned in should be leading to it; but I should think there could be no better reason for founding a college than to remove the slightest craving for such a state of things, by giving a more healthful direction to the minds which might entertain it. The more pains we take to call forth and employ the facilities which belong characteristically to each sex, the less it will be intruding upon the province which, not the conventions of the world, but the will of God, has assigned to the other. . . . Englishmen would not have women surgeons or physicians; they find they must have them as *nurses.*

In Frederick Denison Maurice, *Lectures to Ladies on Practical Subjects* (1857)

WOMAN AS DOCTOR—OR NURSE? (1878)
The Lancet

The Lancet, *a weekly professional journal for doctors, was devoted to the exchange of practical medical information but also included debate on social topics related to the profession.*

Again "the woman question," in relation to the practice of physics and surgery, is forced upon us by the wise decision of the British Medical Association to exclude female practitioners; and, by a curious coincidence, we are, at the same moment, invited, by an able article in the last number of *The Spectator,* to consider the peculiar physical state and mental susceptibilities of "Invalids." The two topics, thrown together, not inopportunely, suggest the comparison, or contrast, as it will be found, of women as doctor and woman as nurse. In the one character she is as awkward, unfit, and untrustworthy, as she is at home, capable, and thoroughly worthy of confidence in the other.

In the economy of nature . . . the ministry of women is one of help and sympathy. The essential principle, the key-note of her work in the world, is *aid*; to sustain, succour, revive, and even sometimes shelter, man in the struggle and duty of life, is her peculiar function. The moment she affects the first or leading *rôle* in any vocation she is out of place, and the secondary, but essential, part of helpmate cannot be filled. . . .

This is not a mere sentimental view of the facts. If women undertake the duties of physicians and surgeons, we shall presently feel the want of nurses. . . . The unsuitability of men as nurses is not due to any want of power or tact on their part; they are stronger, and, therefore, able to perform many services for the sick with less fatigue to the patient than women-nurses, and when feeling and interest inspire the touch of a man's hand, it is steadier, more precise, and not less gentle than that of a woman; but, unless under exceptional circumstances, man's nature rebels against the complete surrender of his own judgment and that implicit obedience in spirit, as well as letter, which are the first essentials of a good nurse. In the same way women will, unconsciously, perhaps, but effectually, cease to play the subordinate part required of them as nurses when their own sex is elevated to the control of the sick chamber and the treatment of disease. Already, since the craze of women to become physicians and surgeons has attained proportions promising success to the movement, we recognise an evil influence on the training and work of female nurses. Subjects of purely medical and surgical concern are beginning to be included in the "studies" of the *nurse,* while other matters, on which mainly the success of treatment must always depend, are regarded as menial, and relegated to the care of servants. . . .

In *The Lancet,* August 17, 1878

SPEECH FOR ADMISSION TO
THE ROYAL INFIRMARY OF EDINBURGH (1871)
Sophia Jex-Blake

I called on Dr. Christison, who told me curtly that the question was entirely decided in his own mind, and that it was useless for me to enter upon it. I did not call on Dr. Andrew Wood; but I was introduced to him in Sir James Simpson's room by Sir James, whose large-heartedness and large-mindedness made him from the first our warm friend and helper. On this introduction, I asked Dr. Wood to favour me with five minutes' conversation, to which his reply was that he would rather not, and turned on his heel and pursued a conversation with other persons in the room. These are specimens of the way in which a few—a very few only—met me on my arrival in Edinburgh; and I must do those few the justice to say that their conduct has been absolutely and uniformly consistent ever since. Never have we applied for educational facilities of any kind but they have done their best to meet us with an uncompromising refusal, so far as it was in their power. When the Senatus Academicus gave me leave to enter as a visitor the Botanical and Natural History classes, it was the members of this hostile clique who got a veto put on the permission. When we applied for permission merely for separate classes, exactly the same dead opposition confronted us. When, through the liberality of public feeling, this boon was granted to us, the same adversaries continued to meet us at every corner, even after one of the chief had stated publicly in the Senatus that, the experiment once begun, he would use every means in his power to give it a fair trial. We endeavoured to make private arrangements at great expense for separate anatomical instruction; we were told repeatedly that our efforts would be useless (as indeed they proved), because certain all-powerful members of the Colleges of Physicians and Surgeons had resolved to ostracise any medical men who agreed to give us instructions. ("Oh, oh.") When the absolute impossibility of getting a complete course of separate instruction drove us to ask admittance to the ordinary classes, to which several Professors would willingly have admitted us, the same phalanx of opponents raised the cry of indelicacy—knowing that thus they might prevail in ranging against us public opinion, which would have been on our side had the real issue—education or no education

—been declared. And now I want to point out that it was certain of these same men, who had, so to speak, pledged themselves from the first to defeat our hopes of education, and render all our efforts abortive—who, sitting in their places on the Infirmary Board, took advantage of the almost irresponsible power with which they were temporarily invested to thwart and nullify all our efforts. . . .

Till then, during a period of five weeks, the conduct of the students with whom we had been associated in Surgeons' Hall in the most trying of all our studies, that of Practical Anatomy, had been quiet, respectful, and in every way inoffensive. They had evidently accepted our presence there in earnest silent work as a matter of course, and Dr. Handyside, in answer to a question of mine after the speeches made at the meeting of the General Council, assured me that, in the course of some twenty sessions, he had never had a month of such quiet earnest work as since we entered his rooms. But at a certain meeting of the managers, when our memorial was presented a majority of those present were, I understand, in favour of immediately admitting us to the Infirmary. The minority alleged want of due notice to the question, and succeeded in obtaining an adjournment. What means were used in the interim I cannot say, or what influence was brought to bear: but I do know that from that day the conduct of the students was utterly changed, that those who had hitherto been quiet and courteous became impertinent and offensive; and at last came the day of that disgraceful riot, when the College gates were shut in our faces and our little band bespattered with mud from head to foot. ("Shame.") It is true that other students, who were too manly to dance as puppets on such ignoble strings, came indignantly to our rescue, that by them the gates were wrenched open and we protected in our return to our homes. But none the less was it evident that some new influence, wholly distinct from any intrinsic facts, had been at work. . . .

This I do know, that the riot was not wholly or mainly due to the students at Surgeons' Hall, I know that Dr. Christison's class assistant was one of the leading rioters—(Hisses and "Order")—and the foul language he used could only be excused on the supposition I heard that he was intoxicated. I do not say that Dr. Christison knew of or sanctioned his presence, but I do say that I think he would not have been there had he thought the doctor would have strongly objected to his presence.

Dr. Christison: I must again appeal to you, my lord. I think the language used regarding my assistant is language that no one is entitled to use at such an assembly as this—(hear)—where a gentleman is not present to defend himself, and to say whether it be true or not. I do not know whether it is true or not, but I know that my assistant is a thorough gentleman, otherwise he would never have been my assistant, and I appeal to you again, my lord, whether language such as this is to be allowed in the mouth of any person. I am perfectly sure there is not one gentleman in the whole assembly who would have used such language in regard to an absentee.

Miss Jex-Blake: If Dr. Christison prefers—

Dr. Christison: I wish nothing but that this foul language shall be put an end to.

The Lord Provost: I do not know what the foul language is. She merely said that, in her opinion—

Dr. Christison: In her opinion the gentleman was intoxicated.

Miss Jex-Blake: I did not say he was intoxicated. I said I was told he was.

The Lord Provost: Withdraw the word "intoxicated."

Miss Jex-Blake: I said it was the only excuse for his conduct. If Dr. Christison prefers that I should say he used the language when sober, I will withdraw the other supposition. (Laughter.)

In *Englishwoman's Review*, April 1871

ON DR. ELIZABETH GARRETT ANDERSON (1868)
Josephine Butler
(See pp. 138, 218, 295, 428, 435, and 436.)

Josephine Butler had consulted nine doctors in three countries about her heart condition before she finally had the opportunity of consulting a woman physician.

But for Miss Garrett I must say of her that I gained more from her than any other doctor; for she not only repeated exactly what all the others had said, but entered much more into my mental state and way of life than they could do *because* I was able to *tell* her so much more than I ever could or would tell to any *man*. . . .

I hope you do not think that ultimately, when women doctors shall have had as many advantages as men, they will not be equally able. They have judgment, and skill in ordinary matters, and I think very often more insight. This is a subject on which I feel very, very much for I have suffered for so long. O, if men knew what women have to endure, and how every good woman has prayed for the coming of a change, a change in this. How would any modest *man* endure to put himself in the hands of a woman medically as women have to do into the hands of men? And are women less modest than men? God forbid. They are *not*, and believe me, the best and purest feelings of women have been torn and harrowed and shamefully wounded for centuries, just to please a wicked *custom*, while those women who are not intrinsically noble and good, are debased, insensibly, by such customs. . . . I wrote on this subject when I was only nineteen; then Miss Nightingale arose and said the same, and I foresaw a hope for the future. O! do not let men crush that hope again! . . . My beloved mother had twelve children and never had a doctor near her. I followed her example and was carried safely through every confinement. [My sister] Mrs. Meuricoffre the same—we trust in God, and if we die we do so willingly in a protest against wicked customs.

From Josephine Butler to Albert Rutson, February 22, 1868, from typed extract in Fawcett Collection at the City of London Polytechnic

CLERICAL WORK

From 1861 on, as census figures dramatically show, the real growth in opportunities for women was in clerical work. Women went from less than 1 percent of the clerical work force in 1861 to 18 percent in 1901. While of the eighty thousand female clerks in 1901, most were employed in private business, about one third were employed by the government, primarily in the post office. Feminists welcomed and encouraged this trend by recruiting women and providing them with clerical training.

Women's clerical work, however, developed separately from men's, not so much in the nature of its duties as in rank, pay, and possibilities of advancement. More than half of all male clerks were earning over £100 a year by 1901, while almost all female clerks earned less than that and consequently had a hard time making ends meet. The dead-endedness of the work was reinforced by some employers' refusal to hire or retain married women workers. Technological change opened up some new clerical occupations for women—for instance, in telegraphy. "Typewriting machines" came into wide use in the 1880s, and women soon succeeded men as "typewriters." Similarly, shorthand, formerly a male skill acquired by such parliamentary reporters as Charles Dickens, was increasingly learned by women. Although clerical work was considered "genteel," requiring some degree of literacy and a formality of dress associated with professional life, working conditions were usually unpleasant. Women worked as long as twelve hours a day in poorly ventilated, dirty rooms with inadequate toilet facilities.

TESTIMONY BEFORE THE CIVIL SERVICE COMMISSION (1874)
Gertrude Jane King

The Society for Promoting the Employment of Women of which Gertrude Jane King was secretary was founded by Jessie Boucherett and others of the Langley Place Circle in 1859 at the offices of the Englishwoman's Journal. It lasted into the twentieth century as a source of referrals, training, and short-term educational loans for women seeking employment in skilled lower-middle-class jobs, such as bookkeeping, law copying, typewriting, and telegraphy.

Q: Is it the business of your office to keep a registry of those women who want employment?
A: Yes, of all who are seeking employment.
Q: And to test their qualifications?
A: Yes, as far as possible.
Q: And to recommend them accordingly?
A: Yes, I always make them write a letter to me of some sort before recommending any one to do writing; and generally if they are likely to have dictation, or anything requiring careful spelling, I give them dictation.
Q: Are most of them that come to you young or old?
A: They vary: we wish that we could get them younger. They generally come to us when they have lost their homes; it is ladies of the middle rank who have had homes until perhaps their parents die, and then at 30 or 35 they are thrown upon the world. . . . We have a

great many girls, but they are chiefly of the tradesman rank; we do not get hold of the ladies as early as we should like, as long as the father can keep them at home he does not feel the necessity of giving his girls a training.

Q: So that that class of women have not the chance of a fair education?

A: I think that the education is improving. The large public day schools, such as the North London College for example, try to make them thoroughly efficient. . . .

Q: Are there any suggestions which you would like to make to us upon the subject of the employment of female clerks?

A: I do not think that I could venture to do that. The only thing is that we should be heartily glad to get suitable employment for ladies, who now very often become governesses and are really unfit to teach, I do not mean from want of education, but every one has not the patience to teach; and many come to me who have been thoroughly well educated and say, "Is there nothing that I can do but teach?" And it is almost impossible to recommend anything except artistic work, for which, of course, all have not talent.

Q: Looking at it not as a matter of fairness, but as a matter of supply and demand, is it not the case that female clerks would enter into clerical employment at a considerably less rate of remuneration than male clerks at present?

A: I hardly know what the male clerks have. I think that ladies would be very glad to earn as much as £100 or £150 a year.

Q: You do not see as a matter of fairness why if a woman is equally efficient as a clerk with a man, she should receive a different salary?

A: I think that if she does the same work she ought to receive the same amount.

Q: As far as your experience goes, do women in fact, get as much as men?

A: No, they do not.

Q: Is the fact of their getting less in consequence of their doing less work, or for any other reason?

A: I think it is from the circumstance that women's work is not paid so well as men's; but I think that women work as hard as men.

Testimony of Miss Gertrude Jane King, Secretary, Society for Promoting the Employment of Women, at Civil Service Commission, November 24, 1874, in *Englishwoman's Review*, July 1875

WOMEN AS TELEGRAPH CLERKS (1871)

Frank Ives Scudamore

Frank Ives Scudamore (1823–1884) was the highly regarded reformer of the post office and a writer of light literature.

The staff employed in Telegraph Street throughout the day, that is, from 8 a.m. to 8 p.m., is mainly, though not entirely, a female staff. . . . [W]e have largely extended the employment of female labour. For many reasons I think it is desirable that we should continue in this course, but looking at the matter from a purely departmental point of view, I think that their employment is desirable on the following grounds:

In the first place, they have in eminent degree the quickness of eye and ear, and the delicacy of touch, which are essential qualifications of a good operator. In the second place, they take more kindly than men or boys do to sedentary employment, and are more patient during long confinement to one place. In the third place, the wages, which draw male operators from but an inferior class of the community, will draw female operators from a superior class. Female operators thus drawn from a superior class will, as a rule, write better than the male clerks, and spell more correctly; and, where the staff is mixed, the female clerks will raise the tone of the whole staff. They are also less disposed than men to combine for the purpose of extorting higher wages, and this is by no means an unimportant matter.

On one other ground it is especially desirable that we should extend the employment of women. . . . There must always be in the Post Office proper, and not less in postal telegraph offices, an immense number of duties which can be and are just as well performed by a lad of 18 as by a man of 40; but when the same person continues to perform the same duty from his 18th to his 40th year, it is impossible permanently to resist his claim for additional remuneration; and when he continues to perform it to his 60th year, it becomes equally impossible to resist his claim for a retiring allowance. Nor would it be possible for long to maintain a rule under which persons employed on certain classes of duties should perforce retire after a short term, say, five or seven years of service. Women, however, will solve these difficulties for the Department by retiring for the purpose of getting married as soon as they get the chance. . . .

On the whole it may be stated without fear of contradiction that if we place an equal number of females and males on the same ascending scale of pay, the aggregate pay to the females will always be less than the aggregate pay to the males; that within a certain range of duty the work will be better done by the females than by the males, because the females will be drawn from a somewhat superior class; and further, that there will always be fewer females than males on the pension list.

In Frank Ives Scudamore, *Report on the Reorganization of the Telegraph System of the United Kingdom P.P.*, 1871

"THE CHEAPNESS OF WOMEN" (1909)
Dora M. Jones

In one of the last issues of the Englishwoman's Review (October 1909) this summary of the results of women's struggle for wider employment appeared. It should be remembered that 20s. a week (£52 a year) was the level of earnings at which working-class families were just able to get by in 1909 when this article was written. Educated middle-class women were not usually able to make much more than this, as Dora M. Jones points out.

The twin questions of Women's Education and Women's Employment, so fiercely debated forty years ago, may seem to have been settled in a sense favourable to the reforming party. With the establishment of the first great girls' day schools, a generation ago, the education battle was practically won; but the fight for a career in professional and business life was only beginning. A long step was taken on the new road when women became teachers in the public day schools; . . . the first woman clerk in a business house was looked on as a portent. In the wake of the women of talent like Miss F. P. Cobbe or Miss Martineau, followed a growing army of journalists. And now you may pick up the *Englishwoman's Year Book* for the current year, and find that the average schoolgirl at the end of her course appears to have the choice of between thirty and forty avocations. She may be a teacher of the elementary or secondary type, a nurse, a journalist, a chemist, a doctor, a bookkeeper, a teacher of *jui-jitsu,* a laundry manager, a rent-collector, a hairdresser, a commercial traveller, the keeper of a teashop, a sanitary inspector, a Post Office clerk, an actress, or an asylum attendant. . . .

The unmarried girl who has entered on a profession touches life at more points, sees more of human nature, lives more intensely, and with a richness and variety of experience which was unknown to her maiden aunts—poor ladies, who lived perhaps to old age, enslaved to the etiquette of a country town and the discipline of an old-fashioned household. . . . It is perhaps because the memory of those days is past, or only lingers as a vague tradition, that one detects a note of disillusion in the tone of educated working women. Now that they have vindicated their right to enter the labour market, what does this freedom amount to? . . .

We find that a Sanitary Inspector, her training over, may expect to begin with an income of from £80 to £100 a year, an Elementary School Teacher with about £90, and a High School Teacher with from £90 to £100. The Inspector may rise to about £150 a year, which is, generally speaking, the high-water mark for Assistant Mistresses in schools, though in the case of some of the more important Girls' Secondary Schools the salary of a second mistress may run up to £200.

Probably, of all women's professions, teaching offers the best prospect to the majority of its members, considering the short hours and long holidays, as well as the salaries paid. At the Conference on the Work of Educated Women held last year, a lady speaker dwelt on the advantages offered by Post Office work. Women clerks in the Postal Service begin at a salary of £65 per annum, rising by yearly increments of £5 to £100. "This," said the speaker, "is the best paid work any ordinary well-educated woman can expect." First-class clerks, of whom there is one to every twelve or fourteen second-class clerks, begin at £115 a year and rise to £130, while there are a few principal clerks and senior assistant superintendents with salaries rising to £200, and in a very few cases to £300.

The probable initial salary of the journalist is set down by a writer in the *Fingerpost*—herself a practical journalist—as £1 a week; and she estimates the earnings of an average experienced woman journalist as from £2 to £3 a week.

Now these are the cream of the women workers, the girls for whom their parents have been able to provide a first-class education or special coaching; or who have displayed some particular aptitude that takes them out of the common rut.

But the test of any social movement is what it does, not for picked individuals, but for the masses. What are the chances offered to the average middle-class English girl, who is expected nowadays, equally with her brothers, to fend for herself and make her own way in the world?

The majority of these girls, in the large towns at any rate, become clerks. One meets them by the hundred, pouring into London between 8 and 9 in the morning—a spectacle that would have astonished our grandmothers. In the case of the vast army, £1 a week is quite a usual salary for a trained shorthand typist, and 30s. a week is the highest wage that many competent women ever rise to. In the provinces salaries are even lower. The following is part of an application received recently from "a lady by birth and education."

"I was educated at a private school and took the Higher Cambridge Local Certificate with honours, including French and German. Since then I have studied shorthand and typewriting, and have had about fifteen months' experience in a large office. *I am now receiving £40 per annum.* I am the daughter of a late doctor in this town, and can give excellent references." . . .

The competent nurse will make £25 when resident in a hospital, or from 30s. a week upwards with private cases.

Assistant dressmakers and milliners begin as "improvers" with a wage of about 10s. a week. A "general assistant" makes from 20s. to 40s. weekly, though of course the earnings of the majority approximate more closely to the lower than to the higher figure. A fitter or head milliner may make £3 10s. a week, but these positions are the plums, and the earnings of the rank and file average from 25s. to 30s. weekly. Fifteen shillings per week is the usual pay of an assistant hairdresser, and "30s. to £2 is good wages." Photographic retouchers, if competent, make from 30s. to £2 per week.

In fact we may say that a very large proportion of the women whose cases we are considering have to live on a weekly income of 30s., 25s., or even less, and to face on this income not only the risks of illness but also the chance of long spells of non-employment. . . .

The lady clerk at 30s. a week must either consent to live below the standard of her class, or pay away the whole of her salary for board, lodging and travelling. The last is impossible, so she chooses the first. She may reduce her living expenses if she devotes all her leisure to cleaning out her own room, cooking her own meals, and making her own clothes. If she has not strength to undertake this extra labour in addition to her bread-winning toil, she must stint herself in food, raiment, and the essentials of refinement to which she is accustomed, or she must accept eleemosynary help in some form or other, either by taking money from her friends, or by living in an institution which is supported, in whole or in part, by charitable contributions.

It is interesting to reflect that the business firms who are piling up dividends by means of the labour of underpaid women are really kept going in part by the relatives of these women, and in part by the contributions of the charitable public.

TWO

The Working Class

Work began at an early age for female members of the working class. Five-year-old girls took care of infants, and slightly older children accompanied their parents to the street corner, the mill, the fields, or even the mines. Although children under ten were gradually rescued by legislation from some of the worst abuses of the time, children's labor continued, throughout the century, to be important to family income.

Girls were expected to work in the home as well as to bring in what money they could. By thirteen, girls often took domestic-service jobs simply to relieve their parents of the need to support them. Because they could earn wages of their own, young working-class girls could gain a greater measure of independence than their more privileged counterparts. Some young factory girls even welcomed jobs at a distance from home, thereby avoiding household chores and close supervision by the primary family. Their wages would go farther, however, if they were still living at home. Then, too, many found that the extra bits of discretionary income that might be spent on attractive clothing, entertainment, or sweets soon disappeared in the face of the need to support other family members or their own children.

Marriage seldom relieved a woman of the need to earn money. Wives in textile-mill towns often provided the primary income for the family during periods of male unemployment. Women who did not work full time for wages often took various by-employments, which provided extra cash for them to buy Sunday's meat dinner or an occasional pair of shoes. Multiple occupations were the rule rather than the exception, and ingenuity was a necessity of survival. A young girl who peddled fruit in the street might also do some scrubbing in exchange for a bed and an evening meal of tea and bread. Charwomen took advantage of their recognized right to the spent tea leaves of a household (which were used in cleaning carpets) and sold them to entrepreneurs who dyed them and mixed them up with fresh tea.

What public (that is, middle-class) debate there was on working-class women's work centered on questions of what was appropriately womanly. Middle-class men and women tended to think of domestic service as the ideal working-class female occupation, but this preference turned more on self-interest than on objective considerations of the relative gentility and ease of the various lower-class occupations. Emptying slops, scrubbing grates, and carrying heavy buckets of coal and water up and down stairs were not considered unduly filthy or taxing to a woman's strength, but sorting coal at the head of a mine seemed scandalously masculine to many observers. Moreover, the public debate was misleading in that it assumed that women had more choice over the circumstances of their lives than they in fact enjoyed. In regions where there was some degree of choice, working-class women usually chose on the basis of wages, family association, or health. A girl from a mining family might work in the mines until her back gave out and then go to the mill. The degree of confinement and supervision was also an increasingly important consideration for young girls as the century progressed. Factories were warmer than fields, but the work was often less healthy and more confining. Both factory work and field work offered more freedom and higher wages in exchange for greater physical discomfort than did domestic service.

In cities, families generally lived close to the man's workplace, forcing women to make longer walks to find employment. Since a new pair of women's shoes cost 6 shillings—which could be a week's wages—women who could not buy or borrow adequate clothing were further restricted in their choices. Aging also narrowed their possibilities as eyesight and stamina began to decline. In general, women took what jobs they could get and worked at them as long as the work was available—or as long as their health held out.

Women obviously worked at a greater variety of occupations than could be represented here. The selections that follow focus on those occupations which extensively employed women and which were the subject of widespread public interest. Though the experiences of working women are presented in their own words, it is important to remember that these women are speaking in a public arena, and are being questioned and edited by representatives of Parliament or the press. For instance, the question of the sexual energy found in the

work-place occurs frequently in investigators' reports, whether they
are discussing factories, mines, or fields. Employers and reformers
alike desired to impose an antiseptic order upon the lives of their
economic inferiors, a desire that seemed most flagrantly frustrated by
unruly sexual playfulness at work. The jokes and sexual play that
were perhaps an inevitable part of the work environment in places
where large numbers of men and women worked together were offensive to some of the workers as well. However, it is probable that
many women did not find the situation degrading or even uncomfortable (except in cases of sexual exploitation by supervisors), but
only a natural expression of vitality and connection between people
who had little other means of personalizing their demanding labor.

As a result of government regulation, union organization, and
feminist agitation, conditions of work became somewhat less brutal
and dangerous during the century. There was also a shift away from
heavy physical labor (except for domestic service and laundry work)
and toward more "genteel" work like shop-assisting. But, in general,
as the century closed, women remained underpaid with respect to
men and continued to bear the double burden of unpaid household
work and paid work at exhausting menial occupations.

DOMESTIC SERVANTS

Domestic service was the most common female occupation, employing in 1881 one out of every three girls between the ages of fifteen
and twenty. Most girls who went to service did it in their youth, leaving to marry. Although both sexes worked as servants, men were
gradually replaced by women in all but the most wealthy homes by
the end of the century, since women could be paid lower wages and
had less choice of work. From the employers' point of view, well-
trained and reliable servants were all but impossible to come by. The
middle-class household aspired to two or three servants and to a style
of life imitative of the feudal self-sufficiency of country estates, including elaborate entertaining that served business as well as social
purposes. But most middle-class people earned less than £300 a year,
and therefore had to make do with only one, overworked, usually
female servant.

From the servants' point of view, domestic work was readily available but overly demanding. As the single servant in a household, a maid would have to get up early to prepare the fires and breakfast, and stay up late cleaning up. Her bedroom would often be in a cramped, cold attic, or even in a corner of the basement kitchen. Her day would be filled with endless occupations, some more arduous or more demeaning than others. Such burdens were increased for those who had charge of young children at the same time. Among the more embarrassing tasks was the scrubbing of the outside steps, which was a mark of good housewifery for Victorians but which exposed the maid to the ridicule of errand boys or other passers-by.

Aside from the physical burden of the work, the confinement of the job was unpleasant. Servants were dependent upon their employers for food and shelter as well as for wages. If they lost their place, they lost their home as well. They ate less well than the members of the family they served, although they had access to table leavings and to a range of food that their own relatives often envied and sometimes profited from. Female servants were often seen as sexually available, particularly by the boys of the household; but a pregnant servant would be fired and would have to hide her child to get her next job. Servants were not supposed to have "followers"—boyfriends of their own class. They usually had to meet their friends in secret during the few hours a week they were at liberty. City servants were often suspected of meeting relatives, friends, or male admirers in the park, where they went with young children.

Servants were expected to follow such rituals of deference as standing in the presence of their masters and wearing uniforms. These rituals were stigmatizing among their nonservant peers. The servant's cap was jeered at as the "badge of a slave"; and though a shop assistant might be addressed by customers as "Miss," a servant was always called by her first name.

It was up to the servants to shield their masters from the "business of living" (as Martineau called it), those earthy, ordinary tasks that servants were believed to be degraded enough to perform. Such tasks were intimate yet impersonal. The slops were to be emptied by unseen hands, the fireplaces scrubbed before anyone awoke, food to appear while the servants hastily withdrew. In addition, the same master and mistress who would demand aid in preparing a bath or pouring a cup of tea might patronizingly adopt the role of spiritual adviser, supervising servants' churchgoing or insisting upon leading them in daily prayers. Even for the elite among the servants, the cooks and housekeepers, or the lady's maid described here, work began at dawn and continued until bedtime; and overwork, dependency, and deference were the conditions of employment. It is little wonder then that, even as domestic work for women grew during this period, the "dislike to domestic service" became more and more noticeable among working-class women.

SERVANTS' WORK (1859)

Harriet Martineau

(See pp. 96, 149, 161, 216, 291, and 364.)

The physician says that, on the female side of lunatic asylums, the largest class, but one, of the insane are maids of all work (the other being governesses). The causes are obvious enough: want of sufficient sleep from late and early hours, unremitting fatigue and hurry, and, even more than these, anxiety about the future from the smallness of the wages. The "general servant," as the maid of all work is now genteelly called, is notoriously unfit for higher situations, from her inability to do anything well. She has to do everything "somehow," and therefore cannot be expected to excel in anything. At the same time, her wages are low, because it is understood that a servant of high qualification in any department would not be a maid of all work. Thus she has no prospect but of toiling on till she drops, having from that moment no other prospect than the workhouse. With this thought chafing at her heart, and her brain confused by her rising at five, after going to bed at an hour or two past midnight, she may easily pass into the asylum some years before she need otherwise have entered the workhouse. "This is horrible!" some of our readers will exclaim, "but it relates to only a small proportion of one out of many classes of maid-servants—a very small class, probably." Not so. Little as the fact is generally understood, the [over 400,000] maids of all work constitute nearly half of the entire number of female domestics. . . . Beginning upon £5 or £6 [yearly] wages in youth, they rarely rise beyond ten pounds. They have no time to take care of their clothes, which undergo excessive wear and tear, so that it is a wonder if there is anything left for the Savings' Bank at the year's end. . . .

Too often we find that the most imbecile old nurses, the most infirm old charwomen, are the wrecks and ruins of the rosy cooks and tidy housemaids of the last generation. This ought not to be. We are not alone in the wonder we have felt all our lives at the exceedingly low rate at which we obtain such a benefit as having the business of living done for us. . . .

In Harriet Martineau, "Female Industry," *Edinburgh Review*, April 1859

A MAID OF ALL WORK (1874)
Ann Thackeray, Lady Ritchie

Anne Thackeray, Lady Ritchie (1837–1919) describes this experienced maid of all work of thirteen years of age as "a neat, bright, clever, stumpy little thing, with a sweet sort of merrie voice."

"Oh, I've been a servant for years!" said the little thing, who was ready enough to tell us all about herself. "I learnt ironing off the lady; I didn't know nothing about it. I didn't know nothing about anything. I didn't know where to buy the wood for the fire," exploding with laughter at the idea. "I run along the street and asked the first person I sor where the wood-shop was. I was frightened—oh, I was. They wasn't particular kind in my first place. I had plenty to eat— it wasn't anything of that. They jest give me an egg, and they says, "There, get your dinner," but not anything more. I had to do all the work. I'd no one to go to: oh! I cried the first night. I used to cry so," exploding again with laughter. "I had always slep in a ward full of other girls, and there I was all alone, and this was a great big house— oh, so big! and they told me to go down stairs, in a room by the kitchen all alone, with a long black passage. I might have screamed, but nobody would have heard. An archytec the gen'lman was. I got to break everything, . . . oh, I was frightened! . . .

Then I got a place in a family where there was nine children. I was about fourteen then. I earned two shillings a week. I used to get up and light the fire, bath them and dress them, and git their breakfasts, and the lady sometimes would go up to London on business, and then I had the baby too, and it couldn't be left, and had to be fed. I'd take them all out for a walk on the common. There was one a cripple. She couldn't walk about. She was about nine year old. I used to carry her on my back. Then there was dinner, and to wash up after; and then by that time it would be tea-time again. And then I had to put the nine children to bed and bath them, and clean up the rooms and fires at night; there was no time in the morning. And then there would be the gen'lman's supper to get. Oh! that was a hard place. I wasn't in bed till twelve, and I'd be up by six. I stopped there nine months. I hadn't no one to help me. Oh yes, I had; the baker, he told me of another place. I've been there three year. I'm cook, and they are very kind; but I tell the girls there's none 'on 'em had such work as me. I'm very fond of reading; but I 'aint no time for reading." . . .

In Anne Thackeray Ritchie, "Maids-of-All-Work and Blue Books," *Cornhill Magazine*, September 1874

A FARMER'S MAID (ca. 1890)
Sybil Marshall

Sybil Marshall transcribed the memories of her mother, Kate Mary Edwards (see p. 249), who knew country-maids-of-all-work at the end of the century.

It were nothing for a girl to be sent away to service when she were eleven year old. This meant leaving the family as she had never been parted from for a day in her life afore, and going to some place miles away to be treated like something as ha'n't got as much sense or feeling as a dog. I'm got nothing against girls going into good service. In my opinion, good service in a properly run big house were a wonderful training for a lot o' girls who never would ha' seen anything different all the days o' their lives if they ha'n't a-gone. It were better than working on the land, then, and if it still existed now, I reckon I'd rather see any o' my daughters be a good housemaid or a well-trained parlourmaid than a dolled-up shop-assistant or a factory worker. . . . Such gals as us from the fen di'n't get "good" service though, not till we'd learnt a good deal the hard way. Big houses di'n't want little girls of eleven, even as kitchen maids, so the first few years 'ad to be put in somewhere else, afore you even got that amount o' promotion. . . . Mostly they went to the farmers' houses within ten or twenty mile from where they'd bin born. These farmers were a jumped up, proud lot who di'n't know how to treat the people who worked for 'em. They took advantage o' the poor peoples' need to get their girls off their hands to get little slaves for nearly nothing. The conditions were terrible. . . .

I 'ad one friend as I were particular fond of, called for some reason as I never did know, "Shady." . . . She went to service when she were about thirteen, to a lonely outlaying fen farm in a place called Black-bushe. The house were a mile or more from the road, and there were no other house near by. A big open farm yard were all round it on three sides, and at the back door, it opened straight into the main drain, about twelve feet wide and ten feet deep with sides like the wall of a house. There were no escape there. Her duties were as follows:

She were woke up at 6 a.m. every morning by the horsekeeper, who had walked several mile to work already, and used a clothes prop to rattle on her window to rouse her. She had to get up straight away and light the scullery fire in the big, awkward old range, that she had to clean and black-lead afore it got too hot. Then she put the kettle on to get tea made for 6:30 a.m. for the horsekeeper, who baited his horses first, come in for his breakfast at 6:30, and went out and yoked his horses so as to be away to work in the fields by seven o'clock. While the kettle boiled, she started to scrub the bare tiles o' the kitchen floor. This were a terrible job. There were no hot water, and the kitchen were so big there seemed nearly a acre of it to scrub—and when you'd finished that, there'd be the dairy, just as big and the scullery as well. Skirts were long an' got in the way as you knelt to scrub, and whatever you done you cou'n't help gettin' 'em wet. In the winter you'd only have the light o' candles to do it by, and the kitchen 'ould be so cold the water 'ould freeze afore you could mop it up properly.

At 6:30 the horsekeeper come in for his tea, and as soon as he's gone Shady had to start getting breakfast for the family. When they'd had theirs, she could have hers, which was only bread and butter, and the tea left in the pot by the family. If there were little children in the house, she'd be expected to have them with her and give them their breakfast while she had her own. After breakfast she washed up, including all the milk utensils and so on from the dairy, and then started the housework. Very often another woman from the farm 'ould be employed to help with this and to do the washing, while the missus done the cooking and housekeeping duties. On churning days Shady had to get up extra early to make time to fit the churning in. There were no time off at all during the day, and after supper she had to wash up all the things and prepare for next morn-ing. This meant cleaning all the family's boots and shoes, and getting things ready for breakfast the next morning. Farmers cured their own bacon and hams so she would be given the bacon taken from a side "in cut," but the custom was to have fried potatoes for breakfast with the bacon. These were supposed to be the 'taters left over from supper, but there never were enough left, so one of her evening jobs was allus to peel and boil a big saucepan of potatoes to fry next morning. . . .

Then if she had any time before it was bed time, she had to sit by herself in the cold dark kitchen in front of a dying fire that she weren't allowed to make up, except in lambing time. In lambing time it were took for granted that any lambs as were weakly 'ould be looked after in the kitchen, and while the season lasted the old shepherd 'ould come in and set in the kitchen while he waited for his ewes to lamb. I'm 'eard Shady say 'ow she dreaded this. The shepherd there were a dirty, nasty, vulgar old man as no decent girl were safe with. . . . The only other choice she 'ad were to go to bed, once she were sure she wou'n't be needed again, but that di'n't offer such pleasant prospects, either. Maids' rooms were allus at the very top, at the back on the north side o' the house. There were nothing in them but a bed with a hard old flock mattress, a table by the side of it, and the tin trunk the girl had brought her clothes in. It was icy cold in winter, and Shady weren't the only one o' my friends an' acquaintances by a long way as told me they slept in all their clothes to keep warm at all.

Though "the woman" done the washing for the family, she di'n't do Shady's. She wern't allowed to do it herself, but 'ad to send it home to her mother once a week by the carrier. This took most o' Shady's "afternoon off," because she had to walk up to the high road and meet the carrier's cart, often hanging about an hour or more waiting for him, to get her dirty washing exchanged for clean. Sometimes her mother 'ould walk the five or six mile with the clean washing, just to see her for a few minutes afore walking it all the other way. On the first time she did this, she found Shady on her knees scrubbing the kitchen floor. Shady got up to greet her, and her mother lifted her skirt and said, "Let's 'ev a look at yer britches." As the poor mother expected, they were wet through with cold water and black as a soot bag with the constant kneeling and scrubbing and black-leading. It were a sort o' test to the experienced mother's eye o' what sort of a "place" she were forced to leave her daughter in. I don't know which of 'em 'ould suffer most, the mother or the daughter. But there were no help for it, and every girl as left home were one less mouth to feed. If she behaved herself and stuck it out a whole year, there did come a day when she'd draw her year's wages, which stood then at £5.

In Sybil Marshall, *Fenland Chronicle: Recollections of William Henry and Kate Mary Edwards Collected and Edited by Their Daughter* (1967)

DUTIES OF THE LADY'S MAID (1861)
Isabella Beeton
(See pp. 83, 93, and 150.)

Mrs. Beeton's advice to a lady's maid included much detailed description of the proper care of hair, clothing, and household goods. The lady's maid had complicated responsibilities in keeping her mistress's delicate wardrobe presentable. Her reward was castoff clothing. French women were preferred for their knowledge of fashion, but a woman trained in dressmaking or a housemaid skillful with a needle was also considered a valuable lady's maid. Unlike the post of cook, which could lead to the pinnacle female position of housekeeper, lady's maid was a dead end. However, an upper-level servant like her could earn as much as £16 to £20 a year instead of the housemaid's usual salary of between £9 and £14.

The duties of a lady's-maid are more numerous, and perhaps more onerous, than those of the valet; for while the latter is aided by the tailor, the hatter, the linen-draper, and the perfumer, the lady's-maid has to originate many parts of the mistress's dress herself: she should, indeed, be a tolerably expert milliner and dressmaker, a good hair-dresser, and possess some chemical knowledge of the cosmetics with which the toilet-table is supplied, in order to use them with safety and effect. Her first duty in the morning, after having performed her own toilet, is to examine the clothes put off by her mistress the evening before, either to put them away, or to see that they are all in order to put on again. During the winter, and in wet weather, the dresses should be carefully examined, and the mud removed. Dresses of tweed, and other woollen materials, may be laid out on a table and brushed all over; but in general, even in woollen fabrics, the lightness of the tissues renders brushing unsuitable to dresses, and it is better to remove the dust from the folds by beating them lightly with handkerchief or thin cloth. Silk dresses should never be brushed, but rubbed with a piece of merino, or other soft material, of a similar colour, kept for the purpose. Summer dresses of barège, muslin, mohair, and other light materials, simply require shaking; but if the muslin be tumbled, it must be ironed afterwards. If the dresses require slight repair, it should be done at once: "a stitch in time saves nine." . . .

The *Chausserie*, or foot-gear of a lady, is one of the few things left to mark her station, and requires special care. Satin boots or shoes should be dusted with a soft brush, or wiped with a cloth. Kid or varnished leather should have the mud wiped off with a sponge charged with milk, which preserves its softness and polish.

These various preliminary offices performed, the lady's-maid should prepare for dressing her mistress, arranging her dressing-room, toilet-table, and linen, according to her mistress's wishes and habits. The details of dressing we need not touch upon—every lady has her own mode of doing so; but the maid should move about quietly, perform any offices about her mistress's person, as lacing stays, gently, and adjust her linen smoothly.

Having prepared the dressing-room by lighting the fire, sweeping the hearth, and made everything ready for dressing her mistress, placed her linen before the fire to air, and laid out the various articles of dress she is to wear, which will probably have been arranged the previous evening, the lady's-maid is prepared for the morning's duties.

Hairdressing is the most important part of the lady's-maid's office. If ringlets are worn, remove the curl-papers, and, after thoroughly brushing the back hair both above and below, dress it according to the prevailing fashion. If bandeaux are worn, the hair is thoroughly brushed and frizzed outside and inside, folding the hair back round the head, brushing it perfectly smooth, giving it a glossy appearance by the use of pomades, or oil, applied by the palm of the hand, smoothing it down with a small brush dipped in bandoline. . . .

TO MAKE POMADE FOR THE HAIR

Ingredients: ¼ lb. of lard, 2 pennyworth of castor-oil; scent.
Mode: Let the lard be unsalted; beat it up well; then add the castor-oil, and mix thoroughly together with a knife, adding a few drops of any scent that may be preferred. Put the pomatum into pots, which keep well covered to prevent it turning rancid. . . .

Having dressed her mistress for breakfast, and breakfasted herself, the further duties of the lady's-maid will depend altogether upon the habits of the family. . . . Where the duties are entirely confined to attendance on her mistress, it is probable that the bedroom and dressing-room will be committed to her care . . . ; she will, therefore, have to make her mistress's bed, and keep it in order; and as her duties are light and easy, there can be no allowance made for the slightest approach to uncleanliness or want of order. . . . After breakfast, except her attendance on her mistress prevents it, if the rooms are carpeted, she should sweep them carefully, having previously strewed the room with moist tea-leaves, dusting every table and chair, taking care to penetrate to every corner, and moving every article of furniture that is portable. This done satisfactorily, and having cleaned the dressing-glass, polished up the furniture and the ornaments, and made the glass jug and basin clean and bright, emptied all slops, emptied the water-jugs and filled them with fresh water, and arranged the rooms, the dressing-room is ready for the mistress when she thinks proper to appear. . . .

Having swept the bedroom with equal care, dusted the tables and chairs, chimney-ornaments, and put away all articles of dress left from yesterday, and cleaned and put away any articles of jewellery, her next care is to see, before her mistress goes out, what requires replacing in her department, and furnish her with a list of them, so that she may use her discretion about ordering them. All this done, she may settle herself down to any work on which she is engaged. This will consist chiefly in mending; which is first to be seen to; everything, except stockings, being mended before washing. Plain work will probably be one of the lady's-maid's chief employments. . . . She will also, if she has her mistress's interests at heart, employ her spare time in repairing and making up dresses which have served one purpose, to serve another also; or turning many things, unfitted for her mistress to use, for the younger branches of the family. . . .

Deference to a master and mistress, and to their friends and visitors, is one of the implied terms of [a servant's] engagement; and this deference must apply even to what may be considered their whims. A servant is not to be seated, or wear a hat in the house, in his master's or mistress's presence; nor offer any opinion, unless asked for it; nor even to say "good night," or "good morning," except in reply to that salutation.

In Isabella Beeton, *Beeton's Book of Household Management* (1861)

"THE DISLIKE TO DOMESTIC SERVICE" (1893)
Clementina Black

Clementina Black (1854–1922) was a suffragist, early trade unionist, and active campaigner for equal pay and better working conditions for women.

That most young women of the working class dislike domestic service is generally admitted; and there is a certain inclination on the part of persons who find this dislike inconvenient, to preach against it as a sort of depravity. The truth, however, is that these young women— like other classes of working people—understand their own needs and their own discomforts a great deal better than these are understood by their middle-class critics.

The conditions of domestic service are still those of an earlier industrial and social system, and this earlier form does not harmonise with the sentiments of today. In other employments, the person employed sells a certain number of hours of labour, and, when those hours are over, all relation ceases between employee and employer. The worker has, in short, a life of her own, absolutely apart from her industrial life. The servant has no such life of her own. . . . She is at beck and call from morning till night: her companions and her immediate supervisor are not of her own choosing, and are not sympathetic. She is exiled from her family and from her personal friends. Smiles and civility are expected from her, whatever her mood or state of health, and whatever the conduct towards her of the persons with whom she is brought into contact, even when one of these is a son of the household in a state of intoxication.

The domestic servant, in short, still lives under a system of total personal subservience. Now, a feeling has gradually grown up that total personal subservience is intolerable and degrading; and it is this feeling which causes domestic service to be held in low social esteem by women who are often harder worked and less materially prosperous than most servants. The servant is despised, not because she cooks, or scrubs, or nurses a baby, still less because she has to yield obedience to orders—every factory worker has to do that in working hours— but because she consents to put herself permanently at some other person's beck and call. . . .

A servant on duty behaves according to rules of strict etiquette—that is to say, she exercises a prolonged self-restraint. Older people—especially older people of a different social grade—are apt to consider such self-restraint very salutary, and to desire that she should remain perpetually within that barrier of etiquette. Nature, however, is of a different mind, and has made young people of all grades averse to a life thus regulated; she has given them an eager hunger for equal companionship, for change, and especially for freedom. . . .

I must confess that, if I were a mother of girls who had to choose between factory work and service, I should give my voice unhesitatingly for the factory. The work would be probably harder, the material comforts less, and the manners rougher, but the girls would be working among their own class and living in their own home; and their health, their happiness, their companionships, would be under their mother's eye. Nor can I think that an unwillingness on the part of girls to cut themselves off from all the natural ties of kindred and surroundings, to dwell among strangers in an unknown house, and to merge their lives completely in that of an alien household, is by any means a sign of perverse folly.

In *Nineteenth Century,* March 1893

FACTORY WORKERS

Factory work for women was unskilled, exhausting, monotonous, and unhealthy. Conditions in pottery factories produced lead poisoning, in match factories caused necrosis (phosphorus poisoning), and in cotton mills resulted in a poisoning of the lungs. Because there was usually little or no protection from the machinery itself, tired workers were exposed to gruesome accidents. Ventilation was often poor and toilets inadequately supplied. There was little time and no clean place to eat. Women's wages were regularly half that of men's, the highest female wage in an industry often being below the lowest male wage. An 1883 American survey of over seventeen thousand English factory workers gave $3.37 as the average English woman worker's weekly wage and $8.26 as the average English man's.

Textiles employed the largest number of women, 385,000 in 1851. In textile factories of the 1840s, the yearly accident rate, because of

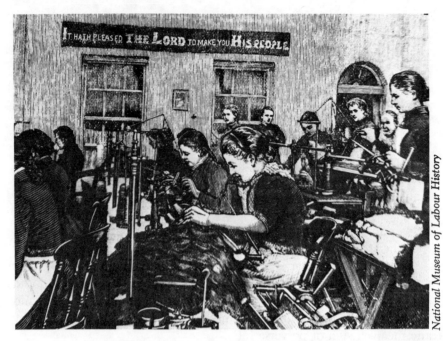

A knitting factory, from All the World, *1893*

overwork and poorly designed machinery, was 15 in 1,000 workers. Working conditions were also quite uncomfortable. Cotton mills, for instance, were extremely hot and humid, temperatures often reaching over 90 degrees; and linen workers were often soaked with water from the wet-spinning process. With the worker pushed to match the pace of the machinery, exhausted young children could be kept at work in the afternoon only by regular beatings. Although parliamentary investigations recorded instances of mothers attacking the supervisors who beat their children, they were often powerless in the situation, since the family needed the child's wages.

The movement for shorter hours began with agitation by working-class men, but it was translated into legislation primarily aimed at shielding first children (in 1833) and then women and children (in 1844) from the worst barbarities of work in the mills. Overlooking the women's need for their wages, early reformers were motivated to cut hours by an idealized, domesticized vision of women. It was certainly true that factory work interfered with good mothering: the unemployment in Lancashire during the "cotton famine" of the

American Civil War caused infant mortality to fall significantly with increased breast-feeding. Still, legislative regulation was not always welcome to women workers. Though the long-range effect of such legislation was to shorten working hours for all workers, the immediate effect was often to close desperate women out of employment in regulated areas. Violations of the Ten Hours Act of 1847 and of the Factory Acts that followed it were widespread, and women workers often cooperated in hiding the true conditions of their employment from the factory inspector. The small sweat-shops which thrived at the end of the century were even harder to regulate.

Unions came later to women's work than to men's. The match workers' strike of 1888 was a key victory that encouraged the work of union organizers in other fields. The work of Emma Paterson, who had founded the Women's Provident and Protective League in 1874; of trade unionists like Clementina Black; and of female factory inspectors and investigators like Clara Collet began to make a difference by the end of the century, although decent hours, conditions of work, and equitable rates of pay still remained largely unavailable to women.

SPEECH ON THE TEN HOURS BILL (1844)
Anthony Ashley Cooper, Lord Ashley

Anthony Ashley Cooper (1801–1885), Lord Ashley and afterward Lord Shaftesbury, was an eminent philanthropist as well as a groundbreaking legislative reformer. He was instrumental in the passage of the Mines Act of 1842 and the Ten Hours Act, finally passed in 1847. As a conservative, religious-minded reformer, he took a paternalistic but tireless interest in the welfare of the poor, and of women and children in particular. He served as chairman of the Ragged Schools Union, and as president of the Society for Promoting the Employment of Women, to mention only two of his numerous interests. He saw reform as a moral duty and as a political necessity for preventing revolution. In the case of reforms concerning women working in factories, he was also afraid of the female usurpation of male behavior and male power. It is important to remember that some radicals and working men held similar views of women's labor. For instance, the Chartist Francis Place wrote in 1835 that "men should refuse to work in mills and factories which employ women" so that "the young

women who will otherwise be degraded by factory labor will become
all that can be desired as companionable wives, and . . . the men will
obtain competent wages for their maintenance."

But listen to another fact, and one deserving of serious attention;
that the females not only perform the labour, but occupy the places
of men; they are forming various clubs and associations, and gradually
acquiring all those privileges which are held to be the proper portion
of the male sex. These female clubs are thus described: "Fifty or
sixty females, married and single, form themselves into clubs, ostensibly for protection; but in fact, they meet together to drink, sing, and
smoke; they use, it is stated, the lowest, most brutal, and most dis-
gusting language imaginable." Here is a dialogue which occurred in
one of these clubs, from an ear witness: "A man came into one of
these club-rooms, with a child in his arms; 'Come lass,' said he, addressing one of the women, 'come home, for I cannot keep this bairn
quiet, and the other I have left crying at home.' 'I won't go home,
idle devil,' she replied, 'I have thee to keep, and the bairns too, and if
I can't get a pint of ale quietly, it is tiresome. This is only the second
pint that Bess and me have had between us; thou may sup if thou
likes, and sit thee down, but I won't go home yet.' " Whence is it
that this singular and unnatural change is taking place? Because that
on women are imposed the duty and burthen of supporting their husbands and families, a perversion as it were of nature, which has the
inevitable effect of introducing into families disorder, insubordination, and conflict. What is the ground on which the woman says she
will pay no attention to her domestic duties, nor give the obedience
which is owing to her husband? Because on her devolves the labour
which ought to fall to his share, and she throws out the taunt, "If I
have the labour, I will also have the amusement." . . .

Observe carefully, too, the ferocity of character which is exhibited
by a great mass of the female population of the manufacturing towns.
Recollect the outbreak of 1842, and the share borne in that by the
girls and women; and the still more frightful contingencies which may
be in store for the future. "I met," says an informant of mine, "with
a mother of factory workers, who told me that all the churches and
chapels were useless places, and so was all the talk about education,
since the young and old were unable to attend, either in consequence
of the former being imprisoned in the mills so many hours, and being
in want of rest the little time they were at home; and the latter being
compelled to live out of the small earnings of their children, and can-

not get clothing, so they never think of going to churches or chapels. She added, 'When you get up to London, tell them we'll turn out the next time (meaning the women), and let the soldiers fire upon us if they dare, and depend upon it there will be a break out, and a right one, if that House of Commons don't alter things, for they can alter if they will, by taking mothers and daughters out of the factories, and sending the men and big lads in.' " . . .

[Women's prolonged labor] disturbs the order of nature, and the rights of the labouring men, by ejecting the males from the workshop, and filling their places by females, who are thus withdrawn from all their domestic duties, and exposed to insufferable toil at half the wages that would be assigned to males, for the support of their families. It affects—nay, more, it absolutely annihilates, all the arrangements and provisions of domestic economy—thrift and management are altogether impossible; had they twice the amount of their present wages, they would be but slightly benefited—everything runs to waste; the house and children are deserted; the wife can do nothing for her husband and family; she can neither cook, wash, repair clothes, or take charge of the infants; all must be paid for out of her scanty earnings, and, after all, most imperfectly done. Dirt, discomfort, ignorance, recklessness, are the portion of such households; the wife has no time for learning in her youth, and none for practice in her riper age; the females are most unequal to the duties of the men in the factories; and all things go to rack and ruin, because the men can discharge at home no one of the especial duties that Providence has assigned to the females.

In Debate on the Ten Hours Bill, House of Commons, *Hansard*, 15 March 1844

TESTIMONY OF A MILL WORKER (1832)
Elizabeth Bentley

This testimony is representative of the evidence gathered to support the passage of the Factory Act of 1833. In 1834 the peak weekly wages for women in Lancashire cotton mills was 9s. 8½d., for men 22s. 8½d.

Q: *What age are you?*   A: Twenty-three.
Q: *Where do you live?*   A: At Leeds.

Q: *What time did you begin to work at a factory?*   A: When I was six years old.

Q: *At whose factory did you work?*   A: Mr. Busk's.

Q: *What kind of a mill is it?*   A: Flax-mill.

Q: *What was your business at that mill?*   A: I was a little doffer.

Q: *What were your hours of labour in that mill?*   A: From 5 in the morning till 9 at night, when they were thronged [busy].

Q: *For how long a time together have you worked that excessive length of time?*   A: For about half a year.

Q: *What were your usual hours of labour when you were not so thronged?*   A: From 6 in the morning till 7 at night.

Q: *What time was allowed for your meals?*   A: Forty minutes at noon.

Q: *Had you any time to get your breakfast or drinking?*   A: No, we got it as we could.

Q: *And when your work was bad, you had hardly any time to eat it at all?*   A: No, we were obliged to leave it or take it home, and when we did not take it, the overlooker took it away, and gave it to his pigs. . . .

Q: *Explain what it is you had to do.*   A: When the frames are full, they have to stop the frames, and take the flyers off, and take the full bobbins off, and carry them to the roller; and then put empty ones on, and set the frame going again.

Q: *Does that keep you constantly on your feet?*   A: Yes, there are so many frames, and they run so quick.

Q: *Your labour is very excessive?*   A: Yes; you have not time for anything.

Q: *Suppose you flagged a little, or were too late, what would they do?*   A: Strap us.

Q: *Are they in the habit of strapping those who are last in doffing?*   A: Yes.

Q: *Constantly?*   A: Yes.

Q: *Girls as well as boys?*   A: Yes.

Q: *Have you ever been strapped?*   A: Yes.

Q: *Severely?*   A: Yes.

Q: *Is the strap used so as to hurt you excessively?*   A: Yes, it is.

Q: *Were you strapped if you were too much fatigued to keep up with the machinery?*   A: Yes; the overlooker I was under was a very severe man, and when we have been fatigued and worn out, and had not baskets to put the bobbins in, we used to put them in the window bottoms, and that broke the panes sometimes, and I broke one one time, and the overlooker strapped me on the arm, and it rose a blister, and I ran home to my mother.

Q: *How long did you work at Mr. Busk's?*   A: Three or four years.

Q: *Where did you go to then?*   A: Benyon's factory.

Q: *That was when you were about ten years old?*   A: Yes.

Q: *What were you then?*   A: A weigher in the card-room.

Q: *How long did you work there?*   A: From half-past 5 till 8 at night.

Q: *Was that the ordinary time?*   A: Till 9 when they were thronged. . . .

Q: *The carding-room is more oppressive than the spinning department?*   A: Yes; it is so dusty they cannot see each other for dust.

Q: *It is on that account they are allowed a relaxation of those few minutes?*   A: Yes; the cards so soon filled up with waste and dirt, they are obliged to stop them, or they would take fire. . . .

Q: *Were the children beat up to their labour there?*   A: Yes.

Q: *With what?*   A: A strap; I have seen the overlooker go to the top end of the room, where the little girls hug the can to the back-minders [carry or hold cans containing carded cotton and measuring about four feet high by one foot in diameter]; he has taken a strap, and a whistle in his mouth, and sometimes he has got a chain and chained them, and strapped them all down the room. . . .

Q: *Were the girls so struck as to leave marks upon their skin?*   A: Yes; they have had black marks many times, and their parents dare not come to him about it, they were afraid of losing their work. . . .

Q: *Did [the card-room] affect your health?*   A: Yes; it was so dusty, the dust got upon my lungs, and the work was so hard; I was middling strong when I went there, but the work was so bad; I got so bad in health, that when I pulled the baskets down, I pulled my bones out of their places. . . .

Q: *It has had the effect of pulling your shoulders out?*   A: Yes; it was a great basket that stood higher than this table a good deal.

Q: *How heavy was it?*   A: I cannot say; it was a very large one, that was full of weights up-heaped, and pulling the basket pulled my shoulders out of its place, and my ribs have grown over it. . . .

Q: *You are considerably deformed in your person in consequence of this labour?*   A: Yes, I am.

Q: *At what time did it come on?*   A: I was about thirteen years old when it began coming, and it has got worse since; it is five years since my mother died, and my mother was never able to get me a pair of stays to hold me up, and when my mother died I had to do for myself, and got me a pair.

Q: *Were you perfectly straight and healthy before you worked at a mill?* A: Yes, I was as straight a little girl as ever went up and down town.

In Minutes of Evidence Taken Before Committee on Factories Bill, 4 June 1832, *P.P.* xv, 1831–1832

THE "WHITE SLAVERY" OF LONDON MATCH WORKERS (1888)
Annie Besant
(See pp. 112, 146, and 294.)

Annie Besant heard about the high dividends and low wages at Bryant and May at a meeting of the Fabian Socialist Society. Her articles and leadership led to a public boycott and a successful strike of fourteen hundred match workers.

Bryant and May, now a limited liability company, paid last year a dividend of 23 per cent to its shareholders; two years ago it paid a dividend of 25 per cent, and the original £5 shares were then quoted for sale at £18 7s. 6d. The highest dividend paid has been 38 per cent.

Let us see how the money is made with which these monstrous dividends are paid. . . .

The hour for commencing work is 6.30 in summer and 8 in winter; work concludes at 6 p.m. Half-an-hour is allowed for breakfast and an hour for dinner. This long day of work is performed by young girls, who have to stand the whole of the time. A typical case is that of a girl of 16, a piece-worker; she earns 4s. a week, and lives with a sister, employed by the same firm, who "earns good money, as much as 8s. or 9s. per week." Out of the earnings 2s. is paid for the rent of one room; the child lives on only bread-and-butter and tea, alike for breakfast and dinner, but related with dancing eyes that once a month she went to a meal where "you get coffee, and bread and butter, and jam, and marmalade, and lots of it." . . . The splendid salary of 4s. is subject to deductions in the shape of fines; if the feet

BBC Hulton Picture Library

Match factory workers, London, 1888

are dirty, or the ground under the bench is left untidy, a fine of 3d. is inflicted; for putting "burnts"—matches that have caught fire during the work—on the bench 1s. has been forfeited, and one unhappy girl was once fined 2s. 6d. for some unknown crime. If a girl leaves four or five matches on her bench when she goes for a fresh "frame" she is fined 3d., and in some departments a fine of 3d. is inflicted for talking. If a girl is late she is shut out for "half the day," that is for the morning six hours, and 5d. is deducted out of her day's 8d. One girl was fined 1s. for letting the web twist around a machine in the endeavor to save her fingers from being cut, and was sharply told to take care of the machine, "never mind your fingers." Another, who carried out the instructions and lost a finger thereby, was left unsupported while she was helpless. The wage covers the duty of submitting to an occasional blow from a foreman; one, who appears to be a gentleman of variable temper, "clouts" them "when he is mad."

One department of the work consists in taking matches out of a frame and putting them into boxes; about three frames can be done in an hour, and ½d. is paid for each frame emptied; only one frame is given out at a time, and the girls have to run downstairs and upstairs each time to fetch the frame, thus much increasing their fatigue. One of the delights of the frame work is the accidental firing of the matches: when this happens the worker loses the work, and if the frame is injured she is fined or "sacked." 5s. a week had been earned at this by one girl I talked to.

The "fillers" get ¾d. a gross for filling boxes; at "boxing," *i.e.* wrapping papers round the boxes, they can earn from 4s 6d. to 5s. a week. A very rapid "filler" has been known to earn once "as much as 9s." in a week, and 6s. a week "sometimes." The making of boxes is not done in the factory; for these 2¼d. a gross is paid to people who work in their own homes, and "find your own paste." Daywork is a little better paid than piecework, and is done chiefly by married women, who earn as much sometimes as 10s. a week, the piecework falling to the girls. Four women day workers, spoken of with reverent awe, earn—13s. a week.

A very bitter memory survives in the factory. Mr. Theodore Bryant, to show his admiration of Mr. Gladstone and the greatness of his own public spirit, bethought him to erect a statue to that eminent statesman. In order that his workgirls might have the privilege of contributing, he stopped 1s. each out of their wages, and further deprived them of half-a-day's work by closing the factory, "giving them a holiday." ("We don't want no holidays," said one of the girls pathetically, for—needless to say—the poorer employees of such a firm lose their wages when a holiday is "given.") So furious were the girls at this cruel plundering, that many went to the unveiling of the statue with stones and bricks in their pockets, and I was conscious of a wish that some of those bricks had made an impression on Mr. Bryant's conscience. Later on they surrounded the statue— "we paid for it" they cried savegely—shouting and yelling, and a gruesome story is told that some cut their arms and let their blood trickle on the marble paid for, in very truth, by their blood. . . .

Such is a bald account of one form of white slavery as it exists in

London. With chattel slaves Mr. Bryant could not have made his huge fortune, for he could not have fed, clothed, and housed them for 4s. a week each, and they would have had a definite money value which would have served as a protection. But who cares for the fate of these white wage slaves? Born in slums, driven to work while still children, undersized because underfed, oppressed because helpless, flung aside as soon as worked out, who cares if they die or go on the streets, provided only that the Bryant and May shareholders get their 23 per cent, and Mr. Theodore Bryant can erect statues and buy parks? Oh if we had but a people's Dante, to make a special circle in the Inferno for those who live on this misery, and suck wealth out of the starvation of helpless girls.

Failing a poet to hold up their conduct to the execration of posterity, enshrined in deathless verse, let us strive to touch their consciences, *i.e.* their pockets, and let us at least avoid being "partakers of their sins," by abstaining from using their commodities.

In Annie Besant, "White Slavery in London," *Link*, June 23, 1888

SEXUAL HARASSMENT IN FACTORIES (1902)
Clara Collet

At the end of the century, the growing employment of women factory and sanitary inspectors, as well as women journalists and private social investigators, brought new kinds of information before the public. In the following selection, Clara Collet (1860–1948), one of the first female factory inspectors, provides a glimpse of the day-to-day sexual politics of factory work.

[Young women factory workers] repeatedly complain about their treatment by foremen. "The masters are kind, but the foremen treat us like animals." It is very difficult to decide in any particular case whether the foreman is in the right or whether the girl is telling the truth. But if in a factory the foremen are habitually tyrannical and subject the girls to rough treatment, the employers must be regarded as represented by the foremen, and many of them deserve the severest censure for their indifference in this respect. Forewomen should superintend girls whenever it is possible; and if suitable women cannot be found for the post, the greatest care should be shown in the selection of the foreman. A very little reflection on the darker side of life in the East End will show to what insult a girl may be exposed by her employer's indifference to the moral character of the man to whom he intrusts the management of young girls. The system of payment adopted by some employers, who pay their foreman by the piece and leave him to engage and dismiss the girls in his department, confers on him a power which the average foreman will be strongly tempted to abuse, unless great watchfulness is shown by the employer. It is not likely that these men should be more incorruptible than other men who have power given them. Bribery of officials is not an unknown thing to employers—they have even occasionally, perhaps, stooped to employ such means themselves; and it might occur to them that if they delegate their functions to their foremen, the latter may be tempted to increase their incomes, or indulge themselves at the expense of the girls, who must find favour in their eyes if they wish to be left unmolested in other ways.

In Clara Collet, "Women's Work," in Charles Booth, *Life and Labour of the People in London* (1902–1904)

NEEDLEWORKERS

In the early 1840s when Thomas Hood published his "Song of the Shirt," there were more than 150,000 women over the age of twenty engaged in sewing for a living. Just after Henry Mayhew's series on "needlewomen" appeared in the *Morning Chronicle* in 1851, the number had risen to 388,302, making it the single largest paid-occupation for women who worked in their homes. A needleworker earned as little as half as much as a factory worker and worked at least as long. "Slop work sewing" (piecework done at home on inexpensive goods), the resort of the least skilled and most house-bound women, was subject to seasonal booms and busts; and the large number of available workers allowed manufacturers to keep lowering the rates paid per piece. Often finished work went unpaid due to real or trumped-up charges of irregularity in execution. Although needlework was thought more respectable than work in the mills, it meant an arduous and more solitary life. Those who sewed in the workshops of the fashionable dressmakers suffered severely from overwork during the great London seasons and from unemployment at other times. Because of their low and uncertain pay, needleworkers were notorious for occasionally dabbling in prostitution (see p. 381).

"THE SONG OF THE SHIRT" (1843)
Thomas Hood

This immensely popular ballad was originally published in the Christmas issue of Punch in December 1843. It presents a pervasive sentimental image of the needleworker as a passive victim of slow starvation.

It was the needleworkers who came to represent the plight of women workers in the popular middle-class mind, partly through Hood's poem, but also through numerous maudlin paintings and sensationalist newspaper accounts of starved seamstresses. Although piecework was particularly low paying and monotonous, it was neither more tiring than domestic service nor more likely to lead to an early tubercular death than factory work (to take the two leading employments of the female poor). But needleworkers were less obviously necessary to middle-class comfort than were servants, and more easy to imagine as feminine domestic angels than factory women who, as we have seen, were thought of as rough and independent.

THE SONG OF THE SHIRT

> With fingers weary and worn,
>   With eyelids heavy and red,
> A woman sat, in unwomanly rags,
>   Plying her needle and thread.
>
> Stitch! stitch! stitch!
>   In poverty, hunger, and dirt,
> And still with a voice of dolorous pitch
>   She sang the Song of the Shirt:
>
> . . . .
>
> "Oh, men, with sisters dear!
>   Oh, men, with mothers and wives!
> It is not linen you're wearing out,
>   But human creatures' lives!

Stitch—stitch—stitch,
In poverty, hunger, and dirt,
Sewing at once, with a double thread,
A shroud as well as a shirt.

. . . .

"Seam, and gusset, and band,
Band, and gusset, and seam,
Work, work, work,
Like the engine that works by steam!
A mere machine of iron and wood
That toils for Mammon's sake—
Without a brain to ponder and craze
Or a heart to feel—and break!"

INTERVIEWS WITH NEEDLEWORKERS (1849)
Henry Mayhew
(See pp. 376 and 398.)

Henry Mayhew (1812–1887) was a journalist with a genius for what we now think of as oral history. His eye for detail, his shrewd appreciation of the means by which poor people provided themselves with the necessities of life, and his Dickensian delight in colorful speech produced (probably with the aid of some invention on his part) portraits of working people that ring true to the conditions of material life and also convey individual character and personality traits. The interviews here are with women in the needle trade, ranging from the poorest pieceworker to the slightly more independent piece-mistress, who gave out the clothes for other women to sew, to a distressed gentlewoman living in someone else's empty house and trying to reconcile her genteel past with her impoverished present. All needleworkers faced the problem of being too weakened by poverty to sew their quota of goods, a futile battle that worsened as a woman aged and her strength declined.

Interview with a woman
making the worst paid convict uniforms

As I had been informed that the convict work was the worst paid of all labour, I was anxious to obtain an interview with one who got her living by it. She lived in a small back room on the first floor. I knocked at the door, but no one answered, though I had been told the woman was within. I knocked again and again, and, hearing no one stirring, I looked through the keyhole and observed the key was inside the door. Fearing that some accident might have happened to the poor old soul, I knocked once more, louder than ever. At last the door was opened, and a thin aged woman stood trembling nervously as she looked at me. She stammered out with a gasp, "Oh! I beg pardon, but I thought it was the woman come for the shilling I owed her." I told her my errand, and she welcomed me in. There was no table in the room; but on a chair without a back there was an old tin tray, in which stood a cup of hot, milk-less tea, and a broken saucer, with some half dozen small potatoes in it. It was the poor soul's dinner. Some tea-leaves had been given her, and she had boiled them up again to make something like a meal. She had not even a morsel of bread. In one corner of the room was a hay mattress, rolled up. With this she slept on the floor. She said,

"I work at convict work, 'the greys'; some are half yellow and half brown, but they're all paid the same price. I makes the whole suit. Gets 7¾d. for all of it [jacket, trousers, and waistcoat], and find [provide] my own thread out of that. . . . There's full a day and a half's work in a suit. I works from nine in the morning till eleven at night. (Here a sharp-featured woman entered and said she wished to speak with the "convict worker" when she was alone. "She came," said the poor old thing when the woman had left, "because I owes her a shilling. I'm sure she can't have it, for I haven't got it. I borrowed it last week off her.") "In a day and a half," she continued, with a deep sigh, "deducting the cost of thread and candles for the suit (to say nothing of firing), I earns 3¾d.—not 2d. a day. The other day I had to sell a cup and saucer for a halfpenny, 'cause crockeryware's so cheap—there was no handle to it, it's true—in order to get me a candle to work with. . . .

"I can't tell what I average, for sometimes I have work and sometimes I an't. I could earn 3s. a week if I had as much as I could do, but I don't have it very often. I'm very often very idle. I can assure you I've been trotting about today to see after a shilling job and couldn't get it. (The same woman again made her appearance at the door and seeing me still there did not stop to say a word. "What a bother there is," said the convict-clothes-maker, "if a person owes a few halfpence. That's what made me keep the door locked.") I suppose her mother has sent for the old shawl she lent me. I haven't no shawl to my back—no, as true as God I haven't; I haven't indeed!"

Statement of a piece-mistress

I was now desirous to see a piece-master, in order that I might find out whether they really did make the amount of money that they were believed to do out of the workpeoples' labour, and found the family in the lowest state of destitution. The party lived in a back-kitchen, in a house over Waterloo-bridge. It was mid-day when I got there, and the woman and her boy were dining off potatoes and some "rind" of bacon that her daughter, who was "in place" had given to her rather than it should be thrown away.

"Poor people," said she, "you know is glad to get anything." Then, observing me notice the crockery, which was arranged on a shelf in one corner, she added:

"Ah, sir, you needn't look at my crockery ware—I'll show it to you," she said, taking down several basins and jugs. They were all broken on one side but turned the best side outwards. "There isn't a whole vessel in the place; only nobody would know but they were sound, you see, to look at 'em. . . . I'm a piece-mistress. I get the work out of warehouse, and give it to the work people. I has a penny a pair out of them. I has twopence out of some—they are the sergeants [uniforms]. Perhaps I'd get 40 pair out in a week, perhaps 30 pair, and maybe 10—when they has them I get them. Before my husband died I've had 100 pair out in a week. . . .

"At the time my husband lived we did pretty well. Was never out of work. If we hadn't it from one warehouse we had it from the others we worked for. He has been three years buried next Easter Sunday, and there's many a night since I've went to bed without my supper, myself and my children. Since then I've had nothing, only just a few odd trousers now and then. I had to go to the workhouse last winter, myself and my children; I couldn't get a meal of victuals for them, and this winter I suppose I shall have to go into it again. If I haven't work I can't pay my rent. Three weeks ago I had only twenty pair to make, and that's 1s. 8d. for myself and boy to live upon (my other's out in the Marine School), and my rent out of that is 1s. 6d. My boy gets 1s. 6d. a week besides this, and only for that I couldn't live at all. And that's drawed before it's earned. I'm obliged to go on credit for my things and pay with my boy's money, and glad to have it to pay. I call it a good week if I get 40 pair of trowsers to give out. This is 3s. 4d. to me, and upon that me and my boy must both live; and there was my other boy to do the same too when I had him. I occasionally get a bit of broken victuals from those that know me round about. I little thought I should be so miserable as I am. That fender is not mine. I borrowed it off my landlady; nor that saucepan neither; I got it to boil my potatoes in. Indeed you may say I very often want. We should be starved entirely if it was not for my landlady, and that's the blessed truth. . . .

A distressed gentlewoman doing needlework

"I work at needlework generally—I profess to do that, indeed that is what I have done ever since I have been a widow. But it is shocking payment. What I am engaged upon now is from a private lady. I haven't, as yet, made any charge. I don't know what the price will be; I did intend to ask 3d. each. The lady has been a great friend to me. . . . They are plain nightcaps that I am making, and are for a lady of rank. Such persons generally, I think, give the least trouble for their work. I can't say how long they take me each to make. I've been very ill, and I've had the children to help me. . . .

"The lady won't put the price herself upon the nightcaps, and I feel timid in asking a price of a lady that's been a friend to me. Latterly I've had no work at all, only that which I got from an institution for distressed needlewomen. They were children's chemises. . . . I did the seven chemises in a fortnight, and got 7s. for them. I have also made within this time one dozen white cravats for a shop; they are the white corded-muslin cut across, and the very largest. I have 6d. a dozen for hemming them, and had to find the cotton of course. I have often said I would never do any more of them; I thought they would never have been done, there was so much work in them. Myself and daughter hemmed the dozen in a day. It was a day's very hard work. It was really such hard work that I cried over it. I was so ill, and we were wanting food so badly.

"That is all myself and daughter have done for this last month. During that time the two of us (my daughter is eighteen) have earned . . . 9s. 6d. for four weeks, or 2s. 4½d. per week. . . . My daughter and I have earned at plain needlework a good deal more than that. But to get more we have scarcely time to eat. I have, with my daughter's labour and my own earned as much as 10s.; but then such hard work injures the health. I should say an industrious quick hand might earn at plain needlework, taking one thing with another, 3s. 6d.

a week, if she were fully employed. But there is a great difficulty in getting work—oh, yes, very great. The schools injure the trade greatly. Ladies give their work to the National Schools, and thus needle-women who have families to support are left without employment. . . .

"Of course we could not have subsisted upon the 2s. 2½d. a week, which we have earned for the last four weeks. I have got many dupli-cates [pawn tickets] in the house to show how we *did* live. . . . I sold my bedstead for 3s. 6d. to a person, who came herself and valued it. That very bedstead, not a month ago, I gave 8s. 6d., and I pledged it for a shilling. Our blankets, too, we pledged for 1s, each; they cost me 6s. the pair; but I've taken one out since. Of course now we sleep upon the floor. Our inside clothing we have also disposed of. Indeed, I will tell you, we are still without our clothing, both my daughter and myself; and I have chewed camphor and drank warm water to stay my hunger.

"What I want is a situation for my eldest daughter. She can speak Spanish, and she works well at her needle. I myself speak Spanish and French. . . . My husband was an officer in the army. . . . He has been dead five years. He left me penniless, with three children. My son is in the West Indies. He is doing well there: he is but young—he is only 17. He has £36 a year and his board. He assisted me last year. I was in hopes to have some assistance this year, according to the last letter I had from him. I do feel it very hard that I—whose father and grandfather have served the country—should be left to suffer as I do. I don't consider, if you understand me, sir, that we have any merit or claim upon the Government; still I cannot but think it hard that the children of those who have served their country so many years should be so destitute as we are.

In Henry Mayhew, "Labour and the Poor," *Morning Chronicle*, November 9, 1849; "The Metropolitan Districts," *Morning Chronicle*, November 16, 1849

SHOP ASSISTANTS

One of the most rapidly growing employments for women in the second half of the nineteenth century was shop assisting. The num-ber of women engaged in retail trades grew from 87,000 in 1861 to 243,000 in 1901, with most of them working as shop assistants, par-ticularly in the new, larger clothing establishments. Shop assistants worked perhaps seventy-five hours a week (or more), standing on their feet all of that time with only forty-five minutes away from their counter for their two daily meals. They received about 10s. a week and were forced to take part of their "salary" in the form of room and board. Near the shop employers provided barracks-style housing, which was usually overcrowded, poorly ventilated, dirty, and inadequately supplied with water and toilets. Meals were served in damp, insect-infested basements and consisted largely of bread and tea. Shop workers were considered more "genteel" than factory workers and had the added expense of providing themselves with "decent" clothing, but their supposed gentility did not exempt them from humiliating and costly supervision, which included an extensive system of fines for such offenses as giving the wrong change, lateness, incivility to customers or floor managers, or even failure to make their own beds. Unemployment was chronic, due to layoffs or inevitable breakdowns in health; and the chances of meeting a husband were poor, especially since male shop assistants were fired upon marriage.

From the 1880s on, a series of inadequate protectionist legislative measures attempted to limit the hours of shop workers and to provide women workers with seats. But shop work continued to be less regulated than factory work well into the twentieth century.

A SHOP GIRL'S LIFE (1894–1902)
Margaret Bondfield

The National Union for Shop Assistants, formed in 1891, was open to women; and Margaret Bondfield (1873–1954) was an early and active member. The daughter of a lace factory worker, she began work at fourteen as a draper's assistant in Brighton and eventually became the first woman cabinet minister in Britain.

London: By dint of rigid economy, at the end of five years of shop life in Brighton I had saved £5, which seemed to me great wealth; but the material side of life did not bother me much. I had reached a stage in my spiritual pilgrimage which I must needs travel alone. . . . I could no longer passively accept contemporary opinion on business morality, to which I applied the harsh judgments of the very young. The outward and visible sign of my protest was a sudden move to London. It was undoubtedly *the* turning-point in my life. . . .

For the next three months I was nearer to starvation than at any time since. I learned the bitterness of a hopeless search for work. The kindness of a landlady who trusted me kept me going when I was penniless, and until I got a job.

In those days the seekers after work had no Labour Exchange to help them. The best plan was to visit the wholesale firms in the City and get information about vacancies from the commercial travellers, and then journey as fast as the old horse buses allowed—perhaps right across London—only to find a queue of 150 to 200 applicants already there. Before we stood in the queue for long a notice would be put up: "No good waiting any longer—places filled."

I have taken the whole of Oxford Street, going into every shop walking West on the one side, and every shop on the other side coming back, on the chance that there might be a vacancy. I was not tall enough. I remember one man saying to me, "We never engage anyone under five feet eight inches."

Even today those first months in the great city searching for work carry the shadow of a nightmare; but finally I got a job—only to find that conditions, which I had thought peculiar to the Brighton shop, were almost universal. . . .

A small thing led me to another adventure of faith. I was hungry and I went across to Fitzroy Street to buy a penn'orth of fish and a ha'p'orth of chips, served to me in a newspaper; munching my feast, I strolled around Fitzroy Square reading the paper, in which was a letter from James Macpherson, Secretary of the National Union of Shop Assistants, Warehousemen and Clerks, urging shop assistants to join together to fight against the wretched conditions of employment. I was working about sixty-five hours a week for between £15 and £25 per annum, living in. Here I felt was the right thing to do, and at once I joined up.

My brother Frank was in London, working at Clement's House Printing Works, where he was "Father of the Chapel" and a member of the Union committee to negotiate terms for the introduction of the Linotype. He encouraged my Trade Union activities. This was a happy time for me.

My Union officers gave me all the work I could do in my scant leisure, and every kind of encouragement. They elected me on to the district council, and once I attended a national conference. For the next two years the Union utilized me for platform work in an ever-increasing degree.

Encouraged by T. Spencer Jones, the editor of our little Union paper, I ventured first to undertake reports of meetings, and later to write a few short stories under the pen-name of Grace Dare. It was quite impossible for me to write in the presence of any who might know what I was doing, and as I had not one inch of space I could call my own, I would wait till one or two of my room-mates were asleep, and then stealthily, with the feeling of a conspirator, and knowing that I was committing an offence for which I could be heavily fined, I would light my halfpenny dip, hiding its glare by means of a towel thrown over the back of a chair, and set to work on my monthly article.

If my room-mates woke they were kind enough not to remember it the next morning, and although this surreptitious writing was kept up for about two years, I do not think any breach of rules was ever reported to the firm. . . .

From this time on I just lived for the Trade Union Movement. I concentrated on my job.

This concentration was undisturbed by love affairs. I had seen too much—too early—to have the least desire to join in the pitiful scramble of my workmates. The very surroundings of shop life accentuated the desire of most shop girls to get married. Long hours of work and the living-in system deprived them of the normal companionship of men in their leisure hours, and the wonder is that so many of the women continued to be good and kind, and self-respecting, without the incentive of a great cause, or of any interest outside their job.

Many of them would toil after business hours to make their clothes, so that, from their small salaries, they could help some member of their family. Some women, much older than myself, would look forward to marriage with hope and dread—hope of economic security, and dread of the unknown ordeal of childbirth. Through what sex knowledge I was able to pass on, [I] resolved their fears, but it was not at all easy to transmit to them the reverence for motherhood, which I had seen at its best and highest, but which to them was too often linked with the obscene.

I had no vocation for wifehood or motherhood, but an urge to serve the Union—an urge which developed into "a sense of oneness with our kind."

In Margaret Bondfield, A *Life's Work* (1966)

"*A Portable Shop Seat—A Suggestion,*"
from the Girl's Own Paper, 1880

"SEATS FOR SHOPWOMEN" (1880)
Englishwoman's Review

Prominent among the working-class causes somewhat sentimentally taken up by philanthropists and feminists was the question of seats for shopwomen. Often seats were provided for show, but the employees were penalized for using them.

A staff of ladies made a tour of all the principal thoroughfares of Edinburgh some days ago, and visited all the shops in them where girls were employed as shopwomen. It appears, as the result of their inquiries, that almost all the milliners, bootmakers, and other shopkeepers who have saloons, allow their young women to sit down in the intervals of business; but that this is the exception rather than the rule where girls are employed behind the counters, as in the shops of drapers, china merchants, stationers, and bakers. Out of 146 shops visited, only twenty-eight cases were found where seats were really allowed and provided behind the counter, though, in some other instances, the owners said the girls were "not forbidden" to sit down, but there was evidently little or no provision for their doing so. In three or four cases it was found that no provision had previously been made, but that arrangements were in progress to provide seats since the owner's attention had been called to the subject by the letters and paragraphs in the daily papers. It is worth notice that in almost every case where shops were owned and managed by women, the necessity for seats was fully recognized and provided for, and in some instances the ladies had very strong statements made to them respecting the suffering and illness arising from the opposite custom.

In *Englishwoman's Review*, July 1880

A BARMAID'S WORK (1876)
Victoria Magazine

Barmaids and restaurant workers suffered from the same long hours and confining circumstances as retail shop assistants. In 1913, their hours of work were limited, in some cases, to a maximum of sixty-

three hours a week. This barmaid's account of her work is from a letter to the editors of a feminist magazine.

Being a barmaid myself for nearly seven years, I speak from experience; and what I write I affirm to be the truth. I live in a city house with six others, and we all work very hard, our hours being seventeen in a day. We open at 5.30 a.m., and close at 12.30 p.m. (midnight). Two of us take it in turns to get up for a week at half-past five o'clock, and retire at 10 p.m. The rest of us get up at 8.00 a.m. and are up till we close. We are supposed to have two hours rest each a day, but this we only get three days out of six, and the other three days we have but an hour. We are supposed to be allowed to go out every third Sunday. Several of us have asked to be allowed to go out in rest time to get a breath of fresh air, but we have been refused for fear we should exceed our time. Therefore, from week's end to week's end, we have to inhale smoke, gas, and the foul breath of the numbers crowding at our bar, and we have no comfort, release, or relaxation from this dreary, wearing toil. I assure you we all feel fit to drop with fatigue, long before the period comes for our short rest.

In *Victoria Magazine*, June 1876

AGRICULTURAL WORKERS

The outdoor physical labor of agricultural women workers was very far from Victorian sentimental notions of womanliness. The female figure most often thought of in this context was the "dairy maid," who was frequently described as a romantic, pastoral creature—a pretty, lightfooted, cheery, singing maiden walking gracefully about the pastures, perhaps with a bucket of milk skillfully balanced on her head. It is against such notions that Martineau presents her truer portraits of the arduous labor and financial insecurity of an agricultural worker's life.

In fact, women had always worked hard at agriculture—as farm wives, cottage farmers, fishwives, and seasonal laborers. Many women preferred agricultural work to factory work under certain conditions, taking pleasure in the open air and the physical battle with nature. For some, hop-picking or other harvesting was a welcome relief from

National Museum of Labour History

Hop-picker, ca. 1900

seasonal unemployment in such occupations as match making. For a robust woman like Molly Nettleton, the young cliff-climbing fisherwoman admiringly observed by A. J. Munby, work could be an exhilarating adventure. But most agricultural workers led grimmer lives.

Part of the traditional satisfaction of agricultural life had been the direct relationship between work and food. However, by the nineteenth century, agricultural production was becoming more and more part of a money economy in which shelter and foodstuffs were no longer available in exchange for labor. Work on the land was wage-labor now, poorly paid and subject to unemployment between seasons.

Before 1834, seasonal unemployment was softened by parish relief in the form of wage supplements to local workers who were unemployed or underemployed. When this relief disappeared with the passage of the new Poor Law, workers were forced to travel in semi-migrant "gangs" to find work. In the eastern counties, gang masters contracted with farmers in labor-poor areas to bring in large numbers of men, women, and children who were paid by the day. Women and children were particularly desirable because they could be paid less than men and yet coerced to work to their limits. In 1843, a woman gang worker was receiving 8d.–9d. a day; a child 3d.–4d. About six thousand people, more than half of them women and girls, were employed in gangs at the height of the system. Gang work was attacked by middle-class reformers because of its severity and because it was believed to promote exposure to "sexual corruption." The Gangs Act of 1867 forbade gangs from employing children under eight years of age, regulated the distance a child was compelled to walk to work, and provided for women licensed as masters to supervise women working under male masters. Such regulation made gang work less profitable. The system came to an end altogether when the Education Act of 1876 made it illegal to employ children under ten in agricultural work. In the second half of the century, rising wages for male laborers made women's agricultural work less necessary for family survival, and the introduction of machinery made it less necessary to farmer-employers. By the beginning of the twentieth century, women had ceased to be employed in agriculture except for small numbers of mostly casual workers, who combined seasonal farm work with other occupations.

DAIRYWOMEN (1859)

Harriet Martineau

(See pp. 96, 149, 161, 216, 291, and 330.)

According to the census of 1841, there were then 66,329 women, above twenty years of age, employed in agriculture, without reckoning the widow-farmers (who are not few), or the farmers' wives. The last census gives 128,418 as the number so occupied, exclusive of the "farmers' wives" and "farmers' daughters," who are specially, but perhaps not completely, returned as being 289,793. Of the independent female agricultural labourers, about one-half, or about 64,000, are dairy women. Neither in America, nor anywhere else, would dairy work be objected to as a feminine employment, conducted within doors, as it is, and requiring feminine qualities for its management: yet it is harder work, and more injurious to health, than hoeing turnips or digging potatoes.

"No end of work," is the complaint; and it is not an unreasonable one. On a dairy-farm, the whole set of labours has to be gone through twice a day, nearly the whole year round; and any one of our readers who has seen the vessels on a Cheshire farm, the width of the tubs, the capacity of the ladles, the strength of the presses, and the size of the cheeses, will feel no surprise at hearing from the doctors that dairywomen constitute a special class of patients, for maladies arising from over-fatigue and insufficient rest. There is some difference between this mode of life and the common notion of the ease and charm of the dairymaid's existence, as it is seen in the corner of a Duchess's park, or on a little farm of three fields and a paddock. The professional dairywoman can usually do nothing else. She has been about the cows since she was tall enough to learn to milk, and her days are so filled up, that it is all she can do to keep her clothes in decent order. She drops asleep over the last stage of her work; and grows up ignorant of all knowledge, and unskilled in all other arts. Such work as this ought at least to be paid as well as the equivalent work of men. . . . But of the 64,000 dairywomen of Great Britain, scarcely any can secure a provision for the time when they can no longer lean over the cheese tub, or churn, or carry heavy weights.

In Harriet Martineau, "Female Industry," *Edinburgh Review*, April 1859

A YORKSHIRE CLIFF CLIMBER (1868)
A. J. Munby

A. J. Munby (1828–1910), a poet and ecclesiastical barrister, was sexually obsessed by women who did physical labor. He carried on a long relationship with a housemaid, Hannah Cullwick, whom he eventually secretly married.

Thursday, 15 October: Filey . . . I went out at 9.30, and through the village and across the fields to Brail Head. Following the path at the edge of the great chalk cliff, I came to the point from which in autumn and winter weather I have so often seen the Flambro' lasses climb the rope. And then, looking down, I saw the new rope, my gift and Molly's treasure, hanging from the stake, and going down the whole height of the cliff, to the broad platform of table rock at the bottom. It was clear that Molly and her friends were below; . . . but as I looked down from the top (which here is about 250 feet up, I think) upon the black weedy scars and pools, I saw no one. . . .

Towards eleven o'clock, however, two bait girls appeared near the foot of the cliff, striding and stooping among the wet seaweed [looking for mussels and winkles]. Both were breeched up to the knee: and she, the tall one with the long legs, was evidently Molly. At that height, one could not hear their voices; but I saw them clamber up to the base of the rock, and there, Molly seized the rope, tried it with her own weight, and began to mount. Hand over hand, sticking her toes into the crevices of the chalk wall, she went up, as easily as one might walk upstairs; and having thus climbed some 50 feet, she turned round, and with her back to the cliff, worked her way along a level ledge that just supported her heels, to an overhanging point. There, stooping forward as coolly as possible, she hauled up her own full basket and her fellow's, which the girl below first tied to the rope-end. When the baskets came up, she just loosened them, and hoisted them up, with one hand, upon a broader ledge above her head; then, grasping the rope again, she climbed up to it, and sat down. . . .

The rope, knotted to the fixed stake at my feet, was trembling with some unseen weight; and very soon the crown of Molly's lilac hood-bonnet appeared above the lower edge of the slope. Thence, holding her basket in one hand and tugging at the rope with the other, she soon climbed up to the stake, grasped it, and then grasped my offered hand, and flung herself down beside me on the little platform of rock, panting for breath, but smiling. Her comrade followed a moment afterward, and did the same . . . when the two had recovered breath, they began a talk, waiting for the others who were still below. . . . Dense mist clouds, borne by the strong northwest wind, had been sweeping over us, and beating on us with small searching rain, for some time; and the lasses, though they went down the Head at daybreak, had not brought their pilot jackets, and were getting wet through above as well as below. So Molly stood up for a moment and showing her tall figure at the cliff edge, shouted to the far off folk, "Noo then, coom on, we're gahin'!" And at last the rope at our feet began to tremble again. Instantly Molly and Nan started up, and saying "Wa min gan an' help 'em," these fearless lasses seized the rope, and before I could speak a word, began to run, Molly first, head-foremost down the dizzy slope of rock, until they both disappeared over the edge of the cliff wall below. I, the man of the party, was left in a ridiculous position; a useless spectator of vigorous athletics.

In A. J. Munby, Diary excerpt, 7 September 1868, as quoted in Derek Hudson, *Munby Man of Two Worlds: The Life and Diaries of Arthur J. Munby 1828–1910* (Boston: Gambit, 1972)

A CHILDHOOD IN FIELD WORK (ca. 1850)
Mrs. Burrows

Mrs. Burrows wrote this account for her fellow members of the Women's Co-operative Guild.

In the very short schooling that I obtained, I learnt neither grammar nor writing. On the day that I was eight years of age, I left school, and began to work fourteen hours a day in the fields, with from forty to fifty other children of whom, even at that early age, I was the eldest. We were followed all day long by an old man carrying a long whip in his hand which he did not forget to use. A great many of the children were only five years of age. You will think that I am exaggerating, but I am *not*; it is as true as the Gospel. Thirty-five years ago is the time I speak of, and the place, Croyland in Lincolnshire, nine miles from Peterborough. I could even now name several of the children who began at the age of five to work in the gangs, and also the name of the ganger.

We always left the town, summer and winter, the moment the old Abbey clock struck six. . . . We had to walk a very long way to our work, never much less than two miles each way, and very often five miles each way. The large farms all lay a good distance from the town, and it was on those farms that we worked. In the winter, by the time we reached our work, it was light enough to begin, and of course we worked until it was dark and then had our long walk home. I never remember to have reached home sooner than six and more often seven, even in winter. . . .

In all the four years I worked in the fields, I never worked one hour under cover of a barn, and only once did we have a meal in a house. And I shall never forget that one meal or the woman who gave us it. It was a most terrible day. The cold east wind (I suppose it was an east wind, for surely no wind ever blew colder), the sleet and snow which came every now and then in showers seemed almost to cut us to pieces. We were working upon a large farm that lay half-way between Croyland and Peterborough. Had the snow and sleet come continuously we should have been allowed to come home, but because it only came at intervals, of course we had to stay. . . . Dinner-time came, and we were preparing to sit down under a hedge and eat our cold dinner and drink our cold tea, when we saw the shepherd's wife coming towards us, and she said to our ganger, "Bring these children into my house and let them eat their dinner there." We went into that very small two-roomed cottage, and when we got into the largest room there was not standing room for us all, but this woman's heart was large, even if her house was small, and so she put her few chairs and table out into the garden, and then we all sat down in a ring upon the floor. She then placed in our midst a very large saucepan of hot boiled potatoes, and bade us help ourselves. Truly, although I have attended scores of grand parties and banquets since that time, not one of them has seemed half as good to me as that meal did. . . .

For four years, summer and winter, I worked in these gangs—no holidays of any sort, with the exception of very wet days and Sundays—and at the end of that time it felt like Heaven to me when I was taken to the town of Leeds, and put to work in a factory.

In Mrs. Burrows, "A Childhood in the Fens About 1850–60," in *Life As We Have Known It* (1931)

TESTIMONY ON GANG WORK (1867)

Elizabeth Dickson, Rachel Clackson Gibson, Sarah Ann Roberts

Elizabeth Dickson: What I say is, these gangs should not be as they are. . . . Sometimes the poor children are very ill used by the gang-master. One has used them horribly, kicking them, hitting them with fork handles, hurdlesticks, &c., and even knocking them down. . . . I have many a time seen my own and other children knocked about. . . . It is if the children play and don't mind their work, or are a little troublesome anyways, or he has set them more than they can do. You see their little spirits get so high, and they will talk to the last, and that is aggravation. Sometimes too they cannot work properly because their hands are cut all across and blistered where they twist the stalk round to pull up the root. Of course he don't knock the big ones, it is the little ones he takes advantage of. . . .

My children were obliged to go to work very young, some before they were seven years old. If you have nothing except what comes out of your fingers' end, as they say, it's no use, you must let them; they want more victuals.

My husband left me a widow with 11 children living, out of 15; nine of them being then under 16 years old, and three under 3 years, two being twins. The parish allowed me 3s. 4d. in money and goods (bread) according to the number of children, but not widow's pay. . . .

Jemima was not more than two months, I think, over six years old when she went out. She said, "Mother, I want some boots to go to school," so I sent her out and saved up what she earned till it was enough to get them. She was a corpse from going in the turnips. She came home from work one day, when about 10½ years old, with dizziness and her bones aching, and died and was buried and all in little better than a fortnight. The doctor said it was a violent cold stuck in her bones. Children stooping down get as wet at top as below. They get wet from the rain too. Perhaps they may have to go out three or four times in a week and not earn 2d., not having made a quarter (of a day), and come home so soaked that the wet will run out of their things. I have often been obliged to take my flannel petticoat off and roll it round a girl's legs and iron it with a warming pan to take off the pain and misery of the bones and let her get to sleep. . . . Some of the work is very hard, as pulling turnips and mangolds, muck shaking, and when turnips are being put into the ground putting muck as fast as the plough goes along—work which women and girls have sometimes to do. Drawing mangolds is the hardest; globe mangolds are fit to pull your inside out, and you have often to kick them up. I have pulled till my hands have been that swelled that you can't see the knuckles on them. I have come home so exhausted that I have sat down and cried; it would be an hour before I could pull my things off; and I have been obliged to have the table moved up to me because I could not move to it. . . .

Rachel Clarkson Gibson: Gangs might be very well for boys, but never for girls. I did not go myself till I was 17 and could take care of myself. The coming home is the worst part, that's when the mischief is done. . . . I know that there is a great deal of badness done in the fields. As for the talk, you can't stand at your door but what you would have to shut your ears for it. I don't think it proper that womenkind should go into the fields at all, in gangs or not, though I have done both. . . . I should just have liked you to have met that gang coming back this afternoon, with their great thick boots, and buskins on their legs, and petticoats pinned up; you might see the knees of some.

Sarah Ann Roberts: Soon after I went out with the gang, when I was 11 perhaps, I got the rheumatism. The work was so wet; we have been dripping through, especially in wheat. When low it would be up to our knees, and sometimes it was up to our shoulders; we have weeded it when in the ear. I have been so wet that I have taken off my clothes and wrung them out and hung them up to dry on the top of the wheat or anywhere while we went in again to weed. We durst not hang up only light things, such as aprons, handkerchiefs, &c., not petticoats. We have had to take off our shoes and pour the water out, and then the man would say, "Now then, go in again." Often when it came on to rain there was no shelter within reach, but, if there was any, sometimes he would not let us go to it till we were drenched. I often blamed him for making my bones sore. . . . The man knocked us about and ill-used us dreadfully with hoes, spuds, and everything, he would not care what. . . . We dared not complain. One ought not to be glad to hear of any one's death, but a good many children were glad when he died.

　[(Investigator's note): This young woman seemed to suffer great pain, and looked quite broken in health.]

In the Sixth Report of the Children's Employment Commission: Evidence *P.P.* xvi, 1867

MINERS

On June 7, 1842, Lord Ashley held the House of Commons in rapt attention for two hours as he detailed the horrors of women's work underground in mines. The speech was so effective that Prince Albert read it aloud to Queen Victoria. Testimony from the miners

Woman with harness pulling a cart of coal through a mine tunnel, from
Lord Ashley's 1842 report. The loaded carts weighed 2–5 cwts
(224–560 pounds).

themselves had been gathered and was issued under Ashley's direction in a two-volume edition complete with illustrations of half-naked women descending into mine shafts with men or harnessed like horses to mining equipment. The result of this sensational treatment of the subject was legislation that prohibited women and children from working underground.

Before this 1842 legislation, women were employed in the mines mainly as hurriers, loading small wagons with coal, or as drawers, drawing the wagons behind them in places too low for horses to go. They worked twelve to sixteen hours a day, often under the direction of their fathers or husbands, who loaded them up with a hundred pounds of coal at a time. The work paid about 2s. a day or less, although men were earning 3s. 6d. There were over six thousand women and girls so employed, primarily in the most primitive and least productive mines. But for the women who lived in otherwise unindustrialized areas, especially in parts of Wales and Scotland, mine work was the best available source of wages.

In the 1880s, the controversy over the moral and physical hazards of mine work for women was renewed when it was discovered that women were being employed for surface work—sorting out coal as "pit brow women." There were less than five thousand women so employed, and they were paid half the wages of men doing the same work. Compared to work inside the mine, pit-brow work was not particularly arduous, but to some male observers it was particularly disturbing because the women sometimes wore trousers and were engaged in strenuous labor in close proximity to men. The pay was 9s. a week, and the workers themselves seem to have found it desirable and respectable labor. Feminists, women workers, and mine owners together succeeded in preventing the passage of legislation that would have prohibited pit-brow work for women.

WORK IN THE MINES (1842)

Elizabeth Day, Margaret Gomley, Patience Kershaw, Betty Harris, Rosa Lucas

Elizabeth Day, aged 17: I have been nearly nine years in the pit. I trapped [operated trap doors for the trains] for two years when I first went, and have hurried ever since. . . . We always hurry in trousers as you saw us today when you were in the pit. Generally I work naked to the waist like the rest; I had my shift on today when I saw you, because I had had to wait, and was cold: but generally the girls hurry naked to the waist. It is very hard work for us all. It is harder work than we ought to do a deal. I have been lamed in my ankle, and strained in my back; it caused a great lump to rise in my ankle-bone once. The men behave well to us, and never insult or ill-use us, I am sure of that. We go to work between five and six, but we begin to hurry when we get down. We stop an hour to dinner at 12; we generally have bread and a bit of fat for dinner, and some of them a sup of beer; that's all; we have a whole hour for dinner, and we get out from four to five in the evening; so that it will be 11 hours before we get out. We drink the water that runs through the pit. I am not paid wages myself; the man who employs me pays my father; but I don't know how much it is. I have never been at school. I had to begin working when I ought to have been at school. I don't go to Sunday school. The truth is, we are confined bad enough on week-days, and want to walk about on Sundays; but I go to chapel on Sunday night. I can't read at all. Jesus Christ was Adam's son, and they nailed him on to a tree; but I don't rightly understand these things.

Margaret Gomley, aged 9: They call me Peggy for my nick-name down here, but my right name is Margaret; I am about nine years, or going nine; I have been at work in the pit thrusting corves [baskets] above a year; come in the morning sometimes at seven o'clock, sometimes half-past seven, and I go sometimes home at six o'clock, sometimes at seven when I do over-work. I get my breakfast of porridge before I come, and bring a piece of muffin, which I eat on coming to pit; I get my dinner at 12 o'clock, which is a dry muffin, and sometimes butter on, but have no time allowed to stop to eat it, I eat it while I am thrusting the load; I get no tea, but get some supper when I get home, and then go to bed when I have washed me; and am very tired. . . . They flog us down in the pit, sometimes with their hand upon my bottom, which hurts me very much; Thomas Copeland flogs me more than once in a day, which makes me cry. There are two other girls working with me, and there was four, but one left because she had the bellyache; I am poorly myself sometimes with bellyache, and sometimes headache. I had rather lake [play] than go into the pit; I get 5d. a-day, but I had rather set cards for 5d. a-day than go into the pit. The men often swear at me; many times they say Damn thee, and other times God damn thee (and such like), Peggy.

Patience Kershaw, aged 17: My father has been dead about a year; my mother is living and has ten children, five lads and five lasses; the oldest is about thirty, the youngest is four; three lasses go to mill; all the lads are colliers, two getters and three hurriers; one lives at home and does nothing; mother does nought but look after home. . . .

I wear a belt and chain at the workings to get the corves out; the getters that I work for are *naked* except their caps; they pull off all their clothes; I see them at work when I go up; sometimes they beat me, if I am not quick enough, with their hands; they strike me upon my back; the boys take liberties with me sometimes, they pull me about; I am the only girl in the pit; there are about 20 boys and 15 men; all the men are naked; I would rather work in mill than in coal-pit.

Betty Harris, aged 37: . . . I am a drawer, and work from six o'clock in the morning to six at night. Stop about an hour at noon to eat my dinner; have bread and butter for dinner: I get no drink. I have two children, but they are too young to work. . . . I have a belt round my waist, and a chain passing between my legs, and I go on my hands and feet. The road is very steep, and we have to hold by a rope; and when there is no rope, by anything we can catch hold of. There are six women and about six boys and girls in the pit I work in: it is very hard work for a woman. The pit is very wet where I work, and the water comes over our clog-tops always, and I have seen it up to my thighs: it rains in at the roof terribly: my clothes are wet through almost all day long. . . . I have drawn till I have had the skin off me: the belt and chain is worse when we are in the family way. My feller [husband] has beaten me many a time for not being ready. I were not used to it at first, and he had little patience; I have known many a man beat his drawer. I have known men take liberties with the drawers, and some of the women have bastards.

I think it would be better if we were paid once a-week, instead of once a-month, for then I could buy my victuals with ready money.

Rosa Lucas, nearly 18 years old, drawer:

Q: *How did the accident happen you are now suffering from?* A: I was sitting on the edge of a tub in the bottom, and a great stone from the roof fell on my foot and ankle, and crushed it to pieces, and it was obliged to be taken off.

Q: *Did you ever see the drawers much beaten?* A: Yes, some gets beaten. Mary Tuity gets beaten nearly every day.

Q: *What do they beat her with?* A: A pick-arm.

Q: *What do they beat her for?* A: I suppose it is for "sauce"; she has a saucy tongue.

Q: *What age is she?* A: She is 23 years old.

Q: *What is your father?* A: He was a collier, but he was killed in a coal pit. I go past the place where he was killed many a time when I am at work, and sometimes I think I see something.

In Evidence on the Employment of Children *P.P.* xvi, 1842

THE SUITABILITY OF PIT-BROW WORK (1886)
Englishwoman's Review

The Englishwoman's Review was firmly opposed to protective legislation for women. In 1885 they wrote:

It seems to us that if legislation has any right to legislate at all about the labour of adults, it should do so impartially, and if it interferes to shut women out from work which they probably would not enter upon if they could get better paid for other

kinds of labour, should prohibit men from undertaking light
and easy employments, adapted to feminine strength.

We have read a good deal of the evidence on both sides, and it seems
to us that there is a conclusive answer to every one of the arguments
in support of legislative interference. They might run thus:

Pro interference: They wear men's dress. *Con:* If it were so, do not
women in the upper ranks wear ulsters, men's cuffs and collars, and
men's hats, and when boating, riding, and tricycling, trowsers also;
because it is a more decent kind of dress than petticoats?

Pro: Their faces are black and dirty. *Con:* So they are in rag and
paper mills, and in many forms of employment with which interference is never proposed.

Pro: The work is beyond their strength, and is continued sometimes even by pregnant women. *Con:* So is laundresses' work, charing,
and some kinds of factory work, which women nevertheless do. *Pro:*
They are exposed to the weather. *Con:* So are the flower girls in our
London streets, and the women engaged in agricultural work to a far
greater degree.

Pro: It keeps women away from their homes. *Con:* So does factory work necessarily. In all cases it is an evil when a mother has to
leave her children; but it is a lesser evil than insufficient food. Compare the conditions of these Lancashire pitwomen's homes with the
one-roomed den of the starving mothers of families who, with their
little ones round them, work at match-box making in London. . . .

Pro: They have to hear much bad language. *Con:* Unfortunately this
appears to be inevitable in any trade or occupation where women
meet the coarse of the other sex; but, short of inventing a different
language for women to that which men use, as is said to be the case
among some African tribes, it is difficult to see how "evil communica-
tions" can fail, in any department of life, to "corrupt good manners."

In *Englishwoman's Review*, February 1886

MARGINAL OCCUPATIONS

Thousands of women in nineteenth-century England did not work at
any of the regular wage-paying occupations for very long and instead
eked out a living as street vendors, scavengers, beggars, or prostitutes

(see Part V). Faced with poverty, childhood neglect, ill health, hunger, cold, and the death of loved ones, they managed to stay alive through sheer endurance, ingenuity, or sometimes with the cooperation of other impoverished people. Their stories, as rendered here from their own words by Henry Mayhew, display a vitality that contrasts strongly with the passive suffering of the poor in governmental blue books and in sentimentalized literature, such as Hood's "Song of the Shirt."

Mayhew described his *London Labour and the London Poor* as "the first attempt to publish the history of a people, from the lips of the people themselves—giving a literal description of their labour, their earnings, their trials, and their sufferings, in their own 'unvarnished' language; and to portray the condition of their homes and their families by personal observation of the places, and direct communion with the individuals." Most of his subjects were people working on the streets of London.

STREET PEOPLE OF LONDON (1862)

Henry Mayhew

(See pp. 352 and 398.)

A WATERCRESS GIRL

The little watercress girl who gave me the following statement, although only eight years of age, had entirely lost all childish ways, and was, indeed, in thoughts and manner, a woman. There was something cruelly pathetic in hearing this infant, so young that her features had scarcely formed themselves, talking of the bitterest struggles of life, with the calm earnestness of one who had endured them all. I did not know how to talk with her. At first I treated her as a child, speaking on childish subjects; so that I might, by being familiar with her, remove all shyness, and get her to narrate her life freely. I asked her about her toys and her games with her companions; but the look of amazement that answered me soon put an end to any attempt at fun on my part. I then talked to her about the parks, and whether she ever went to them. "The parks!" she replied in wonder, "where are they?" I explained to her, telling her that they were large open places with green grass and tall trees, where beautiful carriages drove about, and people walked for pleasure, and children played. Her eyes brightened up a little as I spoke; and she asked, half doubtingly, "Would they let such as me go there—just to look?" All her knowledge seemed to begin and end with watercresses, and what they fetched. She knew no more of London than that part she had seen on her rounds, and believed that no quarter of the town was handsomer and pleasanter than it was at Farringdon-market or at Clerkenwell, where she lived. Her little face, pale and thin with privation, was wrinkled where the dimples ought to have been, and she would sigh frequently. When some hot dinner was offered to her, she would not touch it, because, if she eat too much, "it made her sick," she said, "and she wasn't used to meat, only on a Sunday."

The poor child, although the weather was severe, was dressed in a thin cotton gown, with a threadbare shawl wrapped round her shoulders. She wore no covering to her head, and the long rusty hair stood out in all directions. When she walked she shuffled along, for fear that the large carpet slippers that served her for shoes should slip off her feet.

"I go about the streets with watercresses, crying, 'Four bunches a penny, watercresses.' I am just eight years old—that's all, and I've a big sister, and a brother and a sister younger than I am. On and off, I've been very near a twelvemonth in the streets. Before that, I had to take care of a baby for my aunt. No, it wasn't heavy—it was only two months old; but I minded it for ever such a time—till it could walk. It was a very nice little baby, not a very pretty one; but, if I touched it under the chin, it would laugh. Before I had the baby, I used to help mother, who was in the fur trade; and, if there was any slits in the fur, I'd sew them up. My mother learned me how to needle-work and to knit when I was about five. I used to go to school, too; but I wasn't there long. I've forgot about it now, it's such a time ago; and mother took me away because the master whacked me, though the missus use'n't to never touch me. I didn't like him at all. What do you think? he hit me three times, ever so hard, across the face with his cane, and made me go dancing down stairs; and when mother saw the marks on my cheek, she went to blow him up, but she couldn't see him—he was afraid. That's why I left school.

"The cresses is so bad now, that I haven't been out with 'em for three days. They're so cold, people won't buy 'em; for when I goes up to them, they say, 'They'll freeze our bellies.' Besides, in the market, they won't sell a ha'penny handful now—they're ris to a penny and tuppence. In summer there's lots, and 'most as cheap as dirt; but I have to be down at Farringdon-market between four and five, or else I can't get any cresses, because everyone almost—especially the Irish—is selling them, and they're picked up so quick. Some of the saleswomen—we never calls 'em ladies—is very kind to us children, and some of them altogether spiteful. The good ones will give you a bunch for nothing, when they're cheap; but the others, cruel ones, if you try to bate them a farden less than they ask you, will say, 'Go along with you, you're no good.' . . .

"It's very cold before winter comes on reg'lar—specially getting up of a morning. I gets up in the dark by the light of the lamp in the court. When the snow is on the ground, there's no cresses. I bears the cold—you must; so I puts my hands under my shawl, though it hurts 'em to take hold of the cresses, especially when we takes 'em to the pump to wash 'em. No; I never see any children crying—it's no use.

"Sometimes I make a great deal of money. One day I took 1s. 6d., and the cresses cost 6d.; but it isn't often I get such luck as that. I oftener make 3d. or 4d. than 1s.; and then I'm at work, crying, 'Cresses, 4 bunches a penny, cresses!' from six in the morning to about ten. . . . The shops buy most of me. Some of 'em says, 'Oh! I ain't a-going to give a penny for these'; and they want 'em at the same price I buys 'em at.

"I always give my mother my money, she's so very good to me. She don't often beat me; but, when she do, she don't play with me. She's very poor, and goes out cleaning rooms sometimes, now she don't work at the fur [trade]. I ain't got no father, he's a father-in-law. No; mother ain't married again—he's a father-in-law. He grinds scissors, and he's very good to me. No; I don't mean by that that he says kind things to me, for he never hardly speaks. When I gets home, after selling cresses, . . . I puts the rooms to rights: mother don't make me do it, I does it myself. I cleans the chairs, though there's only two to clean. I takes a tub and scrubbing-brush and flannel, and scrubs the floor—that's what I do three or four times a week. . . .

"I am a capital hand at bargaining—but only at buying water-cresses. They can't take me in. If the woman tries to give me a small handful of cresses, I says, 'I ain't a goin' to have that for a ha'porth,' and I go to the next basket, and so on, all round. I know the quantities very well. For a penny I ought to have a full market hand, or as much as I could carry in my arms at one time, without spilling. For 3d. I has a lap full, enough to earn about a shilling; and for 6d. I gets as many as crams my basket. I can't read or write, but I knows how many pennies goes to a shilling, why, twelve, of course, but I

don't know how many ha'pence there is, though there's two to a
penny. When I've bought 3d. of cresses, I ties 'em up into as many
little bundles as I can. They must look biggish, or the people won't
buy them, some puffs them out as much as they'll go. All my money
I earns I puts in a club and draws it out to buy clothes with. It's
better than spending it in sweet-stuff, for them as has a living to
earn. Besides it's like a child to care for sugar-sticks, and not like one
who's got a living and vittals to earn. I ain't a child, and I shan't
be a woman till I'm twenty, but I'm past eight, I am."

A DOG-DUNG COLLECTOR

*[Dogs' dung was called pure because it was used to clean leather in
tanyards. It was collected from the streets by rag pickers or by specialists called pure-finders, such as the woman who speaks here.]*

"I am about 60 years of age. My father was a milkman, and very well
off; he had a barn and a great many cows. I was kept at school till I
was thirteen or fourteen years of age; about that time my father died,
and then I was taken home to help my mother in the business. After
a while things went wrong; the cows began to die, and mother, al-
leging she could not manage the business herself, married again. I
soon found out the difference. Glad to get away, anywhere out of
the house, I married a sailor, and was very comfortable with him for
some years; as he made short voyages, and was often at home, and
always left me half his pay. At last he was pressed, when at home
with me, and sent away; I forget now where he was sent to, but I
never saw him from that day to this. . . . I got some money that was
due to him from the India House, and, after that were all gone, I
went into service, in the Mile-end Road.

"There I stayed for several years, till I met my second husband,
who was bred to the water, too, but as a waterman on the river. We
did very well together for a long time, till he lost his health. He
became paralyzed like, and was deprived of the use of all one side,
and nearly lost the sight of one of his eyes. . . . Then we parted with
everything we had in the world; and, at last, when we had no other
means of living left, we were advised to take to gathering 'Pure.' At
first I couldn't endure the business, I couldn't bear to eat a morsel,
and I was obliged to discontinue it for a long time. My husband kept
at it, though, for he could do *that* well enough, only he couldn't
walk as fast as he ought. He couldn't lift his hands as high as his

head, but he managed to work under him, and so put the Pure in the basket. When I saw that he, poor fellow, couldn't make enough to keep us both, I took heart and went out again, and used to gather more than he did; that's fifteen years ago now, the times were good then, and we used to do very well.

"If we only gathered a pail-full in the day, we could live very well; but we could do much more than that, for there wasn't near so many at the business then, and the Pure was easier to be had. For my part I can't tell where all the poor creatures have come from of late years; the world seems growing worse and worse every day. They have pulled down the price of Pure, that's certain; but the poor things must do something, they can't starve while there's anything to be got. Why, no later than six or seven years ago, it was as high as 3s. 6d. and 4s. a pail-full, and a ready sale for as much of it as you could get; but now you can only get 1s. and in some places 1s. 2d. a pail-full; and, as I said before, there are so many at it, that there is not much left for a poor old creature like me to find. The men that are strong and smart get the most, of course, and some of them do very well, at least they manage to live.

"Six years ago, my husband complained that he was ill, in the evening, and lay down in the bed—we lived in Whitechapel then— he took a fit of coughing, and was smothered in his own blood. O dear" (the poor soul here ejaculated), "what troubles I have gone through! I had eight children at one time, and there is not one of them alive now. My daughter lived to 30 years of age, and then she died in childbirth, and, since then, I have had nobody in the wide world to care for me—none but myself, all alone as I am. After my husband's death I couldn't do much, and all my things went away, one by one, until I've nothing left but bare walls, and that's the reason why I was vexed at first at your coming in, sir. I was yesterday out all day, and went round Aldgate, Whitechapel, St. George's East, Step- ney, Bow, and Bromley, and then came home; after that, I went over to Bermondsey, and there I got only 6d. for my pains. Today I wasn't out at all; I wasn't well; I had a bad headache, and I'm so much afraid of the fevers that are all about here—though I don't know why I should be afraid of them—I was lying down, when you came, to get rid of my pains. There's such a dizziness in my head now, I feel as if it didn't belong to me. No, I have earned no money to- day. I have had a piece of dried bread that I steeped in water to eat. I haven't eat anything else to-day; but pray, sir, don't tell anybody of it. I could never bear the thought of going into the 'great house' [workhouse]; I'm so used to the air, that I'd sooner die in the street, as many I know have done. I've known several of our people, who have sat down in the street with their basket alongside them, and died. I knew one not long ago, who took ill just as she was stooping down to gather up the Pure, and fell on her face; she was taken to the London Hospital, and died at three o'clock in the morning. I'd sooner die like them than be deprived of my liberty, and be prevented from going about where I liked."

A VAGRANT

"I went to the shirt-making when I was 12 years of age, and that used to bring me about 4d. a-day, and with that I used to buy my bread, for we never got a halfpenny from my father to keep us. . . . The young chap that I first took up with was a carpenter. He was apprenticed to the trade. He enticed me away. He told me that if I'd come to London with him he'd do anything for me. I used to tell him how badly my father treated me, and he used to tell me not to stop at home. I have been knocking about three years, and I'm twenty now, so I leave you to say how old I was then. No, I can't say. . . . I never learnt my ciphering. . . .

"I hadn't many clothes when I left my father's home. I had nothing but what I stood upright in. I had no more clothes when I was at home. When my young man left me there was another young girl in the lodging-house, who advised me to turn out upon the streets. I went and took her advice. I did like the life for a bit, because I see'd there was money getting by it. Sometimes I got 4s. or 5s. a-day, and sometimes more than that. . . . There were a lot of girls like me at the same house. . . . No tramps used to come there, only young chaps and gals that used to go out thieving. No, my young man didn't thieve, not while he was with me, but I did afterwards. I've seen young chaps brought in there by the girls merely to pay their lodging money. The landlady told us to do that. . . . We used to be all in the same room, chaps and girls, sometimes nine or ten couples in the same room—only little bits of girls and chaps. I have seen girls there 12 years of age. The boys was about 15 or 16. They used to swear dreadful.

"I fell out with the gal as first told me to go on the streets, and then I got with another at another house. I moved to Paddington. I lived at a little public house there—a bad house; and I used to go out shoplifting with my pal. I used to take everything I could lay my hands on. We went one night, and I stole two dresses, at a linen-draper's shop, and had two months a-piece for it. Yes, sir, I liked prison very well, because I had such bad clothes; and was glad to be out of the way. . . .

"I had one fancy-man. He was a shoplifter and a pickpocket: he has got two years now. I went to see him once in quod; some calls it 'the Steel.'" I cried a good deal when he got nailed, sir: I loved him. . . . I saw I couldn't get him off, 'cause it was for a watch, and the gentle-man went so hard against him. I was with him at the time he stole it, but I didn't know he'd got it till I saw him run. I got the man down by a saw-mill; he was tipsy. He was a gentleman, and said he would give me five shillings if I would come along with him. My fancy-man always kept near to me whenever I went out of a night. I wasn't to go out to take the men home; it was only to pick them up. My young man used to tell me how to rob the men. I'd get them in a corner, and then I used to take out of their pockets whatever I could lay my hands on; and then I used to hand it over to him, and he used to take the things home and 'fence' them. We used to do a good deal this way sometimes: often we'd get enough to keep us two or three days. At last he got caught for the watch; and when I see'd I couldn't get him off, I went down into the country—down into Essex, sir.

"I travelled all parts, and slept at the unions on the road. I met a young girl down in Town Malling, in Kent. I met her, and then we used to go begging together, and tramp it from one union to another. At last we got so ragged and dirty, and our things all got so bad, that we made up our minds to go in for three months into prison, at Battle, down in Sussex. We used to meet a great many on the road boiling their kettle, and sometimes we used to stop and skipper with them of a night. Skippering is sleeping in barns or under hedges, if it's warm weather. . . . We generally used to steal on the way. If we could see anything, we used to take it. At last, when our clothes got bad, I and the other girl—she still kept with me—determined to break the parson's windows at Battle. We broke one because the house was good for a cant—that's some food—bread or meat, and they wouldn't give it us, so we got savage, and broke all the glass in the windows. For that we got three months. After we got out, the parson sent word for us to come to his house, and he gave us half-a-crown a-piece to take us on our road. He would have give us some clothes—we had no shoes and stockings: we was very bad off: but his wife was in London.

"So we went on the road tramping again, and I have been tramping it about the country ever since. . . . I like the tramping life well enough in the summer, 'cause there's plenty of victuals to be had then, but it's the winter that we can't stand. Then we generally come to London, but we can't call at house to house here as we do in the country, so we make but a poor thing of it. I never was so bad off as I am now, excepting when I was at Battle, for I had no shoes or stockings then. The police is too sharp for us in London. I'm very fond of going through the country in fine weather. Sometimes we don't make much freedom with the chaps in the union, and sometimes we do. They tells us to go along with them, for they knows good houses to call at. What you make is all according to whether you're in a lonesome road. I've travelled a day, and not seen a house that I could get anything at. Some days I've got a shilling given to me, and some days as much as half-a-crown. We can always get plenty of bread and meat, for countryfolks is very good. If I had some good things—that is, good boots—I should like to go into the country again. . . .

"I shouldn't like to give it up just yet. I do like to be in the country in the summer-time. I like haymaking and hopping, because that's a good bit of fun. Still, I'm sick and tired of what I'm doing now. It's the winter that sickens me. I'm worn out now, and I often sits and thinks of the life that I've led. I think of my kind, dear mother, and how good I would have been if my father had taught me better. Still, if I'd clothes I'd not give up my present life. I'd be down in the country now. I do love roving about, and I'm wretched when I'm not at it.

In Henry Mayhew, *London Labour and the London Poor* (1862)

Part V

UNWOMANLY
WOMEN

O f all the classes of women who did not conform to the cultural ideal of the domestic angel, prostitutes were the most disturbing and the most visible. Reformers and journalists at midcentury estimated the number of prostitutes in London alone at between sixty thousand and eighty thousand. Although the actual number (based on more concrete and less impressionistic police records) was probably closer to eight thousand, it was certainly true that there were strikingly great numbers of women making a living at prostitution in the large cities and military towns of nineteenth-century England. However, prostitution was more than an overcrowded occupation; it was a national obsession, occupying the minds of prime ministers, journalists, clergymen, physicians, philanthropists, and social reformers, both male and female.

The popular iconography surrounding the prostitute was sentimental in the extreme. She was usually portrayed as "ruined," her life destroyed by sexual experience, a passive victim of male lust, destined for an early grave. One representative version of this myth was a poem, supposedly written by a dying prostitute, which ended like this:

> Daily debased, to stifle my disgust
> Of forced enjoyment in effected lust;
> Covered with guilt, infection, debt, and want.
> For seven long years of infamy I've pined,
> And fondled, loathed, and preyed upon mankind;
> Till the full course of sin and vice gone through;
> My shattered fabric failed at twenty-two.

Beneath this maudlin attention lay powerful feelings of sexual guilt, anger, and fear. William Blake's prophecy that "the harlot's curse from street to street/Shall weave old England's winding sheet [shroud]" was echoed throughout the century in recurrent references to respectable middle-class families elbowed off the pavement or awakened in their comfortable London homes by an unruly mob of diseased and corrupting women. Many people felt threatened by the vulgar, sexually aggressive women of the streets, including even the august and street-smart Charles Dickens, who in a fit of outrage once pursued a woman across the city of London in order to have her arrested for using indecent language to him.

This sort of fear and revulsion was partly due to the prostitutes' flagrantly "unwomanly" behavior. The raucous indecency of the prostitute mocked not only the power structure of female subservience to men, but also the pretense of female sexual ignorance, passivity, and lack of appetite. Even when prostitutes were not rude, the necessarily public nature of their lives was particularly glaring in a world in which women were expected to be indoor creatures. The gulf between their bold and exposed demeanor and that of "respectable" women, privileged and poor, is apparent in contemporary illustrations in which a prostitute is immediately recognizable by her direct gaze or uncovered head. So strong was this fear of what they were felt to represent that prostitutes were seen as a separate class of womanhood.

As objects of obsessive public scrutiny, prostitutes also served as a focus for otherwise forbidden sexual fantasies. Part of the fascination middle-class women reformers felt for the bands of roving outlaws they imagined to be passing by their windows at night must have stemmed from the sense that prostitutes had a knowledge of life other women were barred from obtaining. By the same token, men were often drawn into reform work from intense sexual curiosity. Prime Minister William Gladstone, at the risk of his political career, regularly patrolled the Haymarket area of London in search of graceful and mannerly prostitutes whom he attempted to reclaim in endless late-night interviews, after which he would often physically flagellate himself. The sincere religious mission to convert sinners was, for Gladstone and others, a way of simultaneously indulging in and repudiating their own vagrant sexuality.

Part of the pressure to view prostitutes as a separate class derived from acceptance of the double standard of sexual behavior. Whether they did it with a sigh or a shrug, most male commentators accepted prostitution as an inevitable feature of society, needed to satisfy men's desire for sexual activity outside marriage. Such a belief demanded that there be two separate sets of women, one of which must be protected from antisocial male sexual impulses and the other of which must be freely available for the satisfaction of male desire. Middle-class writing on prostitution always stressed the impassable chasm between the two classes of women and the impossibility of a "fallen" woman ever rejoining society.

In fact, the barriers against women with extramarital sexual experience varied tremendously along class lines. It was much more difficult for a divorced duchess to be received by Queen Victoria than it was for a common prostitute to find a place to live—or a husband to make an "honest" woman of her. Known prostitutes might be limited to more rundown neighborhoods and rougher husbands, but a woman who could hide her past by moving to a new area would be all the more eligible a bride for having saved some money from her profession.

The sexual prudery of the Victorian age and the desire to view the prostitute as a being separate from all others naturally made the prostitute's world seem more lurid and isolated than it was. Actually, prostitutes were not very different from other women of their economic class. Far from being a separate order of women, they were hop-pickers, seamstresses, mothers, servants—all the things that other poor women workers were. Nor were prostitutes usually troubled by the consciousness of sin and shame, which so obsessed their middle-class reformers. Much like the women textile workers or miners who feared state regulation that would deprive them of their jobs, prostitutes were most bothered by the repeated efforts to control their behavior by those who viewed prostitution as a life-defining spiritual and moral state rather than a part-time occupation of young women.

Significantly enough, women did offer resistance to the double standard. Many writers, such as Eliza Lynn Linton and Ann Lamb, pointed out that mercenary sexuality existed in the respectable marriage market as well as in the disrespectable demimonde. Some saw that the economic dependency of the prostitute upon her male customers was not that different from the general dependency of women upon their husbands or male employers. Feminists were particularly clearsighted when it came to seeing prostitution as an essentially economic rather than moral question. Annie Besant summed up the situation this way:

Remunerative employment would empty half the streets; pay

women, for the same work the same wages that men receive; let sex be no disqualification; let women be trained to labor, and educated for self-support; then the greatest of all remedies will be applied to the cure of prostitution and women will cease to sell their bodies when they are able to sell their labor.*

Feminists were also vocal in demanding that the same standards of sexual conduct be applied to both men and women. Socialists such as Annie Besant argued for various forms of "free love" arrangements, which made marriage a matter of choice rather than of economic or legal compulsion. Advocates of "moral purity"—for instance, Josephine Butler—took the opposite position and insisted on male chastity and on marriage based upon love and complete fidelity on both sides. Either way, the demand from feminists was for equality of sexual arrangements and bonding based solely upon affection and free choice.

The feminist battle against the double standard was most dramatically waged through organized resistance to the Contagious Diseases Acts, which were the most striking attempt to treat prostitutes as a separate class of women and to recognize prostitution as a socially necessary occupation. The fight against the Contagious Diseases Acts was a key feminist victory for several reasons. Not only was it successful, after a sixteen-year struggle, in heading off the establishment of state-regulated prostitution in England, but it also brought women together across the boundaries of class and caste. Respectable women, led by the iconoclastic Josephine Butler, were able to break the sexual taboos of their society by openly discussing prostitution and venereal disease. Such a denial of the accepted decorums of domestic angelhood bore witness to a different sense of womanly goodness: a morality based upon public responsibility and identification with other women as fellow victims of male power. The feminist attack on the Contagious Diseases Acts identified the abuses of male lust with the mistreatment of women as wage earners and with the exercise of organized male power over women in the form of police, courts, Parliament, military, and medical authorities.

Far from being a deviant figure, the prostitute in many ways was highly representative of women in nineteenth-century England, both in her own experiences and in her public situation. The obviously

* Annie Besant, *The Legalization of Female Slavery in England* (1885), p. 7

dehumanizing quality of the prostitute's work, her alienation from her own body and from her capacity for pleasure, differ only in degree from the general situation of women whose sexual and emotional lives were similarly inhibited and defined by their economic dependence on men. At the same time, public responses to widespread prostitution, in the form of condescending missionary efforts, sensational journalism, and overly controlling state regulations, resembles the general cultural responses to women. Like the poor seamstress, the strong-minded feminist, or the domestic angel, the prostitute was seen through an iconography made up of male projections, falsifications, and sentimentalizations, all of which served to reinforce belief in the inevitability of a system by which women were to be easily available to and easily controlled by men.

Most striking of all, the prostitute's pariah status reflected the general status of female sexuality—and even of womanhood itself—as an exploited and despised commodity. The feminist championing of prostitutes is therefore a crucial response to the nineteenth-century oppression of women. By affirming solidarity in disregard of the barriers of respectability, by recognizing the prostitute's oppression as part of their own, the women who publicly opposed the Contagious Diseases Acts were making one of the most radical and imaginative efforts of their time. Whether they did so out of a belief in moral purity or in free love, feminists who embraced the prostitute were flouting perhaps the most potent taboos of Victorian society in order to affirm their own sexual dignity. Even if the campaign against the Contagious Diseases Acts had not been so outstandingly successful, it would have been of tremendous significance as a symbolic breakthrough in women's century-long struggle to resist the circumstances of their oppression and to redefine their place in the social, economic, and cultural world.

The Experience
of Prostitution

Prostitution was ordinarily a part-time, temporary employment of young women that offered a supplement to the low pay of other women's work, a buffer against recurrent unemployment, and an escape from the close supervision of factory work or domestic service. The common prostitute's usual wage of one shilling a customer was attractive to women who would otherwise be working punishingly long hours for perhaps six shillings a week. Prostitutes were generally healthy, if only because they ate better than seamstresses or the mothers of large families and were therefore better protected against tuberculosis, the disease that claimed the most victims in nineteenth-century England. When they left prostitution, as most did after a very few years, they might have accumulated a little bit of money with which perhaps to buy a sewing machine or to get married. In other words, prostitution was not necessarily a "deviant" choice in the context of the miserable choices of employment open to a working-class woman, nor was it necessarily a choice that left a woman an outcast from her family or friends.

At the same time, prostitutes were subject to a variety of harassments. They were made vulnerable by their need for two kinds of workplaces: a public area in which to pick up customers and a private place to take them. Women relied upon the streets, theaters, and public houses of various kinds to meet potential clients. In all these places they were supervised by the police, who had the power to arrest any woman they considered unruly and who were usually bribed to allow the trade to continue. Prostitutes were also subject to economic exploitation and harassment by bar owners and accommodation house owners (who rented rooms for short periods of time). A prostitute might be expected to bring in a certain amount of trade to a bar or to encourage men to buy overpriced trinkets in disreputable gift shops in return for the use of the establishment as a place to make a pickup. To defend themselves against the various hazards of their trade, prostitutes tended to have a strong system of mutual reliance. They shared lodgings, clothes, money, and child care with one another and often with other friends or family members who were not themselves engaged in prostitution.

Acton, Mayhew, Stead, and other investigators and reformers tended to see prostitution in terms of a spectrum running from the toasted courtesan to the syphilitic outcast in the gutter. This approach slighted the woman who was more representative of the profession, the underpaid working woman of about twenty who was using part-time prostitution as a way to supplement her wages. Clearly, investigators found it hardest to accept the notion of women who practiced prostitution without being wholly defined by it. As Mayhew put it, the case of the casual prostitute is

> the most serious side of prostitution. This more clearly stamps the character of the nation. A thousand and one causes may lead to a woman's becoming a professional prostitute; but if a woman goes wrong without any very cogent reason for so doing, there must be something radically wrong in her composition, and inherently bad in her nature. . . .

After recognizing the economic basis of prostitution and the falsity of the sentimental icons that depicted prostitutes as helpless victims of sordid lust and disease, we are nevertheless left to consider what the peculiar nature of her occupation meant to the prostitute herself. Prostitutes functioned by thinking of sexual relationships as commodity relationships. They usually had attitudes much like other con artists or street hustlers. Prostitution could be a degradation or a practical step, depending on the temperament and the situation of the women involved. It clearly signified a different thing to the "typo," who occasionally earned a little spending money by it, than it did to the "wren" living in a hut on the Curragh, entirely dependent on the trade of ill-paid soldiers. Putting aside the investigators' contradictory overlay of bourgeois indignation and man-of-the-world detachment, we can listen in these interviews for what these women have to reveal about their world, their comaraderie, their assertiveness, their matter-of-fact sexuality, their experience of male harassment and evasion of male control, their quickness to seize upon a shilling, and their combination of prostitution with other "dodges"—including the lucky chance of finding a journalist to buy them gin and pay for their stories.

TWO CLASSES OF PROSTITUTES (1870)
Dr. William Acton
(See pp. 127, 427, and 432.)

William Acton, an influential physician and reformer, believed that prostitution should be openly recognized and regulated by the state for the sake of public health.

FASHIONABLE PROSTITUTES

The principal dancing rooms of London are the two casinos known respectively as the Argyll Rooms and the Holborn. They are open for music and dancing every evening, except Sunday, from half-past eight o'clock to twelve. The visitor, on passing the doors, finds himself in a spacious room, the fittings of which are of the most costly description, while brilliant gas illuminations, reflected by numerous mirrors, impart a fairy-like aspect to the scene. . . . The women are of course all prostitutes. They are for the most part pretty, and quietly, though expensively dressed, while delicate complexions, unaccompanied by the pallor of ill-health, are neither few nor far between. This appearance is doubtless due in many cases to the artistic manner of the make-up by powder and cosmetics, on the employment of which extreme care is bestowed. Few of these women, probably, could write a decent letter, though some might be able to play a little on the piano, or to sing a simple song. Their behavior is usually quiet, little solicitation is observable, and all the outward proprieties of demeanour and gesture are strictly observed.

The proprietor, indeed, is careful to maintain the appearance, at least, of decorum among his visitors. Should any woman misconduct herself, she is pointed out to the door-keepers, with instructions not to admit her again to the rooms. No punishment could be heavier, no sentence more rigorously carried out. She will attempt in vain to avoid recognition, or by bribes to soften the watchful janitor. Her efforts will be met with some such rebuke as this: "It's no use trying it on, Miss Polly; the gov'nor says you are not to go in, and, of course, you can't!" Her only chance of obtaining remission of the sentence

Streetwalkers bribing the beadle to let them walk in Burlington Arcade,
Picadilly, London, from the Days' Doings, *1871*

Newberry Library

is to induce some friend to plead with the proprietor on her behalf, who may, but does not always, readmit her after an exile of three months, and on her promising to behave herself in the strictest manner for the future.

On the whole, judging of the women who frequent these rooms by their dress, deportment, and general appearance, the visitor might be inclined to suppose them to belong to the kept mistress rather than the prostitute class. This is, however, not the case, as, with a few exceptions, they all fall without the latter denomination. Many of them, no doubt, have a friend who visits them regularly, and who makes them a fixed allowance, not sufficient to keep them altogether, but substantial enough to make them careful in selecting their customers, and careful about accepting the company of a man in any way objectionable. This arrangement is perfectly understood by the "friend" who pays his periodic visits, and to whom, of course, the woman is always at home. The sum expected by one of these women in return for her favours is about two or three sovereigns. Many will expect those who desire their company to stand them refreshment without stint, not only at the casino, but at some house of call later on in the night, suggesting champagne or "phiz" as agreeable to their palate, and will be indisposed to return home until they have had their full evening's amusement.

One woman merits a passing notice here, who has achieved a sudden notoriety, and given to the casino . . . a pre-eminence over its rival. There she holds a mimic court, attired unlike the rest of the frequenters, who come in their bonnets in full ball dress. She is surrounded by a crowd of admirers, idlers, and would-be imitators, and gives the tone to the establishment that she patronizes. It is said that the diamonds worn by this woman are worth £5,000. She is supplied daily from a florist in Covent Garden with a bouquet of the choicest flowers, amid which are interspersed specimens of the most beautifully coloured beetles, the cost being about 30s., and her habit on entering the rooms is to present this really splendid trifle to the female attendant at the wine bar, as a mark of her condescension and favour. On permission to visit her being requested, she would probably, like another celebrated "fille de joie," take out her pocket-book and, after a careless glance at it, reply that she was full of engagements, but that if the petitioner would call at her house at a given hour that day week, she would, perhaps, spare him some twenty minutes of her society, for which favour she might expect the modest sum of £25.

ARMY TOWN PROSTITUTES

There appears to exist a sort of tacit understanding between these women and the authorities that they shall be suffered to pursue their calling unmolested so long as they abstain from acts of flagrant indecency.

[A prostitute] obtains lodgings at the rate of about 3s. 6d. a week, for the daily accruing quota of which the landlord calls upon her every morning. One of these lodgings into which I was introduced by the inspector may be taken as a fair specimen of the class. It was a small room on the first floor of a cottage, approached by a steep narrow staircase, furnished in the most primitive manner, containing only a bed with the usual covering, one or two rough chairs, and the commonest necessaries of a bedroom. Only one condition beyond punctual payment of the rent is attached to the tenancy. The landlord is usually the proprietor of a beer-house or some other place of public entertainment, which the lodger must patronize during her stay. She is required to spend her evenings there until the tattoo sounds at 9.30, after which hour she is free to go where she pleases. She is also expected to aid the landlord in the sale of liquor, both by inducing the soldiers to drink, and by accepting whatever drink may be offered to her by them. . . . There is at Aldershot no street prostitution permitted; the woman's hunting grounds are the . . . public rooms.

The daily gains are not large. The generous and prodigal son of Mars who has lately received his pay or his loot money will, perhaps, bestow half a crown in return for the favours granted to him, but the usual honorarium is 1s. To obtain a subsistence, a woman must take home with her about eight or ten lovers every evening, returning to her haunts after each labour of love . . . to dance or drink beer until a fresh invitation to retire is received by her. As night approaches, each woman usually seeks her room, carrying with her ale or other stimulating liquor, which she shares with her fellow-lodgers, and wakes up in the morning languid from the night's debauch to breakfast off beefsteaks and beer. . . . For help when her own resources fail her, she depends on the contribution of those of her companions whom chance has for the time being more befriended; and in justice to these women, it must be said that they are always ready to afford each other this mutual assistance.

In William Acton, *Prostitution* (1857, 1870 revised edition)

INTERVIEWS WITH LONDON PROSTITUTES (1862)
Henry Mayhew
(See pp. 352 and 376.)

A CLANDESTINE OR OCCASIONAL PROSTITUTE

"Ever since I was twelve," she said, "I have worked in a printing office where a celebrated London morning journal is put in type and goes to press. I get enough money to live upon comfortably; but then I am extravagant, and spend a great deal of money in eating and drinking, more than you would imagine. My appetite is very delicate, and my constitution not at all strong. I long for certain things like a woman in the family way, and I must have them by hook or by crook. The fact is the close confinement and the night air upset me and disorder my digestion. I have the most expensive things sometimes, and when I can, I live in a sumptuous manner, comparatively speaking. I am attached to a man in our office, to whom I shall be married someday. He does not suspect me, but on the contrary believes me to be true to him, and you do not suppose that I ever take the trouble to undeceive him. I am nineteen now, and have carried on with my 'typo' [typesetter] for nearly three years now. I sometimes go to the Haymarket, either early in the morning, when I can get away from the printing; and sometimes I do a little in the day-time. This is not a frequent practice of mine; I only do it when I want money to pay anything. I am out now with the avowed intention of picking up a man, or making an appointment with some one for to-morrow or some time during the week. I always dress well, at least you mayn't think so, but I am always neat, and respectable, and clean, if the things I have on ain't worth the sight of money that some women's things cost them. I have good feet too, and as I find they attract attention, I always parade them. And I've hooked many a man by showing my ankle on a wet day. I shan't think anything of all this when I'm married. I believe my young man would marry me just as soon if he found out I went with others as he would now. I carry on with him now, and he likes me very much. I ain't of any particular family; to tell the truth, I was put in the workhouse when I was young, and they apprenticed me. I never knew my father or my mother, although . . . I heard that he was hung for killing a man who opposed him when committing a burglary. In other words, he was 'a macingcove what robs,' and I'm his daughter, worse luck. I used to think at first, but what was the good of being wretched about it? . . . Birth is the result of accident. It is the merest chance in the world whether you're born a countess or a washerwoman. I'm neither one nor t'other; I'm only a mot who does a little typographing by way of variety. Those who have had good nursing, and all that, and the advantages of a sound education, who have a position to lose, prospects to blight, and relations to dishonour, may be blamed for going on the loose, but I'll be hanged if I think that priest or moralist is to come down on me with the sledge-hammer of their denunciation. You look rather surprised at my talking so well. I know I talk well, but you must remember what a lot has passed through my hands for the last seven years, and what a lot of copy I've set up. There is very little I don't know, I can tell you. It's what old Robert Owen would call the spread of education."

A HOP-PICKER PROSTITUTE

"I am a native of ——, where my father was a woolcomber. I was an only child. I can't remember my mother, she died when I was so young. My father died more than four years ago. I've heard as much since I left home. I was sent to the National School. I can read, but can't write. My father went to work at Wellington, in Somersetshire, taking me with him, when I was quite a little girl. He was a good father and very kind, and we had plenty to eat. I think of him sometimes, it makes me sorrowful. . . .

"My father married again when I was 12, I suppose. He married a factory-woman. . . . She led me a dreadful life, always telling my father stories of me—that I was away when I wasn't, and he grumbled at me. He never beat me, but my stepmother often beat me. She was very bad-tempered, and I am very bad-tempered, too—very passionate; but if I'm well treated my passion doesn't come out. She beat me with anything that came first to hand, as the hearth-brush, and she flung things at me. She disliked me, because she knew I hated my father marrying again. I was very happy before that, living with my father. I could cook dinner for him, young as I was, make his bed, and do all those sorts of things, all but his washing. I had a bed to myself. . . . I used to tell my father how she used me, but he said it was nonsense. This went on till I was fifteen, when I ran away. . . .

"I was almost as big then as I am now. I had 4s. or 5s. with me, I don't remember just how much, I started in such a passion; but it

was money I had saved up from what my father had given me. I took
no clothes with me but what I had on. I was tidily dressed. It was
in the haymaking time, and I made straight away to London. I was
so young and in such a rage, I couldn't think of nothing but getting
away. . . . I was sitting in Hyde-park thinking where I should go . . .
[when] some girls and some young men, and some older men, passed
me, carrying rakes . . . [and] said, 'We are going half-way to Watford
a-haymaking. Go with us?' . . . I had a fortnight at haymaking. I had
a mate at haymaking, and in a few days he ruined me. He told the
master that I belonged to him. He didn't say I was his wife. They
don't call us their wives. I continued with him a long time, living
with him as his wife. We next went into Kent harvesting, then a-
hopping, and I've been every summer since. He was kind to me, but
we were both passionate—fire against fire—and we fought sometimes. . . . I lived with him, and was true to him, until he ran away
in haymaking time in 1848. . . .

"I came up to London in a boat from Gravesend, with other hop-
pers. I lived on fifteen shillings I had saved up. I lived on that as long
as it lasted—more than a week. I lodged near the Dials, and used to go
drinking with other women I met there, as I was fond of drink then.
I don't like it so much now. We drank gin and beer. I kept to myself
until my money was gone, and then I looked out for myself. I had
no particular friends. The women I drank with were some bad and
some good. I got acquainted with a young girl as I was walking along
the Strand looking out for my living by prostitution—I couldn't
starve. We walked together. We couldn't stay in the Strand, where
the girls were well-dressed, and so we kept about the Dials. I didn't
think much about the life I was leading, because I got hardened. I
didn't like it, though. Still I thought I should never like to go home.
I lodged in a back-street near the Dials. I couldn't take anybody there.
I didn't do well. I often wanted money to pay my lodgings, and food
to eat, and had often to stay out all night perishing. Many a night
out in the streets I never got a farthing, and had to walk about all
day because I dursn't go back to my room without money. I never
had a fancy man. There was all sorts in the lodging-house—thirty of
them—pickpockets, and beggars, and cadgers, and fancy men, and
some that wanted to be fancy men, but I never saw one that I liked.
I never picked pockets as other girls did; I was not nimble enough
with my hands.

Sometimes I had a sovereign in my pocket, but it was never there

BBC Hulton Picture Library

Hop-picker, 1887

a day. I used to go out a-drinking, treating other women, and they would treat me. We helped one another now and then. I was badly off for clothes. I had no illness except colds. The common fellows in the streets were always jeering at me. Sometimes missionaries, I think they're called, talked to me about the life I was leading, but I told them, 'You mind yourself, and I'll mind myself. What is it to you where I go when I die?' . . . I think, by the life I lead—and without help I must lead it still, or starve—I sometimes get twenty shillings a week, sometimes not more than five shillings. I would like best to go to Australia, where nobody would know me. I'm sure I could behave myself there. There's no hope for me here: everybody that knows me despises me. I could take a service in Sydney. I could get rid of my swearing. I only swear now when I'm vexed—it comes out natural-like then. I could get rid of my love of drink. No one—no girl can carry on the life I do without drink. . . . I am strong and healthy, and could take a hard place with country work. That about Australia is the best wish I have. I'm sure sick of this life. It has only drink and excitement to recommend it."

THE MOST VIOLENT WOMAN IN THE NEIGHBORHOOD

A woman who was well known to cohabit with soldiers, of a masculine appearance but good features, and having a good-natured expression, was pointed out to me as the most violent woman in the neighbourhood. When she was in a passion she would demolish everything that came in her way, regardless of the mischief she was doing. She was standing in the bar of a public-house close to the barracks talking to some soldiers, when I had an opportunity of speaking to her. I told her I had heard she was very passionate and violent.

"Passionate!" she replied; "I believe yer. I knocked my father down and well-nigh killed him with a flat-iron before I wor twelve year old. I was a beauty then, an I aint improved much since I've been on my own hook. I've had lots of rows with these 'ere sodgers, and they'd have slaughter'd me long afore now if I had not pretty near cooked their goose. It's a good bit of it self-defense with me now-a-days, I can tell yer. Why, look here; look at my arm when I was run through with a bayonet once three or four years ago."

She bared her arm and exhibited the scar of what appeared to have once been a serious wound.

"You wants to know if them rowses is common. Well, they is, and it's no good one saying they aint, and the sodgers is such— cowards they think nothing of sticking a woman once they'se riled and drunk, or they'll wop us with their belts. I was hurt awful onst by a blow from a belt; it hit me on the back part of the head, and I was laid up weeks in St. George's Hospital with a bad fever. The sodger who done it was quodded [jailed], but only for a drag [three months], and he swore to God as how he'd do for me the next time as he comed across me. We had words sure enough, but I split his skull with a pewter, and that shut him up for a time.

"You see this public; well, I've smashed up this place before now; I've jumped over the bar, because they wouldn't serve me without paying for it when I was hard up, and I've smashed all the tumblers and glass, and set the cocks agoing, and fought like a brick when they tried to turn me out, and it took two peelers [cops] to do it; and then I lamed one of the bobbies for life by hitting him on the shin with a bit of iron—a crow or summet, I forget what it was. How did I come to live this sort of life? Get along with your questions. If you give me any more of your cheek, I'll—soon serve you the same."

In Henry Mayhew, *London Labour and the London Poor* (1862)

THE WRENS OF THE CURRAGH (1867)
Pall Mall Gazette

The army prostitutes in this sensational report were living in crude huts along the border of an Irish military base.

[T]he nests have an interior space of about nine feet long by seven feet broad; and the roof is not more than four and a half feet from the ground. You crouch into them as beasts crouch into cover, and there is no standing upright till you crawl out again. They are rough misshapen domes of furze—like big rude birds'-nests, compacted of harsh branches, and turned topsy-turvy upon the ground. . . . When the nest is newly made . . . and if you happen to view it on a hot day, no doubt it seems a tolerably snug shelter. . . . But all the nests are not newly made; and if the sun shines on the Curragh, bitter winds drive across it, with swamping rains for days and weeks together, and miles of snow-covered plain sometimes lie between this wretched colony of abandoned women and the nearest town. Wind and rain are their worst enemies (unless we reckon in mankind). . . . The beating of the one and the pelting of the other soon destroy their bowery summer aspect. They get crazy, they fall toward this side and that, they shrink in and down upon the outcast wretches that huddle in them, and the doorposts don't keep the roof up, and the clods don't keep it down. The nest is nothing but a furzy hole, such as, for comfort, any wild beast may match anywhere, leaving cleanliness out of the question. . . .

The most important piece of furniture was a wooden shelf running along the back of the nest, and propped on sticks driven into the earthen floor. Some mugs; some plates; some cups and saucers; a candlestick; two or three old knives and forks, battered and rusty; a

few dull and dinted spoons; a teapot (this being a rather rich establishment), and several other articles of a like character, were displayed
upon the shelf: and a grateful sight it was. . . .

Beneath [the shelf] was heaped an armful of musty straw, originally smuggled in from the camp stables: this, drawn out and shaken
upon the earth, was the common bed. A rough wooden box, such as
candles are packed in, stood in a corner; one or two saucepans, and
a horrid old teakettle . . . were disposed in various nooks in the furzy
walls; a frying-pan was stuck into them by the handle, in company
with a crooked stick of iron used as a poker; and . . . a cheap little
looking-glass was stuck near the roof. . . .

In every [nest] an upturned saucepan was used for a seat when
squatting on the earth became too tiresome. In all the practice is to
sleep with your head under the shelf (thus gaining some additional
protection from the wind) and your feet to the turf fire, which is
kept burning all night near the doorway. Here the use of the perforated saucepan becomes apparent. It is placed over the burning
turf when the wrens dispose themselves to rest; and, as there is no
want of air in these dwellings, the turf burns well and brightly under
the protecting pot. . . . All day they lounge in a half-naked state,
clothed simply in one frieze petticoat, and another, equally foul, cast
loosely over their shoulders; though towards evening, they put on . . .
decent attire. . . . None of the women have any money of their own;
what each company get is thrown into a common purse, and the
nest is provisioned out of it. What they get is little indeed: a few
halfpence turned out of one pocket and another when the clean
starched frocks are thrown off at night, make up a daily income just
enough to keep body and soul together.

A community like that which I am attempting to describe naturally falls into some regular system, and provides for itself certain
rules and regulations. Fifty or sixty people separated from the rest
of the world and existing in and by rebellion against society, naturally
form some links of association; and when the means of life are the
same, and shameful and precarious; when those who so live by them
are poor as well as outcast, and when, also, they are all women, we
may assure ourselves that a sort of socialistic or family bond will soon
be formed. . . . Thus the colony is open to any poor wretch who imag-
ines that there she can find comfort . . . or another desperate chance
of existence. Come she whence she may, she has only to present herself to be admitted into one nest or another, nor is it necessary that

she bring a penny to recommend her. Girls who have followed soldiers to the camp from distant towns and villages—some from actual love and hope, some from necessity or desperation—form a considerable number of those who go into the bush; and I also learn that the colony sometimes receives some harvester tired of roaming for field work, to whom the free loose life there has, one must suppose, attractions superior to those of the virtuous hovel at home. . . . Suppose a woman with child who has followed her lover to the camp and loses him there, or is admonished with blows to leave him alone; or suppose a young wife in the same condition is bidden by her martial lord to go away and "do as other women do" (which seems to be the formula in such cases); they are made as welcome amongst the wrens as if they did not bring with them certain trouble and an inevitable increase to the common poverty. It is not long since that a child was born in one of these nests. . . . The mother . . . had followed its gallant father to the camp from Arklow—a fishing village many a mile away; but he unfortunately diverted his benevolence into other channels, and she sought refuge among the bushwomen when her trouble was near. They did what they could for her, and brought her safely through without recourse to the doctor.

Although the birth of an infant is a novel event in the annals of the Curragh, the appearance of a mother with her baby in arms is by no means rare; and though a child is certainly as much an "incumbrance" there as it can be anywhere, no objection is ever made to it. In fact, a baby is obviously regarded as conferring a certain respectability upon the nest it belongs to, and is treated, like all possessions, as common property. At the present time there are four children in the bush. . . . Should the children fall sick they would be taken at once to the workhouse; for the doctor is never seen in the bush. In sickness the wrens administer to themselves or each other such remedies as they happen to believe in, or are able to procure. . . . The medical officers in the camp are, of course, kept too busy amongst the men who are the wrens' friends to have any time to spare for the wrens themselves. . . .

No. 2 nest had . . . its turf fire burning near the door; by the light of which I saw, as I approached it, one wretched figure alone. Crouched near the glowing turf, with her head resting upon her hands, was a woman whose age I could scarcely guess at, though I think by the masses of black hair that [fell] forward over her hands and backward over her bare shoulders that she must have been young. . . .

Of course, I wanted to know how my wretched companion in this lonely, windy, comfortless hovel came from being a woman to be turned into a wren. The story began with "no father nor mother," an aunt who kept a whisky store in Cork, an artilleryman who came to the whisky store, and saw and seduced the girl. By and by his regiment was ordered to the Curragh. The girl followed him, being then with child. "He blamed me for following him," said she. "He'd have nothing to do with me. He told me to come here and do like other women did. And what could I do? My child was born here, in this very place, and glad I was of the shelter, and glad I was when the child died—thank the blessed Mary! What could I do with a child? His father was sent away from here, and a good riddance. He used me very bad." After a minute's silence the woman continued, a good deal to my surprise. "I'll show you the likeness of a better man, far away—one that never said a cross word to me—blessed's the ground he treads upon." And, fumbling in the pocket of her too scanty and too dingy petticoat, she produced a photographic portrait of a soldier, inclosed in half a dozen greasy letters. "He's a bandsman, sir, and a handsome man indade he is, and I believe he likes me too. But they have sent him to Malta for six years; I'll never see my darlint again." And then this poor wretch, who was half crying as she spoke, told me how she had walked to Dublin to see him just before he sailed, "because the poor craythur wanted to see me onst more." The letters she had in her pocket were from him; they were read and answered by the girl . . . who seems to be the only woman in the whole colony who can either read or write. . . .

From this woman . . . I learned, as I sat smoking over the turf fire—and the night was bitterly cold—much that I have already related. I also learned the horror the women have of the workhouse; and how, if they are found straying over the limits allotted to them, they have to appear at Naas to be fined for the offence (a half-crown seems to be the fine commonly inflicted), or to be sent for seven days to gaol. There, according to this woman, they get about a pint of "stirabout" for breakfast, at two o'clock in the afternoon some more stirabout and about a pound of bread, and nothing more till breakfast time next day . . . and yet she spoke of the workhouse as a place still more unlovely. However, she had suffered so much privation last winter that she had made up her mind not to stay in the bush another such season. "At the first fall of the snow I'll to the workhouse, that I will!" she said, in a tone of one who says that in such an event he is determined to cut his throat. "Why, would you belave it, sir, last winther the snow would be up as high as our little house, and we had to cut a path through it to the min [men], or we'd been ruined intirely."

REPORT OF AN EX-DRAGOON

"Driving the wrens," as the phrase went twelve or thirteen years ago, was no unusual pastime. Gentlemen fresh from the hospital, with others who had been jilted or robbed, were always ready to organize parties for this purpose, nor were these avengers ever at a loss for recruits. Generally speaking "the fun of the thing" was irresistible. After evening stables—half-past seven to eight o'clock—the gang, usually a pretty large one, mustered, and well armed with pieces of turf, cabbage-stalks, and similar missiles, marched to the scene of action. That attained, supposing the evening to be wet, a general rush of the mob would tumble the frail edifices about the ears of the occupants, who received an unmerciful pelting as they bolted from the ruins. A dry summer or autumn evening, however, was preferred for perpetrating these acts of wantonness. Of course, at these times the huts would be as inflammable as so much tinder, and the application of a match to the roof would in a very few moments wrap the whole structure in flames. When this happened those inside would dash not only through the door, but through the sides of the burning nest, and plunge along among the mocking cheers and ready missiles of their tormentors, carrying with them in their hair and clothes burning fragments of the wreck. What loss or injury they sustained by these amusements nobody cared.

In *Pall Mall Gazette*, October 15, 16, 17, 19, and 23, 1867

TWO

Theorists and Rescuers

Victorian moralists and social reformers were very much at pains to account for the causes of prostitution. Responsibility was often distributed along class lines. The male aristocracy was blamed for ruthlessly purchasing or seducing young women. The middle classes were accused of encouraging male profligacy by postponing marriage until the young couple could afford an "establishment." But, most of all, the poor were blamed for displaying bad character through faulty parenting, crowded sleeping quarters, love of dress, greed, drunkenness, and natural viciousness, all of which were enumerated and considered at length as contributing causes of vice.

Behind these endless arguments about the causes of vice lay the commonly held assumption that prostitution existed in order to allow men to satisfy sexual needs, which necessarily could not be met by marriage. Engels stated this functional argument most fully in *The Origins of the Family, Private Property, and the State* (1884), pointing out that monogamy as a social institution has always meant monogamy for "respectable" women and multiple sexual contacts for men. William Lecky earlier had celebrated this very dispensation in the passage included here from his *History of European Morals* (1869)— a passage often quoted in its time. By elevating the prostitute to the status of a martyred savior of the home, men like W. R. Greg and William Lecky were providing an ideological framework for the establishment of a regulated, custodial trade in prostitution. Hence their maudlin meditations on the "fallen" are really not that different in assumptions and in effect from the scrupulously matter-of-fact reports of William Acton, the advocate of state medical regulation.

Victorians turned the rescue of the "fallen" into a large-scale activity. In the 1860s, there were more than twenty shelters and asylums in London, and there were missionaries from the established and dissenting churches regularly patrolling the streets around the Hay-market, passing out leaflets and soliciting prostitutes to forsake their sinful lives. The asylums, once entered, were highly punitive. Women were separated from family and friends (including their own chil-dren), awakened early, set to prayers, kept busy with menial occupa-tions, forced to dress plainly in uniform style, and required to keep silent about their former lives and to refrain from cursing and rough manners. In return they were given a clean place to sleep, regular meals, and the sometimes illusory promise of a job when their time (often a year or two) was up. Whether run by individuals or by churches, these private establishments worked in conjunction with the state-run system of prisons and hospitals. Often the job that awaited the rescued woman was an extension of the long institutional surveil-lance, since employers, who were always told of their servant's past life, would be placed in the position of overseeing a woman's moral regeneration while benefitting from her cheap labor.

Because it was the sexuality rather than the misery of the fallen woman that offended most missionaries, all their efforts were bent to-ward submerging the prostitute in the fabric of respectable society. The transformation of the roving, sexual outlaw into the industrious and pious domestic servant was a particularly gratifying prospect. By the same token, many reformers wished to provide free passage to the colonies for "rescued" women. Such a plan, like the similar schemes for transporting "redundant" women, aimed at eliminating a social problem by putting the victims far out of sight.

The class differences between rescuer and rescued—the opportuni-ties for patronizing and meddlesome behavior on the one hand, and hypocrisy and scamming on the other—are well-illustrated by these selections.

WHY WOMEN FALL (1850)
William Rathbone Greg
(See p. 50.)

There is, we think, a very general misapprehension, especially among the fair sex, as to the original causes which reduce this unfortunate class of girls to their state of degradation—the primary circumstances of their fall from chastity. . . . Those who think of this class of sinners as severely as . . . most women are apt to do—fancy the original occasion of their lapse from virtue to have been either lust, immodest and unruly desires, silly vanity, or the deliberate exchange of innocence for luxury and show. We believe they are quite mistaken. . . . Women's *desires* scarcely ever lead to their fall; for . . . the desire scarcely exists in a definite and conscious form, till they *have* fallen. In this point there is a radical and essential difference between the sexes: the arrangements of nature and the customs of society would be even more unequal than they are, were it not so. In men, in general, the sexual desire is inherent and spontaneous, and belongs to the condition of puberty. In the other sex, the desire is dormant, if not nonexistent, till excited; always till excited by undue familiarities; almost always till excited by sexual intercourse.

Women whose position and education have protected them from exciting causes, constantly pass through life without ever being cognizant of the promptings of the senses. Happy for them that it is so! . . . Were it not for this kind decision of nature, which, in England, has been assisted by that correctness of feeling which pervades our education, the consequences would, we believe, be frightful. If the passions of women were ready, strong, and spontaneous, in a degree even remotely approaching the form they assume in the coarser sex, there can be little doubt that sexual irregularities would reach a height, of which, at present, we have happily no conception. . . .

We believe we shall be borne out by the observation of all who have inquired much into the antecedents of this unfortunate class of women—those, at least, who have not sprung from the *very* low, or the actually vicious sections of the community—in stating that a vast proportion of those who, after passing through the career of kept mistresses, ultimately come upon the town, fall in the first instance from a mere exaggeration and perversion of one of the best qualities of a woman's heart. They yield to desires in which they do not share, from a weak generosity which cannot refuse anything to the passionate entreaties of the man they love. There is in the warm fond heart of woman a strange and sublime unselfishness, which men too commonly discover only to profit by—a positive love of self-sacrifice— an active, so to speak, an *aggressive* desire to show affection, by giving up to those who have won it something they hold very dear. It is an unreasoning and dangerous yearning of the spirit, precisely analogous to that which prompts the surrenders and self-tortures of the religious devotee. Both seek to prove their devotion to the idol they have enshrined, by casting down before his altar their richest and most cherished treasures. This is no romantic or over-coloured picture; those who deem it so have not known the better portion of their sex, or do not deserve to have known them. We refer confidently to all whose memory unhappily may furnish an answer to the question, whether an appeal to this perverted generosity is not almost always the final resistless arguments to which female virtue succumbs. When we consider these things, and remember also, as we must now proceed to show, how many thousands trace their ruin to actual want—*the want of those dependent on them*—we believe, upon our honour, that nine out of ten originally modest women who fall from virtue, fall from motives or feelings in which sensuality and self have no share; nay, under circumstances in which selfishness, had they not been of too generous a nature to listen to its dictates, would have saved them.

In W. R. Greg, "Prostitution," *Westminster Review*, July 1850

THE SOCIAL FUNCTION OF PROSTITUTION (1869)
William Lecky

William Lecky (1838–1903) was a historian, essayist, and member of Parliament.

The family is the centre and the archetype of the State, and the happiness and goodness of society are always in a very great degree dependent upon the purity of domestic life. The essentially exclusive nature of marital affection, and the natural desire of every man to be certain of the paternity of the child he supports, render the incursions of irregular passions within the domestic circle a cause of extreme suffering. Yet it would appear as if the excessive force of these passions would render such incursions both frequent and inevitable.

Under these circumstances, there has arisen in society a figure which is certainly the most mournful, and in some respects the most awful, upon which the eye of the moralist can dwell. That unhappy being whose very name is a shame to speak; who counterfeits with a cold heart the transports of affection, and submits herself as the passive instrument of lust; who is scorned and insulted as the vilest of her sex and doomed, for the most part, to disease and abject wretchedness and an early death, appears in every age as the perpetual symbol of the degradation and the sinfulness of man. Herself the supreme type of vice, she is ultimately the most efficient guardian of virtue. But for her, the unchallenged purity of countless happy homes would be polluted, and not a few who, in the pride of their untempted chastity, think of her with an indignant shudder, would have known the agony of remorse and of despair. On that one degraded and ignoble form are concentrated the passions that might have filled the world with shame. She remains, while creeds and civilisations rise and fall, the eternal priestess of humanity, blasted for the sins of the people.

In William Lecky, *History of European Morals* (1869)

A DOUBLE ANSWER TO PRAYER (1860)
John Blackmore

John Blackmore (b. 1815), a retired naval lieutenant, wrote a memoir of the thirteen years he spent cruising the streets of London at night to persuade prostitutes to reform.

Dr. William Acton believed that, because of the naiveté and punitive attitudes of the reformers, only the most sickly, homely, and spiritless girls landed in the asylums. Blackmore's specimen, for example, is a barmaid, a class of women who were often expected to use their sexuality to sell drinks and bring in customers. Her description of losing her place through impropriety is quite unlikely, although it is exactly the sort of story missionaries wanted to hear. Her whole tale, in fact, is representative of a minor literary genre: the prostitute's progress from early piety through seduction, drugging, and abduction—usually at the hands of a man of higher social station—followed by debilitating illness and a rapid descent into the streets, then restoration through the agency of prayer to innocent, forgiving parents. Looking at this story from another angle, though, we might guess that here is a girl down on her luck, unable to pick up customers perhaps because of obvious syphilis (Blackmore says that no penitentiary would admit her) and taking advantage of a chance to recover and eat without working.

Returning home late one night, and while waiting for an omnibus near Charing Cross, I was accosted by a young woman, who . . . seemed half ashamed to speak to me.

"Why are you out at this late hour?" I asked.

"To seek a lover," she replied.

"You are? Well, then, he is not far from you; for the Bible says, . . . 'God so loved the world—so loved you, my friend—that he gave his only begotten Son, that whosoever believed in him should not perish, but have everlasting life.' "

"Oh, yes, I know all that, Sir; but I am really very hungry."

"Come then with me." I took her to a coffee-house, and gave her some refreshment. While she partook of it, I sat on the other side of the table, and thus had an excellent opportunity of speaking to her about her soul. . . . I told her that if she wished to leave her course of sin, I should be happy to see her at my house the following day, and gave her my card for that purpose.

"I will come," she said.

She was true to her appointment; and during our interview gave the following account of her past life.

"I am twenty years of age. My mother was a pious woman, who sent me, and my brothers and sisters, to a Sunday-school. . . . I was brought up to London by an uncle, who kept a public-house. After teaching me the business, he procured for me a situation as a bar-maid. . . . One evening, as I was going to my uncle's house, I was accosted by a gentleman, who asked me to take a walk with him, and proposed that we should go to Astley's Theatre. To this I at first objected. . . . However, upon his promising that I should leave the theatre early, I was induced to go there with him. The time passed away so rapidly, that when we came out, it was much past the hour I ought to have been at home, which threw me into great distress of mind; and I knew not what to do. After much persuasion, he induced me to take something to drink; which produced so powerful an effect upon me, that I knew not what I was about; and whilst in that condition he took me to a bad house. Oh, Sir, the rest is too dreadful to relate."

Here she wept bitterly, and it was some minutes before she could proceed.

"He left me in the morning, and I have never seen him since. When I returned to my situation, I was discharged immediately. I went to . . . my uncle . . . [who] would have nothing more to do with me, and turned me out of his house. Having a little money left, I took a lodging, and lived upon it until all was gone; and then I went on the streets to keep me from starving. Two months afterwards I was taken very ill, and thought I should die. A lady pitied me, and obtained a letter of admission to the —— Hospital, where I remained about a month; but came out again in a bad state, and I feel I am getting worse every day. I know not where to go to obtain food and lodging; I have no money, and no one will trust me. . . ."

At first I knew not what to do; . . . even if the morrow were "reception day" at any of the penitentiaries, she would not have been admitted, because of the state of her health. I therefore found a lodging for her in the house of a Christian widow, and procured the aid of a medical man, under whose care, and a regular and nutritious diet, she speedily recovered. After remaining in these lodgings about two months, her mother was communicated with, and came immediately to town, accompanied by her other daughter. I shall never forget their meeting; the mother burst into tears; her heart overflowing with gratitude, she exclaimed, "This is indeed an answer to my prayers. I asked the Lord to send some Christian minister to rescue my child; and this is the answer to my prayers: for here is my child." Both mother and daughter wept for joy; we prayed together, and the mother and her two daughters returned to their home in the country.

On the evening I met this young woman, I had made it a subject of prayer, that God would be pleased to use me as an instrument of blessing to some poor wanderer. Thus was this my first case a double answer to prayer.

A short time after returning home, she married a respectable person; and when we last heard of them they were doing well. To the Lord be all the glory.

In John Blackmore, *The London by Moonlight Mission* (1860)

FALLEN SISTERS (1860)
Emma Sheppard

The writer, the wife of a magistrate, contributed this report to The Magdalen's Friend, *a monthly magazine edited by a Reverend Tuckniss for the Society for the Rescue of Young Women and Children.*

English ladies, have you ever analysed these two words—"a Sister"—though "fallen"? Yes, high-born, gently-bred, delicately nurtured Ladies, that poor Outcast, upon whom you cast an eye of scorn and loathing as perhaps she tramped up Regent Street this morning, looking wistfully at your luxurious carriage, with its warm wrappings from the cold, carrying you from shop to shop in quest of some small trifle—that poor, weary, outwardly-hardened, sin-debased creature—a victim to man's brutal requirements—is, in the sight of our most holy God, your *Sister*. . . . Oh, think the night after you read this, as you lie, perchance awake, and know that the husband of your youth, the children of your love, lie close by you—when the carpeted room, and the warm bed-hangings, and the ample coverings keep out a breath of the chilly wintry air, which you think would kill you—think for ten minutes of midnight streets, cold pavements, dreary doorsteps, dark corners, on which, perhaps the eye of God alone then looks—picture these filled with women, young girls, your Sisters, once fair and loved as you, now debased, and humbled, and degraded to the level of the brutes, either cursing, or drinking, or quarrelling, or following deeds of darkness such as your mind never *can* picture; and then turn your head on your pillow, and bless that gracious God who has kept you *unfallen* in the eyes of the world. . . .

In November 1858, my husband sent to prison, for the twenty-seventh time, a notorious offender, Matilda H——, only twenty-nine, one of the most disorderly *habituées* of the streets. In jail, she found her first friend, the kind and earnest wife of the Governor of Shipton House of Correction, who spends much of her time among the female prisoners. Her kindly words gained influence over poor Matilda, and secured her tender and most devoted love. After her term of imprisonment was over, the girl came back to Frome, determined to enter the Workhouse, and, if possible, to bear the irksome and galling restraints there, and regain such a character as eventually to allow her to emigrate. *There* I visited her, giving her words of cheering purpose, getting the Master of the Workhouse to alter her work from oakum-picking (that degrading, unwomanly employment) to washing for the house, and taking her up some tea and sugar, now and then, to soften the hardships I knew she was undergoing.

Christmas Eve 1858, when we took up our annual present to every member of the Workhouse, I laid my hand on Matilda, after giving her her little packet, saying, "Be a good girl, and try to stay here." She beckoned me into a corner, and took out of the bosom of her pauper dress a well-worn note, wrapped up in several scraps of paper, and tied with a bit of stocking cotton—her talisman—saying, "Here's what will keep me good—a note from that dear lady at the jail; I promise you, I won't vex her or you, by being naughty."

Was there not here a touching revelation of a soft, tender heart in that rough, rude woman?

But Matilda again fell; the story too long to tell. After two months or more in the Workhouse, really behaving well, she asked leave one day to go out and see her mother, got drunk, returned to use violent language, &c., to the master, and was sent off for the twenty-eighth time to prison. My heart yearned over her. . . . I drove over to Shipton, asked to see Matilda, and was shown alone into her cell. . . . I laid my hand on her shoulder as we knelt side by side, and she shook like an earthquaking, with sobs of loving repentance. Then I offered her Clewer shelter. She gasped at the thought of it. . . . Then came the piteous request, "Do let me see my old mother in Frome; she won't live over the two years I am away." I told her I could not trust her a night in Frome, but would arrange for her, to come from Shipton by earliest train, March 31st.

I returned to make these arrangements—bought some tea, sugar, bacon, &c. for the breakfast—the old parents whitewashed the tiny house, in preparation. I went down to meet her at train by seven a.m., and about eleven, went up to her home. We read a few verses; then I prayed in the midst of the assembled family of parents, brothers, and sisters, and took her down to the station, so as to make *sure* of her. When I had taken her ticket for Windsor, I knew not where to put it for safety; so took off my own glove, put it on her, and placed the ticket inside. She looked at me wonderingly, then kissed the glove tenderly, with "I'll *never* part with that as long as I live." What was this, but as loving a heart as yours or mine, for the first time called out into exercise? . . .

If there was a heart in this poor, wretched, oft-convicted, scorned creature, why should we not seek and find the same in others. . . ?

In Emma Sheppard, "A Fallen Sister," *The Magdalen's Friend*, April 1860

REGULATIONS OF A REFUGE (1853)
Charles Dickens

In 1846, Angela Burdett-Coutts, the wealthiest woman and most important philanthropist of her day, established a home for "homeless" women, which Charles Dickens (1812–1870) undertook to supervise for her at the very height of his writing career. Dickens's writing on the subject of Urania Cottage displays a real pleasure in exercising control over young, errant women. His was a scheme for making them "patient, gentle, persevering, and good tempered." For Dickens, the worst sin was to grumble or to express anger. Although he has been uniformly praised by modern male commentators for his "energy, good sense, patience, and generosity" in supervising the shelter, Dickens merely substituted a cozy paternalism for the bleaker institutional sanctions of more overtly punitive establishments. His connection with the home ended when Angela Burdett-Coutts broke with him for leaving his wife in favor of his mistress, Ellen Ternan. Miss Burdett-Coutts herself does not appear to have been particularly sympathetic to her charges. She kept aloof from them, for fear of moral contamination, and disapproved of their marrying even after exile to Australia. Our information about her ideas and values is, however, limited by the fact that her half of her correspondence with Dickens has been destroyed.

Five years and a half ago, certain ladies, grieved to think that numbers of their own sex were wandering about the streets in degradation, passing through and through the prisons all their lives, or hopelessly perishing in other ways, resolved to try the experiment on a limited scale of a Home for the reclamation and emigration of women. As it was clear to them that there could be little or no hope in this country for the greater part of those who might become the objects of their charity, they determined to receive into their Home, only those who distinctly accepted this condition: That they came there to be ultimately sent abroad (whither, was at the discretion of the ladies); and that they also came there, to remain for such length of time as might, according to the circumstances of each individual case, be considered necessary as a term of probation, and for instruction in the means of obtaining an honest livelihood. . . .

They are allowed to be visited under the following restrictions; if by their parents, once in a month; if by other relatives or friends, once in three months. The principal Superintendent is present at all such interviews, and hears the conversation. . . .

They can write to relatives, or old teachers, or persons known to have been kind to them, once a month on application to the committee. It seldom happens that a girl who has any person in the world to correspond with, fails to take advantage of this opportunity. All letters dispatched from the Home are read and posted by the principal Superintendent. All letters received, are likewise read by the Superintendent; but she does not open them. Every such letter is opened by the girl to whom it is addressed, who reads it first, in the Superintendent's presence. . . .

Formerly, when a girl accepted for admission had clothes of her own to wear, she was allowed to be admitted in them, and they were put by for her; though within the Institution she always wore the clothing it provides. It was found, however, that a girl with a hankering after old companions rather relied upon these reserved clothes, and that she put them on with an air, if she went away or were dismissed. They now invariably come, therefore, in clothes belonging to the Home, and bring no other clothing with them. A suit of the commonest apparel has been provided for the next inmate who may leave during her probation, or be sent away; and it is thought that the sight of a girl departing so disgraced, will have a good effect on those who remain. . . .

When the Home had been opened for some time, it was resolved to adopt a modification of Captain Macconnochie's mark system: so arranging the mark table as to render it difficult for a girl to lose marks under any one of its heads, without losing under nearly all the others. The mark table is divided into the nine following heads: Truthfulness, Industry, Temper, Propriety of Conduct and Conversation, Temperance, Order, Punctuality, Economy, Cleanliness. The word Temperance is used [in the widest sense of] "patience, calmness, sedateness, moderation of passion." A separate account for every day is kept with every girl as to each of these items. If her conduct be without objection, she is marked in each column, three—excepting the truthfulness and temperance columns in which, saving under extraordinary circumstances, she is only marked two: the temptation to err in those particulars being considered low under the circumstances of the life she leads in the Home. If she be particularly deserving under any of the other heads, she is marked the highest number—four. If her deserts be low, she is marked only one, or not marked at all. If her conduct under any head have been, during the day, particularly objectionable, she receives a bad mark (marked in red ink, to distinguish it at a glance from the others) which destroys forty good marks. The value of the good marks is six shillings and sixpence per thousand; the earnings of each girl are withheld until she emigrates, in order to form a little fund for her first subsistence on her disembarkation. . . . The usual earnings in a year are about equal to the average wages of the commoner class of domestic servant.

In Charles Dickens, "Homes for Homeless Women," *Household Words*, April 23, 1853

LETTER TO MISS BURDETT-COUTTS ON A CASE OF INSUBORDINATION (1854)
Charles Dickens

Rhena Pollard, that girl from Petworth jail, had been (as is supposed) the companion of the girl who ran away last Sunday, and had in a most inveterately audacious manner, threatened Mrs. Morson that she would leave—had pretended indeed, that she waited for the Committee day as a kind of obliging favor on her part. Accordingly I summoned Mrs. Morson when the girl appeared in her turn, and said, "Mrs. Morson, this is the girl who wants to go, I believe." "Yes." "Take her at her word. It is getting dark now, but, immediately after breakfast tomorrow morning, shut the gates upon her for ever." I think the girl was more taken by surprise, and more seized with consternation, than anybody I have ever seen in that place. She begged and prayed—was obliged to be taken out of the room—went into the long room, and *before all the rest*, entreated and besought Mrs. Morson to intercede for her—and broke into the most forlorn and dismal lamentations. I told Mrs. Morson to give her no hope or relief all night—to have the rough dress down and air it in the long room—and this morning, if the girl again besought her in the same way *before all the others*, to pause and send to me. This she did. I wrote back a letter, which I arranged with her yesterday that she should read them all. I put the case in the strongest and plainest manner possible, and said that you supported that Home, to save young women who desired to be saved and who knew the misery and degradation out of which they were taken—that it was *not* the place

for those who audaciously slighted the shelter of the only roof inter-
posed between them and the great black world of Crime and Shame—
and that I *would not,* nor would any of the gentlemen who assisted
you in its management allow its blessings to be thus grossly trifled
with. As it was the great forgiving Christmas time, she was to give
this girl one more trial; but only on the condition that if she ever
repeated her threat in any way, she was to be instantly discharged. . . .

I think you will approve of the wretched young creature's having
one more chance in this bitter weather—but in a just remembrance
of what is due to the Home and its Supporter, I could not have given
it to her, if she had been other than a stranger in London, and an
utterly friendless speck in the world.

Snow two feet deep in the streets today!

From Charles Dickens to Angela Burdett-Coutts, January 4, 1854, in *Letters
to Angela Burdett-Coutts, 1841–1865,* ed. Edgar Johnson (1953)

"THE MAIDEN TRIBUTE OF
MODERN BABYLON" (1881)
W. T. Stead

*Journalist W. T. Stead's (1849–1912) reporting for the Pall Mall
Gazette on the white slave traffic in London is perhaps the apotheosis
of Victorian moral reformism. White slavery and brothel prostitution
were probably very limited in England, and involuntary child prostitution even rarer. But despite his exaggerations and over-dramatizations,
Stead appealed to a large public by concretizing common fears and
fantasies of the time.*

THE VIOLATION OF VIRGINS

It is a fact that there is in full operation among us a system of
which the violation of virgins is one of the ordinary incidents; that
these virgins are mostly of tender age, being too young in fact to
understand the nature of the crime of which they are the unwilling
victims; that these outrages are constantly perpetrated with almost
absolute impunity; and that the arrangements are made with a simplicity and efficiency incredible to all who have not made actual
demonstration of the facility with which the crime can be accomplished. . . .

Before beginning this inquiry I had a confidential interview with one of the most experienced officers who for many years was in a position to possess an intimate acquaintance with all phases of London crime. I asked him, "Is it or is it not a fact, that, at this moment, if I were to go to the proper houses, well introduced, the keeper would, in return for money down, supply me in due time with a maid—a girl who had never been seduced?"

"Certainly," he replied without a moment's hesitation.

"At what price?" I continued.

"That is a difficult question," he said. "I remember one case which came under my official cognizance in Scotland-yard in which the price agreed upon was stated to be £20. Some parties in Lambeth undertook to deliver a maid for that sum to a house of ill fame, and I have no doubt it is frequently done all over London."

"But," I continued, "are these maids willing or unwilling parties to the transaction?"

He looked surprised at my question, and then replied emphatically: "Of course they are rarely willing, and as a rule they do not know what they are coming for."

"But," I said in amazement, "then do you mean to tell me that in very truth actual violation, in the legal sense of the word, is constantly being perpetrated in London on unwilling virgins, purveyed and procured to rich men at so much a head by keepers of brothels?"

"Certainly," said he, "there is not a doubt of it." . . .

THE CONFESSIONS OF A BROTHEL-KEEPER

The getting of fresh girls takes time, but it is simple and easy enough once you are in it. I have gone and courted girls in the country under all kinds of disguises, occasionally assuming the dress of a parson, and made them believe that I intended to marry them, and so got them in my power to please a good customer. How is it done? Why, after courting my girl for a time, I propose to bring her to London to see the sights. I bring her up, take her here and there, giving her plenty to eat and drink—especially drink. I take her to the theatre, and then I contrive it so that she loses her last train. By this time she is tired, a little dazed with the drink and excitement, and very frightened at being left in town with no friends. I offer her nice lodgings for the night: she goes to bed in my house, and then the affair is managed. My client gets his maid, I get my £10 or £20 commission, and in the morning the girl, who has lost her character, and dare not go home, in all probability will do as the others do. The brothel-keeper's profit is, first, the commission down for the price of a maid, and secondly, the continuous profit of the addition of a newly-seduced, attractive girl to his establishment. . . .

DELIVERED FOR SEDUCTION

[*After pretending to purchase a young virgin for the sake of his investigation, Stead finds the would-be victim eager to go through with the arrangement.*]

She was a nice, simple, and affectionate girl of sixteen . . . utterly incapable of understanding the consequences of her act. Her father is "afflicted"—that is, touched in his wits; her mother is a charwoman. She herself works at some kind of millinery, for which she receives 5s. a week. Until a month or two ago she had attended Sunday school, and to all appearance she was a girl decidedly above the average. She was to have £4, of which the firm were to have £2. The poor child was nervous and timid, and it was touching to see the way in which she bit her lips to restrain her tears. I talked to her as kindly as possible, and endeavoured to deter her from taking the fatal step, by setting forth the possible consequences that might follow. She was very frank, and, I believe, perfectly straightforward and sincere.

Nevertheless, to my astonishment, the child persisted that she was ready to be seduced. "We are very poor," she said. "Mother does not know anything of this: she will think a lady friend of Miss Z.'s has given me the money; but she does need it so much."

"But," I said, "it is only £2."

"Yes," she said, "but I would not like to disappoint Miss Z., who was also to have £2."

By questioning I found out that the artful procuress had for months past been actually advancing money to the poor girl and her mother when they were in distress, in order to get hold of her when the time came. She persisted that Miss Z. had been such a good friend of hers; she wanted to get her something. She would not disappoint her for anything.

"How much do you think she has given you first and last?"

"About 10s., I should think, but she gave Mother much more."

"How much?"

"Perhaps 20s. would cover it."

"That is to say, that for a year past Miss Z. has been giving you a shilling here and a shilling there; and why? Listen to me. She has already got £3 from me for you, and you will give her £2—that is to say she will make £5 out of you in return for 20s., and in the meantime she will have sold you to destruction."

"Oh, but Miss Z. is so kind!"

Poor trusting little thing, what damnable art the procuress must have used to attach her victim to her in this fashion! But the girl was quite incapable of forming any calculation as to the consequences of her own action. This will appear from the following conversation:

"Now," said I, "if you are seduced, you will get £2 for yourself; but you will lose your character, and you may have a baby which it will cost all your wages to keep. Now I will give you £1 if you'll not be seduced; which will you have?"

"Please, sir, I will be seduced."

"And face the pain, and the wrong-doing, and the possible ruin and ending your days on the streets, all for the difference of one pound?"

"Yes, sir," and she burst into tears, "we are so very poor." . . .

In *Pall Mall Gazette*, July 6, 7, 8, and 10, 1885

THREE

The Contagious Diseases Acts

The organized harassment of prostitutes began in Europe at the time of the syphilis epidemics of the late sixteenth century. Fear of physical and moral contagion led to the establishment of degrading and terrorizing punishments (such as near drowning) and to ever-sterner efforts to segregate prostitution within Europe's growing cities. Since there was very little attempt to punish the customers of prostitutes, the effect of such practices was to create a closely regulated trade. This trend was carried furthest in France. By the beginning of the nineteenth century, a system of state-licensed prostitution had been established under which registered prostitutes were subject to periodic examination for venereal disease and were forced to practice only in specially supervised brothels, where their movements were carefully limited. In England, attempts to institute state-regulated prostitution began in the 1860s.

The Contagious Diseases Acts of 1864, 1866, and 1869 were the work of the military, who were concerned over the righ rate of venereal disease among soldiers and sailors; and of the increasingly powerful medical establishment, who saw garrison-town regulations as the first step in the creation of a system of state-supported medical regulation of prostitution to be extended to the general population. The acts provided for the periodic genital examination of any woman suspected of being a prostitute and living in a town with a large military population. Women who were found diseased were subject to involuntary confinement in special "Lock" hospitals until they were declared cured. Women who refused inspection could be imprisoned and even put to hard labor. At first, the acts went unnoticed; but, by 1869, an opposition was beginning to form—an organized alliance of liberals, moral reformers, feminists, working men, and in their day-today resistance the prostitutes themselves, their families, neighbors, and friends. Although the Contagious Diseases Acts were repealed in 1886, they were instrumental in the professionalization and further stigmatization of prostitution, which occurred in the nineteenth century. In effect, they denied anonymity to women who practiced the trade and turned the community against prostitutes in their midst through harassment of registered women at their homes and workplaces.

One of the most abusive aspects of the acts—the vulnerability to arrest, inspection, and confinement of almost any woman living within the garrison towns—derived from the lack of definition of a "common prostitute." Acton, for instance, quotes this working definition given in testimony before Parliament by a magistrate who was also a visiting surgeon to the Portsmouth Lock Hospital: "[a prostitute is] any woman whom there is fair and reasonable ground to believe is, first of all going to places which are the resorts of prostitutes alone, and at times when immoral persons are usually out. It is more a question of mannerism than anything else."

The police in garrison towns were notoriously intrusive and brutal. They were also careful to limit themselves to the "lower class of girls," many of whom were illiterate and unaware of their right to appear before a magistrate if they refused to sign the "voluntary submission." Of course, even if they had insisted on going to court, there was no guarantee that the magistrate would be any more sympathetic than the police. And the police were not subject to prosecution for false arrest.

Police harassment was instrumental in turning casual prostitutes into professional prostitutes. One woman, a tailoress, reported:

> I went wrong, I confess I did not lead a chaste life, but I was not a common prostitute; but in consequence of the special police coming after me to my place of employment, I was driven from it; my master would not employ me. Since then I have tried the shoe-binding business. I thought perhaps if I could get another course of employment I could evade them, but they followed me to that place, and I lost that also. What was I to do? I could only turn on the streets.*

The possibility of arrest for harboring a diseased prostitute and the

* Quoted in the testimony of Mr. Littleton to Royal Commission on the Contagious Diseases Acts, *P.P.* xix, 1817

notoriety of having the police visiting one's house eventually had
the effect of turning landlords, friends, and relatives against prostitutes. In 1881, the Industrial Schools Act, which sent children found
living in brothels to state-run boarding schools, was passed; as a result, poor people who took in prostitutes as boarders risked losing
their children.

Medical treatment under the acts consisted of confinement during
periods of obvious infection and applications of mercury ointment.
Mercury was somewhat effective in suppressing the symptoms of
syphilis, but it did not contain the progress of the disease and could
cause kidney disease or other ailments. Applications of the mercury
to sore areas caused painful burning. Moreover, even had the treatment been effective, it was compulsory only for women. As one military doctor testified, periodic examination of the soldiers "would
tend to destroy the men's self-respect." The Commission Report of
1871 affirmed a double standard of medical examination in terms of
sexual morality:

> Many witnesses have urged that as well on grounds of justice
> as expediency, soldiers and sailors should be subjected to regu-
> lar examinations. We may at once dispose of this recom-
> mendation, so far as it is founded on the principle of putting
> parties to the sin of fornication on the same footing by the
> obvious and not less conclusive reply that there is no compari-
> son to be made between prostitutes and the men who consort
> with them. With the one sex the offence is committed as a
> matter of gain; with the other it is an irregular indulgence of
> a natural impulse.

The double standard applied to notions of contagion as well. Some
doctors posited that venereal disease could be spread only from
women to men, and Dr. William Acton himself testified that honest
women could not contract syphilis unless they were or had been
pregnant.

Similarly, the struggle to repeal the acts was made more difficult
by Victorian sexual decorum, which allowed medical men to discuss
prostitution and venereal disease but which made such subjects off
limits to others, including even legislators. James Stansfield, for instance, lost his chance for cabinet office by identifying himself with
the cause of repeal. For a woman, the stigma of identification with
diseased prostitutes was even more serious, thereby rendering the

open, energetic, and even theatrical leadership of Josephine Butler all the more striking.

THE NEED FOR LEGISLATION (1870)
Dr. William Acton
(See pp. 127, 394, and 432.)

This Act . . . is something more than a means of imparting health both physical and moral. It forms the commencement of a new legislative era, being a departure from that neutral position previously held by English law with respect to venereal diseases, and admits that there is nothing in the nature of prostitution to exclude it from legislative action, but that, on the contrary, it may be necessary to recognize its existence, and to provide for its regulation, and for the repression, so far as possible, of its attendant evils. It is, in fact, the adoption of the principle . . . that prostitution ought to be an object of legislation. . . .

In considering the attitude which it becomes us to assume toward prostitution, one fact must be carefully borne in mind: that . . . it has existed from the first ages of the world's history down to the present time. . . . The records of the human race, from the Book of Genesis downwards, through the whole range of ancient and medieval literature to the writings of our own day, bear witness to the perpetual presence among men of the daughters of shame. Kings, philosophers, and priests, the learned and the noble, no less than the ignorant and simple, have drunk without stint in every age and every clime of Circe's cup; nor is it reasonable to suppose that in the years to come the world will prove more virtuous than it has shown itself in ages past. . . . Equally irrational is it to imagine that this irrepressible evil can exist without entailing upon society serious mischief; though incapable of absolute repression, prostitution admits of mitigation. To ignore an ever-present evil appears a mistake as fatal as the attempt to repress it. I am, therefore, an advocate of RECOGNITION. . . .

This word RECOGNITION may sound very dreadful, and be regarded by many as the precursor of a coming deluge of continental immorality. But what is the real fact? Is not recognition already accorded by society? Who are those fair creatures, neither chaperones nor chaperoned, "those somebodies whom nobody knows," who elbow our wives and daughters in the parks and promenades and rendezvous of

fashion? Who are those painted, dressy women, flaunting along the
streets and boldly accosting the passers-by? Who those miserable
creatures, ill-fed, ill-clothed, uncared for, from whose misery the eye
recoils, cowering under dark arches and among bye-lanes? The picture has many sides; with all of them society is more or less acquainted.
Why is the State—that alone can remedy a condition of things that
all deplore—alone to refuse recognition? . . .

To give access to and control over the woman whose ameliora-
tion we desire to accomplish, it seems to me absolutely necessary
that the Contagious Diseases Act should be extended to the civil
population, for by means of its machinery alone can we discover and
detail till cured the women afflicted with syphilitic diseases, and in
no other way that has occurred to me can the supervision necessary
for enabling us to work a gradual improvement in their lives be obtained. . . .

The reader who is a conscientious parent must perforce support
me; for, were the sanitary measures I advocate once in operation,
with what diminished anxiety would he not contemplate the progress
of his boys from infancy to manhood? The statesman and the political
economist are mine already, for are not armies and navies invali-
dated—is not labour enfeebled—is not even population deteriorated
by the evils against which I propose we should contend?

In William Acton, *Prostitution* (1857, 1870 revised edition)

THE LADIES' APPEAL AND PROTEST
AGAINST THE CONTAGIOUS DISEASES ACTS (1870)
Josephine Butler
(See pp. 138, 218, 295, 317, 435, and 436.)

*Josephine Grey Butler was born into the landed gentry and grew up
the petted and athletic daughter of a radical family. She underwent
a religious crisis in adolescence and eventually married the fervently
religious, reform-minded scholar George Butler. It was a singularly
harmonious marriage characterized by mutual admiration and a shared
spiritual and intellectual life. As the research assistant of her husband,
Josephine Butler was the first woman to use the library at Oxford.
She was also an early supporter of higher education for women, and
an organizer of Newnham College, Cambridge. The Butlers had*

Josephine Butler

three children, the youngest of whom, the only girl, died in a house-hold accident when she was very little. Butler's grief at her daughter's death intensified her motherly interest in abandoned and "ruined" young women. Her philanthropic rescue work, which included prayer reading in workhouses and the nursing of dying prostitutes in her own home, laid the basis for her championing the cause of repeal of the Contagious Diseases Acts. Butler was also a tireless advocate and leader of the larger European movement against state-regulated prostitution on the continent. She thought of her work as a "great crusade," an *"abolitionist" movement similar to the earlier nineteenth-century battle to eradicate black slavery (in which her father had participated).*

There are two Acts of Parliament—one passed in 1866, the other in 1869—called the Contagious Diseases Acts. These Acts are in force in some of our garrison towns, and in large districts around them. Unlike all other laws for the repression of contagious diseases, to which both men and women are liable, these two apply to women only, men being wholly exempt from their penalties. The law is ostensibly framed for a certain class of women, but in order to reach these, all the women residing within the districts where it is in force are brought under the provisions of the Acts. Any woman can be dragged into court, and required to prove that she is not a common prostitute. The magistrate can condemn her, if a policeman swears only that he "has good cause to believe" her to be one. The accused has to rebut, not positive evidence, but the state of mind of her accuser. When condemned, the sentence is as follows: To have her person outraged by the periodical inspection of a surgeon, through a period of twelve months; or, resisting that, to be imprisoned, with or without hard labour—first for a month, next for three months— such imprisonment to be continuously renewed through her whole life, unless she submit periodically to the brutal requirements of this law. Women arrested under false accusations have been so terrified at the idea of encountering the public trial necessary to prove their innocence, that they have, under the intimidation of the police, signed away their good name and their liberty by making, what is called a "voluntary submission," to appear periodically for twelve months, for surgical examination. Women who, through dread of imprisonment, have been induced to sign the "voluntary submission," which enrolls them in the ranks of common prostitutes, now pursue their traffic under the sanction of Parliament; and the houses where they congregate, so long as the Government surgeons are satisfied with the health of their inmates, enjoy, practically, as complete a protection as a church or a school.

We, the undersigned, enter our solemn Protest against these Acts—

1st—Because, involving as they do, such a momentous change in the legal safeguards hitherto enjoyed by women in common with men, they have been passed, not only without the knowledge of the country, but unknown to Parliament itself; and we hold that neither the Representatives of the People, nor the Press, fulfill the duties which are expected of them, when they allow such legislation to take place without the fullest discussion.

2nd—Because, so far as women are concerned they remove every guarantee of personal security which the law has established and held sacred, and put their reputation, their freedom, and their persons absolutely in the power of the police.

3rd—Because the law is bound, in any country professing to give civil liberty to its subjects, to define clearly an offence which it punishes.

4th—Because it is unjust to punish the sex who are the victims of a vice, and leave unpunished the sex who are the main cause, both of the vice and its dreaded consequences; and we consider that liability to arrest, forced surgical examination, and (where this is resisted) imprisonment with hard labour, to which these Acts subject women, are punishments of the most degrading kind.

5th—Because, by such a system, the path of evil is made more easy to our sons, and to the whole of the youth of England; inasmuch as a moral restraint is withdrawn the moment the State recognises, and provides convenience for, the practice of a vice which it thereby declares to be necessary and venial.

6th—Because these measures are cruel to the women who come under their action—violating the feelings of those whose sense of shame is not wholly lost, and further brutalising even the most abandoned.

7th—Because the disease which these Acts seek to remove has never been removed by any such legislation. The advocates of the system have utterly failed to show, by statistics or otherwise, that these regulations have in any case, after several years' trial, and when applied to one sex only, diminished disease, reclaimed the fallen, or improved the general morality of the country. We have, on the contrary, the strongest evidence to show that in Paris and other continental cities where women have long been outraged by this forced inspection, the public health and morals are worse than at home.

8th—Because the conditions of this disease, in the first instance, are moral, not physical. The moral evil through which the disease makes its way separates the case entirely from that of the plague, or other scourges, which have been placed under police control or sanitary care. We hold that we are bound, before rushing into the experiment of legalizing a revolting vice, to try to deal with the *causes* of the evil, and we dare to believe that with wiser teaching and more capable legislation, those causes would not be beyond control.

[*Signed by 251 women, including Josephine Butler, Harriet Martineau, and Florence Nightingale*]

In *The Shield*, March 14, 1870

THE EXAMINATION (1870)
Dr. William Acton
(See pp. 127, 394, and 427.)

The inspections are conducted in the following manner. The women are introduced one at a time from the wards by one nurse into a special room, containing a properly raised bed, with feet, similar to the one in use on the Continent. The patient ascends the steps placed by the side of the bed, lays down, places her feet in the slippers arranged for the purpose, and the house surgeon separates the labia to see if there are any sores. If no suspicion of these exists, and if the female is suffering from discharge, the speculum is at once employed. In this institution several sizes are used, and they are silvered and covered with india-rubber. The head nurse after each examination washes the speculum in a solution of permanganate of potash, then wipes it carefully, oils it ready for the next examination, so that the surgeon loses no time, and the examinations are conducted with great rapidity. In the course of one hour and three-quarters I assisted in the thorough examination of 58 women with the speculum.

In William Acton, *Prostitution* (1857, 1870 revised edition)

THE CASE OF CATHERINE PICKLES (1870)
The Shield

The Shield was the weekly newspaper of Josephine Butler's Anti-Contagious Diseases Acts Association.

The first witness called was the girl herself, who gave her evidence in a clear and apparently straightforward manner. She stated that she was sixteen years of age on the 29th of last month, and in March last the police came after her and ordered her to go to the examining room at Stonehouse, telling her that if she did not go she would be sent to prison. She was examined by the doctor, and cried very much because she was dreadfully hurt, and because she was obliged to go there. She went again after that. She solemnly and seriously declared, knowing that she was on her oath, that previously to being ordered to be examined under the Act she was a virtuous girl. "After I was examined," said the girl, "I was so ashamed and hurt that I thought I may as well go altogether, and I went on the town. I swear that this—and this alone—was the cause of my becoming a prostitute." She added that after being examined, the nurse, on seeing her crying, said, "Oh! that is nothing, you will soon get used to it." Subsequently, she was sent into the hospital, where she was kept a month and four days; but there was nothing the matter with her; she was as well when she went in as when she came out. [Inspector] Annis presented her the submission paper to sign; she could not write, and he made the cross upon it. He did not read the paper to her, or explain it, and she was ignorant of it. She admitted having gone wrong up to the week before last; but she had forsaken her vicious course of life, and desired to go to a home. She was determined, however, not to be examined again, and would rather go to prison than submit to it.

The mother of the girl—also called CATHERINE PICKLES—was then sworn, and testified that she believed that when the police first came after her child she was virtuous. She had had a little trouble with her because she would "run about and was a little wild," but she solemnly believed on her oath that she was not a prostitute. The fact of her having been compelled to go to be examined had been her ruin, and nothing else. She told the police so; and she told them that she had been virtuous when they first came after her, and that it must have been some enemy to her who had given them false information. But the police deceived her; they led her to believe that she was not going to be taken to be examined. After the girl came back, she screeched with pain, so much was she hurt, and cried bitterly because she had been compelled to go. After this she was bound to go again, and then she went away from her on the town. "I know," said the mother, "that there was nothing wrong with my child before." The daughter had since hid away for days together because the police should not find her and take her to be examined. Both she and the girl had since made efforts to have her name taken off the books but without effect. . . .

The mother stated that on one of the occasions that the police had sworn they had seen the girl out, she was hid away indoors to escape them, and therefore she was certain they had not spoken the truth. They had so hunted her daughter that she was obliged to shift her residence; they pestered her and followed the house so much, that the landlord gave them notice to leave. The police had also so followed another daughter belonging to her—who was of respectable character—that she was obliged to leave the neighborhood to escape them.

The BENCH said there need be no difficulty in the case. [If] the girl went up for examination, and it was found that she was not diseased, and that she was desirous of leaving her mode of life, she would be relieved, Mr. Laity [a magistrate] observing that he knew there was no obstacle thrown in the way of reclamation at the hospital.

Mr. EASTLAKE said they were only too happy to promote it.

The BENCH: Under those circumstances we refuse to grant the application, and the girl must be examined.

The GIRL: I will not go.

The MOTHER: She will go to prison rather.

Mr. EDMONDS: Well, it will only be another prisoner. The girl is determined to go to prison rather than submit to it, and you may as well hear the other case, and send her at once. She will go to prison, very likely on the town again, and another bed will be filled at the hospital. Perhaps that is the object.

The girl then repeated that she would not submit, and left the Court with her mother, both protesting loudly against the decision of the Bench.

(Our readers will observe that Mr. Daniel Cooper had intimated his willingness to place this poor child immediately in a Home. But the Magistrates would not allow her to escape without at least *one* more outrage first. Our readers will be glad to know, however, that she did escape it nonetheless, and that she is now safe, where she will be taken care of and restored to a virtuous life.)

In *The Shield*, August 15, 1870

ABUSES UNDER THE CONTAGIOUS DISEASES ACTS (1870)
Josephine Butler
(See pp. 138, 218, 295, 317, 428, and 436.)

Another Inspector boasted openly to a gentleman (who told me of it) of the excellence of his method of discovering quiet, clandestine prostitutes. In illustration of this, he told an anecdote (much to his own credit truly!) of his having accosted a pretty, quiet-looking girl, and requested to be allowed to take a walk with her in the direction of her home, which was about a mile out of the town. She agreed, and during the walk the spy acted the part of an agreeable but dishonourable man. On reaching the door of her dwelling, she seemed willing to accede to his proposal to walk in. Thus, he said, I knew by her willingness to admit me, that she must be a prostitute, and served her with a summons. . . .

I obtained a Magistrate's order to visit Dover prison. There were then five women imprisoned there under the Acts. The impression produced on my mind was a melancholy one in respect to the injustice and indecency of the law, when I left the open air on a beautiful morning, where the larks were soaring freely in a cloudless blue sky, and entered those dim stone galleries, and the cells, with their grated windows and heavy doors where delicate girls were immured— for what? For refusing the ghastly indecency, the shame and the pain which the Act commands them to endure, without any proof that they are what it pleases to call them. They are in solitary confinement most of the day. Two whom I saw were washing in a dark corner, fenced off by a chain or rail. I leaned over the barrier to speak with them. It was a moment of deep interest to me. The girls drew close to me, looked earnestly through the gloom in my face, and asked, "O Madam, what does the Queen say?" Unhappily I could give them no answer to this, but I could tell them of the sympathy of women throughout the whole kingdom. In expressing this sympathy I never fail to let them feel how we *hate* the sin of their lives while we are indignant at the law which degrades them still further. But many I saw were *not* prostitutes, nor would it have been suitable to say a word to them as if they were sinners more than the most virtuous, after knowing their histories. One of these women told me she had refused the second examination because when she

went through the process the first time she had not been three weeks
risen from childbed, and she suffered so terribly from the instrumental violation that she could not go again. She has never been
well since. She said, "The man might have known that a woman in
my state was not fit to go through all that horrible business." Her
case reminded me of poor Sarah Waters whom I saw, and whom you
will have seen by the papers, promised under threat of imprisonment
to appear regularly for examination for "twelve calendar months."
Now in six or seven months that girl will be confined. I think it is
right that the women of England should know distinctly whether the
law makers of our country have enacted that women shall be periodically violated while pregnant, up to the time of delivery (as Sarah
Waters is condemned to be), and as soon as possible again after
delivery. If so, we women of England assuredly know what steps to
take. That poor girl was threatened with miscarriage, and I much
doubt whether she can ever be a mother after what she has gone
through.

In *The Shield*, May 9, 1870

MEN, MEN, ONLY MEN (1870)
Josephine Butler
(See pp. 138, 218, 295, 428, and 435.)

There is nothing more significant of the nature and intentions of the
Contagious Diseases Acts than the exclusion from the Lock Hospitals
of lady workers. . . . What is the motive for excluding ladies? I should
like Mr. Childers, Mr. Cardwell, and the other guardians of these
Acts, to answer this question honestly. I recall the bitter complaint
of one of these poor women: "It is *men, men, only men*, from the
first to the last, that we have to do with! To please a man I did wrong
at first, then I was flung about from man to man. Men police lay
hands on us. By men we are examined, handled, doctored. . . . In the
hospital it is a man again who makes prayers and reads the Bible for
us. We are had up before magistrates who are men, and we never
get out of the hands of men till we die!" And as she spoke I thought,
"And it was a Parliament of men only who made this law which
treats you as an outlaw. Men alone met in committee over it. Men
alone are the executives." When men, of all ranks, thus band them-

selves together for an end deeply concerning women, and place themselves like a thick, impenetrable wall between women and women, and forbid the one class of women entrance into the presence of the other, the weak, outraged class, it is time that women should arise and demand their most sacred rights in regard to their sisters.

In *The Shield*, May 9, 1870

Bibliography

GENERAL STUDIES

Basch, Françoise. *Relative Creatures: Victorian Women in Society and the Novel.* New York: Schocken, 1974.

Delamont, Sara, and Duffin, Lorna. *The Nineteenth-Century Woman: Her Cultural and Physical World.* London: Croom Helm; New York: Barnes & Noble Books, 1978.

Hartmann, Mary S., and Banner, Lois. *Clio's Consciousness Raised: New Perspectives on the History of Women.* New York: Farrar, Straus & Giroux, 1976.

Kanner, S. Barbara. "The Women of England in a Century of Social Change, 1815–1914: A Select Bibliography." In Vicinus, *Suffer and Be Still.*

Kanner, [S.] Barbara. "The Women of England in a Century of Social Change, 1815–1914: A Select Bibliography, Part II." In Vicinus, *Widening Sphere.*

Mitchell, Juliet, and Oakley, Ann. *The Rights and Wrongs of Women.* Harmondsworth, England: Penguin, 1976.

Palmegiano, E. M. *Women and British Periodicals, 1832–1867: A Bibliography.* New York and London: Garland Publishing, 1976.

Strachey, Ray. *The Cause: A Short History of the Women's Movement in Great Britain,* 1928. Reprint. London: Virago, 1978.

Vicinus, Martha, ed. *Suffer and Be Still: Women in the Victorian Age.* Bloomington and London: Indiana University Press, 1973.

Vicinus, Martha, ed. *A Widening Sphere: Changing Roles of Victorian Women.* Bloomington and London: Indiana University Press, 1977.

Part I   THE WOMANLY WOMAN

Aveling, Eleanor Marx and Edward. "The Woman Question from a Socialist Point of View." *Westminster Review* 69 (January 1886).

Buck, Anne. *Victorian Costume and Costume Accessories.* London: Herbert Jenkins, 1961.

Cobbe, Frances Power. "Celibacy vs. Marriage." *Frasers,* February 1862.

Cobbe, Frances Power. "What Shall We Do With Our Old Maids?" *Frasers,* November 1862.

Fee, Elizabeth. "The Sexual Politics of Victorian Social Anthropology." In Hartmann and Banner.

Grey, Maria. *Old Maids: A Lecture.* 1875.

Hammerton, A. James. "Feminism and Female Emigration, 1861–1886." In Vicinus, *Widening Sphere.*

Kunzle, David. "Dress Reform as Antifeminism: A Response to Helene E. Roberts's 'The Exquisite Slave . . .' ." *Signs: Journal of Women in Culture and Society* 2 (1977): 570–579.

Linton, Eliza Lynn. *The Girl of the Period and Other Social Essays*. 1883.
Payne, Blanche. *History of Costume: From the Ancient Egyptians to the Twentieth Century*. New York: Harper and Row, 1965.
Roberts, Helene E. "The Exquisite Slave: The Role of Clothes in the Making of the Victorian Woman." *Signs: Journal of Women in Culture and Society* 2 (1977): 554–569.
Roberts, Helene E. "Reply to David Kunzle's 'Dress Reform as Antifeminism: A Response to Helene E. Roberts's "The Exquisite Slave." ' " *Signs: A Journal of Women in Culture and Society* 3 (1977): 518–519.
Rubinstein, David. "Cycling in the 1890s." *Victorian Studies* 21 (1978): 47–71.
Sandford, Elizabeth Poole. *Woman in Her Social and Domestic Character*. 1833.
Taylor, Barbara. "The Woman-Power: Religious Heresy and Feminism in Early English Socialism." In *Tearing the Veil: Essays on Femininity*, edited by Susan Lipshitz. London and Boston: Routledge & Kegan Paul, 1978.
Taylor, Mary. *Miss Miles: Or A Tale of Yorkshire Life 60 Years Ago*. 1890.

Part II   WOMAN'S SPHERE

Anderson, Michael. *Family Structure in Nineteenth-Century Lancashire*. Cambridge, England: Cambridge University Press, 1971.
Banks, J. A. and Olive. *Feminism and Family Planning in Victorian England*. New York: Schocken, 1964.
Barr, Pat. *A Curious Life for a Lady: The Story of Isabelle Bird*. London: Macmillan, 1970.
Besant, Annie. *Marriage: As It Was, As It Is, and As It Will Be*. 1879.
Branca, Patricia. "Image and Reality: The Myth of the Idle Victorian Woman." In Hartmann and Banner.
Branca, Patricia. *Silent Sisterhood: Middle-Class Women in the Victorian Home*. Pittsburgh: Carnegie-Mellon University Press; London: Croom Helm, 1975.
Burnett, John. *Plenty and Want: A Social History of Diet in England from 1815 to the Present Day*. London: Nelson, 1966.
Burton, Hester. *Barbara Bodichon 1827–1891*. London: John Murray, 1949.
Clark, Anna K. "Sexuality and Class in the Controversy over the Bastardy Clause of the New Poor Law 1834–1844." Undergraduate honors thesis, Harvard University, 1979.
Davidoff, Leonore. *The Best Circles: Women and Society in Victorian England*. Totowa, N.J.: Rowman and Littlefield; London: Croom Helm, 1973.
Davidoff, Leonore. "Class and Gender in Victorian England: The Diaries of Arthur J. Munby and Hannah Cullwick." *Feminist Studies* 5 (1979): 87–141.
Davidoff, Leonore. "Mastered for Life: Servant and Wife in Victorian and Edwardian England." *Journal of Social History* 7 (1974): 406–428.
Davidoff, Leonore; L'Esperance, Jean; and Newby, Howard. "Landscape with Figures: Home and Community in English Society." In Mitchell and Oakley.
Davin, Anna. "Imperialism and Motherhood." *History Workshop* 9 (1978): 9–65.
Fee, Elizabeth. "Psychology, Sexuality, and Social Control in Victorian England." *Social Science Quarterly* 58 (1978): 632–646.
Frisch, Rose E. "Population, Food Intakes, and Fertility." *Science* 99 (1978): 22–30.
Fryer, Peter. *The Birth Controllers*. New York: Stein and Day, 1965.
Gaskell, Elizabeth. *The Life of Charlotte Brontë*. 1857. Reprint. Harmondsworth, England: Penguin, 1975.
Gaudie, Enid. *Cruel Habitations: A History of Working-Class Housing, 1780–1918*. London: Allen and Unwin, 1974.
Gillis, John P. "Servants, Sexual Relations, and the Risks of Illegitimacy in London, 1801–1900." *Feminist Studies* 5 (1979): 142–173.
Hayek, Friedrich August von. *John Stuart Mill and Harriet Taylor: Their Correspondence and Subsequent Marriage*. Chicago: University of Chicago Press, 1951.
Hill, Michael. *The Religious Order*. London: Heinemann, 1977. Chapter 9, "The Role

of Women in Victorian Society: Sisterhoods, Deaconesses, and the Growth of Nursing."

Himes, Norman E. *Medical History of Contraception*. 1934. Reprint. New York: Gamut Press, 1963.

Holcombe, Lee. "Victorian Wives and Property: Reform of the Married Women's Property Laws." In Vicinus, *A Widening Sphere*.

Hyde, H. Montgomery. *Mr. and Mrs. Beeton*. London: George G. Harrap & Co., 1951.

Johansson, Sheila Ryan. "Sex and Death in Victorian England: An Examination of Age- and Sex-Specific Death Rates, 1840–1910." In Vicinus, *A Widening Sphere*.

Lambertz, Janet R. "Male-Female Violence in Late-Victorian and Edwardian England." Undergraduate honors thesis, Harvard University, 1979.

Liddington, Jill, and Norris, Jill. *One Hand Tied Behind Us: The Rise of the Women's Suffrage Movement*. London: Virago, 1978.

Linton, Eliza Lynn. *The Autobiography of Christopher Kirkland*. 1885.

McLaren, Angus. "Abortion in England, 1890–1914." *Victorian Studies* 20 (1977): 379–401.

McLaren, Angus. *Birth Control in Nineteenth-Century England*. New York: Holmes & Meier, 1978.

Meacham, Standish. *A Life Apart: The English Working Class, 1890–1914*. Cambridge, Mass.: Harvard University Press, 1977.

Myers, Mitzi. "*Harriet Martineau's Autobiography*: The Making of a Female Philosopher." In *Women's Autobiography: Essays in Criticism*, edited by Estelle C. Jelinek. Bloomington: Indiana University Press, 1980.

Myers, Mitzi. "Unmothered Daughter and Radical Reformer: Reconstructing Some Interconnections in Harriet Martineau's Career." In *Embraced and Embattled: The History of Mothers and Daughters in Literature*, edited by C. N. Davidson and E. M. Boroner. New York: Frederick Ungar, 1979.

Norton, Caroline. *A Plain Letter to the Lord Chancellor on the Infant Custody Bill*. 1839.

Oakley, Ann. *Woman's Work: The Housewife, Past and Present*. New York: Vintage, 1976.

Oren, Laura. "The Welfare of Women in Laboring Families: England, 1860–1950." In Hartmann and Banner.

Piers, Martha W. *Infanticide: Past and Present*. New York: Norton, 1978.

Ravetz, Alison. "The Victorian Coal Kitchen and Its Reformers." *Victorian Studies* 11 (1968): 435–461.

Showalter, Elaine. "Victorian Women and Insanity." *Victorian Studies* 23 (1980): 157–181.

Stevens, Joan, ed. *Mary Taylor, Friend of Charlotte Brontë: Letters from New Zealand and Elsewhere*. Auckland, New Zealand: Auckland University Press; Oxford, England: Oxford University Press, 1972.

Walters, Margaret. "The Rights and Wrongs of Women: Mary Wollstonecraft, Harriet Martineau, Simone de Beauvoir." In Mitchell and Oakley.

Webb, Catherine. *The Woman with the Basket: The Story of the Women's Co-operative Guild, 1883–1927*. London: Women's Co-operative Guild, 1927.

Westwater, A. Martha. "Surrender to Subservience: An Introduction to the Diaries and Journal of Eliza Wilson Bagehot." *International Journal of Women's Studies* 1 (1978): 517–529.

Wohl, Anthony S., ed. *The Victorian Family: Structure and Stresses*. New York: St. Martin's Press, 1978.

Part III WOMAN'S MIND

Alaya, Flavia. "Victorian Science and the 'Genius' of Women." *Journal of the History of Ideas* 38 (1977): 261–280.

Beale, Dorothea. *Reports Issued by the Schools Inquiry Commission on the Education of Girls: With Extracts and a Preface*. 1869.

Bradbrook, M. C. *That Infidel Place: A Short History of Girton College.* London: Chatto and Windus, 1969.

Burstyn, Joan N. "Education and Sex: The Medical Case Against Higher Education for Women in England, 1870–1900." *Proceedings of the American Philosophical Society* 117 (1973): 79–89.

Burstyn, Joan N. *Victorian Education and the Ideal of Womanhood.* London: Croom Helm, 1980.

Cobbe, Frances Power. "Female Education and How It Would Be Affected by University Examinations." A paper read at the Social Science Congress, 1862.

Davin, Anna. "Board School Girls." Unpublished manuscript.

Davin, Anna. " 'Mind that you do as you are told': Reading Books for Board School Girls, 1870–1902." In *Feminist Review* 1 (1979): 89–98.

Delamont, Sara. "The Contradictions in Ladies' Education." In Delamont and Duffin.

Delamont, Sara. "The Domestic Ideology and Women's Education." In Delamont and Duffin.

Dyhouse, Carol. "Good Wives and Little Mothers: Social Anxieties and the Schoolgirl's Curriculum, 1890–1920." *Oxford Review of Education* 3 (1977): 21–35.

Ellsworth, Edward W. *Liberation of the Female Mind: The Shirreff Sisters, Educational Reform, and the Women's Movement.* Westport, Conn. and London: Greenwood Press, 1979.

Grey, Maria. *Last Words to Girls, or Life in School and After School.* 1889.

Grey, Maria, and Shirreff, Emily. *Thoughts on Self-Culture.* 1854.

Kamm, Josephine. *Hope Deferred: Girls' Education in English History.* London: Methuen, 1965.

Kamm, Josephine. *How Different from Us: Miss Buss and Miss Beale.* London: Bodley Head, 1958.

McWilliams-Tullberg, Rita. *Women at Cambridge: A Men's University—Though of a Mixed Type.* London: Victor Gollancz, 1975.

Patterson, Elizabeth C. "The Case of Mary Somerville: An Aspect of Nineteenth-Century Science." *Proceedings of the American Philosophical Society* 118 (1974): 269–275.

Patterson, Elizabeth C. "Mary Somerville." *British Journal for the History of Science* 4 (1969): 311–339.

Pederson, Joyce Senders. "Schoolmistresses and Headmistresses: Elites and Education and Nineteenth-Century England." *Journal of British Studies* 15 (1975): 135–162.

Ridley, Annie E. *Frances Mary Buss and Her Work for Education.* 1895.

Senior, Jane Elizabeth. "Report on the Education of Girls in Pauper Schools, 1873–74." In *Third Annual Report* of the Local Government Board. P.P. 1874.

Shirreff, Emily. *Intellectual Education and Its Influence on the Character and Happiness of Women.* 1858.

Silver, Pamela and Harold. *The Education of the Poor: The History of a National School, 1824–1974.* London and Boston: Routledge & Kegan Paul, 1974.

Part IV   WOMAN'S WORK

Abel-Smith, Brian. *A History of the Nursing Profession in Great Britain.* New York: Springer, 1960.

Alexander, Sally. "Women's Work in Nineteenth-Century London: A Study of the Years 1820–1850." In Mitchell and Oakley.

Anderson, Olive. "Women Preachers in Mid-Victorian Britain: Some Reflexions on Feminism, Popular Religion, and Social Change." *Historical Journal* 12 (1969): 467–484.

Butler, Josephine, ed. *Women's Work and Women's Culture.* 1869.

Carpenter, Mary. *Red Lodge Girls' Reformatory.* 1875.

Cobbe, Frances Power. *Essays on the Pursuits of Women.* 1863.

Collet, Clara E. *Educated Working Women: Essays on the Economic Position of Women Workers in the Middle Classes.* 1902.

Collet, Clara E. "Report on the Conditions of Work in London." Royal Commission on Labour: The Employment of Women. *P.P.* xxxvii, 1893.

Davidoff, Leonore. "Class and Gender in Victorian England: The Diaries of Arthur J. Munby and Hannah Cullwick." *Feminist Studies* 5 (1979): 87–141.

Davidoff, Leonore. "Mastered for Life: Servant and Wife in Victorian and Edwardian England." *Journal of Social History* 7 (1974): 406–428.

Donnison, Jean. *Midwives and Medical Men: A History of Inter-Professional Rivalries and Women's Rights.* New York: Schocken, 1977.

Edelstein, T. J. "They Sang 'The Song of the Shirt': Visual Iconography of the Seamstress." *Victorian Studies* 23 (1980): 183–210.

Foster, John. *Class Struggle and the Industrial Revolution: Early Industrial Capitalism in Three English Towns.* London: Weidenfeld and Nicolson, 1974.

Fredeman, William E. "Emily Faithfull and the Victoria Press: An Experiment in Sociological Bibliography." *The Library* 29 (1974): 139–164.

Hewitt, Margaret. *Wives and Mothers in Victorian Industry.* 1958. Reprint. Westport, Conn.: Greenwood, 1980.

Holcombe, Lee. *Victorian Ladies at Work: Middle-Class Working Women in England and Wales, 1850–1914.* Hamden, Conn.: Archon Books; Newton Abbot, England: David and Charles, 1973.

Horn, Pamela. *The Rise and Fall of the Victorian Servant.* Dublin: Gill and Macmillan; New York: St. Martin's Press, 1975.

Ignatieff, Michael. *A Just Measure of Pain: The Penitentiary in the Industrial Revolution, 1760–1850.* New York: Pantheon, 1978.

James, Anna. *Sisters of Charity and the Commission of Labour.* 1859.

Jex-Blake, Sophia. *Medical Women: A Thesis and a History.* 1886.

John, Angela. *By the Sweat of Their Brow: Women in the Victorian Coal Mines.* London: Croom Helm, 1980.

Kitteringham, Jennie. "Country Work Girls in Nineteenth-Century England." In *Village Life and Labour,* edited by Raphael Samuel. London and Boston: Routledge & Kegan Paul, 1975.

Klein, Viola. *Britain's Married Women Work.* London: Routledge & Kegan Paul, 1965.

Lowenhak, Sheila. *Women and Trade Unions: An Outline History of Women in the British Trade Union Movement.* New York: St. Martin's Press, 1977.

McBride, Theresa M. *The Domestic Revolution: The Modernization of Household Service in England and France, 1820–1920.* New York: Holmes & Meier, 1976.

McBride, Theresa M. "The Long Road Home: Women's Work and Industrialization." In *Becoming Visible: Women in European History,* edited by Renate Bridenthal and Claudia Koonz. Boston: Houghton Mifflin, 1977.

McDougall, Mary Lynn. "Working-Class Women During the Industrial Revolution." In *Becoming Visible: Women in European History,* edited by Renate Bridenthal and Claudia Koonz. Boston: Houghton Mifflin, 1977.

Milne, John. *Industrial and Social Employment of Women in the Middle and Lower Ranks.* 1857, 1870 (revised).

Neff, Wanda. *Victorian Working Women.* New York: Columbia University Press, 1929.

Nightingale, Florence. *Notes on Nursing: What It Is and What It Is Not.* 1860.

Papworth, Lucy Wyatt, and Zimmern, Dorothy M. *Women in Industry: A Bibliography.* London: Women's Industrial Council, 1915.

Parkes, Bessie Raynor (Mrs. Belloc). *Essays on Women's Work.* 1865.

Peterson, M. Jeanne. "The Victorian Governess: Status Incongruence in Family and Society." In Vicinus, *Suffer and Be Still.*

Pinchbeck, Ivy. *Women Workers and the Industrial Revolution 1750–1850.* London: Routledge, 1930.

Pope, Barbara Corrado. "Angels in the Devil's Workshop: Leisured and Charitable Women in Nineteenth-Century England and France." In *Becoming Visible: Women in European History,* edited by Renate Bridenthal and Claudia Koonz. Boston: Houghton Mifflin, 1977.

Pratt, A. E. *A Woman's Work for Women: Arms, Efforts, and Aspirations of Louisa Hubbard.* 1898.

Radcliffe, Mary Ann. *The Memoirs of Mrs. Mary Ann Radcliffe in Familiar Letters to Her Female Friend.* 1810.

Showalter, Elaine. "Florence Nightingale's Feminist Complaint: Women, Religion, and Suggestions for Thought." *Signs: Journal of Women in Culture and Society* 6 (1981): 395–412.

Smart, Carol. *Women, Crime, and Criminology: A Feminist Critique.* London and Boston: Routledge & Kegan Paul, 1976.

Stafford, Ann. *A Match to Fire the Thames.* London: Hodder and Stoughton, 1961.

Stanley, Liz, ed. *The Diaries of Hannah Cullwick.* London: Virago, forthcoming.

Taylor, Barbara. "The Men Are as Bad as Their Masters . . . : Socialism, Feminism, and Sexual Antagonism in the London Tailoring Trade in the Early 1830s." *Feminist Studies* 5 (1979): 7–40.

Thompson, Dorothy. "Women and Nineteenth-Century Radical Politics: A Lost Dimension." In Mitchell and Oakley.

Tilly, Louise A., and Scott, Jean W. *Women, Work, and Family.* New York: Holt, Rinehart, and Winston, 1978.

Todd, Margaret. *The Life of Sophia Jex-Blake.* 1918.

Twining, Louisa. *Workhouses and Pauperism and Women's Work in the Administration of Poor Law.* 1898.

Webb, Beatrice. *My Apprenticeship.* 1926.

Woodham-Smith, Cecil. *Florence Nightingale, 1820–1910.* London: Constable, 1950.

Part V   UNWOMANLY WOMEN

Besant, Annie. *The Legalization of Female Slavery in England.* 1885.

Collins, Philip. *Dickens and Crime.* London: Macmillan; New York: St. Martin's Press, 1962.

[Dickens, Charles]. "The Ruffian." *All the Year Round*, October 10, 1868, pp. 421–424.

Engel, Arthur. " 'Immoral Intentions': The University of Oxford and the Problem of Prostitution, 1827–1914." *Victorian Studies* 23 (1979): 79–107.

Engels, Frederick. *The Origin of the Family, Private Property and the State.* 1884.

Finnegan, Frances. *Poverty and Prostitution: A Study of Victorian Prostitutes in York:* Cambridge, England: Cambridge University Press, 1979.

Gorham, Deborah. " 'The Maiden Tribute of Modern Babylon' Re-examined: Child Prostitution and the Idea of Childhood in Late-Victorian England." *Victorian Studies* 22 (1978): 353–377.

Greenwood, James. *The Seven Curses of London.* 1869.

Kanner, Selma Barbara. "Victorian Institutional Patronage: Angela Burdett-Coutts, Charles Dickens, and Urania Cottage, Reformatory for Women, 1846–1858." Ph.D. dissertation, University of California at Los Angeles, 1972.

Millman, Marcia. "She Did It All for Love: A Feminist View of the Sociology of Deviance." In *Another Voice: Feminist Perspectives on Social Life and Social Science,* edited by Marcia Millman and Rosabeth Moss Kanter. New York: Anchor, 1975.

Petrie, Glen. *A Singular Iniquity: The Campaigns of Josephine Butler.* New York: Viking, 1971.

Tait, William. *Magdalenism: An Inquiry into the Extent, Causes, and Consequences of Prostitution in Edinburgh.* 1842.

Walkowitz, Judith. "The Making of an Outcast Group: Prostitutes and Working Women in Nineteenth-Century Plymouth and Southampton." In Vicinus, *A Widening Sphere.*

Walkowitz, Judith. *Prostitution and Victorian Society: Women, Class, and the State.* Cambridge, England: Cambridge University Press, 1980.

Walkowitz, Judith and Daniel J. " 'We Are Not Beasts of the Field': Prostitution and the Poor in Plymouth and Southampton Under the Contagious Diseases Act." In Hartmann and Banner.

Whyte, Frederic. *The Life of W. T. Stead.* 1925.

FURTHER ACCESS TO SOURCES

Recent Reprints

Acton, William. *Prostitution.* 2nd ed. 1870. Reprint. London: MacGibbon & Kee, 1968, edited and abridged by Peter Fryer.

Beeton, Isabella. *Beeton's Book of Household Management.* 1861. Reprint. New York: Farrar, Straus & Giroux, 1974.

Davies, Margaret Llewelyn. *Life As We Have Known It.* 1931. Reprint. London: Virago, 1977. Reprint. New York: Norton, 1975.

Davies, Margaret Llewelyn. *Maternity: Letters from Working Women Collected by the Women's Co-operative Guild.* 1915. Reprint. London: Virago, 1978.

Davies, Emily. *Thoughts on Some Questions Relating to Women, 1860–1908.* 1910. Reprint. New York: Kraus, 1971.

Hughes, M. Vivian. *A London Girl of the Eighties.* 1936. Reprint. Oxford: Oxford University Press, 1978.

Mayhew, Henry. *London Labour and the London Poor,* 4 vols. 1862. Reprint. New York: Dover, 1968.

Mill, John Stuart and Harriet Taylor. *Essays in Sex Equality.* Edited by Alice S. Rossi. Chicago and London: Chicago University Press, 1970.

Murray, Janet Horowitz, and Stark, Myra, eds. *The Englishwoman's Review of Social and Industrial Questions,* 1866–1910. Complete run with index. New York and London: Garland, 1980.

Nield, Keith, ed. *Prostitution in the Victorian Age: Debates on the Issue from 19th-Century Critical Journals.* Westmead, England: Gregg International Publishers, 1973.

Nightingale, Florence, *Cassandra.* 1852. Old Westbury, N.Y.: Feminist Press, 1979.

Reeves, Maud Pember. *Round About a Pound a Week.* 1914. Reprint. London: Virago, 1979.

Other Anthologies of Related Materials

Bauer, Carol, and Ritt, Lawrence. *Free and Ennobled: Source Readings in the Development of Victorian Feminism.* Oxford: Pergamon Press, 1979.

Burnett, John. *Annals of Labour: Autobiographies of British Working-Class People, 1820–1920.* Bloomington: Indiana University Press, 1974.

Burnett, John. *Useful Toil: Autobiographies of Working People from the 1820s to the 1920s.* Harmondsworth, England: Penguin, 1977.

Hellerstein, Erna Olafson; Hume, Leslie Parker; and Offen, Karen M. *Victorian Women: A Documentary Account of Women's Lives in Nineteenth-Century England, France, and the United States.* Stanford, Calif.: Stanford University Press, 1981.

Hollis, Patricia. *Women in Public: The Women's Movement, 1850–1900.* London: George Allen & Unwin, 1979.

Humphreys, Anne. *Voices of the Poor: Selections from the* Morning Chronicle. *"Labor and the Poor"* (1849–1850) *by Henry Mayhew.* London: Frank Cass, 1971.

MacKenzie, Midge. *Shoulder to Shoulder: A Documentary.* New York: Knopf, 1975.

Pike, E. Royston. *"Golden Times": Human Documents of the Victorian Age.* New York: Schocken, 1972.

Thompson, E. P., and Yeo, Eileen. *The Unknown Mayhew: Selections from the Morning Chronicle, 1849–1850.* London: Merlin, 1971.

Index

Anthologized selections by indexed authors are indicated in italics.